A Biocultural Approach to Literary Theory and Interpretation

A Biocultural Approach to Literary Theory and Interpretation

NANCY EASTERLIN

The Johns Hopkins University Press

Baltimore

2 4 6 8 9 7 5 3 1

The Johns Hopkins University Press
2715 North Charles Street
Baltimore, Maryland 21218-4363
www.press.jhu.edu

Library of Congress Cataloging-in-Publication Data

Easterlin, Nancy.
   A biocultural approach to literary theory and interpretation / Nancy Easterlin.
     p. cm.
   Includes bibliographical references and index.
   ISBN-13: 978-1-4214-0472-1 (hdbk. : acid-free paper)
   ISBN-13: 978-1-4214-0504-9 (electronic)
   ISBN-10: 1-4214-0472-9 (hdbk. : acid-free paper)
   ISBN-10: 1-4214-0504-0 (electronic)
   1. Literature—History and criticism—Theory, etc. 2. Literature and society.
3. Empiricism in literature. 4. Social science literature. I. Title.
   PN51.E24 2012
   809'.93355—dc23   2011034745

A catalog record for this book is available from the British Library.

*Special discounts are available for bulk purchases of this book. For more information,
please contact Special Sales at 410-516-6936 or specialsales@press.jhu.edu.*

The Johns Hopkins University Press uses environmentally friendly book materials,
including recycled text paper that is composed of at least 30 percent post-consumer
waste, whenever possible.

For Peter, and for Keaton
Ever the best of friends

AUDREY

What Jane Austen novels have you read?

TOM

None. I don't read novels. I prefer good literary criticism—that way you get both the novelists' ideas and the critics' thinking. With fiction I can never forget that none of it really happened— that it's all just made up by the author.

Whit Stillman

What is literature *for*?

The study of literature isn't typically cast in terms of its usefulness, but litera-ture is a thing made for human use, like an airplane or a soup pot or a belt. In the sense that I mean the term *literature*, written text, the phenomenon of literature dates back further than the airplane, to a degree that we judge significant cultur-ally but not evolutionarily. However you look at it, though, given the penchant for cultural analysis that has grown and spawned numerous disciplines since the late nineteenth century, it is striking how little scholars have concerned them-selves with the *utility* of literature.

Although functionalist hypotheses about the arts began emerging soon after publication of *The Origin of Species,* the predominant approach to aesthetics has been essentialist or idealist throughout human cultural history. According to this view, the question at the heart of aesthetic inquiry is this: What are the core quali-ties that constitute the beauty or the artfulness of the object, whether a painting, a symphony, a lyric poem, a dance, or a production of another kind? Certainly, by the twentieth century the core concept of beauty posed its own set of prob-lems. But it is not simply the disintegration of this criterion in the face of mod-ernist movements in the arts and the failure to identify any core set of features for aesthetic evaluation within each artistic medium that should make us uneasy. The anxious desire to hastily spirit the artwork out of the human arena in which it was so painstakingly crafted and intended for use itself only makes sense in the contexts of evolved human needs and cultural history.

So what is *art* for?

The anthropologist and art historian Ellen Dissanayake provides the only thorough evolutionary account of the function of the arts, one that takes account of the differences between the artifacts of prehistory and those of the modern spheres of art. In the last section of chapter 1, I provide a brief outline of Dissanayake's theory and present a few other important functionalist accounts of art and literature. But the purpose of this book is not to answer such grand questions about the function of art and literature, which I view as too multifunctional in their varied forms in our current cultural situations to be comprehended under one or two single theoretical accounts. I hope to do something more useful for my readers, by example, if those readers are willing to situate their understanding within the framework of a generally functionalist account. This book illustrates biocultural theory and interpretation as I practice it, and as I hope others will practice it in their own way, combining cultural, historical, and literary analysis within a cognitive-evolutionary framework, after reading it. In the first chapter, I explain why the time is right for such a biocultural approach, both within the historical development of literary studies as a discipline and in the context of the more recent rise of cognitive and evolutionary approaches to literature.

This volume has had a long germination, and there are many colleagues whose encouragement was vital to its realization. My first and most profound debt is to Lisa Zunshine, who urged me to propose a book to the Johns Hopkins University Press in early 2005. Brian Boyd, Joseph Carroll, Ellen Dissanayake, David Miall, Jack Stillinger, Robert Storey, Alan Richardson, and William Zimmerman also gave indispensible support for this project in its earliest stages. Joshua Gass, Peter McNamara, and, again, Robert Storey read the manuscript in full, and David Herman, Leslie Heywood, Cynthia Hogue, and Judith Saunders read individual chapters. All offered valuable insights and suggestions. With typical generosity, and at a busy time for himself, Josh delivered particularly attentive and meticulous remarks.

Several grants and awards were vital to my being able to achieve the scope of the project and yet complete it within a reasonably timely manner. I am grateful to the University of New Orleans for a sabbatical in spring 2006 and for the award of a research professorship in 2008, which provided me with a reduced course load for a three-year period. A Guggenheim Fellowship in 2008 granted me a full year of leave, an unknown luxury without which, I believe, the conclusion of this project would be receding into the distance.

Over the years, many other colleagues in evolutionary and cognitive approaches, ecocriticism, narrative studies, and romanticism have formed a central network of intellectual exchange and support. In addition to those already mentioned, I would also like to acknowledge H. Porter Abbott, Frederick Luis Aldama, Michael Austin, Frederick Burwick, Brett Cooke, Kathryn Duncan Stasio, Harold Fromm, Marilyn Gaull, Jon Gottschall, Elizabeth Hart, Kathleen Hart,

Patrick Hogan, Tony Jackson, Suzanne Keen, Beth Lau, Clint Machann, Brian McHale, David McWhirter, Katja Mellman, Anja Mueller-Wood, Marcus Nordlund, Lalita Pandit, James Phelan, Dana Phillips, Brian Richardson, Ellen Spolsky, Brad Sullivan, Frederick Turner, and Blakey Vermeule. Denis Dutton, who also shared and disputed, is now sadly missed. Among literary societies, the International Society for the Study of Narrative deserves special thanks for providing a home for cognitive and evolutionary theory and practice for many years.

I began writing this book after my return to New Orleans in spring 2006, subsequent to my family's evacuation for Hurricane Katrina. I am grateful to the University of Southern California for providing me with a Visiting Scholar appointment in fall 2005, when I was just beginning my research. To Wayne Raskind, Joseph Boone, and the faculty of the USC Department of English, I am thankful for the resources and collegiality that were especially important at that difficult time.

To the editors at the Johns Hopkins University Press—Michael Lonegro, who acquired this project for the press during his tenure there, and Matthew McAdam, who saw it through to completion—I am grateful for their confidence, patience, and guidance. For her meticulous copyediting, Joanne Allen deserves my profound thanks. I received several semesters of capable research support from Katie Chosa, Amanda Bourgeois, and Carin Chapman, my UNO graduate assistants.

The text always both begs attention and points outside itself, and for letting those be my guiding assumptions throughout my life I am indebted to my family and my friends. My father, Richard Easterlin, who contributed Thorstein Veblen to this particular endeavor, more generally showed me a whole way of relating ideas across intellectual domains. Since my first days at university, Bob Storey, my generous mentor, has demonstrated that breadth of mind and lack of pretention that open up the avenues of inquiry. Never much in the way of ivory-tower aesthetes, my husband and daughter, to whom this book is dedicated, every day demonstrate how literature has, in William James's phrase, "cash-value" for experience. And for those who live prior to the sign—Rudy, Musetta, and Lloyd Cole McNamara—thank you for your company and for calling me back to your meanings. To their brother, the spirit-cat Al, thank you for sticking around.

*A Biocultural Approach to Literary Theory
and Interpretation*

CHAPTER ONE

Literature, Science, and Biocultural Interpretation

> But within the field of learning proper there is a similar predilec-
> tion for an air of scientific acumen and precision where science
> does not belong. So that even that large range of knowledge that
> has to do with general information rather than with theory—what
> is loosely termed scholarship—tends strongly to take on the name
> and forms of theoretical statement. . . . The students of literature,
> for instance, are more and more prone to substitute critical analy-
> sis and linguistic speculation, as the end of their endeavors, in the
> place of that discipline of taste and that cultivated sense of literary
> form and literary feeling that must always remain the chief end of
> literary training, as distinct from philology and the social sciences.
>
> *Thorstein Veblen*

Literature and Science?

In the conclusion to "Literature and Science," an address delivered in the United States in 1882, Matthew Arnold surmises that "humane letters" will remain at the center of education in the future, though "they will someday come, we may hope, to be studied more rationally." Arnold suggests that "while we shall all have to acquaint ourselves with the great results reached by modern science, and to give ourselves as much training in its disciplines as we can conveniently carry," the humanities will not only prevail but become more necessary than in the past, because "the majority of men will . . . have the more and the greater results of science to relate to the need in man for conduct, and to the need in him for beauty."[1] For Arnold, the likelihood that science would produce findings with direct bearing on questions of ethics and aesthetics, matters he envisioned at the heart of "humane letters," boded well for the future health of our division of learning.

Few humanists today are likely to feel comforted by Arnold's remarks, for few, if any, imagine that the rise of science has been accompanied by a productive, mutually beneficial, wide-ranging interdisciplinary exchange in the academy. Just as few, for that matter, are likely to believe that "conduct" and "beauty"— terms we might more comfortably construe today as *ethics* and *aesthetics*—form, self-evidently, the core rationale for humanistic endeavor. As Robert Scholes remarks, commenting in his 2004 presidential address to the Modern Language Association of America on Arnold's *Culture and Anarchy,* "The assumption that human beings are driven by a desire for perfection is a charming notion," but one that is impossible to sustain in our post- or antihumanist culture.[2] Hewing, on one hand, to his beloved Hellenism, Arnold could not but believe that contact . with culture was quite simply ennobling.[3] The case is hardly so simple for us today, though it is perhaps even more pressing. But before we deploy Arnold's least durable idea as an implement to heave his others into the dustbin of historical irrelevance, we should consider whether a more rational literary criticism is still desirable; whether it might be achieved, in some measure, through a considered and intelligent exchange with science; and whether such rationally interdisciplinary literary study might begin to demonstrate the purpose of literature and the humanities as a whole.

Put bluntly, if the Aristotelian ennoblement born of the integration of ethics and aesthetics in the work of art's formal unity strikes us today as a lovely fiction, what role, if any, remains for the humanities to fill?[4] With respect to the area of study that concerns me here, what is the function of literature specifically? And what place, if any, should science have in defining or facilitating current literary study? For Scholes, the answer to the first question is simple: "interpretation is at the heart of the humanistic enterprise" ("Address," 732). But the foundational justification for interpretation and the augmentation of interpretive practices resolve themselves, for Scholes, into a greater emphasis on language, reinvigorated by a return to the trivium of grammar, rhetoric, and logic, which defined the elementary division of the liberal arts in the Middle Ages. There does not appear to be a role for science in explaining why interpretation might be of such central human importance and in elucidating the processes or meanings of interpretable phenomena. As Scholes says in reply to Harold Fromm, who impatiently urges him to look toward bioevolutionary explanations of culture to find answers for the crisis in the humanities, "Yes, we were natural for eons before we were cultural— before we were human, even—but so what? We are cultural now, and culture is the domain of the humanities."[5]

I share Scholes's view that interpretation is at the core of the humanities, and I would further claim that literary interpretation (as opposed to cultural interpretation in general) constitutes a focal activity in literary studies specifically. However, Scholes's method of refocusing the interpretive enterprise and shoring up the humanities is problematic in an era dominated by the sciences, for several reasons. At the very least, the suggestion that we reorganize the humanities along the lines of their original conception seems rhetorically weak, especially as an argument that might hold sway outside of our own disciplinary confines. The current marginalization of the humanities makes many of us painfully aware that we cannot simply be learned, but must be learned *for* one purpose or another, and that that purpose must be not only demonstrable but attractive to administrators and students alike. While on the face of it this version of the life of the mind might seem deplorable to some, the fact of the matter is that no one today believes (or would admit to believing) that knowledge is a pure and disinterested affair. Certainly, Scholes does not suggest that it is, but his ability to argue for the relevance of interpretation is drastically weakened by the assumption that our cultural present divides us neatly from our natural past.

Variations on this two-cultures theme have been echoed by other members of the Modern Language Association leadership in recent years as the question of the role of science in the humanities has become more pressing. Says Louis Menand, "Culture is not an add-on to the biological and sociological conditions of existence; it is constitutive of species identity."[6] No very clear sense of the emergence of culture underlies this assertion, according to which "culture" and "biological and sociological conditions of existence" are apparently monolithic and independent entities (although the pragmatists that Menand has written about so brilliantly would point to their thoroughgoing status as conceptual constructions).[7] But surely the assertion that culture "is constitutive of species identity," which evinces a sort of secular intelligent design creationist mentality, is patently false. Strikingly, the willingness of the Modern Language Association leadership to fall back on long-held but meaningless dichotomies, notably kept intact throughout the recent era of now-moribund postmodernist theorizing, amounts to more than a reassertion of the traditional two-cultures claim that the kinds of knowledge provided in the humanities and the social sciences are incommensurate. The implication of both Scholes's and Menand's claims is that culture constitutes our human essence.

I do not intend to explore the notion that we are essentially cultural any more than I will explore the opposite, that we are essentially natural, partly because such manufactured categories provide an unproductive ground for argument and partly because I do not really accept that either Scholes or Menand believes such a thing.

Any sustained consideration of the emergence of human culture reveals that it is, so to speak, a development and extension of the rather remarkable characteristics of the human species. Scholes sensibly calls for a renewed disciplinary emphasis on language; language itself is hardly least among the phenomena that emerged to serve the evolving needs of species fitness.

Why the insistence on a two-cultures stance? Menand actually wants subject matter from other disciplines, including scientific ones, brought into literary studies, claiming that the traditional boundaries between disciplines "are dumbing us down" (14), yet in the same breath he condemns interdisciplinarity and forwards his claim that "culture is constitutive of species identity," in the process cordoning off vast tracts of learning from any humanist relevance. Why the dogmatic insistence that a strict (and wholly untenable) line must be drawn between investigations of natural and cultural phenomena? Part of the explanation lies in the historical longevity of the rivalry between the humanities and the sciences, which was already nearly a hundred years old when Arnold sought, in 1882, to reassure his audience about the abiding relevance of "humane letters." But another good portion of the explanation lies in the general failure to clarify the central terms and issues that lie at the heart of interdisciplinary study. (Menand's presumed definition of *interdisciplinarity* would seem to be a case in point, but to be fair, the burden of clarification lies with those of us who are conducting innovative interdisciplinary work.)

The recent resurgence of the debate about the role of science in literary studies is largely due to the 1998 publication of E. O. Wilson's *Consilience,* in which the renowned biologist called for a unification of knowledge across the academic disciplines. The enduring antipathy that Wilson's book—a popular press publication that does not attempt systematic argument—has occasioned would be curious were it not for the endorsement Wilson's project has received from within literary studies. Most particularly, Wilson's call for consilience has been championed by Joseph Carroll, the leading figure in Darwinian (or adaptationist) literary studies. From a 1998 debate in the *Wilson Quarterly* to a 2008 special double issue of the journal *Style* containing a target article by Carroll as well as responses from numerous scholars and including a number of journalistic forays in between, the topic of the role of scientific theories and methods in literary study has been much debated.[8] Yet at the center of this debate lies a series of questions that have never been clearly articulated, much less satisfactorily answered. Any productive proposal for interdisciplinary literary studies should take the following questions into consideration:

1. What has been the traditional *aim* of literary studies?
2. Currently, how do the *aims* of the humanities and the sciences differ?
3. Are the current *aims* of literary studies justified?
4. How are differences in the *aims* of literary studies and the sciences related to the nature of the principal *objects* of investigation?
5. To what extent do differences in the *aims* and *objects* justify or necessitate differences in research methods?
6. To what extent do proposals for the transformation of *methods,* where such are part of an interdisciplinary program, inform pedagogical and curricular concerns?
7. Are the uses of key terms and concepts and their practical implications, as they are adopted within literary studies, relatively unambiguous? (With respect to the current discussion, these would include *consilience, unity of knowledge,* and *interdisciplinarity.*)

As I suggest in what follows, Wilson's book *Consilience* does not provide a comprehensive basis for biocultural literary criticism and theory, because Wilson does not consider these basic questions. Irritatingly, this renders the task of outright dismissal of such interdisciplinary approaches extremely easy on the part of those traditional humanists who were probably hankering after such an opportunity in the first place. But traditionalists who recognize that evolutionary and cognitive literary scholars do not represent a unified radical front will, I hope, be inspired by what we can learn about ourselves and our artifacts through a reasonable (or, as Arnold says, "rational") application of social science to literary studies. As I have conceived them from the beginning, biocultural criticism and theory strengthen the aims and practices of literary studies by combining scientific psychology and evolutionary studies with literary criticism, history, and other areas of the humanities and sciences.

Because the institutional study of literature is relatively recent, dating from about the time of Arnold's address, many of the foundational issues and conflicts of English studies provide an important context for the current discussion. For this reason, the next section of this chapter briefly traces the history of literary studies as an academic discipline. Since the last decades of the nineteenth century, English (now literary studies) shifted its aims and altered its methodology substantially, but remnants of the original conflicts at the heart of English, defined in good part by the ascendance of science, remain today, perhaps most obviously in the vigorous opposition to any form of scientifically oriented interdisciplinary research. Having established that the first eighty years of English resulted in a number of developments vital to a coherent field of literary studies, including a focus on the study of literature as opposed to language or human values and an orientation to textual interpretation, I return to the current debate over the two cultures, inspecting Wilson's definition of *consilience* and Carroll's most recent mission statement for Darwinian literary studies, which draws centrally from Wilson. In the process, I speak to the interrelated questions of objects, aims, and methods and map out an alternative theoretical stance that suggests that the very nature and diversity of literary artifacts, which are themselves only fully constituted via a complex cognitive process of production and consumption, a process itself inherently interpretive, militates against a programmatically scientific approach to literature.

The avowed purpose of this book is to demonstrate that, given the nature of the literary object, a reasoned, fair-minded, creative biocultural criticism has great potential value for the many subfields of literary studies. In contrast to the relatively strong emphasis on quantitative research championed by some Darwinian literary critics, then, I suggest that biological and cultural evolution together highlight the centrality of meaning-making processes for our species and, by extension, provide ample justification for interpretation as the core aim of our discipline. Following this, I offer a brief overview of theories of the evolutionary function of the arts, because consideration of the possible adaptative functions of art provides a larger context for the more local uses of literature analyzed in this volume. Additionally, these theories illuminate the conflict over science and values with which literary studies has struggled since its inception. The last portion of the chapter briefly explains the book's organization and offers a rationale for the range of approaches herein addressed.

The Emergence of "English" and the Two Cultures

Current debates about the relation of literature to science commonly take C. P. Snow's 1959 Rede lecture, *The Two Cultures,* as their point of departure, largely because Snow sought to remind his listeners of the destructive divide between intellectual orientations. Intent on asserting the significance of science in an intellectual atmosphere where, in his view, eminent literati such as T. S. Eliot held the day, Snow, a research scientist and novelist, provided no historical analysis of the divide between science and the humanities. It is therefore not surprising that recent discussions, rather than offering systematic consideration of the matter, typically acknowledge "the costs of our captivity to a residual two-culture mentality, with its self-stultifying provincialisms and antagonisms" before summarily condemning Wilson's call for the unity of knowledge.[9]

In many respects, the conflicts at the core of English during its formation as a discipline in the nineteenth century mirror the larger cultural conflict between scientific and humanistic modes of understanding. In Gerald Graff's words,

> The appearance of departments of language and literature in the last quarter of the nineteenth century was part of the larger process of professionalization by which the old "college" became the new "university." In literary studies, as everyone knows, the advance guard of professionalization was a German-trained cadre of scholarly "investigators," who promoted the idea of scientific research and the philological study of the modern languages. Yet the philologists' right to define the terms of professionalism in literary studies was contested from the very beginning. A competing model was defended by a party of "generalists" . . . who were also committed to the idea of departments of English and modern languages, but who upheld the old college ideal of liberal or general culture against that of narrowly specialized research. . . .
>
> This generalist group . . . formed a "dissenting tradition" . . . which defended appreciation over investigation and values over facts.[10]

Although Graff describes a fairly clear divide by the 1870s between rigorous forms of research influenced by science and professionalization on the one hand and a quasi-spiritual view of the humanities stemming back through Renaissance humanism to ancient Greece on the other, from the beginning of the formation of English as a discipline the problem was not quite so clear-cut. For the original justification for the study of language as well as literature presumed a spiritual and formative nature to the enterprise. Influenced by Hegel's romantic theory of language, the study of the classics in the 1840s presupposed that noble qualities inhere in ancient literatures and languages alike. Thus, while philology was to become associated with rigor and professionalization over the next three decades, its original principles, though perhaps more thoroughly theorized, were hardly less spiritual than those of the generalist orientation. Furthermore, philologists themselves began to argue for the inclusion of literature in English studies by the last decades of the nineteenth century, albeit on different grounds than the generalists': "the same specialized rigor and impatience with amateurism that had produced the scientific study of the modern languages led to the conclusion that literature should be treated as a domain in its own right" (Graff, 77).

In sum, if the later opposition to emerge in the formative years of English studies pitted the longstanding socializing mission of the humanities, given new voice in Arnoldian humanism, against the presumed rigor of professional study promoted by the modern research university, the presumption of spiritual and social benefits was a motive force in both cases. The values providing the impetus for English studies fostered confusion about its object of study, its methods, and its aims. As Scholes explains in *The Rise and Fall of English,* "Literary study . . . has never quite defined its objects as neatly as the sciences have defined theirs. It has hovered between the forms of canonicity proper to science and those proper to religion, sometimes regarding its objects of study as specimens, but more often giving them the status of quasi-religious texts, not grounded in the Word of God, exactly, but in the Imagination, which, as Coleridge so explicitly argues, is analogous to and partakes of the creativity of God the Creator."[11] Certainly, over the past century professors of literature have become far less inclined to overtly embrace the ethical and aesthetic justifications for literary study and have repeatedly aimed to make the field rigorous more or less along the model of the sciences. As Roger Seamon notes, "When vernacular literatures were introduced to the curriculum of research universities in the late nineteenth century they had to overcome the objection that literature in one's native language, unlike the classics, did not require disciplinary study. Since vernacular works were addressed to and readily understood by educated adults, what would one be tested on—one's taste?"[12] The solution to this dilemma was to combine the study of English language with the study of English literature.

In Seamon's assessment, worries that English constitutes, in F. W. Bateson's words, "the soft option" have motivated a century of efforts at a rigorous criticism along scientific lines. But the perennially defensive posture Seamon identifies in his contemporary colleagues and traces to the institutionalization of literary studies was preceded by a gnawing consciousness among the romantic poets that "humane letters" were losing ground amidst the scientific successes of the Enlightenment. The mere fact that Wordsworth found it necessary to distinguish between the poet and the scientist attests to the consciousness that one sort of thinker is liable to dissolve in the identity of the other: "The Man of Science seeks truth as a remote and unknown benefactor; he cherishes it and loves it in his solitude: the Poet, singing a song in which all human beings join with him, rejoices in the presence of truth as our visible friend and hourly companion. Poetry is the breath and finer spirit of all knowledge; it is the impassioned expression which is in the countenance of all Science."[13] Claiming that poetry is the gracious expression of our shared, intuitive connection with the life of things, Wordsworth offered no help to those who, almost a hundred years later, wished to argue for the inclusion of literature in the discipline of English. If it is so close to our intuitions and so readily apprehended in our native language, what justification could there be for systematic study? By the same token, Shelley's claim that poetry provides the groundwork for "ethical science" by enlarging sympathy and thought through the action of imagination suggests that poetry is a necessary prerequisite to social reform, but it likewise sets the stage for the defensive posture that apparently has been a hallmark of the discipline from its very beginnings.[14] If poetry acts so effectively upon us, the implication seems to be, why bother to study it?

Finally, the sense of literature's marginality and the fear that it might prove elusive as a valid object of study are defining features of our disciplinary origins, and the conflicted stance that literary studies must avoid impressionism and remain rigorous without selling out to science has been, in the long view, surprisingly intransigent. I find this surprising, because in spite of the prominence of poststructuralist and postmodern perspectives in the past thirty-some years, many of which return us to a new brand of impressionism under the guise of scientistic rigor, real gains have been made since the nineteenth century in defining the discipline through the focal and interconnected activities of research and teaching. The fact that some philologists endorsed the study of literature in the 1890s as a remedy to the increasing divide between their research and the interests of their students may not have served as a very fortuitous foundation for literary studies. But in the same period, the emergence of the social sciences legitimated human psychology, behavior, and culture as distinct areas of study. Recognized intellectual fields, in short, develop in the effort to know more about what humans are and what they create.

To put this in perspective, whereas in the late nineteenth century English departments were debating the merits of including literature in their curricula, by the middle of the twentieth literary study had come to constitute the central activity of the discipline of English. Furthermore, throughout the twentieth and into the twenty-first century there have been debates about and adjustments in the methods of literary study, and many of these have been productive. While some practitioners of New Criticism went too far in their efforts to isolate literature from history and other forms of cultural discourse, literary history and textual interpretation still largely shape curricula and classroom teaching and define a considerable number of scholarly endeavors. Many current professors of literature, perhaps even the majority, would assent to Seamon's assertion that "the purpose of literary study is the transmission, transformation, and even creation of literary traditions. . . . Literary study is not 'about' those traditions, it is a constitutive part of them" (261). We create those traditions by selecting specific works and writers for critical attention, by tracing commonalities between writers and connecting these to historical contexts, and by shaping conceptual categories (the Renaissance, romanticism, Victorianism, modernism, postcolonialism, and so on) that help to organize vast amounts of writing in a cognitively coherent fashion. Seamon's emphasis on (and acceptance of) the constitutive nature of literary scholarship tacitly endorses the role of scholars' values and judgments in this process, for given the volume of writing produced in recent centuries, the creation of critical traditions assumes selective processes on the part of the critics. And since critical values may be more divergent in some periods than in others—such as the last third of the twentieth century, when postmodern critics challenged the aestheticism promoted by New Criticism and pointed attention to the ideological functions of both texts and the process of canon formation itself—those traditions remain open to some degree of reorganization and reconceptualization.

To Seamon's description of the discipline I would add that literary appreciation has a central role in the professional mission of literary studies, and literary interpretation provides a robust mechanism for teaching the value of the traditions and the individual works. The close reading of literary works is our chief inheritance from New Criticism, and that critical movement's combination of an empirical approach influenced by a scientific culture with a quasi-spiritual notion of the poetic text should seem less odd in light of the conflicts between scientific rigor, impressionism, amateurism, spiritual values, and socialization that Graff identifies as foundational to literary studies. The claim that we teach appreciation is apt to produce discomfort among literary scholars, who may suspect that this crystallizes the endeavor's identity as impressionistic, unstructured, and anti-intellectual. But the analysis of what humans value and why they value the things they do is, again, a legitimate subject for intellectual inquiry.

As the preceding overview suggests, during the past century, literary studies has defined itself in relation to a reasonably clear set of purposes, and it has done so by focusing on its objects of study, literary works and the traditions within which they are integrated. In spite of three decades of postmodern theory, some of which has proclaimed that the notion of literariness is an ideological stunt that artificially cordons off some bits of writing from the totality of text, the basic activities of the field have not fundamentally altered from those established between 1790 and 1970. Cultural studies has not, on the whole, replaced curricula designed around works conventionally considered literary and their traditions, and it has not come to dominate literary scholarship.

Interdisciplinary approaches to literature have had their own somewhat erratic history alongside the development of literary studies. The desire, as Arnold put it, to see literature studied more rationally sponsored (and still sponsors) many of these, whether the results appear particularly rational or not. But although interdisciplinarity "appears in the oldest critical texts we possess," and although traditional humanists no longer labor under the stigma of amateurism that plagued the field's founding, many are antipathetic to interdisciplinary studies that draw on the sciences in any shape or form.[15] From this perspective, interdisciplinary effort between humanities disciplines is all very well, and indeed unavoidable, for reasons having to do with the nature of literary practices and the objects of study. But a line should be drawn between the study of natural and the study of cultural objects, whether for practical or philosophical reasons. Just as interdisciplinary critics should take seriously the concerns of traditionalism, traditionalists should not homogenize the diverse theoretical perspectives and practices of individual interdisciplinary scholars as a preliminary maneuver to issuing a blanket dismissal of all such work.

What Is Consilience?

Opponents of cognitive and evolutionary approaches to literature enjoy homogenizing its various practitioners, who, in point of fact, have only one shared assumption: that findings about human psychology and behavior might prove illuminating for the study of human artifacts. There is no particular agenda or approach shared by this growing number of scholars, many of whom hold different views about such fundamental matters as the epistemological legitimacy of poststructuralist theory; the utility of specific interpretive and theoretical models for literary studies; and the areas of psychology most fruitfully explored in interdisciplinary research. Nevertheless, in spite of such fundamental differences among cognitive-evolutionary scholars, traditional humanists have assumed that the outlook and goals of critics align with Wilson's *Consilience,* and they have used that book as a convenient weapon against anyone today attempting criticism informed by the sciences of the mind.

So just what is consilience? In his book of that title, Wilson issues a call for the unity of knowledge through the process of "consilience," which he defines as "literally a 'jumping together' of knowledge by the linking of facts and fact-based theory across disciplines to create a common groundwork of explanation" (8). On the face of it, then, consilience appears to propose nothing more dramatic than a classically pragmatic theory of knowledge, wherein truth is made by a process of continued mediation between endeavors. "Truths emerge from facts," asserts William James, "but they dip forward into facts again and add to them; which facts again create or reveal new truth . . . and so on indefinitely." For James, truth is a function of ideas that agree with reality, and "our ideas must agree with realities, be such realities concrete or abstract, be they facts or be they principles, under penalty of endless inconsistency and frustration."[16] Unlike the neopragmatism of Stanley Fish and Richard Rorty, classical pragmatism does not cast its lot with radical skeptical epistemology, because the shared, mutually agreed-upon perceived reality is a good enough, and long-enduring, basis for assessing the relative validity (or truth) of ideas.[17] Along these lines, Wilson's consilience, like pragmatism, entails the abandonment of propositions like the Oedipus complex, which does not agree with fact-based theory in developmental psychology, in favor of the view that parents typically serve as models for future love objects rather than being the primary objects of love and sexual attraction themselves.

That things held to be true in one discipline or area of experience are not contradicted by those in another is a necessary component of the intellectual enterprise, and it certainly constitutes one feature of Wilson's proposed consilience. But an evolving set of background assumptions about the nature of things based in a shared concept of knowledge is not necessarily the same thing as a "common groundwork for explanation," which may imply a shared starting point for inquiry as well as shared goals and objectives, since the starting point of inquiry is always relative to the proposed object of study and the purpose for studying it.

On the whole, *Consilience* tenders an inconsistent message regarding the degree to which the adoption of scientific methods and purposes is integral to Wilson's envisioned renovation of the humanities. On one hand, he asserts the functional independence of the branches of learning; on the other, he champions the reductions of the scientific method so forcefully while remaining silent about the traditional procedures of literary scholarship and pedagogy that, by inference, he appears to tacitly propose the importation of scientific method into literary studies to fill the imagined void. For instance, in the chapter entitled "The Arts and Their Interpretation," Wilson claims that "scholars in the humanities should lift the anathema placed on reductionism. . . . [Science and the arts] have radically different goals and methods. The key to the exchange between them is not hybridization, not some unpleasantly self-conscious form of scientific art or artistic science, but reinvigoration of interpretation with the knowledge of science and its proprietary sense of the future. Interpretation is the logical channel of consilient explanation between science and the arts" (211). On its face, this passage seems to suggest that humanists should recognize the gains in science resulting from reductionism, while maintaining their own distinct methods. Yet Wilson's emphasis throughout the chapter on universals and near universals in art (including archetypes, incest avoidance, parent-infant bonding, cooperation, and conflict), themselves probably the product of evolved psychological adaptations, suggests a potentially "common groundwork for explanation" and presumes some reorientation of the goals of literary studies toward those of evolutionary social science.

As it stands, Wilson's sketch for the renovation of the arts operates at such a high level of generality that the typical professor of literature, who likely devotes the majority of each semester to teaching three or four courses in literature and composition, is left perplexed over the proposal's practical implications. In Wilson's conception, are courses organized around the literature of historical periods and specific genres to be jettisoned in favor of a program aimed at documenting the correspondences between a universal psychological architecture and the features of literary works? Is literary study to become, then, a social science? As Tony Jackson asks, "Can [scholars] make a legitimate use of the science without requiring literary interpretations to be judged by the criteria of scientific method?"[18] Although Wilson argues against the hybridization of art and science in the passage just cited, he seems to favor the hybridization of literary theory and criticism with evolutionary social science, which takes human beings rather than literary works as its object of study.

Since the publication of *Consilience,* Joseph Carroll, widely recognized as the father of Darwinian literary studies, has aligned his conception of the unity of knowledge closely with Wilson's statement. Although he has criticized Wilson for neglecting higher cognitive functions in his list of human motivational systems and for the sketchiness of his proposal on the arts, Carroll endorses Wilson's concept of consilience to the extent of consistently incorporating it into his own descriptions of adaptationist criticism.[19] He has made the concept central to his mission statement for adaptationist literary criticism, incorporating it into the target article on evolutionary literary criticism in the special double issue of *Style:*

> [Literary Darwinists] aim at fundamentally altering the paradigm within which literary study is now conducted. They want to establish a new alignment among the disciplines and ultimately to subsume all other possible approaches to literary study. They rally to Edward O. Wilson's cry for "consilience" among all branches of learning. Like Wilson, they envision an integrated body of knowledge extending in an unbroken chain of material causation from the lowest level of subatomic particles to the highest levels of cultural imagination. And like Wilson, they regard evolutionary biology as the pivotal discipline uniting the hard with the social sciences and the humanities. They believe that humans

have evolved in an adaptive relation to their environment. They argue that for humans, as for all other species, evolution has shaped the anatomical, physiological, and neurological characteristics of the species, and they think that human behavior, feeling, and thought are fundamentally constrained and informed by those characteristics.[20]

Many interdisciplinary literary scholars who place their work on the continuum of evolutionary literary criticism, like me, would be disinclined to accept this paragraph in its entirety as a statement of their theoretical perspectives and ultimate goals. For this reason, I shall work through the paragraph's separate assertions, beginning with those that strike me as least problematic. All evolutionary and many cognitive critics probably concur with the final claim: that a distinct human nature is a product of species adaptations and that that nature "constrains and informs" human actions (physical and affective-cognitive). This claim, in fact, embodies evolutionary literary study's major point of departure from the constructivist hegemony of the late twentieth century. Likewise, most who agree to this proposition reject philosophical dualism and, alternatively, accept in theory the view that material causation underlies all visible processes. Such a theoretical stance, however, does not entail the belief that we will soon (or ever, for that matter) be able to articulate the precise sequence and relationship of causes contributing to even a fairly local behavior (such as the writing of a novel, for instance). Even Wilson himself suggests that this is unlikely.[21] For this reason, Carroll's visionary claim for "an integrated body of knowledge extending in an unbroken chain of material causation from the lowest level of subatomic particles to the highest levels of cultural imagination" makes me, and I imagine many others, profoundly uncomfortable. If this is not simply hyperbole—and I assume it is not, since it is part of a mission statement—it seems rather grandiose and premature, given the extent of our knowledge about individual phenomena and our related ability to link them causally to one another at the present time. Finally, many would disagree with the agenda to replace the current paradigm in literary studies by aligning it along with the rest of the humanities with the sciences—assuming, that is, that our understanding of "the current paradigm" is compatible with Carroll's.

Since Carroll hews closely to *Consilience*, and since he endorses empirical research projects, it is not surprising that respondents to his article in the *Style* special issue question the degree to which he envisions a disciplinary transformation. Jonathan Gottschall, the Darwinian literary critic most closely aligned with Carroll philosophically, maintains that they both advocate "a fairly radical solution to the malaise in academic literary study: we should study the successes of the sciences and, insofar as possible, we should try to emulate them." Further stressing the radicalism of Carroll's proposal, Gottschall comments that "Carroll is not only arguing for reinterpreting texts through the lens of consilient knowledge, he is arguing for a wholesale disciplinary migration toward a scientific ethos."[22] Gottschall himself, in fact, the leading proponent and practitioner of quantitative approaches in Darwinian literary criticism, is a more vocal advocate of disciplinary change, for which he has argued at length, than Carroll. In his view, doing literary study well entails a restructuring of the discipline that requires "much education in scientific thinking, in the processes of hypothesis testing, and in the intricacies of statistics and probability."[23] But aside from Gottschall, very few respondents express enthusiasm for empirically oriented disciplinary change, even though many of these respondents have an active engagement with evolutionary literary criticism. For example, Edward Slingerland, who is also sympathetic to the sort of integrated conception of knowledge I have aligned with pragmatism, differentiates between such "vertical integration" and "greedy" reductionism and confesses that "one sometimes gets the sense that [Carroll] is advocating the stronger, 'biology subsumes all' position that humanists rightly want nothing to do with."[24]

In his reply article, Carroll notes immediately the concern of respondents about the degree to which literary studies conducted under a scientific ethos can account for the specific historical, aesthetic, and semantic features of literature, and he seeks to reassure skeptics that adaptationist literary studies, as he envisions it, would include both interpretation and empirical, quantitative research. To restate his position, he quotes a passage from an essay first published in *Biopoetics* in 1999:

> If literary studies are ever to satisfy the criteria for empirical validity, they will have to include a range of activities that can be located on a scale of empirical constraint, and these activities will have to be interdependent. At the lower end of the scale, with the least empirical constraint, we can locate most of what we now think of as literary criticism. At the upper end, with the greatest constraint, we can locate the kinds of experimental study—in psychology and linguistics—that are already being conducted but that have not often been expanded to include literature. As a behavioral science, experimental literary study would affiliate itself closely with observational disciplines like ethology and cultural anthropology. Such disciplinary connections would make it possible to pose and answer empirical questions about how art functions in social

groups, what kinds of social needs it satisfies, and how it interacts with other social factors. The results of such study would supply us with the basic facts for the statistical generalizations that are indispensable for causal explanations of cultural and literary history.[25]

In answer to the question of how students inspired by literature might respond to this reorientation, Carroll further stresses, in notable contrast to Gottschall, the modesty of his proposal, which would include basic courses in statistics and experimental method, providing options in literary scholarship but not dictating the nature of scholarly projects along the range of empirical constraint.[26]

Several aspects of Carroll's proposal for literary studies contribute to, rather than resolve, the ambiguity that has been central to it since he first articulated it more than a decade ago. To wit: is he calling for a reorientation of the discipline based on an empirically verifiable "groundwork for explanation" and a substantial shift in research projects toward empirical methodology, or is he instead proposing, more modestly, an acceptance of empirically verifiable background assumptions about human nature and the nature of reality? In the 1999 *Biopoetics* essay quoted here, Carroll restates Wilson's appraisal of literary studies in his 1978 book *On Human Nature*. Wilson believes, according to Carroll, "that all knowledge should be assessed by universal standards of empirical validity and that it should be integral with contiguous disciplines. Applying this standard to the finest literary journal articles of the time, he observes that they consist 'largely of historical anecdotes, diachronic collating of outdated, verbalized theories of human behavior, and judgments of current events according to personal ideology—all enlivened by the pleasant but frustrating techniques of effervescence.'" Carroll accepts the biologist's negative appraisal of literary scholarship as "a historically accurate diagnosis of a crucial intellectual failure" and issues the call for an "empirically grounded study of literature."[27]

First, to what extent is literary studies concerned with producing new, empirically verifiable knowledge? To the extent that interpretation continues to form a core activity of the discipline, any strong call for the negative test is apt to be problematic. Although the model of interpretation that Carroll himself has been developing in his interpretive essays suggests that critics should begin the interpretive process from a set of common assumptions about human motivational systems (about which I will say more in the next section), these readings are not empirically verifiable, as Carroll would be the first to acknowledge. Yet Carroll has expressed misgivings about discursive methodology repeatedly and consistently for the past ten years. Most recently, in the target article for *Style,* Carroll refers to the conclusion of a collaborative forthcoming project, "Graphing Jane Austen," to explain the value of empirical research for both literary studies and social science:

> Research that uses a purely discursive methodology for adaptationist literary study remains passively dependent on the knowledge generated within an adjacent field, and it does not contribute in any very substantial way to that primary source of knowledge. The methodological barrier that separates discursive literary study from the adaptationist program in the social sciences limits the scope and significance both of literary study and of adaptationist social science. The production and consumption of literature is a large and vitally important part of our specifically human nature. An artificial barrier that leaves adaptationist literary scholars in the stance of passive consumers of knowledge also leaves adaptationist social scientists cut off from any primary understanding of one of the most important and revealing aspects of human nature.   ("Paradigm," 134)

On the whole, this passage issues a reasonable call for the inclusion of empirical research within the range of scholarly activities in literary studies. However, the disparaging characterization of interdisciplinary scholars who practice a synthetic, discursive methodology as "passively dependent" and "passive consumers" of scientific knowledge seems misguided. From the time people rise in the morning until they go to bed at night, they evaluate all sorts of ideas, and often they are not privy to the facts and methods underlying them. The more educated people are, the more likely they are to be skeptical of new scientific discoveries reported in the newspaper (such as a gene for intelligence, for example) and the better able they are to assess the value of sources. It is fallacious to assume that scholars who are not specialized practitioners of scientific methodologies cannot assess the worth of theories in the hard and soft sciences, where, after all, poor or misguided research is also as regular a part of the intellectual enterprise as it is in the humanities. And it is impractical to suggest that engaging in empirical research will necessarily strengthen the analytical component of cognitive-evolutionary literary studies.

Notwithstanding Carroll's own long alliance with Arnoldian humanism, his consistent, if ambivalent, misgivings that the speculative dimension of literary scholarship smacks of "inspired amateurism" echoes the late nineteenth-century fear that research on and teaching of vernacular literatures were not real intellectual work. By his own reckoning, Carroll does not overtly embrace the radical stance that Gottschall describes, "a wholesale disciplinary migration toward a scientific ethos"; however, his uneasiness about discursive methodology, his view of literary studies as a failure, and his strong appeal for scientific study ultimately point in the direction of a very different kind of discipline, one that perhaps locates human nature rather than literature as its primary object of study. For the difficulty of maintaining a scientific standard of verification becomes rapidly obvious when we consider its feasibility in light of Wilson's exposition of the process of consilience by reduction. As Wilson acknowledges, "Biology is almost unimaginably more complex than physics, and the arts equivalently more complex than biology" (*Consilience*, 67).

Using the extended metaphor of Ariadne's thread to illustrate the increasing complexity of intellectual effort, Wilson explains:

> The accelerating growth of forward-bound complexity, from entrance to end points, is illustrated with textbook clarity by cell biology. Researchers have used the reductionist principles of physics and chemistry to explain cellular structure and activity in admirably brilliant detail. . . . They expect in time to explain everything about any particular kind of cell chosen for study, reducing it organelle by organelle and finally reassembling it holistically, thus traveling toward the labyrinth entrance and simplicity. But they nourish faint hope of *predicting*—as opposed to explaining and reconstructing retrodictively—the character of any complete cell from physics and chemistry, hence traveling away from the labyrinth entrance toward rising complexity. . . .
>
> Put briefly, the questions of interest are how the cell is put together and what was the evolutionary history that led to its prescription. . . .
>
> To dissect a phenomenon into its elements, in this case cell into organelles and molecules, is consilience by reduction. To reconstitute it, and especially to predict with knowledge gained by reduction how nature assembled it in the first place, is consilience by synthesis.   (67–68)

My understanding is that this is an entirely material process in biology, and it is therefore hard to see how this method might work for a literary text, whose constitutive material elements—words, punctuation marks, pieces of paper, and sometimes pictures—are its vehicle rather than its substance. Since the object of analysis is not the physical thing but our cognitive apprehension of the communication from another consciousness, it is already an interpreted object about which readers will agree on many things (e.g., the basic story line) and disagree about others (e.g., the author's overall purpose or the appeal of certain characters). In other words, there is, relatively speaking, a far greater degree of subjectivism involved in the initial apprehension of the object alone than is the case in cell biology. It follows that any attempt to reduce the text to its fundamental elements will be guided rather strongly by the interpreter's a priori assumptions. What would be analogous, in other words, to "the reductionist principles of physics and chemistry" in helping us arrive at the constituent elements of a literary text? On the one hand, almost all scholarly fields have a potential relevance; on the other, none, arguably, isolates the core structural or dynamic elements of a literary text.

Beginning with the assumption that "literature is a product of human nature," Carroll has developed, with progressively increasing sophistication, an approach to reading that incorporates "a necessary minimum of analytic concepts—five in all—that must enter into a reasonably competent literary analysis informed by a Darwinian understanding of human nature."[28] Divided fairly equally between concepts drawn from evolutionary social science (e.g., human nature as a structured hierarchy of motives) and from literary analysis (e.g., " 'point of view,' or the location of meaning within three distinct centers of consciousness"), Carroll reduces down to basic elements of human nature and builds back up to textual specifics in his analysis of the exemplary text, *Pride and Prejudice*. Since Carroll is proposing that Darwinian approaches replace the paradigm in literary studies, he is prospectively suggesting that these analytic concepts must register in any "reasonably competent literary analysis."

This returns us to the problem of a "groundwork for explanation," which can, presumably, be arrived at by the process of consilience by reduction. Critical of Carroll's call for a "Grand Theory" of literature premised on social science, Frederick Crews retorts that "the subject matter of literary study is not human nature; it is literature," and he asks whether evolutionary themes deserve a special status in literary interpretation.[29] But another critic attempting to reduce the text down to its constituent elements might arrive at a very different set of features and might share Crews's view that Carroll's proposal would reconfigure literary studies at least in part around the study of human nature. This seems to be indicated in the analysis of *Pride and Prejudice,* where Carroll establishes a rubric of five general categories. As Crews notes, Carroll's five minimal analytic concepts generally inform criticism at the commonsense level, so it is unclear whether they need enter explicitly into the interpretation for the critic to pass the test of competence.

Among the problems bedeviling Carroll's program for adaptationist literary study organized around the concept of consilience, then, are several that recall the questions I framed at the outset of this chapter. For example, the insistence that literary scholars should engage in empirical research raises practical, philosophical, and pedagogical problems. Neither Carroll nor Gottschall fully articulates the benefits of such empirical study in terms of the goals of literary study in the past or in the future as they envision it. In my view, the attempt to formulate a Grand Theory of interpretation that mimics scientific processes of consilience by reduction and synthesis ignores fundamental differences in the nature of the objects of study in these disciplines.

The "Unimaginable Complexity" of Interpretation

Adopting a biocultural approach to literary interpretation does not necessitate acceptance of scientific methodology; adoption of a specified set of analytic concepts or a prescribed interpretive model; or adoption of a common groundwork for explanation. Indeed, I believe that doing any of these is not only inherently undesirable for the study of literature but also unjustified in view of the nature of that object and the process of apprehending it. In "Consilient Literary Theory," the evolutionary literary critic Marcus Nordlund sketches a simple model of reading and interpretation that briefly elucidates the semantic complexities inherent in any valid interaction with texts. Leading us back to a fuller consideration of the nature of the object, Nordlund suggests precisely why the nature of the object and the process by which it takes on significance militate against the methodological rigor that some humanists have yearned for not only in the current era of interdisciplinary enthusiasm but, as the brief foregoing overview of the discipline suggests, for more than a century.

Nordlund's triad contains a reader, a text, and a world (for purposes of his basic model, the author is included in the third category); among these, only the text itself "can be regarded as a reasonably finite creation with a fixed content" (318). The other two categories involve "a complexity that seems infinite to all human intents and purposes since it cannot be grasped by a finite, temporal mind" (318). All aspects of this model are dynamic, reciprocal, and necessary for all acts of reading, because the reader must relate to the text, on which she projects her understanding of the world, and the text also has a necessary relationship to the world. Hence, in keeping with the postmodern dictum that interpretation is always already theoretical, Nordlund's pragmatic triadic model posits three implicit theories: between reader and text, a theory of reading; between text and world, a theory of context; and between reader and world, a theory of reality. These theories, always operant in the reading process, shade into one another (a reader's theory of reality is prerequisite to her theory of context, for instance), but "a consilient theory of literary interpretation must not sacrifice or elide this complexity and must avoid any premature grafting of concepts from the natural sciences onto literary texts" (325). Because of the unimaginable complexity of the process, interpretation requires methodological reduction, "since it is impossible to deal with a single text while keeping all these parameters at work" (326). In light of this, Nordlund counsels a "self-conscious pluralism" in approach that avoids conflicts over different emphases in favor of constructive debate.

Nordlund offers this model to demonstrate to biocultural and adaptationist critics specifically that their interpretations will necessarily emphasize one or another aspect of the interpretive process, but because this is a model of reading per se, it effectively applies to literary interpreters of all stripes. Thus, the reasonable pluralism that Nordlund recommends for biocultural critics applies, in my view, to interpretive criticism at large. The critic may choose to emphasize the relation between reader and text, as in New Criticism; the text and the world, as in New Historicist contextualism; the reader and the world, as in evolutionary criticism; and so on. The reader will be all the better for her choice of reduction if she does not utterly neglect other dimensions of the process and if she acknowledges that the text under consideration should have a substantial say, so to speak, in the methodological choice. "Hudibras" and "Easter, 1916" cry out for text-world orientations; realistic novels from *Lazarillo de Tormes* to *The Heather Blazing*, for reader-world orientations; and lyric poetry, *Finnegan's Wake*, and other works of surface density for reader-text orientations, but all readings will fall flat if they focus on one dimension to the exclusion of others.

The importance of attending to all orientations while perhaps inevitably emphasizing one holds true for biocultural and adaptationist criticism specifically as well as literary criticism generally. Carroll, for instance, began from a specific reader-world assumption and has incorporated text-world and reader-text aspects more fully into his interpretive model and practice since 1995. Nordlund, a Shakespearean biocultural critic, pays more attention to historical context in *Shakespeare and the Nature of Love* than Carroll in his recent interpretive essays, partly because "Shakespeare's texts are more culturally and historically specific for me than they were for Ben Jonson" ("Consilient," 322). Carroll's focus has been on the Victorian novel since he began developing as an evolutionary critic, and the realities of the nineteenth century are a bit closer to home for most of us than are those of Shakespeare's day. Additionally, subjective factors such as personality influence the critic's choice of literary specialization as well as his or her critical orientation. While such factors influence the choice of pursuits for scientists, it is probably to a lesser degree than for many literary critics, because biology, unlike literature, does not deal directly with the contents of human experience.

In sum, any attempt to reduce the literary object down to its basic elements for the purposes of criticism is largely a deductive process, guided by the critic's angle of approach, which, one would hope, has a special relevance to the literary work in question.

Of course, the physical text acts as a stabilizing element in this process (the words on the page retain a fixed order supplied by the author, and these constrain and guide meanings considerably), but it should be noted that the literary work only becomes manifest as an object of significance in the reading process, where interpretation necessarily *begins.* Nordlund's model thus implicitly highlights the complexity of literary phenomena themselves, which are, in fact, *cognitive objects.*[30] As the products of individual consciousnesses that reach fruition when their material instantiations are apprehended by other consciousnesses, they are rather unlike cells produced by the blind process of natural selection or complex organisms with an intentionality of their own. Noting that literary scholars "inevitably expand the range of their studies to include philosophy and social and psychological commentary" because of the overlap between imaginative literature and other forms of humanistic discourse, Carroll points out that "critics tend to get absorbed into their subject.... They have no Archimedean point of critical leverage" ("'Theory,' Anti-Theory," 34). As Nordlund's model implies, however, the nature of the object is so fundamentally defined by different consciousnesses with varied relations to the world and by aspects of the reading process that absorption into the subject seems, to a significant degree, a fundamental aspect of reading and interpretation.

In this light, the notion of anything resembling scientific objectivity in interpretive criticism—Carroll's "Archimedean point of critical leverage"—seems unachievable. As Nordlund notes, quoting Robert Trigg, "being 'a realist about one class of entity does not commit one to being a realist about every class,' and it is perfectly possible (at least in theory) to be a scientific realist as well as a literary relativist" ("Consilient," 314). Put in terms of the entities themselves, cells, organisms, and books are all demonstrably real, but the latter, as the products of what Merlin Donald calls "theoretic culture," have a complex material-cognitive phenomenology whose essence, its iteratively constructed meanings, is not amenable to objective testing.[31] If humans succumb to extinction but other species of animals and plants survive, the cells within those surviving organisms will retain their full functional utility and thus will be real in a sense that books left to decay in unused libraries and empty homes will not be. Whereas modified scientific realism enables new knowledge to accumulate through the iterative process of hypothesis, experimentation, falsification, and proof in the sciences, attempts at a symmetrical process for literary studies, one aspiring to grasp the essence of its objects, accede to reductionism in their neglect of the unimaginable complexity of the object of study.

This is not the same as saying that literary meaning is endlessly deferred in any radical sense; rather, literary works are intentionally constructed not only in light of the endless complexity of world and reader but largely because of that complexity. And interpretive criticism is the attempt to shed some significant but relative light on that complexity. Thus, when Carroll asserts that "the primary purpose of literary criticism, as an objective pursuit of true knowledge about its subject, is to identify the specific configuration of meaning in any given text or set of texts" ("Human Nature," 205), I think he overstates the case for a unitary knowledge about literary works. As Nordlund points out, "There can be no 'empirical criticism' as long as that criticism also defines itself as an interpretive criticism" ("Consilient," 317); in other words, interpretation is the process of explaining what is not plain or explicit, such as the possible meanings generated by strings of words. Interpretive criticism addresses a core feature of literature, *meaning,* but the immateriality and relative instability of this core feature makes it impossible to adjudicate between rival and reasonable interpretations. How, for instance, do we get to the bottom of "Beauty is truth, truth beauty," when so much of Keats's ode suggests the sterility of the art object, while so much in Keats's writing and outlook underscores the poet's aestheticism? Although contemporary readers might tend toward an ironical reading, Keats may have meant this unironically, or he may have wanted to evoke an experience of negative capability in his readers. Who is the final arbiter of the configuration of meaning that will contribute to "true knowledge"? Reading is a dynamic, interpretive process, and it is in that process that meaning is configured and, perhaps, knowledge is glimpsed.

In retrospect, then, it is perhaps less than shameful that literature has been somewhat difficult to grapple with as an object of study. Nevertheless, as departments of English came to focus more fully on literature and interpretive criticism rather than philology through the first half of the twentieth century, they settled on a set of practices that speaks to the complexity of literary phenomena, strives for a degree of analytic distance from the object of study, and acknowledges as well that a relative degree of absorption into the subject is constitutive of the critical process. Literary history and close reading address reader-text and text-world dimensions of the reading process. Today, evolutionary and cognitive research is already expanding greatly our knowledge of all three dimensions of the unimaginable complexity of reading and interpretation.

The Centrality of Interpretation: Glimpsing Knowledge

I concluded the introductory section of this chapter with a list of questions about the aims, methods, and objects of inquiry in literature compared with those of the sciences that often are not distinguished in talk about "consilience" or about a successful means of resolving the divide between the two cultures. So far, I have suggested that, postmodernist trends notwithstanding, the development of literary studies since the late nineteenth century has become increasingly focused on the literary object and that because of fundamental differences in the objects of inquiry, the kind of knowledge produced by literary inquiry will continue to differ from that produced by scientific inquiry. In the previous section, I suggested that Nordlund's model of textual dynamics produces a strong rationale for the centrality of interpretation in literary study, since it illuminates the inextricability of interpretation in the process of the work's realization. At the most basic level, literary works are phenomenologically insignificant until they are instantiated through the informal interpretive process of reading. Scholarship and criticism, then, are a natural, formal extension of the informal process of interpretation that takes place during basic reading. Considered as a whole, the semantic power of imaginative literature bears witness to the centrality of meaning-making for the human species, for the business of producing and consuming texts is primarily about extending our meaning-making capabilities, not about something else during which meaning-making happens to become some secondary kind of adventure.

Curiously, however, the centrality of interpretation and meaning-making in our lives results in the paradox of our profound unconsciousness, or at least underconsciousness, of our perpetual meaning-making activities. In a sense, this is not particularly surprising, because reflection inhibits immediate action. Literature often plays a part in reawakening us to the sense of meaning-making, and this may well be one of the functions of imaginative literature, with its peculiar phenomenology: to bring back into consciousness some of what, for purposes of expediency, has been pushed out of conscious thought. In his novel *Stoner,* set in the first decade of the twentieth century, John Williams depicts a fairly dramatic version of such an awakening, one that speaks strongly to our underconsciousness of meaning-making and the unusual phenomenology of literature. A young man, William Stoner, leaves his small Missouri farm to attend the University of Missouri's new agricultural college. Boarding with his mother's cousin, he earns his keep by attending to the relative's farm and performs reasonably well in his university subjects until he is required to take a survey of English literature in his second year. Although he studies so hard that his other courses begin to suffer, he cannot understand the purpose of the course or earn satisfactory grades. Singled out in class one day for the contemptuous attentions of his English professor, Archer Sloane, Stoner cannot summon the most meager response to Sloane's question:

> Sloane's eyes came back to William Stoner, and he said dryly, "Mr. Shakespeare speaks to you across three hundred years, Mr. Stoner; do you hear him?"
>
> William Stoner realized that for several moments he had been holding his breath. He expelled it gently, minutely aware of his clothing moving upon his body as his breath went out of his lungs. He looked away from Sloane about the room. Light slanted from the windows and settled upon the faces of his fellow students, so that the illumination seemed to come from within them and go out against a dimness; a student blinked, and a thin shadow fell upon a cheek whose down had caught the sunlight. Stoner became aware that his fingers were unclenching their hard grip on his desk-top. He turned his hands about under his gaze, marveling at their brownness, at the intricate way the nails fit into his blunt finger-ends; he thought he could feel the blood flowing invisibly through the tiny veins and arteries, throbbing delicately and precariously from his fingertips through his body.
>
> Sloane was speaking again. "What does he say to you, Mr. Stoner? What does his sonnet mean?"
>
> Stoner's eyes lifted slowly and reluctantly. "It means," he said, and with a small movement raised his hands up toward the air; he felt his eyes glaze over as they sought the figure of Archer Sloane. "It means," he said again, and could not finish what he had begun to say.[32]

The text under discussion is Shakespeare's sonnet 73, in which the poet enjoins his lover to look upon his aging body. The concrete details of Williams's passage convey how fully the sonnet "means" for Stoner, whose physical response—his attention to his hands and his consciousness of his circulation—demonstrates his understanding of the poem's metaphors and their connection to human decay. Although he is dumbstruck, Stoner's sensory awakening to the reality of the place and to his own body promise that his epiphany will be more than equal to the humiliation to which Sloane is subjecting him. Inured to the brutalizing labor of farm work, he has never thought about his body at all. But perhaps the poem has made him aware of his body as a living thing that will age and die as other living things will. Whatever else William Stoner has understood about the sonnet in his informal interpretive process, the passage suggests at least that he has connected it to his physical body. Entirely incapable of reformulating a linguistic paraphrase of the sonnet, Stoner has nonetheless experienced something physiologically meaningful through the abstract medium of language.

This example has a particular poignancy, because the eponymous character has previously given apparently little more thought to his body than have the animals on his parents' farm, so Shakespeare's meditation on the body's decline, which Sloane reads in full before questioning Stoner, contrasts with Stoner's inarticulate yet sensorily immediate response. Ultimately, Stoner's desire to articulate his response, to become a formal interpreter of literature (for he does finally become a professor of literature), is especially strong, but the reader does not have to be an English professor to understand the character's impulse to grasp the poem cognitively. Stoner has understood the connection between at least some of Shakespeare's metaphors—autumnal tree, setting sun, and the deathbed—and felt their meaning. Providing a coherent paraphrase or explication would, in addition to saving him from public embarrassment, complete an entire circuit of literary experience.

I have used Williams's novel as an example of our unconsciousness of meaning-making processes, but this scene also offers a promising opportunity for cognitive and evolutionary interpretation itself. One sort of interpretation along these lines might point to the linguistic priming effects of the Shakespeare sonnet and their possible connection to Stoner's attention to his hands once he stops nervously gripping the desk. Such an analysis could furthermore distinguish as well between the cognitive effect on the character in contrast to that on the reader, as I do in chapter 4, where I consider these effects. In this manner, a nuanced biocultural criticism can reveal how the quintessentially abstract process of reading has a physiological impact and, through that impact, produces a reemergent consciousness of meaning-making.

Rather than seeing texts and meaning as a distinguishing feature of literary or humanistic culture, a point of view that ultimately further marginalizes literature and the other arts, we might ask what impulse has led to the creation of symbolic artifacts for purposes of interpretation. But considered in light of our unique features as an evolved species, the drive to create cognitive objects that offer themselves up for interpretation is of a piece with our distinct species logic. Artworks of this kind have an unusual capacity to bring back into the consciousness aspects of selves, bodies, behaviors, and the like that may otherwise remain hidden. As I discuss more fully in chapter 4, focusing on the external environment rather than on one's psyche and body is generally adaptive for a biological organism. This may be all some animals need; humans are exceptional, however, in that over millions of years of evolution they developed the capacity for long-term planning and environmental manipulation. In the metaphor of John Tooby and Irven DeVore, humans came to occupy the "cognitive niche."[33] Capable of sophisticated cause-effect situation modeling, humans long applied instrumental intelligence to coordinated group activities, such as tool and weapon manufacture, hunting, locating and utilizing shelter, and food preparation, before the relatively recent evolution of language (approximately 60,000–30,000 years ago), which greatly enhanced social cohesion and cognitive power.

Over time, however, instrumental intelligence does seem to push noninstrumental meaning-making, self-consciousness, and bodily awareness into the background, but the emergence of art, and perhaps especially literary art, indicates that they could not stay there. *Stoner* supplies an example of someone who expected to keep using intelligence instrumentally to run the family farm and turned instead toward the pursuit of meaning and knowledge in literature. And yet today the study of literature and the arts, a pursuit seen as secondary to other human concerns, is being eliminated from American universities at breakneck speed. Certainly, those scholars who emphasize that literature should be studied as a cultural phenomenon might want to consider how we strengthen our arguments for its value by articulating its emergence from our evolved nature.

Are Art and Literature Adaptations?

There are now several evolutionary theories of the arts and a few of literature specifically. The first challenge to such theorists is that of scale, since a complete theory must encompass the evolutionary time frame as well as the modern spheres of art. For the literary scholar (whose notion of the arts is invisible on any evolutionary time line), this means placing literary art on a continuum with other arts that are (or were) quite different from one another in their media and practices, such as self-mutilation, pottery design, ritual, and cave painting.

No matter how one defines art, it functions within the richly semantic world of human life, and literature, although an extremely recent subset of all the arts, nonetheless evinces marked similarities in function to its forebears. A second difficulty in attempting to formulate an adaptive account of art is that our concept of it is protean, just as its place and function in culture are protean. For most of our species' existence, what we now retrospectively identify as the arts—dance and ritual, body adornment, chants and songs, cave paintings—were not produced by individual artists or consumed by solitary users. Today, the arts are no longer bound up in the unified practices of daily life, but, as Johan Huizinga notes, "a gradual process extending over many centuries has succeeded in de-functionalizing art and making it more and more a free and independent occupation for individuals called artists."[34] Art activities in the contemporary world, such as film and performance viewing, museumgoing, and the "as if" pursuit of imaginative narratives, all occur in spheres separated off for most people from work and the everyday. Yet in spite of the differences between modern art activities, typically segregated from communal and work life, and premodern arts, integrated with community and work, and in spite of the division between popular, middle-brow, and high art forms, theorists recognize and strive to express the common elements in these diverse manifestations. As the evolutionary philosopher of art Denis Dutton points out, many twentieth-century scholars who criticize a universalist notion of art themselves reproduce elitist assumptions by comparing the artifacts of tribal and premodern human groups to museum pieces rather than to the Western arts to which they are akin, such as handicraft and folk-song traditions.[35]

The first scholar to develop a full-scale functionalist account of the arts in recent decades is Ellen Dissanayake, whose theory still supersedes in its comprehensiveness all other attempts to provide an evolutionary explanation of the arts. In *What Is Art For?* (1988) and *Homo Aestheticus: Where Art Comes From and Why* (1992) Dissanayake develops her phylogenetic account of art, one that she follows up with an account of the ontogenetic rhythms and modes that she proposes undergird and pattern all art behaviors in *Art and Intimacy: How the Arts Began* (2000). In Dissanayake's account, all of the activities, adornments, and decorations of preindustrial cultures that we recognize as the ancestral forms of modern art exemplify a predisposition toward elaboration, or in her chosen phrase, *making special.* Carvings on tools; nonfunctional, decorative features of baskets and pottery; and the visual, aural, and performative patterns of ritual, for example, are all evidence of the propensity to *make special,* which in some sense removes objects from the world of the everyday and places them, for members of traditional societies, within a magical or supernatural world, yet not within a separate sphere of art. In Dissanayake's words,

> Making special implies intent or deliberateness. When *shaping* or giving artistic expression to an idea, or *embellishing* an object, or recognizing that an idea or object is artistic, one gives (or acknowledges) a specialness that without one's activity or regard would not exist. Moreover, one intends by making special *to place the activity or artifact in a "realm" different from the everyday.* In most art of the past, it would seem, the special realm to be contrasted with the everyday

was a magical or supernatural world, not—as today in the advanced West—a purely aesthetic realm. In both, however, there is a sort of saltation or quantum leap from the everyday humdrum reality in which life's vital needs and activities—eating, sleeping, preparing or obtaining food—occur to a different order which has a different motivation and a special attitude and response. In both functional and nonfunctional art an alternative reality is recognized and entered; the making special acknowledges, reveals, and embodies this reality.

(What Is Art For?, 92)

A universal and distinguishing feature of humans, making special has, according to Dissanayake, two adaptive functions. First, in imposing a civilizing order on everyday things and experience, it promotes a psychological sense of mastery and control; and second, through group activities, shared images, and the like, it promotes social cohesion.

Dissanayake's further elaboration of her theory in the subsequent two books bolsters her original account as she draws on cognitive science, neurophysiology, and developmental psychology to claim the adaptive and central function of aesthetic activities in premodern cultures and in human infancy. For preindustrial persons who are highly intelligent and capable of conscious reflection yet simultaneously subject to numerous threats from their environments, the need for perceived control over experience is paramount. Dissanayake borrows the concept of *dromena,* translated as "things done," from Jane Ellen Harrison to articulate the sense of mastery that making special provides, and she theorizes that a human predisposition to separate the extraordinary from the ordinary began to develop about 250,000 years ago:

> I suggest that the standard and unexceptional animal inclination to differentiate ordinary from extra-ordinary, to recognize specialness, would have been developing over tens of thousands of years, along with other higher-level cognitive abilities that were evolving, such as planning ahead or assessing causes and their consequences. At some point in their evolution, humans began deliberately to set out to *make things special* or extra-ordinary, perhaps for the purpose of influencing the outcome of important events that were perceived as uncertain and troubling, requiring action beyond simple fight or flight, approach or avoidance.   (*Homo Aestheticus,* 51)

Play and ritual both constitute arenas where making special occurs and mastery is enacted, and Dissanayake offers a general psychobiological discussion of the response to art, pointing out that the empathy theory of the early twentieth century is now less easy to dismiss than it once was. As her research shows, and as mine supports in various specific applications to literary works in the chapters of the present book, art elicits a strongly emotional response initially, often through a variety of sensory inputs that then become cognitive and are stored afterward as higher-order representations.

Although our modern notion of art is narrow and culture bound, consideration of its origins suggests that it has many filaments—manipulative, affective, perceptual, cognitive (Dissanayake, *What Is Art For?*, 108)—and that it draws on a broad range of characteristics developed to a high degree in humans. As the passage above intimates, much of the earliest human art developed in the arena of ritual, as the hominids of the Upper Pleistocene attempted to master the forces of their environment and direct their own lives. In cranial deformation, ablation and filing of the teeth, chant, rhythmic dance, and narrative thought, which would propel humans toward myth construction and, thus, the evolution of language, the arts emerged as a central component of the entwined evolution of human consciousness, sociality, and language. Dissanayake's first two books were published in 1988 and 1992, and her theory of art is given support by contemporaneous developments in cognitive psychology and cognitive archaeology. The cognitive psychologist Merlin Donald, for instance, surmises that the drive toward myth construction drove the evolution of language, not vice versa. In this scenario, humans gradually augmented their early forms of mastery, which had provided *dromena* through chant and prelinguistic ritual communion, with explanation of the organization of the natural order.

Among literary scholars, Robert Storey has recently written a brief commentary on the origin of the arts that bolsters and further elaborates Dissanayake's theory of their religious origins. Drawing on the work of Conrad Montell and emphasizing the fact that many early aesthetic practices, such as cranial deformation and sharpening of teeth, were painful and time-consuming, Storey follows Montell in suggesting that human art evolved to solve a metaphysical question: "How to confront or escape a predator—death—that, unlike every other predator, cannot apparently be defeated?"[36] With the emergence of higher levels of consciousness, self-awareness, and social organization, this elusive predator posed the most dramatic threat to the human sense of order and control. Whereas Candace S. Alcorta and Richard Sosis argue that religion, along with all its aesthetic dimensions, arose to strengthen groups in a response to increased competition between groups, Storey disagrees and sensibly suggests that material competition could have met with a material solution (i.e., "well-armed conscripts of zealous thugs" [293]). Without a doubt, once in place religious rituals would help to organize the in-group against outsiders, but it is hard to justify the argument that religious rituals, with all their many filaments of making special, arose entirely for this purpose. Aesthetic-religious behaviors are both too expensive, requiring enormous time and energy, and too indirectly related to between-group competition to make this argument likely. As both Dissanayake and Storey indicate, only a psychological argument sufficiently explains the particular development of the arts.

The most fully elaborated recent alternative theory to the evolution of the arts, which overlaps with Dissanayake's in many respects, is Brian Boyd's, put forth in *On the Origin of Stories: Evolution, Cognition, and Fiction.* Boyd defines art as cognitive play designed to gain attention and appealing to a documented preference for patterned information. Boyd maintains that phylogenetically and ontogenetically, art begins in solitary and shared patterned cognitive play, whose self-rewarding nature reshapes the mind and over time raises the status of individual artists and the general human willingness to cooperate. These rewards of art can occur either via religion or not, but in Boyd's view art is a precursor to religion.

In common with the most important current functionalist accounts of art, then, Boyd stresses its communality or attention-sharing and its psychological or cognitive efficacy. Distinguishing human from animal play, Boyd points out that instances of nonhuman mammalian art are not representational and social, even among primates. Citing experiments with chimps who mime the use of pull toys, Boyd notes that even these animals are unprepared to share attention. While the young chimp Viki elaborately mimed pulling a string toy and guiding it through a house, Viki could not reengage in the game when her human caretaker tried to reinvent it a few days later (99–100). The inability of a chimpanzee, who, unlike most other animals, has some metarepresentational capabilities, to engage in this level of imaginative interaction indicates that it would be necessarily closed off from any psychological or cognitive rewards that the arts could offer.

Boyd tends to draw a stronger distinction between play and religion than either Dissanayake or Storey or than I do in my preliminary exploration of the adaptive analogy between play and literary experience, and at the same time he wants to separate the origin of art from that of religion.[37] But the point of disagreement on the matter of art's religious origin appears to be semantic rather than substantive. Boyd seems to suppose a cosmological order and set of beliefs and practices by the term *religion,* a word he does not define for the purposes of his own argument. From this perspective, the religion argument seems, understandably, illogical. Boyd asks,

If a group of early humans had begun to believe in supernatural forces, why *would* and how *could* they then have invented art to serve the purposes of religion? Why would they have thought of art as a next step, if there had not *already* been ways of embellishing surfaces and altering shapes and producing sounds and movements that elicited a deep response in human eyes and ears? Religion, on the other hand, needs art as a precursor. Without the existence of stories that diverge from the true, without the first fictions, religion could not have arisen. Religion depends on the power of story.   (114)

The confusion here derives from the assumption that *religion* in these hypotheses refers to a coherent cosmology and set of beliefs, however rudimentary in their formulation, rather than an impulse of a holistic, nonanalytic, and fairly primitive mind to solve core metaphysical and psychological conflicts. Such a mind does not move from conceptual understanding to execution of aesthetic (much less symbolic) product, or from fictional story to religious myth. The argument of Dissanayake, Storey, and others is that the various aesthetic practices emerged in tandem with the development of ritual and myth and that these processes drove the evolution of language. This accords with the present-day estimate for the evolution of language (within the past 60,000–30,000 years) in contrast to the much longer time frame for aesthetic or making-special activities that Dissanayake posits (approximately 250,000 years).

The individual and shared properties of play behaviors, whose value Boyd fully documents, provide many of the same cognitive and social benefits as early ritual and religion, and thus there is no conflict in seeing play behavior as an analog to the art function in later evolution. However, Storey does raise a relevant objection to the hypothesis that play is the sole source of art behaviors: unlike the arts, play has no product. Whereas the theory that art evolved through play behavior posits functional utility, it may not answer to the complex productivity of the arts. On the other hand, the suggestion that art may have originated in what we call *religion,* in our ancestors' desire to control the natural forces that bore down on them, is likely to attract resistance not only in a secular age but in an era when literary criticism still aspires, however ambivalently, to scientific credibility. In my estimation, we need to honestly confront what some of our best scientific theorizing suggests about literature: that its objects are unimaginably complex and that its origins are bound up with the deepest human fears and longings.

Perhaps these analyses about the evolutionary origins of art help explain not only the hovering effect that Scholes notes in literary canonicity between treating the objects of study as if they were specimens and holy texts but also the prolonged struggle in English and literary studies between rigor and research on the one hand and spiritual ideals on the other that ultimately materialized as the two-cultures debate in the mid-twentieth century. It is not likely that the religious resonance in the passage from Williams's *Stoner* escaped my readers: "Light slanted from the windows and settled upon the faces of his fellow students, so that the illumination seemed to come from within them and go out against a dimness; a student blinked, and a thin shadow fell upon a cheek whose down had caught the sunlight." We can easily chalk this recognition up to our cultural training in the religious and literary traditions on which Williams draws, but if the link between epiphany and illumination is not simply trite (more overuse of an overused tradition), we need to ask why this is the case. One important answer, of course, has to do with the tension between elements in the scene, because Stoner is failing and blinded in his limited insight. But the evolutionary critic would point out that the psychobiological correlates between epiphany and illumination and the original choice that led to the convention of linking light to revelation were certainly constrained by adaptive predispositions, although they have been inverted (by E. M. Forster and Robin Lippincott, among others). Addressing this passage from a biocultural perspective invites the critic to bring these forms of knowledge together. This does not mean, however, that the end result will be a scientific interpretation, offering true knowledge. And it does not mean that the critic, if he or she felt it in the first place, will have explained away the feeling of awe attendant upon reading the passage, which, cognitive object that it is, derived from filaments of making special, may call up our gravest doubts, manifesting itself variously as specimen or holy text in consciousness over time.

What Is Literature For?

Over the course of recent hominid evolution, the arts have manifested themselves in a variety of forms as expensive behaviors, worthy of a great investment of time and effort for groups and individuals without extraneous time and resources. Whether the arts evolved primarily out of metaphysical needs or within the overlapping activities of ritual and play, the message seems fairly clear as we look to the anthropological record: in the line connecting human prehistory and human history the arts exhibit enduring importance.

As the art form that attests to our ability to use compositional, recursive language and to multiply our cognitive abilities within cultural symbolic systems, literature is of special *evolutionary* importance. Ironically, however, because human beings have been so successful in performing discrete manipulations on the environment, they are led into the fallacy that our natural status is a thing of the past and "we are cultural beings now." This two-cultures mentality is simply wrong, dismissing the complex and fascinating psychobiological factors that bear on our production and consumption of literature. But it is also terribly trivializing to see interpretation and meaning as aspects of language and texts and the special provenance of the humanities, when they are distinguishing features of the human species.

What is literature for? Literary works are complex cognitive objects, dependent on a dynamic process of production and consumption, of reading and interpretation, for their instantiation. But the case is even far more complicated than this today, for if we glimpse just the current output of literature in the broad use of the term—speculative, horror, thriller, mystery, and other genre fiction; memoir and other creative nonfiction; lyric and narrative poetry; literary novel; drama; graphic novel; humor—we can begin to envision many overlapping reading groups and a variety of potential functions for literature and the experiences available through it.

A biocultural approach to literature sheds light on the virtue of this variety, because it counsels a pragmatic approach that entails combining traditional humanist methods and research with aspects of cognitive neuroscience and evolutionary social science that are relevant to the project at hand. Most critically, biocultural criticism, as I envision it, does not employ an a priori model that it presumes has application to the vast majority of literary texts. The drawback of many pseudoscientific twentieth-century programs was to work deductively from such models, and many of us have been left bored and unenlightened by such approaches.

Thus, the goal of the following chapters is to demonstrate to literary specialists that literature may be *for* many things and that a biocultural approach has broad application across literatures, topics, and subfields. The chapters maintain a philosophically coherent view of human beings while illustrating how different applications of interdisciplinary research can illuminate the human problems dramatized in literary texts. In this way, I hope to suggest that an acknowledgment of our shared human nature does nothing to reduce the diversity available in criticism, although it may well provide a little continuity to a remarkably fragmented discipline.

Aiming for depth and variety, I address four fields of current literary study, with the hope that my examples will encourage readers to pursue their own biocultural methods of criticism. Each of the following chapters has at its center an issue or topic that has been of focal concern since the ascendance of Theory in the early seventies and around which schools of criticism have taken shape. The topics are aesthetics and ideology, the environment, cognition, and Darwinism; and the subdisciplinary movements that have been energized by these topics are Marxist and New Historicist criticism, ecocriticism, cognitive approaches to literature, and Darwinian literary criticism and feminism. Chapters 2–5 each have three main parts: a survey of the state of the field, including some dominant concepts or models; a reconsideration of specified dominant concepts or models in light of cognitive neuroscience, evolutionary psychology, or other related fields; and one or more extended literary readings that draw specifically on the new concepts introduced in the second of these main parts.

Although each of these chapters can be read in isolation, the book as a whole seeks to illustrate how biocultural criticism brings to the fore the complementary aspect of literary subdisciplines that too often have seemed like competing domains. The chapters are organized so that they move from perhaps the single most important shift in theoretical perspective four decades ago, from aesthetic to ideological considerations, to the most recent call for a perspectival shift from literary Darwinists. Furthermore, while chapters 2–4 draw on a broad range of resources and make quite different arguments about how ideologically driven historicism, ecocriticism, and cognitive approaches might be enhanced by research in the social sciences, the chapters together paint a progressively complex picture of the sources and function of narrative cognition's instrumentality. Beginning in chapter 2 with an understanding of how narrative thought might enhance ideological criticism, I augment this sense of narrative's functionality in chapters 3 and 4 through an expanded research base in developmental psychology, ecological psychology, and cognitive neuroscience, showing its centrality to operant selfhood and relations to the nonhuman natural world. Finally, in chapter 5 I take up the issue of sex-differential mating strategies from an explicitly Darwinian feminist perspective, thus both illustrating another mode of biocultural criticism and returning to the issues raised by adaptationist literary criticism in the present chapter.

In chapter 2, "'It Is No Tale': Narrative, Aesthetics, and Ideology," I argue that while the ascendance of ideological criticism led to the neglect of aesthetic aspects of literary art, a biocultural approach has special worth in revealing the relationship between cognitive predispositions, historical situations, literary artifacts, and the aesthetic value of individual texts. Drawing on research in cognitive and evolutionary psychology, I not only describe the strong human predisposition toward narrativity (narrative thinking) but elaborate the troubling ideological and epistemological implication of this finding: that we are exceptionally

biased toward material delivered in story form. The transition into modernization spurred by the industrial revolution bred a more cognitively demanding,
epistemic literature, evident pervasively in texts from the romantic era and especially in a distrust of systems and narrative. In their poetry, poets such as Byron
and Wordsworth, for instance, evince both ideological and epistemological skepticism about the efficacy of narrative. In an extended analysis, I compare two
comic poems in ballad form, Wordsworth's "Simon Lee" and Mary Robinson's
"Old Barnard," to illustrate how the refusal to satisfy the reader's narrative bias
simultaneously constitutes the aesthetic and the ideological superiority of Wordsworth's poem.

If in chapter 2 I suggest that scholars need to explore the relationship between
ideology and aesthetics and that a biocultural approach can assist in that endeavor, in chapter 3, "Minding Ecocriticism: Human Wayfinders and Natural
Places," I recommend that ecocritics ground their field in knowledge of evolved
human psychology in an effort to understand the species' relationship with the
nonhuman natural world. On the whole, ecocriticism has struggled with the concept of mind and has been suspicious of literary works that reflect mental process, sometimes misguidedly favoring literary realism over other modes; but as
I argue in chapter 3, drawing on classical pragmatism and Darwin's *Origin of
Species*, concepts like "environment" are always constructed in light of species
prerogatives. The behavioral and cognitive plasticity characteristic of human evolution goes hand in hand with general adaptability to varied environments, but
human attitudes toward nonhuman nature are typically affected by the strength
and stability of human relations. Ecocritics have recently turned to the concept
of place, and in much of chapter 3 I seek to illustrate how human social connections, which evolved in the species past to protect the group, often have a central
importance in the attitude toward place. Drawing on developmental psychology
to explain that there is initially no distinction between the love for the mother
and the love the infant first feels for the world around it, I extend this observation to a reading of Wordsworth's Lucy poems and Jean Rhys's *Wide Sargasso Sea*.
These works illustrate how human loss and disordered social relations deform
our sense of the nonhuman natural world, coloring it with ambivalence and
antipathy.

In chapter 4, "Remembering the Body: Feelings, Concepts, Process," I survey
some of the many different practices that now fall under the rubric of cognitive approaches to literature and discern, in spite of the demise of cognitivism
(computer-modeled, first-generation cognitive science), a tendency to reconstruct machinelike models of the mind in literary studies. Drawing on ecological

psychology, environment psychology, the embodiment paradigm in cognitive science, cognitive archaeology, and cognitive neuroscience—fields employed in chapter 3 to explain human wayfinding cognition—I challenge these machinelike models of mind. Arguing that many of them are, however unwittingly, indebted to the assumption that thought is predominantly language based, I focus on Gilles Fauconnier and Mark Turner's conceptual blend theory, a model of human cognition that presumes an evolutionary ground. Whereas Fauconnier and Turner argue for coherent cognitive concepts that must be blended in a third space, I suggest that in many human contexts attention to language may not be the most salient factor for message comprehension. Drawing on Donald's theory of a mind comprising vestiges of three distinct stages and now engaged with an external storage system (extended mind), I develop a dynamic model of reading that I apply to two first-person texts, Coleridge's "Dejection: An Ode" and Raymond Carver's "I Could See the Smallest Things." In texts such as these, which explore the drama of consciousness, the process of reading is in some respects like physically moving through and perceiving a physical environment.

In chapter 5, "Endangered Daughters: Sex, Mating, and Power in Darwinian Feminist Perspective," I explain the emergence of evolutionary literary criticism in the context of Theory and clarify that the specific focus of that chapter, sex-differential mating strategies, is not necessarily the inevitable topic of Darwinian approaches. However, this topic has overshadowed other legitimately evolutionary directions in literary criticism and theory (just as cognitive processing and environmental relations have dominated cognitive approaches and ecocriticism respectively); thus, in chapter 5 I take the opportunity to address the more problematic literary representations of mating. Although Carroll, the recognized leader in adaptationist approaches, insists that the theory of life history provides a paradigm for interpretation, I argue against his life-history reading of *Wuthering Heights* in my opening section on evolutionary grounds and reconsider all the novel's relationships and psychology through existing criticism and Storey's theory of the evolved function of comedy and tragedy. Next, in the theoretical section, I lay out the basic differences in mating strategies between men and women and explain how these are related to their different roles in reproduction, emphasizing especially the normative conflict at the heart of male-female relations. While all individuals are psychologically organized and motivated to serve their own fitness objectives, on the whole, men seek to acquire resources as a means of acquiring and controlling women. Recognizing that unconscious fitness motivations might conflict not only with the desired partner's (i.e., the woman's) interests but also with the man's own need for emotional fulfillment in the pair bond establishes the context for the literary reading of D. H. Lawrence's *The Fox*. The existing readings of this novella are many and varied, but a Darwinian feminist interpretation highlights Henry Grenfel's proprietary, predatory approach to Nellie March, which in the long run undermines the fulfillment both characters seek.

Given the variety of theoretical considerations and practical applications brought to bear on literature in this book, no reader can complete it without coming to understand that biocultural criticism is fundamentally a creative enterprise, not a matter of mastering a model and then slapping it down onto unsuspecting texts. Criticism needs to be rational and judicious in its approach to science, as Arnold seems to have anticipated, while not forgetting the awe or love of beauty that draws us to art and maybe even toward the sciences that some of us want to use to help elucidate it. Because of the complexity of literature that Nordlund illustrates so well, there are many ways to begin biocultural inquiry, and patience, feeling, and the love of literature all assist one another in this endeavor. Whatever you find to disagree with in these pages, perhaps somewhere I have succeeded in bringing together the love of beauty and a more rational form of criticism that Arnold once anticipated, and perhaps, most of all, some of you will now want to contribute to this enterprise.

CHAPTER TWO

"It Is No Tale"

Narrative, Aesthetics, and Ideology

> The myth is the prototypal, fundamental, integrative mind tool.
> It tries to integrate a variety of events in a temporal and causal
> framework. It is inherently a modeling device, whose *primary*
> level of representation is thematic.
>
> *Merlin Donald*

Aesthetics under the Sign of Ideology

Literary scholars have been notably silent on the question of aesthetics in the past thirty-five years and have taken particular care to avoid evaluation of literary works based on aesthetic criteria. This is a product of a pervasive constructionist perspective that assumes the cognitively formative influence of sociocultural entities. Direct theoretical expression of constructionism is manifest in a great number of schools, ranging from the interpretive communities of Stanley Fish to the Foucauldian concept of discourse; but more importantly, a tacit constructionist code is maintained even by scholars with fairly traditional commitments. Thus, the general success of the constructionist ethos is itself powerful testimony to the element of truth in the poststructuralist doctrine of groupthink. However, it is not impossible to recognize the impact of our economic system and political culture on values, beliefs, and perceived knowledge and, at the same time, to make discerning judgments about poems, plays, and novels, except when the prevailing critical culture suggests that values and beliefs are nothing more than the manifestation of political power in another guise. In other words, although it is unlikely that most literary scholars would, if pressed, espouse strong constructionist commitments, the ideology governing professional decorum, in placing topics like aesthetics off limits, currently pervades the profession in this extreme form. If perceived knowledge, truth, and values are nothing more than a reflection of the sociocultural environment, then there is no possibility of a large-scale mediation of their validity.

Again, while few literary scholars would endorse such epistemic and moral relativism, the ideological thesis of constructionism has influenced literary critical culture in a strong way; gathered in small groups, research colleagues are often willing, even eager, to discuss the merits of various literary works, but professional forums have been notoriously silent about such matters.

The impossibility of pure objectivity notwithstanding, overt discussions of our judgments, aesthetic and otherwise, are crucial to the health of literary studies. Such discussions, certainly never easy, are now likely to be far more contentious and confusing than they were forty years ago, which is all the more reason why they should be central to any vision of literary studies as it is constituted now or might be constituted in the future. I am not arguing for a monolithic set of criteria, aimed at selected texts, intended to serve a narrow range of disciplinary goals and purposes, but I am suggesting that we need to think somewhat more comprehensively and perhaps systematically about our goals and purposes. In a basic sense, all disciplines need to do this to justify their existence. Viewed more pragmatically, the trend of the past several decades emphasizing the rediscovery of neglected authors has fostered an impulse toward inclusivity, one that, while taxing program design, simultaneously creates the illusion that discriminating judgments between works have been avoided, when in fact the criteria for value judgments have merely shifted from the aesthetic to the political.

Is it true that we can know, teach, and produce scholarship on it all? The implication of Willie van Peer's research suggests that this is highly unlikely. Noting that the total volume of literary works increases in literate cultures over time, van Peer finds that such cultures "are constantly engaged in selection processes, the outcome of which is a heavily skewed subset of the total number of literary works produced within that culture."[1] In other words, canon formation occurs whether we actively promote it or not. If van Peer is right, then, we can engage consciously in the formation of canons for research and teaching, or we can let the canons take care of themselves, so to speak. Since a certain amount of the latter will occur anyway—since canonization is a cumulative process involving many people, we cannot know with certainty what our influence will be or how things will play out over time—it does seem that literary scholars might want to think about how their decisions regarding what works to study have an impact on the discipline as a whole. This reasoning applies as incontrovertibly to those who take a strong cultural-studies perspective as it does to those of us who believe that aesthetic criteria should play a significant role in determining the canon; the only difference is that cultural studies has been promoting its values all along, whereas the aesthetes, silenced by poststructuralist ideology, have retreated shamefacedly to the corner.

Those of us who wish to argue that determinations of artfulness or beauty should have a role in what gets discussed, studied, and taught need to start formulating better theories about what contributes to aesthetic value than have been available in the past. As a subdiscipline of philosophy, aesthetics has been hindered by essentializing and transcendentalizing tendencies and by the corollary failure to consider aesthetic judgments in the light of apparent real-world considerations, including cognitive predispositions and cultural context. A pragmatic, functionalist account assumes at the outset that while evaluative criteria do not remain constant, they are not culture-relative in an extreme sense. Thus, special skill in handling the medium, an awareness of formal patterning, and evidence of novelty (in style, form, or content) are all significant in aesthetic evaluations; moreover, all likely have some origin in our evolved psychology, but the particular value of any given instantiation is relative not only to canonical precedents but to other aesthetic criteria as well. In addition to criteria that relate to a biopsychological substrate, the sociocultural, political, technological, and intellectual milieux, as well as social and technological change, are all central features in aesthetic judgments. In other words, the more we speculate about evaluative criteria, the clearer it becomes that aesthetics and ideology are bound up with each other not in any singular or straightforward way but in a manner that might be teased apart on a case-by-case basis.

Skill and the capacity for innovation in the primary medium are perhaps the most enduring features in attributions of aesthetic value, but what counts as innovation is demonstrably culture-relative to a significant degree, since it is influenced by technological and intellectual developments of the historical period in which it emerges. In the nineteenth century, the production of vivid new paints, packaged for the first time in tubes, enabled artists to work outdoors for extended periods. In combination with the rise of psychology and theories of light and perception, this technical innovation effected not only the emergence of impressionism but its ultimate celebration as a major aesthetic achievement. In literature, the awareness of the predominantly nonlogical nature of mental process and of the related ambiguity of human motivations led to the stylistic innovations of Henry James, James Joyce, Virginia Woolf, D. H. Lawrence, and William Faulkner, among others. In this manner, new cultural contributions to knowledge not only affect the forms, style, and method of artworks but transform standards of judgment. Moreover, some art forms have a number of significant aesthetic dimensions, and frequently trade-offs are made in the evaluative process. The opera is a good example of this. Richard Wagner would have made a poor showing as a novelist, but his erratic handling of dramatic action, his penchant for exposition, and his engagement with an ideology most today find repulsive are superseded in aesthetic judgments by his profound capacity for musical innovation combined with a gift for spectacle. Narrative defects—absurdities of plot, poor pacing, and the like—abound in many operas deemed great, since music is primary in this medium.

By contrast, literature, especially nondramatic literature, depends on the handling of language for its evaluation. Percy Shelley held that poetry was the highest form of art because "language is arbitrarily produced by the Imagination and has relation to thoughts alone; but all other materials, instruments and conditions of art, have relations among each other, which limit and interpose between conception and expression."[2] Shelley's high estimation of literature rests, of course, on a hope that poetry might grasp universal truth, a hope few, if any, poets and scholars share today. Influenced by Hume's insight that only thoughts can be known directly, Shelley overstates his case by ignoring the aural dimension of language. One might wonder, too, how a phenomenon such as language, designed evolutionarily for the purpose of group cohesion and social mediation, "has relation to thought alone," and certainly as a practicing poet Shelley himself could not maintain his faith in the mediatory purity of language. Yet in spite of his idealism, Shelley does point to a distinctive feature of literary art, its fundamentally abstract nature, which perhaps makes it more reliant than other media on conscious cognition for processing and appreciation. Although humans respond enthusiastically to the rhythms of artful language well before they consciously understand its meanings—read a two-year-old a few poems from Blake's *Songs of Innocence* to witness this—a developed appreciation requires some level of engagement with the semantic content. This is not true to the same degree for visual art or even for operatic or choral music. All of which does not make literature better than painting, music, or dance, as Shelley seemed to think, although it does suggest that the ideas both motivating and presented within a work of literature will have greater salience in determinations of literary value than in aesthetic judgment for works in other media.

If we assume that ideas are likely to take a central place in literary value judgments, we still need to ask what the role of a cognitive approach is in considerations of aesthetic value. After all, most of the research in evolutionary and cognitive psychology points to prototypical, unconscious mechanisms and mental predispositions, and such theories of general architecture or propensities seem far removed from the culturally inflected ideas manifested in specific literary texts.[3] As Jon Gottschall points out, literature supplies vast evidence of these mechanisms; however, as I argued in the introductory chapter, the valuable project of revealing these mechanisms in the databases of literature and other arts, of which Gottschall is a strong proponent, moves in the opposite direction from the question what makes literature *literature* and the related matter of aesthetic judgments because it focuses solely on commonalities.[4] In fact, a recurrent argument against a broadly defined interdisciplinarity is that it undermines the study of literature in its own right, redirecting attention toward generalities and away from the individual dynamics of works of art. As Northrop Frye memorably put it, "There can be no such thing as a sociological 'approach' to literature. There is no reason why a sociologist should not work exclusively on literary material, but if he does he should pay no attention to literary values. In his field Horatio Alger and the writer of the Elsie books are more important than Hawthorne or Melville, and a single issue of the *Ladies' Home Journal* is worth all of Henry James. The literary critic using sociological data is similarly under no obligation to respect sociological values."[5] Although literary critics today are unlikely to accept Frye's sharp distinction between literary scholarship and the endeavors of other disciplines, his general point deserves serious attention and is directly related to the endorsement of a strong program of quantitative research advocated by some Darwinian literary critics. If research activity were to become focused solely on the common features of literary works, there would be little rationale for literary studies as a distinct discipline, whether the common features were attributed to social patterns, evolved predispositions, or some other phenomena.

In short, it is not possible to justify the study of literature without engaging with specific features of individual texts, and ideas are one centrally significant feature of individual works. However, an understanding of how cognitive predispositions inform the structure or content of a work of art provides the background against which the presumed innovations of culture, including its developing ideas, can be assessed. As anthropologists and Darwinian literary scholars point out, the enduring themes of literature repeat the basic themes and motivations of human life, just as the typical formal patterns reflect basic human ways of shaping and organizing experience. What special skill in handling language and what engagement with ideas, then, make canonical works stand out?

The following analysis proceeds in several stages. First, basing my argument on a substantial body of research in cognitive psychology, I assert that humans have a strong propensity for narrative thinking and that while our predisposition for narrativity is functionally adaptive, it is also prone to act as an epistemic limit and to serve a conservative ideological function. Second, I assert that narrative's tendency to conserve ideology and perceived knowledge is seriously constrained by the dynamics of social change, particularly when linear explanation no longer answers to the real-world experiences and the intellectual developments attendant on modernization. Finally, I suggest that the eighteenth- and nineteenth-century recognition of the epistemic and ideological limits of narrative is in fact part of the reason why some texts are regarded so highly. Concluding with an analysis of the narrative strategies of Wordsworth's "Simon Lee" and Mary Darby Robinson's "Old Barnard," I suggest that the ongoing cultural relevance of Wordsworth's eschewal of narrative is a central feature in the aesthetic evaluation of the poem. In contrast to "Old Barnard" and other comic poems published in the *Morning Post*, "Simon Lee" illustrates the complex relationship between narrative, received ideology, ideological change, cultural and intellectual development, and aesthetic merit.

Narrative Knowing and Epistemic Constraints

The study of narrative provides an excellent test case for the value of a cognitive approach to aesthetics, because both literary studies and psychology have developed bodies of research on and theories about this subject in the twentieth century. Both Vladimir Propp's formalist analysis of folk tale and Lévi-Strauss's structuralist analysis of myth laid the groundwork for later efforts to analyze the elements of narrative, and indeed, narratology became the chief beneficiary of structuralism, extending the project to the study of modern literatures. Yet as early as 1966 Girard Genette pointed to the limitations of the binary categorizations *diegesis-mimesis* and *narrative-discourse*, thus raising the question of the usefulness, or even basic validity, of rational categories for the analysis of literary techniques.[6] In the long run, of course, deconstruction's conclusion—that if categories are not rational and discrete, they have no meaning at all—was unhelpfully extreme. Recently, David Herman and Alan Palmer, among other scholars, have suggested that the study of narrative can benefit from cognitive science, and Palmer particularly recommends that an understanding of how human minds function both within and outside fiction might provide a useful, revisionary perspective for narratology, steering that subdiscipline away from an overemphasis on language and a somewhat coldly analytic view of character, which tend to separate, for example, characterization from the presentation of consciousness and perception (focalization or point of view) from other aspects of mental life.[7] Palmer's holistic emphasis on intermental functioning compels us to ask to what extent any formal analysis of narrative structure actually reflects the workings of literary texts.

"Ideally rational is what we long to be," says the cognitive psychologist Dan Lloyd, "but it is another question whether ideal rationality even approximates what we are."[8] If the history of narratology indicates that the components of story structure are not as strictly amenable to rational categorization as scholars might have hoped, is there nevertheless a useful definition of narrative? Lloyd's own description of narrative is the best place to start, because it is cautious and minimalist. First, at the most basic level, the theory of narrative is not one of artistic genre; since narrative is evident in much that is nonliterary, a preliminary definition requires that it be set apart from specifically literary considerations. Lloyd is even hesitant to call narrative a *structure,* preferring to designate it as a *texture,* because unlike sentences, narratives do not have discrete structural elements. Yet narrative does exhibit central tendencies in form and content, most especially formal and semantic constraints: its representations are singular and affirmative, identifying or describing its subjects and stating what *is* the case (the affirmativity constraint) and giving information about the temporal ordering of events; and it militates against the representation of unattached events, showing them instead to be causally connected (210–21). According to Lloyd, the theories of both structuralists and cognitivists exclude some narratives, because "narrative is nearly unlimited in its forms, including the banal, boring, and brief. ... 'During the thaw, a sheet of ice on the roof loosened and fell. It struck a parked car, cracking the windshield.' Though hardly the stuff of great novels, this nonetheless seems to be a narrative" (225). Lloyd's definition calls attention to the broad range of phenomena sharing the basic features of narrative, thus importantly qualifying the somewhat narrower definitions of other theorists.

Typically, as Lloyd suggests, many theories of narrative reflect specific disciplinary perspectives. For example, like Lloyd, the social psychologist Jerome Bruner emphasizes the inherently sequential nature of narrative, but whereas Lloyd seeks to characterize narrative based on its objective manifestations and thus apart from its human function, Bruner is mainly concerned with narrative's psychological and social purpose.[9] Humans are, according to Bruner, essentially meaning-making animals who order events and mental states by casting them into plots, thus demonstrating that for our species sequentiality is indispensable to significance. In keeping with this psychological perspective, Bruner adopts Kenneth Burke's definition of narrative, or of the well-formed story: actor, action, goal, scene, and instrument, plus trouble (in Bruner, 50).

It is worth noting that although Bruner's chief concern is narrative thought and its social function, he draws his definition of narrative, which at times elides the distinction between narrativity (narrative thinking) and intentionally constructed fictional and nonfictional narratives (Burke's primary object of study), from a literary critic and theorist. For the benefit of both psychological and literary studies, it is often important to distinguish between a basic mode of thought on the one hand and the artful manipulation of that cognitive mode on the other. While it is true that all narrative (in thought, conversation, or written modes) tends to ratchet up the purposiveness of human behavior by casting events into a linear and causal structure, literary narrative, unlike our day-to-day thinking, is the product of a conscious shaping of characters and events, and as a result it may emphasize, complicate, or subvert the prototypical characteristics of narrative. Interestingly, the tendency to obscure the distinction between narrativity and constructed story is perhaps itself testimony to our desire to find purpose and cause everywhere.

As Lloyd, Bruner, and Roger Schank suggest, narrative structure is ubiquitous, determining the mode of all discourse, whether fictional or factual. Its pervasiveness suggests that narrative discourse is the result of a built-in propensity for narrativity, or linear and causal thinking.[10] E. O. Wilson calls predispositions like the causal rule "epigenetic rules," which he defines as "the regularities of sensory perception and mental development that animate and channel the acquisition of culture" (*Consilience,* 157). Epigenetic rules can be modified over time, because "culture helps to determine which of the prescribing genes survive and multiply from one generation to the next." Since genetic change is extremely slow— biologists maintain that it takes about fifty generations for minor genetic alterations to occur—perceptual or cognitive orientations, such as seeing in gestalt-like arrangements or organizing experience in causally based narrative sequence, would have to demonstrate a functional disutility for tens of thousands of years to be significantly altered. In other words, our perceptual and cognitive orientations, which preceded the development of human culture and arose to assist adaptation to a far different environment from the one we now inhabit, are still firmly in place.

Wilson's assertion that a mental predisposition to search for causes is a basic rule of human thought provides an evolutionary rationale for a long philosophical tradition identifying causal connection as a primary mode of the association of ideas. As David Hume reaffirms, restating basic notions of the association of ideas that hark back to classical philosophy, "To me, there appear to be only three principles of connexion among ideas, namely, *Resemblance, Contiguity* in time or place, and *Cause* or *Effect*."[11] At the level of common sense, the persistent viability of the causal mode of association as an intellectual concept within philosophy of mind and psychology and adaptationist explanation and, most importantly, the survival of the human species suggest that causal inference offers a functionally accurate interpretation of the world outside the mind. Here is one example of a nonfictional narrative with apparent functional benefits, one probably accepted by most Americans: A hurricane barrels into the Gulf of Mexico and plows through New Orleans, destroying lots of trees, houses, and businesses and killing many people. The impact of this storm is exacerbated by past human negligence, which resulted in substandard levees that in turn were overpowered by Hurricane Katrina, resulting in the destruction of about 80 percent of the city. Although we can never know, in an absolute sense, whether causal narratives like this accurately represent past events, this story and others like it are generally taken to be true functionally and pragmatically, as the strenuous efforts of politicians, volunteer groups, and the citizens of southern Louisiana—working on such projects as wetlands restoration, levee upgrades, and home rebuilding above the flood plain—attest.

In short, narrative thinking arose, presumably, because it facilitated interpretation of events in the environment and consequently promoted functional action. Importantly, from an evolutionary perspective, environment includes all those entities to which a natural population group must respond in order to survive. For human individuals, then, not only members of other species but humans themselves, whether cooperative members of the in-group or antagonistic outsiders, are part of the world negotiated by linear and causal thinking. Once we recognize that for early humans attributions of cause and temporal events were not limited to nonhuman nature but crucially concerned the actions of other humans, we have the logical basis for understanding how, in the process of evolution, narrative's most central function has become the negotiation of human social life, and it is this central function that is the focus of much psychological research. The cognitive psychologist Michael Carrithers defines narrativity as the capacity to cognize complex human interactions carried out over long periods of time, promoting the ability to perceive a given action as part of an unfolding story.[12] Thinking in storylike sequences about our lives and those of others not only enables articulation of the links between external events but also facilitates the connection between thought and actions: "By means of stories humans cognize not just thoughts and not just situations, but the metamorphosis of thoughts and situations in a flow of action" (311–12). Perhaps most importantly for the narrativizing individual or group, the capacity to construe "a direction in events and a coherence in persons" precipitates new human action, as cognizing agents apply the narrative construction to their immediate situation (316).

In this sense, then, narrativity arose to support basic human psychological assumptions, called "folk psychology," and the inferential procedures that this theory of mind supports. Folk psychology (or "folk social science," "common sense," or "theory of mind") includes the following beliefs and premises: that humans have beliefs and desires; that they want certain things; that people should not want and believe irreconcilable things; that there should be coherence to people's beliefs and desires. Furthermore, folk psychology assumes that there is a world outside us that modifies our beliefs and desires and that knowledge of that world affects desire and action (Bruner, 39–43). This basic, unconscious psychology is narrative rather than logical or categorical; that is, we make assumptions about how people will behave based on their previous actions and on our inferences about their mental state related to those actions. For instance, five years ago, when my daughter was ten, I regularly inferred that she would forget to put her homework in her booksack once it was completed, because although she had attended school and had received homework assignments for many years, she had not yet remembered on her own to put her work away after completing it. I did not place her in a category (all ten-year-olds?) and draw my inference from a set of rules about that category. (And while I was engaged in my process of narrative mentation-into-action, it is likely that she was mentally fashioning a quite different narrative of her own.) Indeed, developmental cognitive research indicates that narrative thinking emerges quite early in human life, well before categorical thinking; after developing the ability for object-oriented pretense, children begin to imagine states of desire, perceptions, and beliefs, and by the age of two or three they can imagine states of mind not their own.[13]

Although the suggestion is that the rudiments of narrative thinking preceded language both ontogenetically and phylogenetically, the evolution of language vastly extended the possibility of narrative—as a tool of negotiation (and therefore power) and as a medium of social exchange that enables unifying myths but also organized dissent. Bruner distinguishes between canonical and exceptional narratives, and thus between those articulating the dominant stories (and therefore, most likely, the prevailing ideology) of a culture and the competing stories of individuals or subgroups. But narratives do not so readily fall into or, perhaps more importantly, remain within one or the other of these two groups. In a qualification to Bruner's distinction between culturally canonical and exceptional narratives, Robert Storey asserts that "the more actively engaged that most members of a culture are in elaborating and construing its narratives, the more ambiguous will those narratives be: the line between the 'exceptional' and the 'canonical' (as 'multiculturalism' has shown) will become harder and harder to draw."[14] History bears out this observation about the ambiguous cultural status of conflicting stories, because a high level of a general population's engagement in narrative construal corresponds to modernization and an egalitarian world-view, which provide the intellectual and political conditions under which individuals have, theoretically, both access to the necessary information and the right to construe cultural narratives. Furthermore, Storey suggests that the representation of narrative "usually through the usefully (if meretriciously) stabilizing medium of language . . . [causes] the 'ambiguity' I have ascribed to it" (84). Storey's remarks are provocative because even if this "innate *way of knowing*" (84) is fundamental, as Bruner maintains, to meaning-making—to making sense of our selves, our lives, and our social spheres—the proliferation of stories, especially in written form, in combination with the proliferation of interpreters, makes meaning more and more difficult to construe.

Moreover, as Bruner claims and as the above discussion suggests, stories in their socially meaningful sense have an epistemic as well as a moral status, because they involve both cultural convention and individual deviation. For example, according to Michelle Scalise Sugiyama, the oral precedents to "Little Red Riding Hood" offered a lesson essentially about predation (and thus a cautionary story close to the literal level of the tale's characters and events); eighteenth-century literary versions likely altered the content of the original oral tales enough to refocus the moral on the imperative of virginal purity.[15] In spite of considerably different messages (or perceived messages), both tales operate epistemically and morally within their cultural contexts, and the latter particularly illustrates narrative's capacity to subserve and conserve dominant culture values, because its domain contains the real and the imaginary, promoting as it does the culture's preconceptions about girls and women. Human susceptibility to narrative, certainly, gives one pause about its epistemic and moral influence, which seems uncomfortably culture-relative and might at first blush appear to support the strong interpretation of Foucault's claim that knowledge is directly relative to power.

Narrative exhibits, in Bruner's words, a "shadowy epistemology," for two reasons: first, as the above suggests, narratives are not unbiased but serve particular interests (whether these interests be individual, political, or of some other sort); and second, they are our means of construing both the real and the imaginary (55). Thus, our awareness that narratives are *someone's or something's* stories in combination with their ambiguous relationship to perceived reality complicates our sense of their epistemic and moral utility. In *Experiencing Narrative Worlds* Richard Gerrig underscores Bruner's claim about the problematic nature of narrative epistemology in his summary of a range of experiments and in his theoretical conclusions about some of the psychological processes underlying story interpretation. Citing Coleridge, Searle, and others, Gerrig calls into question "toggle" theories, thus disputing the long-held view that fictional information is compartmentalized apart from factual information. As he points out, such theories cannot explain either the place of real-world knowledge in fiction or the demonstrable effects of fictional stories on real-world behavior.

Moreover, studies by a number of psychologists suggest that fictional information is frequently persuasive, although it is treated more critically when it is related to the personal situation of the reader than when it is not. Most striking (and amusing) is Gerrig's discussion of *perseverance effects,* including biased search and causal scenario construction. In the instance of biased search, subjects accept information they have been told is false if that information fits with their existing belief structures. For example, although viewers knew that *Jaws* was a fictional story, the movie increased fear of shark attacks (even among lifeguards!) because actual shark attacks do occur. In other words, subjects search cognitively for the belief structure that fits the information, even when they know the story under consideration is fictional. This finding, incidentally, further supports the psychological observation, beginning with nineteenth-century pragmatism and confirmed by research in social psychology today, that people seek to maintain their existing belief structures.[16] Similarly, experiments in causal scenario construction indicate the strength of our predisposition to create causal explanations and to maintain them once they are in place. In one experiment, subjects were asked to create a scenario to explain information but were subsequently told that they had been provided with false information; in spite of this revelation, they nonetheless retained the causal explanation. Ultimately, Gerrig suggests that if any toggle exists, it is between narrative and preexisting information. That is, while we may be disturbingly prone to persuasion by material presented in narrative form, we tend to be skeptical about new information.[17]

In addition to a built-in bias for causal scenario construction, cultural conventions contribute to our predisposed modes of interpreting and perceiving and thus further direct the epistemic trajectory of stories or particular types of stories. Narratives have been identified as generalized knowledge structures, and while a variety of generalized knowledge structures—including serial, categorical, and matrix structure as well as spatiotemporally organized schemas, such as stories, scripts, and scenes—may be universally evident and hence potentially founded on biologically based predispositions, the content of some schemas, and sometimes the entire schema itself, may be derived from and only relevant to a particular culture. For example, an event schema for a birthday party will vary from culture to culture and be entirely absent from some cultures, yet the likelihood that all humans have event schemas—"hierarchically organized [sets] of units describing generalized knowledge about [event sequences]"—in their knowledge base is a strong claim among many cognitive scientists.[18] So, too, with stories: their base structure is apparently invariant, but formal, substantive, and semantic dimensions are apt to be culturally inflected and sometimes culturally determined. Stories perform a central function in the maintenance of religious belief, binding the community together; within evangelical communities, the recitation of a story with which all members of the congregation identify binds the members of the group together and, in drawing a conclusion, provides closure (Schank, 212–18). Significantly, the conservative function of stories in the maintenance of belief has been demonstrated in instances in which millennial expectations have been disappointed.

In the case of written literature, preconceptions about structure, content, and genre may not only direct the reader's response but, in fact, predetermine all or part of that response. This is probably especially true of children's, adolescent, and popular literature, all of which rely heavily on formulae. Even before the reader's expectations are cued during the reading process, the very framing of the experience invites a set of assumptions about the artifact: the purple hardcover version of *Harry Potter and the Goblet of Fire* sports a dustjacket depicting Harry (whom we all already know) and an elderly character, probably Dumbledore, gazing wide-eyed into an urn out of which swirls a white vapor that merges with the dustjacket background. This illustration heightens the expectation of magic and adventure, already well prepared by readings of the first three or four novels, and primes the reader for another round of contests endured and evil creatures subdued. Someone may, in fact, die, but suspense and fear are controlled by the assurance that it will not be Harry. Adult reading experiences are similarly framed, whether we prefer Virginia Woolf or Robert Ludlum, and thus we often anticipate our own responses. (This may not be so for the first-time reader of Woolf, although her experience might be framed by other factors, such as a course syllabus for an upper-level English class or the spectacle of Nicole Kidman walking into the Ouse at the beginning of the film version of *The Hours*.) Responses to films are also framed by reviews and generic expectations; as Noël Carroll points out, the expectation that a horror film will produce fear helps to produce fear.[19] Culture's tendency to exploit the disturbingly suasive structure of narrative raises the specter of skepticism once again, compelling us to ask whether our own minds shut out more knowledge than they provide.

Gerrig's research on the procedures humans employ as they move between information and causal scenarios seems to suggest that narrative is highly unlikely to coincide with anything approximating empirical validity. But just as a half-filled glass is always half empty, it is always half full: if our bias toward narrative thinking results in interpretive errors (e.g., that the federal government, in not financing and building a modern levee system, intended the destruction of New Orleans), it also enables knowledge. Several points are worth making here. First, without a set of generalized knowledge structures to provide orientation to the external environment, there is only confusion. Second, as what appears to be our most basic generalized human knowledge structure, narrativity is certainly powerful, but it is only one of a number of such generalized structures, all of which arose because of their practical utility; other cognitive predispositions, such as the tendency to categorize or to form dichotomies, also shape our mental architecture, which suggests that for the adapting human organism narrativity alone has never provided sufficient solutions to environmental challenges. Put another way, no single brain-mind thinks in purely narrative terms. Third, Rousseau notwithstanding, humans have never lived in isolation, a fact to which the preeminence of narrative thinking attests; we think about our lives and needs in relation to the environment outside the self, and all the goals that narrative helps to shape must take that environment into account and must negotiate the levels and types of narratives on the same subject. Thus, among the many narratives about the failures of city, state, and federal governments throughout the Katrina crisis and into its interminably long aftermath, the story claiming that the city was intentionally destroyed is unlikely to become canonical.

Those who speak of narrative as an "intersubjective map" or an "intermental" function have gleaned, therefore, the relational significance of narrative: it makes possible the maintenance and management of human life by mediating the interactions of individuals and groups vis-à-vis the environment, that is, both the physical world and other individuals and human groups.[20] Therefore, while specific stories certainly do work to conserve the status quo, their perceived validity is regularly undermined by forces of change, whether these are cultural, natural, individual, or communal. When Rosa Parks refused to give up her bus seat in Birmingham in 1955, her physical action in a well-defined place challenged the canonical story of the segregationist South and created the opportunity for the developing narrative of the civil rights era, which, in turn, became canonical. Interestingly, Parks herself had not planned her action and had no goal-driven story (she was not even the first to protest in this manner), but she acted anyway, and because her action was in keeping with a growing dissatisfaction about entrenched inequality, her refusal to move sparked the Birmingham Bus Boycott and thus played a significant part in disrupting the canonical story and became a central event in the replacement narrative. And the new story, since it held up well against the observed conditions under which African Americans were living, began the work of renegotiating the place of blacks in American society with the aim of establishing their rights in relation to American society as whole. The importance of Parks's action and the narrative construction of the need to remediate a situation of continued inequality for black Americans persisting since emancipation would not have gotten much of a hearing if neither the action nor the narrative corresponded to the observed condition of this population.

What holds true for the dynamics of narrative in political and social change pertains to the realm of cultural artifacts as well, and thus the complex interactions governing the production, consumption, and evaluation of literary narratives mitigate the conservative effects of story. In what follows I suggest that while literary narratives can certainly limit knowledge and reinforce outdated and even patently false beliefs, they can also challenge the beliefs of the literate population, even when generic structural conventions appear to serve the maintenance of existing ideas and values. Moreover, if we consider literary canons in the past two to three hundred years—since the rise of literacy and the proliferation of print material—originality and creativity seem to have been consistently valued. Keeping in mind that every literary work, being shaped by its culture and by the life experiences of its authors, will display continuity with that culture, it is striking not so much that literature has changed in the past five hundred years but that novelty or change has become increasingly valued as an aesthetic criterion. If art is a human adaptation for making *special,* as Dissanayake argues, then we might want to ask why artists since the emergence of modernism have been glorified for making *extra special.* With much justice, Marxist critics point out the ideological utility of an aesthetic of change in a rapidly transforming culture, but claims that such an aesthetic represents a reification of the dominant ideology need to be weighed against the evidence of specific literary works. Because social structure, ideology, and culture have been massively transformed since the industrial revolution, any given analysis of the ideological content of a literary work needs to consider authorial manipulations of form relative to the work's content, as well as the short- and long-term reception of the work.

In the following analysis I suggest that even though narrative has the capacity to channel us into received modes of thought, and even though it does in daily life frequently function that way, many of our most prized literary narratives of the past several hundred years promote critical reflection and the ideal of knowledge in a broad sense and that this ideal tends to run counter to the bland acceptance of the status quo, including received assumptions about a perceived dominant ideology, an essentialized human nature, or other preconceptions. The great paradox of industrialization is that while it spawns and perpetuates an unthinking and destructive consumerism on the one hand, it gives birth to the culture of criticism on the other.

Cognition, Modernization, and Aesthetic Transformation

From the perspective adopted in this book, the desire to know is in the most general sense integral to human origins, because knowledge seeking and knowledge acquisition are necessary features of survival for a wayfinding, social animal who not only traverses a large domain and must therefore process a complex environment but also must negotiate successfully the kinship network on which he or she depends. At the same time, the desire for broader and deeper knowledge— for abstract ideas, a greater comprehension of human minds, and a variety of perspectives on political, social, and individual conflicts—is a luxury founded on the security of cultural comforts. Modernization relies on widespread education, and thus the desire for more knowledge of all kinds coincides with the complexity of modern culture.

But while the desire for profound knowledge is therefore certainly linked to the values governing postindustrial life, I take issue with the Foucauldian supposition that knowledge is an *effect* of power, that the complex "power-knowledge" operates in varying ways at all levels of culture. Foucault's chief terms are broadly applied, compelling us to ask what kinds of knowledge directed at what purposes he had in mind.[21] Surely knowledge cannot be a manifestation of ideology in any simple sense, for whereas the desire to know how to design websites may simply subserve pecuniary goals, the desire to know, for instance, the status of the U.S. government's information about nuclear-weapons development in Iraq before the beginning of the Iraq War, or perhaps more to the point, about the government's efforts to *limit* knowledge of this episode in recent history, serves rather different interests. By the same token, the urge to know why humans pursue imaginative experience in literature and the urge to know whether grief has an adaptive function appear to have quite distinct goals from my two preceding examples. Among these, only the second example provides a clear instance of authority attempting to *produce* (or manage or contain) knowledge, but even in that example the knowledge-power relation seems to have eroded, albeit later than the American public might have hoped.

In short, various types of knowledge are in demand in modernized cultures, and it is unlikely that all of them contribute to the subterranean regulation of a police state either as direct and conscious state action or through the invisible operation of discourse that Foucault seems to envision. If narrative itself provides the conceptual and discursive mode for public misinformation, it is nonetheless simultaneously the mode of dissenting views. In the process of cultural transformation, new ideas emerge in the sociopolitical, personal, and intellectual spheres as they gain credibility, and they do so in the form of narratively ordered explanations, exceptional stories that over time may become canonical.

Literature (in the traditional sense) has been no less a vehicle for the dissemination of new ideas than have factual modes. Given the sociocultural need to align values with shifts in social and economic culture, the presentation or enactment of new ideas in literature has had a legitimately important role in determinations of literary value. This is true even when such modes test and challenge our cognitive capacities, although the intellectual challenges presented by modern art have hardly been uniformly praised. Bruner claims that the novel has become more epistemic since the time of Flaubert, as it has moved increasingly away from exposition and toward the representation of intentional states (51–52). Bruner here addresses what literary critics refer to as the novel's inward turn, its explicit focus on human minds as the locus of action, but as Palmer points out, even narratives that eschew representation of mind place high demands on the human mind-reading ability, that is, the capacity to make inferences about intentions, beliefs, and desires. Asserting that literature "capitalizes on and stimulates [theory-of-mind] mechanisms that evolved to deal with real people," that we "'intuitively' connect people's behavior to their mental states," Lisa Zunshine proceeds to identify the complex and embedded intentional states of several characters that a reader must comprehend to make sense of a brief passage from *Mrs. Dalloway*.[22] Considering the passage in light of recent research on mind reading, Zunshine concludes that writers like Woolf test the limits of our mind-reading ability.

What is the potential value in testing our cognitive limits? In fact, since the 1960s an array of psychologists, anthropologists, and arts scholars interested in the evolutionary and cognitive aspects of art have deplored the intellectually demanding quality of the last century's productions, insisting that the arts have gone astray in manipulating and subverting perceived cognitive norms.[23] However, not one scholar that I know of has presented a convincing argument explaining why the artists should reaffirm baseline characteristics—in visual art, the recognizable gestalts we seek out in our environment; in narrative, an emphasis on causally related external events accompanied by a minimal psychological dimension; in lyric poetry, the presentation of a brief narrative or epiphanic moment in conventionalized meters based on built-in patterns. Underlying these complaints against difficult art are unarticulated assumptions about the nature and function of art that are, if not downright erroneous, highly questionable. First, it is simply untrue that nature, either in the mind or in the world, is a coherent entity whose stable and unified qualities should be enforced and preserved. As Gerrig's research on causal scenario construction suggests, some cognitive predispositions may at times be unhealthily robust. Indeed, the dynamism of actuality is the greatest challenge to minds. Second, while detractors of modern art most frequently assume that enjoyment and/or quasi-religious unification experiences are the function of the arts, this is hardly self-evident. While the significance of pleasure and transport should not be eschewed in evaluation of artworks, neither should intellectual difficulty. In this sense, the third assumption of these scholars, that art dependent on the explanations of specialists for its coherence is somehow flawed, is anachronistic, even atavistic, in a cultural milieu dependent on specialists for all other forms of explanation.

Aesthetic artifacts are a product of distinct human environments, and cultural history indicates that modifications in the environment result in radically different aesthetic artifacts. Those that test our cognitive limits may, in fact, have an important place in modern culture, which itself tests human limits in ways that would have been inconceivable just a few hundred years ago. Let us first pause to consider the transformation undergone by many cultures in the past three hundred years. Modernization proceeds in a distinct pattern: The Enlightenment produced the knowledge necessary for the means of industrial production, precipitating the shift from an agrarian to an industrial economy with the development of factories and large-scale cities. Efficient management of factories and laborers requires levels of organization and employees with skill and technical knowledge, and hence industrialization catalyzes the movement toward universal education and precipitates the growth of the middle classes. Over time, the increasing sophistication of production techniques, the application of technical knowledge to new areas, such as transportation and communication, and the need to regulate and organize modern life by supplying the physical and social infrastructure it requires (large buildings, roads, sanitation, law enforcement) created the need for universal mass education. This pattern of change, first witnessed in eighteenth- and nineteenth-century Europe and America, has proceeded in the same fashion in later-developed and developing nations, and it is typically though not always accompanied by economic capitalism and democratic political systems.[24]

In my view, it is not possible to exaggerate the cognitive and emotional demands placed on people by the rise of industrialization, for the process of modernization results in the most dramatic changes in social and political organization and lifeways that humans have known in approximately ten thousand years of culture.[25] The human relation to places and the types of environments people must negotiate differ vastly from those of the past, so the psychological impact and epistemic demands of the shift to modern living had to be substantial. Prior to industrialization, the structure of farm life maintained the continuity between home and work in a manner consistent with the lives of our early ancestors. Over the course of industrialization, however, the home and the workplace became increasingly separate, requiring people not only to negotiate unfamiliar terrain, often alone, but to deal successfully with a far greater range of human groups and individuals than had formerly been the case. Although, of course, much small-scale business persisted within the industrializing city—families ran small shops (purveying food or providing tailoring, for instance) conjoined with their domestic environment—the movement was increasingly toward mass production and hence the separation of environments and persons, as well as the different and complex conjunctions of persons and environments, that that pattern entails.

The rise of print culture in the eighteenth century was itself a product of the scientific knowledge stemming from the Enlightenment and the perceived need for information, knowledge, and entertainment that accompanies industrializing culture. New technologies made mass print culture possible, but those technologies themselves would never have been invented without the existence of increasing literacy and the desire for knowledge. By the same token, new forms of imaginative literature depended on this reading audience as well as on less expensive forms of printing. But the availability of readers and the production technology alone do not explain why imaginative literature specifically should proliferate. Viewed rationally, the situation suggests that nonfictional media could supply the information and analyses necessary to learn how to negotiate the industrializing environment. Viewed rationally, it would seem that the Gradgrind system would answer to the case. But as philosophers and psychologists have increasingly observed since the eighteenth century and as Lloyd and other cognitivists remind us, we are not primarily rational creatures, whatever our longings. Imaginative literature engages with our everyday modes of thinking and feeling but, locating the reader's experience in as-if situations, resides a safe distance from everyday social and practical interactions.[26] Whatever the ultimate source of these types of making special in our evolutionary past—as ritual and religion, play, and interwoven filaments of other aesthetic activities—hypothetical experience through literary and other media has been of enduring and possibly increasing value to humans with the acceleration of culture. Imaginative literature addresses the emotional and social complexities of modern life while providing information about and views of that transforming world from a variety of perspectives. To give just one brief example, Dickens's imaginative rendering of the deleterious effects of utilitarian education provides, theoretically, the opportunity to experience and know those failures without having to live through them directly.

In short, the transformation in human social structure as a consequence of Enlightenment science resulted in cultural transformations as well, and it should not be surprising that simple forms derived from oral culture, themselves reliant on our cognitive predispositions, would be of limited use in such an environment. Furthermore, whereas oral forms operate under the constraint of memorability, written literature faces no such demands, and the writer is free to complicate form and content in any ways that suit his or her purpose. Nonetheless, human thought and action, including the act of writing or reading literary texts, are only possible within the parameters of human intelligence, and narrative is a foundational feature of human cognition. Whereas writers beginning in the eighteenth century have exploited print and the proliferation of middle-class readers to subvert basic modes of cognitive organization and reasoning, those subversions are always, and necessarily, premised on the forms of thought they question.

Suspicious of received cultural forms, many romantic-era writers equated conventions of language and literature with reigning political and social conventions. Their methods of highlighting the perceived alliance of sociopolitical conservatism and aesthetic practices were diverse; nevertheless, the conviction that specific features of literary art—forms, genres, rhetorical structures, and so on—not only limited thought but often channeled it toward pernicious and destructive ends is pervasive in writers otherwise quite distinct. Romanticists are accustomed to this view and are apt particularly to note its application to Blake and Shelley, in certain respects the most radical of the romantic poets. "I must Create a System or be enslaved by another Man's / I will not Reason & Compare: my Business is to Create," Blake's Los announces,[27] yet the paradox of commanding so as not to be commanded and the concomitant fear that all systems entailed tyranny resulted in the persistent corrosive effects of Blake's work. As scholars have long noted, the unfinished magnum opus and the fragmentary lyric are hallmarks of romanticism, illustrating both the drive toward and the distrust of not only large syntheses and grand narratives—Wordsworth's *Recluse,* Charlotte Smith's *Beachy Head,* Byron's *Don Juan,* Keats's *Fall of Hyperion*—but also unified personal expression.

In *The Marriage of Heaven and Hell,* for instance, Blake consistently challenges his reader's preconceptions, disturbing the desire for received forms containing unambiguous messages.[28] At the outset, he subverts the convention of inserting a brief prose summary (or *argument*) at the beginning of each section of a long poem. Whereas the argument traditionally summarizes action and thus typically directs and guides the reader's attention, Blake opens instead with a cryptic, allegorical narrative poem entitled "The Argument." Although this brief poem is prophetic in tone, intimating the imminent release from the hypocrisy and duplicity of the reigning order—"the sneaking serpent walks / In mild humility"— linguistic transvaluations in combination with the disruption of formal conventions render the status of its prophetic claim anything but clear (plate 2, ll. 17–18, p. 85). More important than Blake's disruptions of form and his ironization of argument is his refusal to invent a new pattern, to reconstitute the stabilities of language and form on other grounds. Almost every section of this idiosyncratic literary work undermines its own presumed assertions, but the "Proverbs of Hell" provide a particularly good example of the drive to unsettle reader preconceptions. Brief and aphoristic, proverbs typically encapsulate received truths for ready consumption, yet Blake's proverbs range across commonplace wisdom, outrage, nonsense, and distinctly Blakean truth. The net effect is the demolition of truth in a monolithic and static sense and its replacement with a view that wisdom is relative to the point one has reached in a process.

Whereas Blake unravels received forms and the preconceptions he believes they tend to encourage, Shelley exposes the destructive effects of conventionalized discourse through its systematic use in *The Cenci.* After Beatrice is raped, she accedes to the rhetoric of religious justification previously identified only with her father. Adopting the language of retribution does not cause Beatrice's transformation from a figure of divine suffering to one of vengeance in any simple sense, but the rhetoric of divine justice fills the gap left by the annihilation of self and sanity resulting from the rape. In so doing, the conventional language of divine retribution, in effecting her reconstitution as the mirror image of her father and in supplying justification for violent action, provides the necessary conceptual framework for the murder of Count Cenci. If Blake suggests that received ideology is embedded in literary structure, Shelley exposes rhetoric's powerful sway. By incorporating doubts about the suasive aspects of language and form into the method of their works, writers such as Blake and Shelley demonstrate an emergent realization that prototypical modes of cognition and expression do not or should not comprehend the possibilities of human thought.

While for Blake and Shelley the conventions they expose perpetuate tyranny and a structure of beliefs that upholds it, other writers demonstrate how received modes downplay the significance of individual experience. Seemingly depicting the era's transformation in consciousness on a much smaller scale and offering a more modest social criticism than *The Marriage* and *The Cenci*, a poem like Anna Laetitia Barbauld's "Washing Day" ultimately reverses the values on which it is premised by undermining mock-heroic conventions. Typically employed to undercut human vanity by applying high rhetoric to commonplace occurrences, the mock heroic focuses on external realities of place and action. Jonathan Swift's "Description of a City Shower" employs heroic couplets, inflated rhetoric, and classical allusion to underscore the filthy state of industrializing London, thus exposing the degraded state of modern man. Omitting the couplets but retaining other heroic trappings, Barbauld begins "Washing Day" in this mode and maintains the mock-heroic diction and figures for more than half the poem (ll. 1–57) even though her opening words bid farewell to neoclassicism in announcing a transition to the everyday subjects that will form the core of Wordsworthian romanticism: "The Muses have turned gossips; they have lost / The buskin'd step, and clear high-sounding phrase / Language of the gods" (ll. 1–3).[29] However, after this mocking depiction of the enormity of washing day, which supersedes and cancels all habitual pursuits and courtesy, Barbauld shifts the perspective and drops the mock-heroic devices, thus transforming the poem into a romantic lyric:

> I well remember, when a child, the awe
> This day struck into me; for then the maids,
> I scarce knew why, looked cross, and drove me from them;
> Nor soft caress could I obtain, nor hope
> Usual indulgencies; jelly or creams,
> Relique of costly suppers, and set by
> For me their petted one; or butter'd toast,
> When butter was forbid; or thrilling tale
> Of ghost, or witch, or murder. . . .
>
> .   .   .   .
>
> Then would I sit me down, and ponder much
> Why washings were. . . .   (ll. 58–79)

The reader is left to balance points of view—that of the utter mock seriousness of washing and its displacement of all other activities on the one hand and that of the puzzled child used to special attentions but now neglected and adrift amidst the flurry of household activities. Although Barbauld's final image of the poem itself as a soap bubble asserts the ephemerality of her composition, the lines just preceding these insist on the basic dignity and integrity of all points of view:

> Sometimes thro' hollow bole
> Of pipe amused we blew, and sent aloft
> The floating bubbles, little dreaming then
> To see, Montgolfier, thy silken ball
> Ride buoyant thro' the clouds—so near approach
> The sport of children and the toils of men.
>
> (ll. 79–84)

These lines suggest not only a similarity between the invention of the hot air balloon and the child's play but also, potentially, a causal connection between such childhood play and adult invention, reinforced by the closeness in age of Barbauld (b. 1743) and the Montgolfiers (b. 1740 and 1745) as well as the year of their first launch and the time frame of the poem's composition (after 1783). Thus, although Barbauld's closing lines contrast the "toils of men" with, perhaps, the literary amusements of women and the play of children, the logic of the comparison, in combination with the genesis of the soap bubbles and, implicitly, the poem in an experience of inwardness and perplexity, insists on the validity of the child's point of view.

Within this context of a general challenge to the interrelated conventions of conceptualization, language, and literary expression, a distinct subset of romantic-era poets evince a distrust of narrative specifically. In some ways, it is hard to imagine two writers more different than Blake and Byron, yet both harbored a distrust of systems, and both believed that mental and literary constructs could subserve existing tyrannies or institute new ones. In Byron's major long poems, *Childe Harold's Pilgrimage* and *Don Juan*, narrative construction is a primary (though certainly not the only) target of the poet's criticisms. Setting up a competition between the eponymous heroes and their supposed conventional trajectories on the one hand and the first-person speakers, both uncomfortably resembling the real Lord Byron, the poet manages to challenge the validity of narrative at multiple, overlapping levels, including selfhood, history, quest or heroic deed (purposive action in the service of the spirit of the nation), and literature. In *Childe Harold* particularly, the incompatibility between the visual perception, the memory triggered by distinct scenes, and the effort to construct a conventional quest of healing and renewal results sooner rather than later in the reconstitution of the work in the speaker-poet's sense of historical and personal crisis. In the final analysis, Harold himself becomes a kind of cartoon, without consciousness or, for that matter, much capacity for conscious thought. His very emptiness seems to have equipped him for the successful completion of his quest.

Paradoxically but not illogically, this resistance to narrative coincides with the emergence of the novel in English literature. Just as social conditions produced the technical knowledge, as well as the need, for exhaustive, realistic narratives in print, the same conditions and intellectual changes produced a suspicion of long narratives—of causally integrated stories in which individual human actions have discernible consequences and according to which a cohesive sense of human meaning results from story-making. On one hand, the eighteenth century witnesses the rise of the novel and thus the intricate representation of social reality and the intersecting stories of various social groups and classes. With the rise of literacy, the written word generally and the novel specifically provide the means for narrative to become an intersubjective and geographical map of the changing world of physical and social relations. While it would be foolish to suggest that the emergence of the novel in the industrial era is equivalent in importance to the emergence of narrativity in human evolution, the genre did to some extent serve a correlative function for its growing readership. On the other hand, if the realistic novel shows us how narrativity can bind us to places and persons previously beyond (quite literally) our imagination, it also dramatizes how hard this process is. *Jane Eyre*, in which the eponymous heroine nearly marries the wrong man for the wrong reasons, has many fairy-tale aspects, but it has about it none of the episodic regularity of fairy-tale narrative structure. The genesis of Pip's story in *Great Expectations* is, in fact, the need to correct the false story according to which he lived his youth and adolescence. The simple causal trajectory of orphans making good and rising in the world shadows these novels, simplified versions of far more tenuous tales. Similarly, in the even more psychological milieu of later Victorian culture, *Middlemarch*'s Lydgate and Dorothea demonstrate the fragile connection between personal desires and conscious goals and ideals, a connection upon whose reasonable reliability the successful attainment of the object depends.

In sum, if the novel's development in England, beginning in the eighteenth century and extending through the nineteenth, attests to the binding agency of narrative, it also exposes the strains on narrative knowing and on the construction of self and social relations resulting from industrialization. The case is even clearer when we consider other instances of the genre's development: the earliest manifestations of the novel, the Spanish picaresque of the sixteenth century, or the quite different development of the genre in America. Similarly, Victorian long poems, such as *The Ring and the Book* and *Aurora Leigh,* in depicting a multiplicity of viewpoints and conflicting philosophies, strain narrative cohesion. Extended literary narrative acts as an imaginative binding agent in Victorian culture, but it must work hard to perform this function and thus stands as the counterpart to, rather than a stern rejection of, romantic-era disruptions of narrative structure.

Unknowing the Narrative Habit: Wordsworthian Configurations

The question of our mental predispositions and their effect on interpretation and formulation reflects, on the whole, a late-Enlightenment awareness that previous human notions of the actual drastically simplified a complex universe and a corresponding collapse of the Cartesian divide between matter and spirit as a result of eighteenth-century brain science. As Alan Richardson explains in *Romanticism and the Science of Mind,* researchers of the day contributed to a generally affiliated set of theories, including the following: the mind is in the brain; the mind is an active processor; body-mind functions are biological rather than mechanical; the brain is complex and constantly active. Moreover, all held proto-evolutionary views of human development and adaptation. Although the associationist psychology David Hartley theorizes in *Observations on Man, His Frame, His Duty, and His Expectations* is mechanistic in comparison with the work beginning in the 1790s, Hartley's goal, as early as 1749, was to reground philosophy in the nervous system by describing how motions from the external environment cause vibrations along the nerves.

Richardson's recent elucidation of 1790s brain science importantly modifies the literary critical tradition that identified Hartleyan associationism as the primary influence on Wordsworth's psychological conceptualizations. Hartley posits a quasi-mechanical process whereby environmental stimuli trigger vibrations along the nerves; over time, the repetition of contiguous sensations generates ideas in the mind. Forty years later, thinking on the nature and activity of the human mind had changed substantially. In *Zoonomia* (1794), Erasmus Darwin, whose reconceptualization of mind and its material nature was in keeping with his belief in evolution and adaptation, moved decisively away from the passive, Lockean conception of mind, positing internal senses, innate desires, and unconscious processes. According to Richardson, Wordsworth, who read *Zoonomia* in the 1790s, was directly influenced by Darwin's conception of mind.

Thus, although Wordsworth employs the word *association* repeatedly in his discussion of a variety of mental processes, his use of the term is multivalent and reflects a strong sense of the actively engaged, dynamic nature of human mental function. Instructively, Wordsworth uses *association* to describe not only the creative interaction of feelings and ideas that produces profound poetry but the cognitive constraints resulting from literary conventions as well. The Preface to *Lyrical Ballads,* written for the second (1800) edition of the poems and subsequently revised, is best known for claiming the centrality of feeling to the writing process, for the assertion that common subjects and forms are appropriate to serious poetry, and for its conception of mental process, presumably derived from Hartley. All of these are central features of Wordsworth's revolutionary poetic enterprise. However, the poet first employs the term *association* in his introductory remarks about encultured expectations. Before summarizing his own poetical program, Wordsworth pointedly remarks that his poems will not adhere to the conventions established for that genre, and he casts this opening in terms of audience expectations. In the second portion of the passage below, added to the 1802 Preface, Wordsworth emphasizes the discrepancy between his project and reader habituation:

It is supposed, that by the act of writing in verse an Author makes a formal engagement that he will gratify *certain known habits of association,* that he not only thus apprizes the Reader that certain classes of ideas and expressions will be found in his book, but that others will be carefully excluded. This exponent or symbol held forth by metrical language must in different æras of literature have excited very different expectations. . . . I will not take upon me to determine the exact import of the promise which by the act of writing in verse an Author in the present day makes to his Reader; but I am certain it will appear to many persons that I have not fulfilled the terms of an engagement thus voluntarily contracted. They who have been accustomed to the gaudiness and inane phraseology of many modern writers, if they persist in reading this book to its conclusion, will, no doubt, frequently have to struggle with feelings of strangeness and aukwardness: they will look round for poetry, and will be induced to inquire by what species of courtesy these attempts can be permitted to assume that title. (emphasis added)[30]

Wordsworth's primary violations of the conventions of form and subject matter in *Lyrical Ballads* have long been identified and include the decision to adapt the native folk ballad to the aims of literary verse even while simultaneously reenvisioning the appropriate subject matter of serious poetry as "incidents and situations from common life" composed in "the real language of men." The poem Wordsworth presents as an example of outmoded conventions, Gray's "Sonnet on the Death of Richard West," repeats tired Augustan techniques of syntactic inversion and personification; in the first four lines alone, mornings smile, Phoebus lifts his golden fire, birds sing an amorous descant, and the fields, like so many merry men, "resume their green attire" (749). Noting that Gray was "more than any other man curiously elaborate in the structure of his own poetic diction," Wordsworth recognizes that the tortured syntax and cartoonish figures distract the reader from, and therefore have no honest relation to, the presumed subject of the poem, the speaker's grief. I do not think it is too much to say that Wordsworth, for whom the cognitive process of the true poet is repeated in the reader's experience, as that reader's "understanding . . . [is] in some degree enlightened, and his affections ameliorated," saw through the gratifications of Gray's poem, which encourages the reader to think well of him- or herself by indulging in a shallow pity masquerading as sympathy (745). Nothing could be further from the process of righting one's world that Wordsworth depicts in the Lucy poems or from the barren psychological truth expressed in his memory of his mother's death: "She left us destitute, and as we might / Trooping together."[31]

As the multiple forms of innovation and experimentation in his own verse suggest, Wordsworth apparently recognized that "known habits of association" can operate within various aspects of a poem (including diction, form, and subject matter) to constrain understanding and the emotions upon which such understanding depends. Whereas Gray's conventional diction, his "gaudy and inane phraseology," deflects attention from the subject and therefore artificially limits the reader's emotional involvement, Wordsworth's own poetry illustrates how a range of preconceptions often blocks the ability to learn from experience. It is worth noting that, far from excluding himself from the failure to think and see profoundly, Wordsworth tends to dramatize the inhibiting nature of preconceptions in poems that adopt a first-person speaker who in many respects resembles or is the poetical reconstruction of the real William Wordsworth. In the 1802 poem "Resolution and Independence," the speaker's naïve, egotistical, and clichéd presuppositions about the poet's lot initially inhibit his receptivity to experience, and in poems as different as "We Are Seven" and *The Prelude,* Wordsworth suggests that the cultivation of reason promotes a reductive and compartmentalized approach to life.[32] Elsewhere in *The Prelude,* Wordsworth suggests that our culturally primed expectations, like the forms of rational analysis, are inadequate in the face of experience, sometimes woefully so. In the crossing of the Simplon Pass in book 6, the failure of sublimity results in disappointment, loss, and temporary psychic annihilation, a pattern repeated in numerous "spots of time."

Ironically, in *The Prelude* it is the stark insufficiency of such "known habits of association" that determines their value, for the mismatch between expectation and experience catalyzes a restructuring of the self.[33]

Thus, Wordsworth's poetry demonstrates, as does that of Blake, Shelley, and Barbauld, an acute awareness that all manner of perception, cognition, and expression can become tired "habits of association," inhibiting our ability to know more or feel more; when constitutive of a poetic practice, such habits stunt and even destroy the moral value of verse. Wordsworth's sensitivity to the cognitive, emotional, and moral limits of intellectual and linguistic conventions anticipates the Russian formalist critic Viktor Shklovsky's twin concepts of habituation and defamiliarization. Writing in 1917, Shklovsky notes that "the process of 'algebrization,' the over-automatization of an object, permits the greatest economy of perceptive effort."[34] Indeed, current research in neuroscience and philosophy of mind accords with the intuitions of Wordsworth and Shklovsky that overly familiar forms and concepts enable processing at a low level of consciousness. The capacity to process much input below the level of consciousness is functional because efficient, as Palmer explains, quoting the neuroscientist Antonio Damasio. In cognitive terms, "the lack of dependence on conscious survey automates a substantial part of our behavior and frees us in terms of attention and time—two scarce commodities in our lives—to plan and execute other tasks and create solutions for new problems" (Damasio, in Palmer, 108).

However, what stands as an advantage in day-to-day human living may not be so in art, and certainly many writers and theorists who have recognized this tendency toward automatic processing have taken a dim view of its place in literature. The problem with such automatization, according to Shklovsky's aesthetic, is that "the purpose of art is to impart the sensation of things as they are perceived and not as they are known. The technique of art is to make objects 'unfamiliar,' to make forms difficult, to increase the difficulty and length of perception because the process of perception is an aesthetic end in itself and must be prolonged" (12). To slow the process of perception through defamiliarization is, in Damasio's terms, to demand attention, requiring the thinking subject to sort through what appears unusual and strange.[35] Hence, a long line of writers and critics from the eighteenth century up to today question the sufficiency of our habituated modes of thought and place an aesthetic premium not only on novelty but on forms of novelty that disable automatic mental processing and instead command attention. The question becomes, then, whether the aesthetic imperative to subvert "known habits of association" or to defamiliarize is an artifact of modernity or a legitimate criterion in present-day aesthetic evaluation.

As eighteenth-century philosophers and writers suggest, confidence that our constructions of events accord well with the actual is seriously in question by this period in history. This attention to the confining nature of our conceptions is itself a phenomenon of a psychological culture, for without the realization that psychological experience can be, and often is, qualitatively and substantively different from objective events—that psychological experience can constitute, in essence, a competing set of events—there is little reason to suspect the adequacy of our conventionalized ways of seeing and explaining, our "known habits of association." If we assume that the mind gives us the world as it is, including a direct account of human rhythms in it, the possibility of alternative conceptual habits is not likely to arise. On the other hand, as long as we perceive that alternative modes of constructing art and experience exist, the question of the sufficiency of one's chosen mode will continue to pose itself. Since the question how we know and whether our mode of knowing will bring us into a productive and ethical relationship with the world has not simply come and gone but has continued to occupy a central place in intellectual culture, it is of legitimate importance in our evaluations of literary works. In their formal creativity, many romantic-era poets developed dramatic techniques that highlighted their substantive statements. This was, in effect, not simply novelty for novelty's sake—the like of which might be supplied by the handy application of a sugary layer of "gaudiness and inane phraseology"—but a form of novelty that arose in response to the central epistemic, ethical, and personal dilemmas of modernity. As such, it is entwined with those subjects "really important to men."

The "known habits of association" that Wordsworth seeks to undermine in his verse comprise a loose group of phenomena, but linear narrative is significantly represented. Poems diverse in form and subject dramatize the interrelated limitations—epistemological, ideological, and moral—of basic narrative sequence. In his extension of the nonlinear, dramatic presentation of mind developed first by Coleridge in "Frost at Midnight" and identified by M. H. Abrams as a distinctive technical innovation of the romantic era, the greater romantic lyric,[36] Wordsworth demonstrates that chronological narrative is epistemically limited. Wordsworth's commitment to this aesthetic innovation, first employed by the poet in "Tintern Abbey" and subsequently developed with increasing complexity in all the versions of *The Prelude,* is inseparable from his belief that genuine poetry must articulate significant human truth. Because internal events do not occur in tandem with external events, the construction of linear story can tend to mask various psychological realities, including states of stagnation, conflict, and crisis. But in "Tintern Abbey" Wordsworth uses the narrative "habit of association" to highlight the discrepancy between mental preconceptions on the one hand and the internal conflicts motivating communication on the other. Just as in "Resolution and Independence," the Immortality ode, and the crossing of the Simplon Pass in *The Prelude*, the insufficiency of the cognitive frame acts as an irritant, prompting the autobiographical speaker to arrive at a better order, one that succeeds as psychological regeneration precisely because it fails as linear narrative.

In the poem's opening, the speaker seems preoccupied with establishing a spatiotemporal framework, with mapping the self via chronological time back into the physical reality of the Wye Valley. The somewhat obsessive emphasis on the exact span of time between departure and return (five years), on the familiarity of the place ("again," "once again"), and on detailed description attests to the impulse to narrativize the moment and restore the dislocated self to the forward-directed world of actions, goals, and meaning:

> *Five years* have past; *five summers*, with the length
> Of *five long winters*! And *again* I hear
> These waters, rolling from their mountain-springs
> With a sweet inland murmur.—*Once again*
> Do I behold these steep and lofty cliffs,
> Which on a wild secluded scene impress
> Thoughts of more deep seclusion; and connect
> The landscape with the quiet of the sky.
> The day is come when I *again* repose
> Here, under this dark sycamore, and view
> These plots of cottage-ground, these orchard tufts,
> Which, at this season, with their unripe fruits,
> Are clad in one green hue, and lose themselves
> Among the woods and copses, nor disturb
> The wild green landscape. *Once again* I see
> These hedge-rows, hardly hedge-rows, little lines
> Of sportive wood run wild . . .   (ll. 1–17, emphasis added)

But even as the first line prepares the narrative ground and begins to establish reader expectations for a chronological story—And what has happened in those five years?—it simultaneously erodes its own temporal markers with other qualifying terms that highlight the difference between quantified time and psychological duration. All seasons may be the same length in fact but far different from human experience and memory, and plotting action and meaning in time that appears stretched and distorted is no simple matter.

Of course, Wordsworth was as well equipped as anyone to tell a chronological story, and he could have narrated "Tintern Abbey" in this manner: I went away, I did X and Y while I was away, I missed this place very much, and although I am back and recognize the scene in front of me, it seems not quite the same as it was before. I feel a little sad and out of place. He must, ultimately, create a narrative of a kind—the past self connected to the present self and to Dorothy and her future through the agency of nature—but since the story relies on memory and association rather than temporal sequence, it is up to the reader to do the challenging work of reconstructing the causal chain. Yet should the reader fail to perceive such a chain, he or she will experience the poem as nonsense. As Gerrig points out, in the construction of narrative worlds "the perception of causality is critical: experimentation has shown that comprehension is guided by the search for causal relations and that those causal relations, once recovered, provide much of the global coherence of memory representations" (46). Although Gerrig's research concerns fictional prose, in which narrative structure is dominant, the basic features of narrative thinking, temporal sequence and causality, are engaged in all literary processing, as Patrick Hogan suggests. In effect, in "Tintern Abbey" Wordsworth recognizes the known habit of everyday narrative and proceeds to defamiliarize it because the problem of narrativizing itself is part of what Wordsworth would have us know; difficult and ultimately necessary, narrative structure pulls us toward the objectification of experience, which is, for Wordsworth, essentially an inner phenomenon.

Narrative requires, in short, the segmentation and temporal plotting of experiences that most often are subjectively known holistically, particularly at the time of the initial experience. Flattening experience into the domain of the actual, story structure gives observable events a priority they do not necessarily deserve, robbing the reader of other sorts of understanding, such as the emotional knowledge of a self in a difficult moment. This tendency of story sequence to objectify is in keeping with the evolutionary explanation for why narrative is so robust: in negotiating and coordinating the actions of members of kinship groups, and in thus mapping individuals into a physical and social reality, it was a powerful mechanism of survival. But there is a world of difference between the original purpose of a cognitive adaptation and the expressive goal of a romantic poet. What matters to evolution is the survival of populations, not the representation of individual states of mind, and the inner reality of persons inhabiting settled culture is not always so easily adjusted to the externalizing direction of sequential structure. To shape a poem like "Tintern Abbey" as a traditional story would eliminate its primary subject matter. By selecting a disruptive, psychologically associative technique for his major autobiographical blank-verse poetry, Wordsworth's exposes the epistemic limits of basic narrative structure.

Given that Wordsworth immediately grasped Coleridge's experimental structure in "Frost at Midnight" and proceeded to adopt it in increasingly complex ways in his own work, his decision to write simultaneously within the ballad form might seem curious. After all, the fundamental purpose of the traditional ballad was to tell an elemental story, and the constraints of orality militate against those features of written literature that slow or even stop time, such as detailed description, complex characterization, and psychological presentation. The short lines of ballads (typically alternating tetrameter and trimeter) and the quatrain form encourage the segmentation of the story into memorable, economical episodes, and rhyme, repetition, and music also have a centrally mnemonic function in sung ballads. A wide array of contemporary cognitivists emphasize the connection between narrative and the retention of experience in memory, and I suspect that selectivity in plotting causal relations is a large part of what enhances memorability. That is, simplification is fundamental to remembering, and in the construction of brief narratives, humans simplify events and cast them into a linear sequence. Hence, traditional forms such as the ballad and the fairy tale are "designed" according to these mental proclivities for encapsulated depictions of character and action that serve as units in the causal frame.

Like all oral literature, then, the ballad is formulaic, and its major formulae were derived from just the kinds of preconceptions and predispositions that many romantic-era writers, Wordsworth among them, were questioning. If Wordsworth sometimes employs "known habit of association" to create a productive tension that ultimately highlights epistemic and moral concerns, the strictures of the ballad might appear to present special challenges for this approach. And although Wordsworth certainly wrote his share of conventionally structured narrative poems, including those in ballad form, his decision to write less storylike poems in quite different forms deserves further consideration. The flexible blank verse of "Tintern Abbey," which readily allows for rumination, digression, and added length, stands in marked contrast to the formal requirements of the ballad. That Wordsworth chose to include a great many ballad-form poems in *Lyrical Ballads* but at the same time "refuse[d] to use the common generic tag 'tale' [and was] exceedingly and uncommonly chary of any genre designations" at all suggests the extent to which he was working against a variety of traditions and assiduously avoiding conventional classification in his most productive decade.[37] Given that the ballad, the tale, and rustic poetry were enjoying enormous popularity, Wordsworth almost certainly made a decision to undo these modes from within. As Andrew L. Griffin comments, "The real concern of these poems is tale-telling and tale-listening, in confused conflict with the poetic imagination: in other words, the problem of imaginative story."[38]

In the three ballad-form poems I discuss here—briefly "The Two April Mornings" and "We Are Seven" and at greater length "Simon Lee"—Wordsworth intentionally confronts conventional assumptions specifically related to the ballad form itself. In each case, the poet both economically establishes character and setting in the opening stanzas, priming "known habits of association" by deceptively inviting the reader to expect the sort of simple story typical of the ballad and tale traditions, and institutes an alternate current arising from the character or point of view of the speaker. In each case, the form's traditional effectiveness as a vehicle for narrative is superseded by the speaker's interaction with or reflection on the story's ostensible main character, as well as by the speaker's ability or failure to incorporate new psychospiritual or moral knowledge into his own perspective.

In "The Two April Mornings" and "We Are Seven," Wordsworth subsumes narrative structure to psychological and spiritual imperatives and, not incidentally, the need for such imperatives to retain meaning through interpersonal exchange. The initial stanzas of both of these poems pose existential questions that are not in keeping with traditional ballad and that work at cross-purposes with the narrative elements Wordsworth also presents. In the first four stanzas of "The Two April Mornings," opposition between philosophical matters and the outward direction of sequential narrative, and the capitulation of the former to the latter, is literally signaled by the start and stop of a walk:

We walk'd along, while bright and red
Uprose the morning sun,
And Mathew stopp'd, he look'd, and said,
"The will of God be done!"

A village Schoolmaster was he,
With hair of glittering grey;
As blithe a man as you could see
On a spring holiday.

And on that morning, through the grass,
And by the steaming rills,
We travell'd merrily, to pass
A day among the hills.

"Our work," said I, "was well begun;
Then, from thy breast what thought,
Beneath so beautiful a sun,
So sad a sigh has brought?"   (ll. 1–16)

The first-person narrator's description of the setting, his companion, and the day's purpose provide all the key introductory elements of a brief tale, but that narrative is cut short the moment the speaker is prompted to ask the meaning of Mathew's sigh. In the ensuing ten stanzas, which comprise the bulk of the poem, Mathew explains how the morning has reminded him of "A day like this which I have left / Full thirty years behind" (23–24)—a day on which he stopped by his daughter's grave, felt a love for her that seemed even to exceed the love he had felt for her before, turned away from the grave and encountered "A blooming Girl, whose hair was wet / With points of morning dew" (43–44), who was transcendentally beautiful but nonetheless no worthy replacement for his Emma even in imagination. Thus, these elements of memory and loss tell a different story from that of the "spring holiday." The final stanza returns us to the speaker, who is now imagining Mathew as though he were palpably present, when he is in fact "in his grave" (57).

If, in "Tintern Abbey" Wordsworth resists narrativizing to highlight internal struggle, in "The Two April Mornings" he subverts it to celebrate the atemporal continuities of shared memories and experiences that transcend individual lives. For a poem of sixteen ballad quatrains, "The Two April Mornings" is extremely subtle and complex, and Wordsworth's personalization of the narrator shifts the terms of the ballad from the poem's opening. The speaker's question to Mathew precipitates, not, as the reader is first led to believe, the poem's story, but what turns out to be the same implied story of loss and continuity, altered only by the details of Mathew's version, as the final stanza makes clear: this is, or perhaps should be, everyone's story of memory, life, and death. Wordsworth's manipulation of temporal perception is surely strategic: the reader is likely to assume at the outset that the events to be narrated occurred in the recent past—"We walk'd along, while bright and red / Uprose the morning sun" (1–2)—but the meditative perspective of the poem's final stanza suggests that Mathew has been dead for some time. Yet when Mathew recounts his memory of the other April morning, the abundance of detail—in the described setting, in remembered emotion, in the visionary beauty of the "blooming Girl"—overwhelms the expanse of thirty years that lies between the two April mornings. So, too, the final stanza shocks "known habits of association" as it suddenly shifts the time frame once again, and as Mathew's narrative, which has subsumed the speaker's narrative, is subsumed by the speaker's narrative memory of both, triggered, as the logic of the poem suggests, by a third April morning. Thus, as in "Tintern Abbey," external events serve as a catalyst for memory, but in this case the memory is of another's story.

"We Are Seven" follows a similar pattern in its subversion of narrative. The first stanza poses an existential question, whereas the second and third stanzas depict just the sort of rustic character appropriate to a brief anecdote. While there is initially no reason to think that the speaker's question will subvert the expected story, this is in fact what happens, as in "The Two April Mornings":

A simple child, dear brother Jim,
That lightly draws its breath,
And feels its life in every limb,
What should it know of death?

I met a little cottage girl,
She was eight years old, she said;
Her hair was thick with many a curl
That cluster'd round her head.

She had a rustic, woodland air,
And she was wildly clad;
Her eyes were fair, and very fair,
—Her beauty made me glad.   (ll. 1–12)

The subsequent twelve stanzas contain a good deal more back and forth between speaker and girl than the parallel section of "The Two April Mornings," largely because the speaker is intent on the proper enumeration of living siblings. In spite of this, the child manages to tell her own story, about who and where her brothers and sisters are and how she spends the day with them. And whatever the speaker thinks he has told his audience about the willful child at the poem's close, his audience is unlikely to share his interpretation of events. Narrative sequence is arrested by the irreconcilable differences in point of view, and Wordsworth's decision to dramatize this stand-off rather than provide a narrative account reveals the logic of the cottage girl's thought and the experiential priority of her psychospiritual relationship to her brothers and sisters living and dead. But whereas Wordsworth thus offers knowledge that direct narrative would mask, the speaker of the poem is himself unaware of his stumbling story's significance. Indeed, the oddness of his tale in "We Are Seven" illustrates his dependence on "known habits of association," on the consolations of rationalist dichotomies and simple stories that package events and forestall experience in the Wordsworthian sense.

By divorcing causality from chronology in "Tintern Abbey" and "The Two April Mornings," then, Wordsworth reveals the epistemic limitations of basic narrative, which in habitually aligning causality and temporality in observable sequence leads away from the achronological, invisible processes of self- and fellow-knowledge. But if narrative subversion in these poems serves the purpose of questioning received modes of knowledge, in "Simon Lee" Wordsworth adds another dimension to his implied critique of narrative by highlighting the inter-relationship between epistemic, ideological, and moral limitations. As Bruner's discussion of canonical and exceptional narratives indicates, human social experience is framed and given meaning by cultural beliefs rendered as stories about who and what we are. Some stories are, accordingly, the instruments of power and its perpetuation, while others challenge dominant stories and seek to replace them. Indeed, a culture's canonical stories can be reinforced or challenged by many aspects of the societies in which they emerge, and in modern cultures the impulse to revise or provide alternative stories is especially strong.

More pointedly than in "We Are Seven," Wordsworth calls attention in "Simon Lee" to the persuasive force of canonical narrative and challenges his reader to accept an exceptional story in its stead. By ultimately refusing to tell the story he embarks on in the first stanza of the poem, Wordsworth exposes the overlap between his culture's received story about the justice of, and rationale for, class differences and the subgenre of the short comic poem.[39] As in "The Two April Mornings" and "We Are Seven," Wordsworth's treatment of the speaker is central to the developing antinarrative, but whereas Wordsworth personalizes the speakers of these ballads, he manipulates the first-person voice in "Simon Lee," so that ultimately the reader is confronted with his or her "habits of association" and the opportunity for a new form of knowledge. As Danby points out, Wordsworth's combination of narrative and dramatic monologue enables him to "take up and lay down his masks," and in "Simon Lee" the dramatic act of switching masks in the course of the poem establishes the ground of a story competing with the expectations of a humorous tale set up at the beginning of the poem.[40]

The initial stanzas introduce the character of Simon and celebrate his past accomplishments as a huntsman, and the first stanza especially establishes the expectation of a jocular tale, employing nursery-rhyme rhetoric, meter, and repetition in its characterization of Simon. These techniques, issuing in an economical and nearly nonsensical depiction of the old huntsman, prepare the way for superficial amusement, most likely at the expense of the now-shrunken Simon Lee:

IN the sweet shire of Cardigan,
Not far from pleasant Ivor-hall,
An Old Man dwells, a little man,
'Tis said he once was tall.
Full five-and-thirty years he lived
A running Huntsman merry;
And still the centre of his cheek
Is red as a ripe cherry.

No man like him the horn could sound,
And hill and valley rang with glee
When Echo bandied, round and round,
The halloo of Simon Lee.
In those proud days, he little cared
For husbandry or tillage;
To blither tasks did Simon rouse
The sleepers of the village.

                                                                    (ll. 1–16)

The nursery-rhyme phrasing of lines 3 and 4—"An old Man dwells, a little man,— / 'Tis said he once was tall"—deflects attention from the facts they impart, that Simon is no longer quite so robust as he once was, and lines 7 and 8, suggesting that he still glows with health, further mask his diminished state.

But just as Wordsworth delineates character neatly and economically in "The Two April Mornings" and "We Are Seven" only to subvert the narrative expectations that such handy characterizations promise, his sketch of Simon as a quaint ancient, the handy subject of an amusing anecdote, succumbs to a shift in perspective that undermines the comic impulse and, in so doing, erodes the narrative logic of the poem's premises. In stanzas 2 and 3, Wordsworth regales the reader with Simon's glorious past as "a running Huntsman merry," and the modulation out of overtly nursery-rhyme rhetoric, as well as the romanticized emphasis on Simon's past, indicates the discrepancy between what Simon once was and what he now is, even if this appears unwitting on the part of the speaker. Up to this point, the speaking voice remains relatively consistent, but the shifts in perspective from here to the end of the poem make it impossible to sustain a unified image of the speaker.

The transition into stanza 4 decisively signals the shift away from comic tale and introduces four and a half stanzas inspecting, sometimes in embarrassing detail, Simon's economically, socially, and physically diminished condition. Tonally, stanza 4 is the most complex in the poem, creating a tension between the plain, even painfully direct statement of the emptiness of Ivor Hall on the one hand and the return to comic use of rhyme and meter on the other. Wordsworth here arrests the narrative, not only frustrating the reader's desire for an event but chastening the reader for that desire:

> But, oh the heavy change!—bereft
> Of health, strength, friends, and kindred, see!
> Old Simon to the world is left
> In liveried poverty.
> His Master's dead,—and no one now
> Dwells in the Hall of Ivor;
> Men, dogs, and horses, all are dead;
> He is the sole survivor.   (ll. 25–32)

In light of the jocular tone established at the outset of the poem, the exclamation serving as the transition into this stanza sounds like a trite acknowledgment of Simon's social and physical decline, for the apparently gratuitous nod toward suffering is in poor taste in a mode that has little time for such considerations. But the fact that this line alludes to Milton's "Lycidas" compounds the problem, allowing us to read it in three possible ways: as a poetical affectation on the part of the speaker (similar to Wordsworth's later, more extended consideration of such affectation in "Resolution and Independence"); as evidence that another speaker, closer to Wordsworth himself in sensibility, is now taking over the poem; or as an instance of self-ironization that combines the two. A pastoral elegy written on the untimely death of one of Milton's Cambridge classmates, "Lycidas" is far removed from "Simon Lee" in its mode and basic concerns. If "Lycidas" follows the cyclical structure of pastoral as "a ritual conducted on the vital surface between air and water," invoking such fancy mythifications consorts oddly with the relentlessly material persistence of Simon's life.[41] Wordsworth, aware that his own middle-class reader would certainly have recognized the Miltonic allusion, apparently intended to startle and offend his reader with the sudden shift from low to high mode.[42]

In the stanza overall, the combination of plain statement with nursery-rhyme meter asks the reader to adopt the conflicting stances of amused observer and sympathetic fellow human, just as it demands that the reader see the speaker simultaneously as unfeeling elitist and revolutionary humanitarian. However, the stanza's final lines enact a resistance to sympathy, in the process crystallizing such resistance as the primary theme of the poem. Even though it is in fact shocking to learn that only Simon is left of the animal and human life once animating the

hall, the incongruous rhyming of *survivor* with *Ivor* in lines 6 and 8, whose prosodic awkwardness is especially emphatic given the extremely simple diction of
most of the stanza, pulls the reader toward the continued objectification of Simon
that most of the stanza renounces. It is perhaps a belated attempt on the part of
the speaker to recuperate the comic mode and continue with his amusing story.
The ubiquity of death—"Men, dogs, and horses, all are dead"—which logically
excludes the still-living Simon from the category of the human, further defamil-
iarizes, in combination with prosodic exaggeration, the term *survivor* and further
reverts to the thinglike portrayal of the huntsman in stanza 1. In sum, the discrepancy between the content of the statement in the last lines and the poetical
method cannot help but produce amusement, even as that amusement is shad-
owed by the eloquent if implicitly accusatory directness of lines 3 and 4—"Old
Simon to the world is left / In liveried poverty"—a sentence suggesting that the
existing social structure sees poverty as a legitimate occupation. While the comic
use of *survivor* cheerfully asserts Simon's endurance, these lines ask us to reflect
on his abandonment by institutions, customs, and individuals neglectful of his
needs.

Thus, although the speaker does not address his restive reader for another
three and a half stanzas, the subject of the poem has shifted by the fifth stanza
from an amusing anecdote about Simon to the huntsman himself. As John Jordan
notes, many of Wordsworth's narrative poems are more rightly descriptive tab-
leaux than linear stories; in "Simon Lee" the poet shifts from one mode to another
in the course of the poem (169). Whereas the second and third stanzas emphasize
Simon's active youth, stanzas 5–7 offer primarily description of Simon's debility
and helplessness, as the initial objectification of him as folk type—a "running
huntsman merry" whose cheek is "red as a ripe cherry"—is replaced by the image
of him as discarded object, nearly used up and left "to the world," to its many
unknowns and to the unforgiving nature of material process. Implicitly, Wordsworth asks his reader to consider what it really means for a person to become
literally objectlike, to be reduced to a waning physical existence. The detailed
description of Simon's body, robbed of proportion and alignment, is embarrassing and painful because it has the force of caricature, recalling the crooked man
in the nursery rhyme, except that it lingers over his decrepitude as no nursery
rhyme would. Wordsworth requires his reader to infer the causes of this debility
and to acknowledge the pain that accompanies Simon's odd appearance.

In contrast to the narrative subversions of "Tintern Abbey," "We Are Seven,"
and "The Two April Mornings," which Wordsworth effects through dramatizing
psychospiritual reality and interpersonal conflict, in "Simon Lee" the speaker's

interruption and diversion of his own story in the eighth and ninth stanzas directly questions the reader's expectation of a conventional comic tale:

> Few months of life has he in store,
> As he to you will tell,
> For still, the more he works, the more
> Do his weak ancles swell.
> My gentle Reader, I perceive
> How patiently you've waited,
> And now I fear that you expect
> Some tale will be related.
>
> O Reader! Had you in your mind
> Such stores as silent thought can bring,
> O gentle Reader! You would find
> A tale in every thing.
> What more I have to say is short,
> And you must kindly take it:
> It is no tale; but, should you *think*,
> Perhaps a tale you'll make it.
>
> (ll. 57–72)

In other words, this "is no tale" in the traditional sense, but you may judge it to have sufficient storylike meaning, or, alternatively, if you are a thinking person, you will see that *it is* a tale. The speaker's direct address, suggesting a sudden shift in course, is more than a little disingenuous, for Wordsworth, as we have seen, has subtly manipulated the tale from the beginning, so that, in fact, he has already considerably eroded the promise of comic story by the time of this interruption.

When the speaker finally confesses that he does not intend to tell a conventional tale, he intimates that the thinking person may have already reconstructed the true story. But because of the strength of our "known habits of association" and the canonical narratives they so readily contain, the "gentle Reader," although perplexed by what might seem a lack of focus in the first seven stanzas of the poem, might still expect that conventional tale. As Danby reminds us, the word *gentle* has two meanings, "genteel" and "kindly"; if the reader is the former but not the latter, he or she may well have suppressed the implication of the poem's shift away from narrative in stanzas 4–7. The last three stanzas, Wordsworth explains, offer another kind of story, a culturally exceptional one, to employ Bruner's terminology, in which the speaker assists the incapacitated Simon Lee with a troublesome tree stump and Simon Lee is overcome by gratitude.

Although the brief narrative related in the final three stanzas has meaning in its own right—and is, incontrovertibly, a narrative—its full significance depends on the violation of the canonical expectations laid out in the beginning. These violations are interrelated but multiple, as I have suggested: as Wordsworth modulates out of the initial comic mode, he substitutes description for concise narration, thus eroding momentum and redirecting attention from the anticipation of an event to Simon's existential state, at the same time shifting gradually into a prototypically Wordsworthian speaking voice. Whereas the opening stanzas of "The Two April Mornings" and "We Are Seven" prepare the reader for a poem that might do more than tell a simple story, the shifting narrative voice of "Simon Lee" asks the reader what, in the final analysis, it is that he or she wants to hear.

In terms of Bruner's definition of the anthropomorphic structure human narratives typically take—actor, action, goal, scene, and agent—the presumed actor is too decrepit to engage in a comic action, and the scene too closely described to serve as a backdrop for such a story. Indeed, Simon's inability to act in a traditional sense is largely the point of Wordsworth's revisionary "tale in everything." Wordsworth seems aware that narrative structure, as employed in the short, unadorned comic tale, prioritizes action and objectifies humans through the superficial presentation of character, and he exposes the means by which the epistemic limitations of the comic tale cohere with ideological limitations. By discouraging a human and social awareness of characters such as Simon Lee, the traditional comic tale complies with a social hierarchy according to which sympathy does not extend beyond the bounds of one's own class. In thus frustrating his reader's desire for a comic story by overtly refusing to adhere to the generic and canonical conventions of a tale, Wordsworth reveals the potential for cruelty in story form.

Mary Robinson's *Lyrical Tales*

Although Mary Robinson selected the title *Lyrical Tales* in a calculated effort to reinforce a sense of relationship between her volume of poems and *Lyrical Ballads,* the influences—not just between Robinson and Wordsworth but among a group that included these two as well as Coleridge and Robert Southey—are hardly unidirectional or easy to summarize, as Stuart Curran explains.[43] When Wordsworth learned of the title of Robinson's volume and hastily requested a revised title for the second edition of *Lyrical Ballads,* his publishers refused, demonstrating their desire to trade on the reputation of existing poets for financial advantage. But this was not simply a matter of using one poet's reputation to promote another: to varying degrees, the three male poets had been associated with Robinson through the poetry pages of the *Morning Post* since 1797. Of these four, Southey and Robinson embraced newspaper publication enthusiastically, serving successively as chief correspondents to the Poetical Department, Robinson's tenure in that appointment beginning in 1797. In spite of his wish to avoid connection to Robinson, Wordsworth was certainly influenced by her work, while she on her side sought to compete with both Southey and Wordsworth. If Southey's *English Eclogues* influenced the others, in a broader sense they were all engaged in the attempt to negotiate an existing tradition of rustic poetry from a middle-class perspective.

Wordsworth's uneasiness about association with Robinson stems from both her social reputation and her aesthetic modus operandi, but the two are intertwined to a significant degree. As with so many talented women of her time, Robinson's subordination and attendant dependence on her family, combined with financial uncertainties and lack of guidance, essentially sealed her fate at an early age and perhaps determined the sort of poetry and prose she would write. Born Mary Darby in 1758 to a middle-class family in Bristol, she was married to Thomas Robinson in 1773, when her maintenance became a burden after a failed business venture of her father's. Her child Maria Elizabeth was born the following year, and by 1775 Thomas Robinson had landed in debtor's prison. In the next few years Robinson began publishing poetry as well as acting; in 1779, much taken with her performance as Perdita in *A Winter's Tale*, the Prince of Wales pursued her romantically, and the resulting two-year liaison left Robinson a ruined woman at twenty-three.[44]

Clearly, the financial and social difficulties of Robinson's life were fixed even as she came to occupy a peculiar place in the public imagination. Glamorous, beautiful, and—let us not forget, given the increasing prudery of late eighteenth- and nineteenth-century England—sexual, yet a mourning woman of talent and accomplishment, Robinson was both accessible and remote, unlike the emergent type of the Angel in the House. Since Robinson was certainly in both fact and imagination more interesting than the period's primary roles for and stereotypes of women, a sense of her presence and aura can only have fueled many a wish-fulfilling fantasy of men and women of her day. In her Della Cruscan poetry of the 1780s as well as her work for the *Morning Post* in the 1790s, Robinson cultivated the public's fascination. Noting that the *Post* of this era, in its combination of "high tragedy and cultural frivolity," was governed by a "theatrical imperative" that encouraged the aura of celebrity among its poets, Judith Pascoe points to the extent to which Daniel Stuart, the *Post*'s editor, and Robinson herself fostered her cult of personality: "Over the course of two or three days, a *Post* reader and Robinson fan might come across a front-page advertisement for a subscription to a new Robinson volume, a poem, a puff, a promotion for a soon-to-be-published poem, and a medical prognosis [of Robinson's ailments]. The reader might also come across a poem written by an idolatrous fan in response to a poem previously published by Robinson."[45]

Psychologically fascinating as this cultural situation is to a person of the twenty-first century, it is hardly one designed to encourage a focused and aesthetically absorbed attention on the work of literature itself, on the part of either the writer or the reader. Once she was socially ostracized, the message to Robinson from her larger public, it seems, was that image counted over substance, and it was the promotion of her own mythos that enabled her to support herself. Leaving aside the liberal-minded intellectuals and writers, including William Godwin and Coleridge, who did not condemn Robinson for her affair with George IV, we have to imagine a situation in which the majority of Robinson's readers, eager to bathe in her aura in print, would have been keen to avoid her in person. In a culture in which women writers were expected to acknowledge that their abilities were inferior to those of their male contemporaries, the specific difficulties of Robinson's situation must have contributed to a sense that the only possible professional identity and poetic practice rested on the circulation of images. Discredited and ignored in person, Robinson acquired a curious kind of power through what Pascoe aptly identifies as her performative approach to the *Post,* and while this vicarious power surely aided her mentally and materially, it was based on and traded on the public's fundamental dishonesty in its attitude toward Robinson. Since Robinson of necessity participated in this fundamental dishonesty, it set serious limitations on the quality of her verse.

One example of the sacrifice of literary standards to commercial appeal is Robinson's tendency to allude to her own romantic past in poems that offer themselves on other premises. Scholars are quick to point out the self-referential quality of the story in "The Poor Singing Dame," which relates how a lord, after imprisoning a poor old woman because "he hated that Poverty should be so chearful," wastes away and dies of shame after the old woman's death, his marble stone nonetheless overshadowing her grave (1.35). But this is far from the only instance of self-reference in *Lyrical Tales;* "The Fortune-Teller, A Gypsy Tale," a story in which an unfaithful young woman gets her comeuppance, begins thus:

LUBIN and KATE, as gossips tell,
    Were Lovers many a day;
LUBIN the damsel lov'd so well,

That folks pretend to say
The silly, simple, doting Lad,
Was little less than loving mad:
A malady not known of late—
Among the little-loving Great!   (ll. 1–8)

The reference to "the little-loving Great" would likely have perplexed the reader deficient in her knowledge of the fashionable world, for this is a poem ostensibly about rural folk. But the Robinson fan would have known that the innuendo in lines 7 and 8 is directed both at the Prince of Wales and at Banastre Tarleton, the war hero who was Robinson's lover from 1782 to 1797. Unlike Byron's violations of narrative illusion or Wordsworth's disruption of story structure, these allusions only serve the appetite for gossip. Such references in verse published in the *Post* direct attention to the person of Robinson at the expense of the poem at hand; in light of this, it is worth pondering whether Robinson perceived a trade-off between the roles of celebrity poet and literary artist. Taking into account her special fondness for *Lyrical Tales,* as well as her self-characterization as a great writer, it seems more than possible that she did not.[46]

Just as Robinson fostered the reading public's interest in herself, she encouraged and reinforced the "known habits of association" Wordsworth intends to frustrate. While it is possible to praise *Lyrical Tales,* as a number of scholars have done, for its thematic and metrical variety, its expression of thwarted potentiality, and its underlying themes of alienation and loss, a more coldly objective survey of the poems collected there suggests an approach designed primarily to please.[47] Certainly images of suffering are common, but they are contained by Robinson's larger narrative and metrical patterns and her overall strategy of arrangement. The themes and modes of these poems include pathetic, tragic, comic, political, gothic, meditative, and pastoral, the last of these to a very limited extent. The poems are arranged to underscore variety, the comic poem "The Mistletoe," for instance, directly succeeding the pathetic "All Alone," which, as Robinson's response to Wordsworth's "We Are Seven," tells of an orphan child in an extreme state of abandonment. Variety and arrangement in *Lyrical Tales,* in short, contribute not to a genuine engagement with the sufferings in the serious poems but to a fleeting indulgence in the topics and feelings there presented that, while not entirely gratuitous, demands little from the reader. Importantly, the pervasively narrative approach of *Lyrical Tales,* emphasizing as it does external, linear action, combines with poetical excess to limit identification and contain emotions within temporal constraints. If Wordsworth could afford to subvert canonical stories built on an innate propensity for narrative, Robinson, a disgraced woman poet, could not, and she caters more consistently to her readers' habituated responses. One strong means of fulfilling her audience's expectations is through the conventional use of narrative structure and content, particularly in the comic tales.

However, Robinson was not unaware that downplaying narrative affects the experience of the reader and is thus related to the epistemic possibilities of literature. In "The Widow's Home" and "The Haunted Beach," for instance, she eschews the sequential structure of narrative to enhance moral, psychological, or political understanding at the expense of the enjoyment of story. Yet many of the "tales," written first for newspaper publication and therefore for a popular audience, emphasize the narration of external, sequential events. The reader's absorption in events and anticipation of closure, which bounds and contains a sequence of events, supersedes contemplation of moral, psychological, political, or other purposes. Interestingly, the poems that are predominantly nonnarrative, while on the one hand inviting the reader to new forms of experience and modes of knowing, adopt closural strategies that are at odds with the primary method of the poems, abruptly terminating feelings of uneasiness by shifting the register of experience. As Herman says of closure in general, "Any particular telling of a narrative has to end, even if the narrative being told is presented as unfinished or unfinishable. In coming to a conclusion, tellings mark even the most painful or disturbing experiences as endurable because finite. In such contexts, narrative is a tool for representing events not as over and done with, but as reaching a terminus that imposes a limit on the trauma-inducing (and cognition-disrupting) power of the events at issue" (173–74). Robinson's strategy in several poems that downplay narrative is, in effect, the opposite of Wordsworth's in the ballads discussed here: whereas Wordsworth disposes of the sequential story he promises at the outset, thus eliciting cognitive disruption, Robinson imposes closure on situations that have not developed toward a terminus.

The inclusion of poems such as "The Widow's Home" and "The Haunted Beach" in *Lyrical Tales* demonstrates Robinson's convergent awareness that tale may be where event is not. The blank-verse poem "The Widow's Home," remarkably similar in its content to Wordsworth's "Ruined Cottage," describes a bucolic setting in which the soldier's widow and son await the father's return. In the initial paragraphs of the poem, Robinson affectingly establishes a mood of waiting, conveying the simultaneous strain and pleasure the mother and son feel as they innocently await the father's return. The tension between the pastoral setting and the calm rhythms of the blank verse on the one hand and the differential levels of understanding—the child eagerly scanning the horizon, the mother anxiously harboring her last hopes, and the speaker, who knows of the father's death, anticipating their future grief—on the other create a strong sense of suspended animation. As the boy watches from the hills,

> if a distant whitening sail appears,
> Skimming the bright horizon while the mast
> Is canopied with clouds of dappled gold,
> He homeward hastes rejoicing. An old Tree
> Is his lone watch-tow'r; 'tis a blasted Oak
> Which, from a vagrant Acorn, ages past,
> Sprang up, to triumph like a Savage bold
> Braving the Season's warfare.   (ll. 54–61)

The poem's initial focus on this gap in knowledge points attention to the vulnerability of the son and the mother and to the pathos of their unresolved situation, but the last twenty-two lines of the poem veer away from the immediate situation into a generalized encomium to the humble soldier and a concomitant condemnation of affluence and power. In this manner, the moralizing conclusion discourages the sympathy it has just aroused and invites the reader's righteous indignation. Even though the precise method of subordinating emotion to other factors is different from that adopted in Gray's "Sonnet on the Death of Richard West," both employ conventions of style, rhetoric, and sentiment to deflect the impact of unresolved feeling.

"The Haunted Beach" especially exhibits Robinson's ability to downplay events in the service of depicting the psychological or emotional matters that tend to be elided by traditional narrative modes. If the suspension of story in the first verse paragraphs of "The Widow's Home" enhances an uneasy sense of longing, anxiety, and suspended grief, in "The Haunted Beach" the avoidance of linear sequence focuses attention on the impact of guilt. Although clearly influenced by "The Rime of the Ancient Mariner," the poem is far from simply derivative and stands out in Robinson's oeuvre for "the uncanny way in which subject and technical treatment reinforce each other" (Curran, 28), for the consistent development of mood and state of mind, achieved through the compatibility of meter, language, and subject. Depicting the desolate seascape in the first two stanzas, Robinson creates a subtle sense of mystery, first through the anomalous persistence of the "little shed" on the site where "lofty Barks were shatter'd," then through the image of the "shiver'd mast" somehow perpetually rolling toward the shore "at ebb of tide." The next two stanzas exploit the sense of mystery through the introduction of the fisherman and the specters he sees or imagines. The fifth stanza informs the reader of the murdered man lying in the hut, and stanzas 6 and 7 cryptically narrate the past events, relating the murder itself with especial subtlety:

> The winter moon, upon the sand
>   A silv'ry carpet made,
> And mark'd the Sailor reach the land,
> And mark'd his murd'rer wash his hand
>   Where the green billows play'd.   (ll. 59–63)

Prioritizing scene and mood, enticing the reader toward the satisfaction of his or her curiosity, and minimizing the fatal event, Robinson avoids the sensationalism and melodrama she elsewhere exploits, inviting her reader, not to know a temporal sequence of events, but to experience the disquiet of the guilty fisherman. In the final stanza, however, Robinson reverts to direct statement, underscoring the moral and thus removing the reader from the experiential dimension of her story:

> Full thirty years his task has been,
>   Day after day more weary;
> For Heav'n design'd, his guilty mind
>   Should dwell on prospects dreary.
> Bound by a strong and mystic chain,
>   He has not pow'r to stray;
> But, destin'd mis'ry to sustain,
> He wastes, in Solitude and Pain—
>   A loathsome life away.   (ll. 73–81)

The moralizing conclusion of "The Haunted Beach," like that of "The Widow's Home," is not a logical outgrowth of Robinson's method in the poem; to the contrary, it encourages the reader to place the poem's psychological and supernatural elements within a conventional Christian context even as evil receives its just deserts. As in "The Widow's Home," Robinson curtails the unresolved feelings by directly assigning blame for the destabilizing experience at the heart of the poem, effectively closing off the experience and in the process inviting the reader to enjoy a sense of moral superiority. Whereas Herman suggests that conclusions by their nature provide consolation because they signal an end to pain, Robinson effectively cancels the feelings aroused by the two poems by superimposing the values inherent in cultural stories onto them.

Robinson's willingness to foster readerly self-satisfaction in this manner is in keeping with the requirement to write popular poetry. As Pascoe explains, "The poetry columns of the *Morning Post,* then, aimed both to satisfy a large, heterogeneous reading audience and to fabricate of this undifferentiated group of readers a select coterie of the book-buying public, whose allegiance to the *Post* would sell advertising space" ("Marketplace," 256). In the final analysis, the endings of both poems constitute significant (though not the only) aesthetic flaws, for the moralizing conclusions only make sense in terms of expectations and values that lie elsewhere. Whereas Wordsworth's subversions of narrative constitute aesthetic innovations that simultaneously expose the epistemic and the moral limits of canonical stories, Robinson undermines her experiments with conclusions that conform to canonical narratives of her culture.

As Pascoe notes, Robinson readily penned "occasional and whimsical poetry aimed at entertaining a general audience," and it is thus not surprising that fully a third of *Lyrical Tales* is made up of comic stories that "can be read as bits of comic business meant primarily, if not solely, to amuse" (258, 266). Robinson frequently published pseudonymously and employed specific pseudonyms for distinct types of poems, although her readers were well aware of the identity of the true author. The comic poems written in the guise of the gossipy spinster Tabitha Bramble, a figure borrowed from Tobias Smollett's *Humphry Clinker,* all follow a conventional tale pattern, beginning with the superficial introduction of character, followed by a brief development of the situation and action and a facetiously moralizing conclusion. In "Old Barnard," the eponymous character tricks his miserly grandson out of his ill-got wealth. In "Deborah's Parrot," a mean-spirited woman is hoisted on her own petard when her method of inciting scandal is turned upon herself. In "Mistress Gurton's Cat," a hypocritical spinster, in a fit of rage, kills the cat whose presumed loss she had recently deplored.[48]

Like "Simon Lee," "Old Barnard" is the story of an impoverished, elderly rustic whose needs are ignored by those of superior means; in the case of Robinson's poem, however, the negligent squire is Old Barnard's own grandson. The first eleven stanzas of this poem develop the contrasting material and spiritual states of Old Barnard and his grandson, the former poor, healthy, cheerful, and purportedly clear in conscience, the latter wealthy but beset by fears and ailments. Just as the initial stanzas of "Simon Lee" depict a quaint, rosy-cheeked old man, Robinson draws a character apparently impervious to the sufferings of age and poverty in her first stanzas:

OLD BARNARD was still a lusty hind,
Though his age was full fourscore;
   And he us'd to go
   Thro' hail and snow,

> To a neighb'ring town,
>   With his old coat brown,
> To beg, at his GRANDSON's door!
>
> OLD BARNARD briskly jogg'd along,
>   When the hail and snow did fall;
>   And, whatever the day,
>   He was always gay,
>   Did the broad Sun glow,
>   Or the keen wind blow,
> While he begg'd in his GRANDSON's Hall.   (ll. 1–14)

But whereas Wordsworth modulates out of his initial comic tone and shifts his subject matter to effect a closer inspection of Simon Lee and his diminished condition, Robinson stays within the comic mode and accordingly explains why Old Barnard does not suffer from hunger, age, and freezing temperatures:

> But BARNARD a quiet conscience had,
>   No guile did his bosom know;
>   And when Ev'ning clos'd,
>   His old bones repos'd,
>   Tho' the wintry blast
>   O'er his hovel past,
> And he slept, while the winds did blow!   (ll. 29–35)

Of course, familiar or not with Robinson's Tabitha Bramble persona, readers will recognize that there is a trick here, because the too-simple contrast between the upright Barnard and the wealthy grandson, who "fear'd some evil / And dream'd of the Devil / Whenever he clos'd his eyes" (ll. 40–42), is bound to collapse. And indeed, the poem turns on a trick played on the grandson by Old Barnard and a monk. Unable to endure his guilty conscience any longer, the grandson visits the monk, who asks him to return the next day. The monk hurries to Old Barnard, who then dresses in the monk's garb and waits for his grandson in the monk's cell, subsequently tricking him into giving up half his wealth:

> "Get home young Sinner," OLD BARNARD said,
>   "And your GRANDSIRE quickly see;
>   *Give him half your store,*
>   For he's old, and poor,
>   And avert each evil

And cheat the Devil,—
By making him *rich as thee.*"

The SQUIRE obey'd; and Old BARNARD now
Is rescued from every evil:
> For he fears no wrong,
> From the weak or strong,
> And the Squire can snore,
> When the loud winds roar,
For he dreams no more of THE DEVIL!   (ll. 106–19)

Poems like "Old Barnard" clearly serve as a foil for Wordsworth's reverential attitude toward rustic persons, for the "lusty hind" who "quiet conscience had" is not ethically hampered from tricking his grandson out of half his wealth. Like all Robinson's comic tales, then, this poem casts a jaded eye on human probity and dignity, for it is only a dishonest trick, urged on Old Barnard by the monk, that restores the aging farmer to material comfort. All Robinson's comic stories, in fact, avoid serious moral considerations, emphasizing a brief action and the superficial presentation of character necessitated by the brevity of the genre and consistent with the objective of amusement. Robinson's inventive, fast-paced but lurching meter, following a regular pattern of tetrameter, trimeter, and dimeter lines and making heavy use of anapests, derives from nursery-rhyme meters rather than from the allied but less exaggerated meter of the ballad stanza. Whereas Wordsworth's selection of the ballad stanza provided him with a form whose singsong effects could be understated by enjambment, shifts in word choice, and limited rhyming, Robinson places a core of dimeter couplets, whose exaggerated rhythm and rhyme cannot be downplayed, at the center of the "Old Barnard" stanzas. This meter drives the story forward and contributes significantly to the comedy. Yet we might ask at whose expense we enjoy this story. The comic meter alone intentionally subverts sympathy, even in stanza 4, where Robinson relates Old Barnard's impoverished state:

Old BARNARD had neither house nor lands,
Nor gold to buy warm array;
> Nor a coach to carry,
> His old bones weary
> Nor beds of feather
> In freezing weather,
To sleep the long nights away.   (ll. 22–28)

In contrast to Wordsworth's shifts in and out of nursery-rhyme meter in "Simon Lee," which signal a transformation in the subject of the poem, Robinson's meter prevents an emotional response to the fact of Old Barnard's physical discomfort, successfully circumscribing the facts related as information in the service of the story. Whereas Wordsworth modulates into an elevated but direct language and employs enjambment to subvert the singsong effects of the ballad in the first four lines of stanza 4 of "Simon Lee," Robinson's syntax and word order both serve the formal constraints of the comic form. Robinson's purpose is to get the story told, not to challenge innate and encultured preferences for narrative construction but to reinforce those preferences, entertaining her audience with a canonical story about the wily ways of rustics.

In their attention to the neglected works of women authors, literary historians since the 1970s have vastly enriched our understanding of the contexts of literary production, and the light they have shed on every established period makes possible a reassessment of what works have become canonical and why. But in terms of aesthetic considerations, little such assessment has taken place. This is partly because the legitimacy of aesthetic factors as a criterion of value has itself been questioned. I have tried to suggest here that while aesthetic values are indeed related to the values and needs of a culture, that relationship may be reason more for endorsing these standards of judgment than for dismissing them as the product of ideological bias. The epistemic and moral challenges Wordsworth insists upon, his refusal to allow the automatic processing of narrative, is part of the reason why he so frustrated the critics of his day and part of his greatness. Conversely, until very recently the originality of women writers was constrained by their lack of freedom, by their limited education, and by the perceived inferiority of their sex, to which they themselves were obligated to accede if they expected to get their work published. To teach a poet like Robinson without discussing the limitations of her verse ultimately does a disservice to the history of women as well as to our understanding of the complex context from which works of excellence emerge.

CHAPTER THREE

Minding Ecocriticism

Human Wayfinders and Natural Places

For the old woodlanders, there is no division between human intercourse and local environment. The presence of memory means
that the countryside is inhabited rather than viewed aesthetically.
The condition of the modern man, with his mobility and his displaced knowledge, is never to be able to share this sense of belonging. He will always be an outsider; his return to nature will always
be partial, touristic, and semi-detached.

Jonathan Bate

Mental Maps for Critical Footpaths

Although ecocriticism only began to develop seriously as a subdiscipline of literary studies in the 1990s, it is inspired by the spirit of activism that spurred the
development of numerous literary approaches two decades earlier. Feminist,
Marxist, and postcolonial theories, for example, all highlight aspects of sexual,
racial, and economic inequality and explore the various ways that these are represented, revealed, or suppressed in literary works. Similarly identified by a set
of political commitments, ecocriticism (or studies in literature and the environment, as it is sometimes called) is nevertheless fundamentally different from
these other activist-inspired schools in that its central focus has been on nonhuman nature rather than on human beings. Thus, while ecocriticism exhibits,
in my view, the same sort of unacknowledged conflict between activist values and
intellectual prerogatives apparent in several other recent schools, it also faces a
special challenge whose source is nothing less than its purported object of study.

The difficulty of explaining the relevance of that object, the environment, to
literature departments is in no wise simplified by the constructed nature of the
object, amply attested by its rate of mutation in ecocritical practice over the past
fifteen years. If, writes Michael Bennett, "the first wave of ecocriticism embraced
those environments at furthest remove from human habitation—the pastoral and

the wild—as represented by a narrowly defined genre of nature writing . . . the new wave of ecocriticism is interested in the interconnections between urban and non-urban space, humans and nonhumans, traditional and experimental genres, as well as the impact of race, class, gender, and sexuality on how we use and abuse nature."[1] Whereas in the early 1990s many within the fold believed that the sub-discipline would become more centrally based in an informal knowledge of the natural world and the natural sciences, the field has not thus crystallized. Also writing about five years after the emergence of this second wave and its implicit reconstruction of the object of study, Ian Marshall offers this assessment: "It seems that ecocriticism is not so much continuing along its path in the woods, traveling onward in a consistent direction (towards the natural sciences?), as it is constructing a web, with threads radiating in all directions from a common center, the whole thing held together by the numerous points where the threads intersect."[2]

While it is standard form today for ecocritics to celebrate this diversity of projects, Marshall's web metaphor is not particularly encouraging, not least be-cause this same metaphor has served as a conceptual barrier rather than a tool in scientific ecology, as Dana Phillips explains. A scientist like Paul Colinvaux finds the information-theory concept of the food web, which transforms limited ma-terial resources into timeless essences and thus wishes away consumption and competition, "not only unreal, but absurd."[3] So, too, the idea of the "web of life, which has become one of the pet notions of environmentalism and popular ecol-ogy," poses serious conceptual problems: in attempting to describe the web, writes Phillips, "one becomes preoccupied with discovering and describing the various interstices of the web in the absence of any concrete evidence of the existence of the web as a whole, and still worse, in the absence of any concrete evidence that the web *is* a whole" (75). In other words, the web metaphor has provided not only a weak but probably misguided characterization of both specific biological pro-cesses and the general organization of organic life. Although academic research programs such as the study of literature and the environment are in many re-spects very different from biological systems, both exhibit a dynamism that is ill-served by the ultimately static web metaphor, and literary studies might well heed Phillips's suggestion that ecology has been hampered by the poor fit between metaphorical construct and natural phenomena.[4]

Given this state of affairs, according to which ambiguity about the object or objects of study diffuses the research practices and purpose of the subdiscipline, a perspective like mine, drawing broadly on contemporary psychology, might seem especially unwelcome. After all, in spite of the considerable broadening of the field, Cheryll Glotfelty and Harold Fromm's early definition of it in the seminal *Ecocriticism Reader* as "the study of the relationship between literature and the physical environment" still generally defines the field's core, just as a glance at the articles and books cataloged in the *MLA Bibliography* affirms Lawrence Buell's remark that ecocriticism retains, on the whole, an "up-country-and-out-back orientation."[5] With nonhuman nature, then, still generally at its center and threads radiating out to the various nodes (built environment, environmental justice, etc.), would it not be best to let well enough alone? Are not these fields—ecocriticism, with its initial focus on the nonhuman natural world, and a cognitive-evolutionary biocultural criticism, with its theoretical and interpretive foundation in the evolution and cognitive processes of the mind—polar opposites, motivated by different principles and focused on quite distinct phenomena?

Let us return to the curious fact that among those schools of criticism currently in operation, ecocriticism, motivated originally by a desire to sustain a very large material object, the planet Earth, has at its center not just one but a number of complex conceptual-linguistic constructs, chief among them *environment, ecology, nature,* and *culture.* This in and of itself might begin to suggest the value of cognitive research for the field, for no other current subdiscipline has central objects and concepts with quite such metamorphic talents as these four terms. Try as we might, for instance, to will away the concrete type *woman* via postmodern performatives, the human object underlying feminism is not largely a subject of debate. Likewise, while subaltern studies has rightly stressed the constructed nature of racial and ethnic categories, the real-world functioning of terms such as *African American* and *Latino* for persons who share some combination of racial, cultural, linguistic, and geographical identity is relatively stable. By contrast, the denotative values of ecocriticism's key terms are hardly stable or concrete, as Marshall's weblike characterization of the field indicates. Rather than constituting a shortcoming, however, the conceptual plasticity of ecocriticism's key terms defines the ground of possibility for a cohesive yet complex articulation of the field of study, suggesting that, somewhat ironically, knowledge of human perception, cognition, and conceptual articulation is more crucial to the key issues underlying ecocriticism than it is to perhaps any other area of contemporary literary study.

I do not wish to suggest that ecocritics have simply failed to acknowledge the importance of the human mind in perception of the environment. To the contrary, the prominent scholar Scott Slovic not only notes that nature writers address the phenomenon of awareness rather than nature itself but also draws on central research in environmental psychology to develop the point. Many other ecocritics likewise acknowledge the mediatory role of consciousness.[6] Nevertheless, the exploration of human perception and cognition for their relevance to both human knowledge of and attitudes toward nonhuman nature has occupied, at best, a distinctly marginal place in the field. Understandably, ecocritics will be averse to the view that they should pay particular attention to the human mind, for to many such an orientation smacks of a pernicious anthropocentrism. The general practice, therefore, has been to note the intervening role of consciousness and to move on to other matters, as though anthropocentrism were a hurdle on the track, cleared with a little bit of effort and skill. Yet if ecocritics wish to get closer to the apparent realities that mental and linguistic constructions such as *nature* and *environment* represent and to understand the reasons why these terms have been constructed in these specific ways, they need to learn about the human brain-mind, the negotiating and orienting tool that creates and utilizes those constructions. The sooner ecocritics begin to grapple with the how and why of the mind's constructions, the sooner they will be able to formulate a workable epistemological stance and promote an informed awareness of the dynamic and mutually modifying sets of relationships—the ecologies—that shape life on Earth.

The central purpose of this chapter, then, is to argue that knowledge of human psychology and evolution establishes the basis for dynamic, coherent accounts of human relations with nonhuman entities. In addition, understanding not only the fluid and protean nature of relations and entities but also the centrality of human perception, cognition, and experience in the construction or representation of environment provides the epistemological and theoretical ground for my claim that psychological literature is an overlooked resource for ecocriticism. Since a primary goal of ecocriticism is to raise awareness of the value of the nonhuman natural world and the human treatment of it, literary works that explore the mind's positive and troubled relationships with nonhuman nature importantly illuminate the conditions that shape human attitudes—enthusiasm, caring, antipathy, indifference, and so on—toward the environment. In my reading of Wordsworth's Lucy poems and Jean Rhys's *Wide Sargasso Sea* later in this chapter, I aim to demonstrate that human relationships and cultural factors profoundly influence attitudes toward nonhuman nature.

Constructing *Minds*

Although a well-intentioned desire to avoid putting human priorities above those of the nonhuman environment may be a cause for ecocriticism's unwillingness to explore its own constructions, it is not the only cause. Quite simply, like practitioners of any scholarly method influenced by poststructuralism, many ecocritics are averse to making positive knowledge claims of even the most modest kind, assenting either tacitly or overtly to the truism that "everything is constructed." To varying degrees, and in spite of a strong countertendency within the field to indulge in a wholesale rejection of theory, many ecocritics have been influenced by the strong constructionism and radical skeptical epistemology that have emerged from poststructuralism and postmodern philosophy. It is hard to believe that any contemporary intellectual might accept either of the two epistemological extremes still bandied about by philosophers, for even intuitively it seems unlikely, on the one hand, that mental representations correspond exactly to external phenomena (naïve realism) or, on the other hand, that the mind's representations have no greater or lesser degree of reference to mind-independent realities (strong constructionism or radical skepticism). As I have argued in "Making Knowledge: Bioepistemology and the Foundations of Literary Theory," bioepistemology, the view that knowledge is relative to human knowers, provides a solution, but it has hardly been welcome in an era of blanket antihumanism. Because of this, contemporary critics of various schools often proceed with the attitude that it does not really matter whether we have an operative theory about how humans know and what sorts of knowledge might be available to them, but in fact it matters all the time, in all our endeavors. For instance, if someone were to suggest to me that my understanding of Hurricane Katrina has been constructed, I might interpret this statement in a variety of ways. In a weak constructionist sense, the conversationalist might have meant that information from the National Hurricane Service disseminated by news media had produced fear and a plan to flee New Orleans in advance of Katrina (thus facilitating, I would argue, rather than constructing my emotional and cognitive response). But if I understood the speaker's words in a strong constructionist sense—that my fear of hurricanes, my decision to act, and indeed the hurricane itself were simply media inventions—I would probably verbalize my objections to the point of view.[7] At the other extreme, I have difficulty accepting that everything reported by the news media accurately reflects the hurricane and the events that transpired in its wake, just as the label *natural disaster* is a construction that conceals at least as much as it reveals. But I can only challenge such an insidious construction and try to correct it with a better one (*natural, human, and governmental disaster?*) if I believe that some constructions more accurately represent mind-independent realities than do others.

The strong constructionist underpinnings of poststructuralism consort particularly oddly with ecocriticism, for I am willing to wager that, like myself, all (or nearly all) ecocritics believe that some constructions are more accurate than others. To my knowledge, no ecocritic embraces a bona fide radical skepticism, which amounts to entertaining the view that the material world environmentalists are trying to sustain may not actually exist or is constructed in radically different ways by different observers. As ecocritics are well aware, this position robs the field of its central object and, along with it, the grounds of effective action. For the truth of the matter is that an environment conceived in the strong constructionist sense is *made up*, and no one can intervene meaningfully on behalf of an imaginary object; nor, for that matter, is meaningful intervention possible if cognition and perception are highly subjective or extremely culturally relative. In short, intellectual inquiry and effective political action require some degree of informed faith in the regularities of observers and objects.

Contemporary critics have preferred to sidestep epistemological debates and proceed with critical projects, but the unresolved contradictions about how and what humans might know leads to some unproductive arguments, some of them about matters that might reasonably be set aside. Like other socially and politically motivated literary scholars, for instance, ecocritics tender evaluative judgments about texts based on the presumed degree to which the texts will raise consciousness about the environment. Ironically—since such an effort assumes that there are minds in which consciousness can be raised and that those minds are therefore critical to the construction and treatment of the environment— ecocritics have generally looked askance at the phenomenon of modern self-consciousness that first emerges forcefully as a literary subject matter in romantic-era writing, and many have done so by championing a realist aesthetic. Christopher Hitt, one critic of this strain within ecocriticism, notes that "these critical responses focus on representation, the relationship between literature and empirical reality, privileging or censuring literary texts according to how fully and accurately they represent the real world."[8] Best are the texts in which mind is least evident, the reasoning seems to go. In a qualified defense of this position, Lawrence Buell suggests that the predilection for realism stems from the ecocritical belief that actual environments and the environmental imagination (a vague and therefore problematic term in Buell's recent writing) are linked.[9] But no sooner has Buell made this claim than he qualifies it, acknowledging that "realism can heighten the divide between narrative consciousness and the text's represented world even as it purports to serve as a bridge" (*Future*, 40). Seeming in one breath to eschew modern self-consciousness and endorse art in which the physical environment is represented in accordance with a realist aesthetic, in the next Buell not only acknowledges the intervening function of mind but admits that some realist figurations may actually damage the cause of environmental awareness.

Thus nodding to the presence of mind in literature while simultaneously wishing it away, Buell's both/and construction hardly clarifies the central question here: How do we come to know and value presumed mind-independent reality through the representations of literary texts? The endorsement of a realist aesthetic in ecocriticism seems to be founded on the fossilized vestiges of a naïve realist epistemology, for it requires the fallacious assumption that eschewing the representation of mind *in* the text reduces or constrains the amount of mental activity invested in the entire textual transaction (including principally but not exclusively its creation by the writer and reception by the reader). The view that properly selected realist texts will result in a salutary imprinting of environmental images on a relatively inert "consciousness" necessarily rests on the notion that specific aesthetic characteristics, in predictably limiting mental activity, draw closer to the real. In short, the conviction that a realist aesthetic will produce political results assumes that the mind is at least sometimes a simple, passive organ that produces and exchanges representationally accurate images of mind-independent reality free of both subjective and species-typical biases and motives.

Although something of a standard-bearer within the field, Buell is hardly the only ecocritic who has claimed that specific modes and techniques harmonize especially well with the values of the field. In addition to realism, comedy, pastoral, and nature writing have all been championed for their presumed fidelity to life and an implicit conviction that their capacity to palliate the soul will culminate in an environmentally friendly perspective.[10] Since literary modes are not only notoriously malleable but also subject inevitably to change, it is often a certain literary or historical period's conception and instantiation of the mode that is singled out, and, notably, the favored mode is commonly celebrated for its perceived alignment with actuality. Thus, there is considerable overlap between the endorsement of a realist aesthetic and the modes identified as eco-friendly by certain critics. Glen Love, who as an ecocritic championing an evolutionary perspective departs considerably from Buell on theoretical grounds, nevertheless likewise connects ethics with style and mode.[11] According to Love, the classical instantiation of pastoral, which connects human with animal life and embraces the reality of death, provides a promising model for literature bent on ecological awareness. Love's selective definition of pastoral, in effect, sidesteps central features of that mode (indeed, perhaps its central manifestations) in the Anglo-European tradition from the Renaissance until well into the eighteenth century, when writers employed the stock natural images of pastoral to convey Christian doctrine and belief symbolically and allegorically.[12] By contrast, the permutation of pastoral that Love endorses eschews symbolic representation and employs the descriptive practice of realism, and in his view Willa Cather's *The Professor's House* exemplifies this model of pastoral. Admiring the focus on bodily senses and perception in the novel, whose form and increasingly minimalist style mimic Cather's "unfurnishing process," Love notes the near renunciation of language over the course of the book (114). What Love especially admires is Cather's effort to bring the novel as close as possible to the status of a natural object by stripping away language and hence the signs of consciousness as far as possible.

The issue here is not whether Cather's experiment is well accomplished but whether it is advisable to theorize aesthetics on the basis of ethics. Additionally, it is not clear what is gained by presenting an example of these aesthetics, especially when the selected work seems not only to counsel the abandonment of language and discourse but also to be valued specifically for its antilinguistic direction. From a practical point of view, the push toward representationalism insistently reveals an uneasiness about literature, language, and human beings, and thus its implicit logic suggests that an abandonment of literary activities in favor of direct activism might be the wisest course. For the end result of such thinking is that literature and its medium are indeed so much furniture barring us from transparent engagement in the Real. As Phillips puts it, "The scandal that alarms ecocritics of the realist stripe only arises if one assumes that the fictional dimension of literature—of all literature, even the nonfictional, paradoxical as this may seem—is somehow the source of its faults. Only then will one seek to treat literature as no more than a kind of writing, and writing as no more than a form of bookkeeping" (16). I would take the point even farther. Inasmuch as even the most apparently objective human account of any phenomenon is distinct from the next person's account, it bears evidence of a subjectively creating consciousness. And inasmuch as any group of critics views subjectively creating mind as an imposition on rather than a portion of the reality in question, they will view all its productions as suspect.

Some recent schools of criticism had an available and intellectually viable (though temporary) solution to this tangled problem of dogmatically driven aesthetics premised on an outdated realist epistemology: set aside questions of knowledge and literary value and focus instead on recovering the works of women and others whom literary history has neglected. Those engaged in these projects have greatly enriched our knowledge of literature, but at the same time the questions how, why, and what we value, having been readmitted through the back door simply by virtue of the attention paid to certain texts, must be addressed at some point, as I suggested in chapter 2. However, this approach is not available to ecocritics, whose politics are not focused on a subordinated human population and who therefore do not have a wealth of neglected texts to put at the center of the field. Precisely because there is a greater difference between their central object of concern and the processes of literary production and dissemination than there is for politically motivated critics of other schools, ecocritics should be able to see the flawed logic in endorsing particular modes and styles as sources of enlightenment. As the foregoing analysis suggests, the assumption that any given mode or style is inherently superior to others for raising political consciousness rests on a series of misconceptions about the nature of thought and mind. The first is a fallacy about the creative mind. Since human beings create original works of literature within an individual and cultural context, they fashion mode, style, and technique to their own purposes. Thus, the content and potential meaning of any work of literature is not constrained by conventions of mode, style, and technique, which are too general and too substantially modified by other factors to reliably convey a particular semantic content or to result in a predictable subconscious impact. The second is a fallacy about the mechanism of human enlightenment. It is by no means necessarily true that the most literally representative rendering of the thing or event will produce the greatest appreciation of the actual phenomenon on the reader's part and thus result in the greatest degree of desired political awareness. Such awareness may depend more significantly on other factors, including the frame of mind of the reader and the context in which he or she encounters the text, than the mode or style of the text itself. Indeed, the framing of a text by the experience of a course on literature and environment could quite plausibly determine the level of raised awareness better than the specific texts being studied. The third is a fallacy about human mind in general, which sees it as intervening between the perceiving agent and mind-independent reality. Instead, the human mind provides our only means of knowing that reality at all.

Furthermore, the history of literary theoretical approaches in the twentieth century already demonstrates the problem of assuming a correlation between aesthetic practices and the ideological implications of artworks. The vagaries of Marxist criticism serve as the most prominent example and suggest that ecocritics would do well to avoid further the pitfalls of a proscriptive approach. Marxist criticism gained momentum after the Russian Revolution in 1917, and in the three subsequent decades arguments that unusual and nonrepresentational techniques exposed class struggle kept pace with contrary arguments that mainstream realism served as the best mechanism for enlightenment. Soviet Socialist Realism, based on the premise that nineteenth-century Russian realism provided detailed illustrations of social class, represented the orthodox Communist view and thus diverged from the Russian formalist emphasis on defamiliarization, with its stress on unusual uses of language and images. Marxist-inspired aesthetics continued along these two tracks: in the 1930s through the 1950s, at the same time that George Lukács became the most sophisticated theorist of a realist aesthetic, Bertolt Brecht developed the theory and technique of the alienation effect, which endorsed breaking the illusion of reality as a means of raising consciousness. During the same period but extending through the sixties, the work of the Frankfurt school reversed the judgment of Socialist Realists regarding modernism, holding that the works deemed decadent in 1917 revealed the fragmentation and dehumanization of modern life. After the late sixties, the argument over the relationship of text to world, as well as the didactic value of distinct texts, continued unabated, although the influences of structuralism, deconstruction, Althusserian Marxism, neo-Freudianism, and other strains of thought rendered the arguments increasingly arcane.

Thus the history of Marxist attempts to align ideological commitments with specific textual practices attests to the inadvisability of pinpointing a correct aesthetics, for the simple fact of the matter is that the semantic content of an artwork cannot be discerned on the basis of something so general as a style or a mode. Meaning does not inhere in specific modes and styles; photographically realistic paintings of men and tractors may suggest strength, triumph, anger, despair, and all manner of emotions and attitudes. In its insistent literalism, Soviet Socialist Realism did indeed aspire to the bookkeeping aesthetic that Phillips disparages among present-day ecocritics, but as an aesthetic theory with political aims it was notoriously short-lived. Detailed specifications for the configuration and depiction of persons and objects may constrain the range of meanings but still cannot determine them, and at the end of the day readers (who all come from somewhat different orientations and experiences) must try to make sense of the exact words put down in a specific order, an arrangement of words whose type is not repeated anywhere else in literary history.

Rather than fruitlessly debating about what kinds of texts will best serve their goals and thus ironically limiting the resource that might illuminate the human relationship to the world, then, ecocritics should give thorough and thoughtful consideration to how and why we construct the world the way we do. The term *construction* itself has been so popular, I believe, because it is so fundamentally vague that it masks a multitude of intellectual confusions. These days, the term *construct* might denote any number of things within a range of cognitive, linguistic, and cultural phenomena, including words, complex concepts, theories, imaginative worlds and texts, and so forth. Moreover, all of our constructions have species-level, individual, and historical dimensions, and from an ecological point of view, no one of these contextual factors should lead to the exclusion of the others. With this in mind, it is worth noting that British romanticist ecocritics have criticized the tendency of their Americanist colleagues to condemn the presumed transcendentalizing of British writers and to downplay their influence on American environmental writing, often in the service of promoting a realist aesthetic. In fact, arguing in 1991 that Wordsworth was at the head of a tradition connecting nature, community, and social emancipation, Jonathan Bate seems to have anticipated the emergent realist literalism of many ecocritics and thus to have initiated a theoretical and historical countercurrent.[13] It is not surprising that romanticists in particular and Wordsworthians specifically would be well represented among those questioning the advocacy of realism, since psychological-imaginative functioning was so central a subject matter at the end of the eighteenth century in Britain, as both contemporaneous developments in brain science and the evidence of literature demonstrate. While a framework relativist or strong constructionist historicism might simply point to the convergent emergence of these phenomena and reduce their significance to their cultural and ideological origins, a pragmatic epistemology enables us to inquire whether attention to the brain-mind has produced any knowledge that is apparently more accurate than what went before. Intelligently historicizing the characteristic features of any era compels us to explain not only the contingent reasons for the emergence of the phenomenon but the possible long-term contribution such phenomena make to our understanding.

Undergirding the perspective of many of these romanticist ecocritics, as well as a number of their Americanist colleagues, I believe, is the view that the results of Enlightenment science in, among other things, the cultural shift to modernization and the active nature of human mind not only profoundly changed our perception of the human relation to nature but furthermore fundamentally require that we acknowledge the implications of that changed relationship. In his comments on Thomas Hardy's *Return of the Native* quoted in the epigraph to this chapter, Bate points attention to the problem of the modern person's relation to nature, his or her consciousness of separation and difference; unlike that of "the old woodlanders," "the condition of modern man, with his mobility and his displaced knowledge, is never to be able to share this sense of belonging."[14] The loss of "a sense of belonging," or perhaps more accurately, the emergence of the affective, perceptual, and cognitive separation that attends the loss of experiential holism, marks a major shift in consciousness that results from the relocation of great numbers of our species to the built (or "carpentered") domains of cities. Not only are ecocritics aware of this shift but they have widely recognized it as the source of the dichotomous *nature-culture* construction, which rests on, not separate or separable entities, but two terms that hardly had the same signification in pre- and postindustrial eras.[15] Before industrialization, Bate informs us, *culture* referred to a cultivated tract of land and thus to a physical expanse continuous with uncultivated and wild portions of nature. The shift in meaning to denote the human attainments of refinement and education thus attests to the conceptual bifurcation of the totality of nature into a human (cultural) domain and a non-human (natural) one. J. Scott Bryson's observation that the historical development of the term *nature* coincides with the sense of the human as separate from all else further supports the view that the conception of humans as apart from and different from nature is by and large a quite recent phenomenon whose development may be identified in the shifting usage of various terms.[16]

In sum, it is not too much to say that the reconstruction of these two words into a dichotomy fosters a conception of humans and their creations in relation to the rest of actuality that is predominantly false, for in the larger picture most of us would agree that everything cultural is contained within and subject to the forces we term *natural.* Perceiving the falsity of the nature-culture dichotomy, ecocritics have tended to respond with a moral outrage that is understandable but also something of a stumbling block to further analysis. If we temporarily set aside our frustration at the enormous hubris of human beings, who deign to imagine that they are cordoned off from other natural phenomena, we can hypothesize several probable causes of this construction. For among the many puzzles resulting from the Enlightenment contribution to knowledge is this conundrum: just when humans have begun to acquire knowledge of the natural world that indicates its complexity and the interdependence of its elements, language comes to reflect and reinforce the restructuring of conceptual categories in a way that *contradicts* modern scientific knowledge. At the psychological level, however, this development is less curious than it might appear, exposing the discrepancy between scientific knowledge and the impact of applied science, which, in transforming human life—through the mass production of manufactured goods, modern transportation, medical technologies, and the like—understandably leads to a disproportionate sense that people actively control natural forces and resources. Since our minds, bodies, and intelligences are directly engaged in day-to-day experiences, these experiences have great persuasive force in our conceptual understanding, whereas the notion of our subservience to larger external forces has become relatively more and more abstract as a result of real or perceived control of the proximate environment. At least as importantly, humans, like all other species, try to control their environment and the resources it affords and thus resist acknowledging their apparent insignificance. In this sense, the nature-culture dichotomy supports the illusion of control.

Additionally, language serves a paradoxical function in relation to conceptualization. Because language provides the means for the description and labeling of phenomena, it clarifies and stabilizes the concepts we use to understand apparent mind-independent reality (Storey, *Mimesis*, 70–71). This feature of language likely provided functional efficiency in human evolution, resulting in shared concepts that were adequate enough to enhance communication and facilitate action. But at the same time that language enables greater precision as a mechanism of shared concepts and meanings, its very functionalism rests on a process of generalization, often conferring objective status on entities or processes that are not bounded and static. Indeed, on the basis of experiments in auditory perception, the psychologist Merlin Donald reports that "words, and more complex auditory events such as sentences and longer utterances, take on the perceptual characteristics usually attributed to three-dimensional visual and tactile objects. . . . Most environmental sounds are aspects of events, rather than events in themselves; words stand out as events on their own" (246). Put simply, people are predisposed to view words (and thus the concepts they name) as things. These findings suggest that the evolutionary and everyday pragmatic functionalism of language is in some respects at odds with human efforts to comprehend the complexity of phenomena, for language's generalizing tendency regularly fosters the hypostatization of complex entities such as *nature* and *culture*. If required to specify what we mean by *nature*, most of us would include the sensate and insensate phenomena of the nonhuman natural world, as well as a variety of forces and processes, and a good many others would include humans and their cultural accoutrements as well. Yet the commonplace use of *nature* and its modern conceptual yoking to *culture* so diminishes the concept that it leads to the routine, ubiquitous distortion of the relation between humans and everything else. Paradoxically, then, the generalizing function of language sometimes conflicts with its capacity to foster precision.

How do we know when, if ever, our linguistic and conceptual constructions represent the actual with relative fidelity? As both this discussion of the nature-culture dichotomy and my discussion of narrative in chapter 2 suggest, the self-interested quality of human knowing results in limited and perhaps distorted characterizations of mind-independent reality. For instance, the nature-culture dichotomy, while so nicely in accord with a theistic conception of reality that places man above the rest of creation, conflicts fundamentally with the theory of evolution by natural selection, according to which all human attributes, including all of culture, only emerge because of their utility in a context defined by other species. However handy the nature-culture dichotomy may be in some everyday contexts, it has no utility in contemporary science, and its efficacy as both a concept in and a structural notion enforcing the distinction between the humanities and sciences is a subject of debate, as the work of evolutionary and ecocritical scholars demonstrates.

This functional view of knowledge, in accordance with which ideas and concepts are not absolute but operate as tools to bring into relation the various aspects of experience, is an inheritance of classical pragmatism as it developed in the nineteenth-century thought of William James, C. S. Peirce, John Dewey, and their respective circles. As Louis Menand relates, pragmatism emerged in the contexts of the disillusioning experience of the Civil War and, most significantly, developments in scientific thought over the course of the eighteenth and nineteenth centuries. In the social and scientific realms, figures such as Wendell Holmes and William James saw how absolute ideas had both dangerous and unproductive consequences; in response they emphasized instead the social character of ideas, which are contingent upon the environment and gain credence through their capacity to explain phenomena. The development of statistical and probabilistic methods in the sciences paved the way for pragmatic philosophy but just as crucially, in providing an alternative to the language of types and essences, enabled the formulation of the theory of evolution by natural selection, which both exemplified and spurred on the development of pragmatism. As Menand points out, although natural selection is no less abstract than typology, since evolutionary change is too slow to be observed in action, it does a better job than previous theories of explaining what we know. Thus, central assumptions of Darwinian evolution, including the dynamic rather than fixed nature of natural phenomena and the self-interested nature of species, are foundational to pragmatic philosophy.

The epistemological and psychological implications of evolution's central assumptions were hardly lost on the pragmatists, who clearly recognized that our identification and naming of entities has primarily instrumental value rather than absolute validity. Humans name not only material things but also unobservable events, phenomena, or properties, and pragmatic philosophers astutely recognized the unavoidable tendency toward misapprehension that came with naming conceptual entities. Peirce, a trained mathematician, took pains to point out that for him terms like *cause, chance,* and *certainty* indicated points on a curve, not fixed properties (Menand, *Metaphysical,* 222–23). Both Dewey and James, psychological in their orientation, were attuned to the human bias toward imagining a correspondence between terms and static, concrete entities once terms have been applied to aspects of a process. James, in fact, applied this understanding of the hypostatizing and rigidifying features of human cognition and expression to the mental research of his day in his criticism of what he identified as the "psychologist's fallacy," the habit of treating the terms of inquiry in psychology as distinct mental features rather than parts of a psychical process that do not, in effect, exist independent of the process as a whole (Menand, *Metaphysical,* 329). John Dewey drew on James's insight and continued to criticize false distinctions throughout his long career; not incidentally, one of the false distinctions he addressed was that between *nature* and *culture.*

In their closely related philosophies, then, the pragmatists, unlike other thinkers of their day, were influenced by a correct understanding of natural selection and its implications for human knowledge. Like Pierce and James in their discussion of probability and psychological theory, Darwin explained that the words *species* and *variety* had meaning only in relation to one another and within the theory as a whole. Populations of organisms inevitably change; they are identified as new species rather than varieties of an existing species at a point in the evolutionary process marked as substantively different by human perception. As Darwin puts it, "I look at the term species, as one arbitrarily given for the sake of convenience to a set of individuals closely resembling each other, and that it does not essentially differ from the term variety, which is given to less distinct and more fluctuating forms. The term variety, again, in comparison with mere individual differences, is also applied arbitrarily, and for mere convenience sake."[17] It is hardly incidental that Samuel Taylor Coleridge, writing decades before Darwin, favored the distinctions between degrees rather than kinds, for he was immersed in the schools of thought and theory, such as German organic philosophy and the evolutionism of Erasmus Darwin, that were formulating the view of reality as process rather than static hierarchy. Coleridge was pointing attention to the relative rather than absolute difference between entities, just as Darwin would later point attention to the relative nature of the difference between species and varieties.

In one light, the nature-culture dichotomy and the theory of evolution by natural selection may be seen as competing constructions of the nature of reality that emerged contemporaneously. The first handily assumes a split between human things and the rest of nature; the second seeks to explain the emergence, survival, and transformation of life forms in relation to one another. Yet although the two constructions contradict each other at one level—that is, it is not possible to see humans or any other entities outside of the process of finding a viable niche amidst numerous other species doing the same—their role in human life and knowledge must be considered in an assessment of their utility. After all, it is not always inaccurate to consider cultural phenomena apart from natural ones, just so long as we do not seek support for that distinction as part of a general explanation of life.

Viewed pragmatically, then, these constructions have different kinds of utility, and humans seem to have a chronic difficulty in distinguishing what terms and constructs apply at what levels or in what contexts. At the highest level, the theory of evolution by natural selection, which describes life as a complex, ongoing process in which entities are by turns interdependent and in conflict and frequently difficult to view in isolation, has the greatest utility, because for more than a hundred and fifty years it has best explained natural observation and the fossil record, which together provide evidence of species transformations and extinctions over long periods of time and in accordance with the driving force of climate change. By contrast, at this level of explanation the nature-culture dichotomy, compatible only with the traditional notion of the Great Chain of Being or a similarly hierarchical concept that identifies humans as essentially different from and higher than other species, does not accord with the facts and has little utility. Because evolutionary theory is the only full-scale description of the emergence of life that claims the fundamental similarity of humans and other species, it presents a solution to the epistemological, ethical, and aesthetic dilemmas of ecocriticism; emphasizing change through process rather than static and discrete entities, it disbands the nature-culture dichotomy. Most importantly for the discussion here, moreover, natural selection assumes that mind and behavior are embedded in and shaped by the material and temporal context of evolution, reminding us that human minds and bodies, like all other minds and bodies, are part of the environment.

Constructing *Environment*

If consideration of the nature-culture dichotomy elucidates the historical reason for its emergence and reveals its paradoxical status as a practically and emotionally useful but scientifically false construct, contemplation of the term *environment* uncovers a similar complexity. According to David Mazel, the word *environment* emerged in the nineteenth century and initially denoted "the act of environing," but its meaning has contracted over time, thus coinciding with the historical development of the terms *culture* and *nature* and attesting at the level of commonplace usage to a corollary conceptual diminution and rigidification. As Mazel points out, "The very idea of environment divides the world into an inside and an outside."[18] Since Darwin's *Origin*, which painstakingly theorizes a natural world characterized by complex process over and above interactions of distinct entities, was published in 1859, it is more than a little ironic that the same era gave birth to such narrow constructions of *nature, culture,* and *environment,* and we would do well to follow Mazel's urging, recognizing *environment* as a construct and asking such self-reflective questions as, "What has counted as the environment," and why (143)? Although we tend to assume automatically that this word applies to a physical place or to nonhuman nature in general, it actually has a number of different contemporary uses that, taken together, illustrate simultaneously the conceptual variability of the term and the extent to which humans are unavoidably embedded in natural process.

The term *environment,* like *nature* or *culture,* differs in kind from those words referring to a wide range of natural and artificial entities, such as *tree, valley, cat, baby,* and *Cheerio,* all of which apparently refer to discrete, bounded entities whose character remains relatively fixed in accord with the regularities of human perception, cognition, and communication. Although skeptics rightly insist that we cannot know, in an absolute sense, whether the objects to which these words refer actually exist, for functional purposes and for my purpose here the skeptic's point is not significant. As James points out, what counts psychologically and functionally in human life is what we take to be real, whatever its status in absolute terms. I assume that the magnolia tree outside my window exists as a discrete, bounded entity and that the phrase *magnolia tree* enables me to communicate about that object to others; if in some absolute sense beyond the domain of human cognition that object has no reality, that fact would in no way alter our shared human perception of the thing as a bounded entity defined by such specific qualities as a trunk, spreading branches, large white blossoms, and glossy leaves. Other terms, such as *hurricane,* for instance, refer to complex and evanescent systems rather than distinct, bounded entities, yet their meanings are still quite stable because of their specific reference to perceived mind-independent phenomena.

In contrast to words referring to observable, mind-independent realities, *environment* is a perceiver-relative term admitting to a range of distinct uses. *Environment* not only frequently refers to places varying in physical size and characteristics, thus failing to designate an apparently self-contained object, but also at times denotes the human rather than the material qualities of a place. Including humans in the environment concept in everyday speech is, in fact, rather common; indeed, in such usages it is often the *human* factor that is paramount. Were another mom to say to me, "I took Priscilla out of Itsy Bitsy Spider Daycare because I didn't like the *environment*," I would know that she was complaining about more than the color of the plastic chairs, and I might tend to think of her language choice as euphemistic, prompted by the wish to avoid direct criticism of persons. But the language choice is only euphemistic inasmuch as it employs a general and flexible term to refer to something more specific (bad teachers and kids that bite, and maybe, secondarily, beat-up furniture and toys or unhealthy snacks). By the same token, if one of the teachers said, "I resigned from Itsy Bitsy Spider Daycare because I didn't like the *environment*," in her case too it would be unlikely that she was referring simply to the physical space and its appurtenances. She might be implying poor treatment of staff by administration or a history of complaining parents (including Priscilla's mom?) or even kids that bite. In any case, we would infer that these comments reflect negatively on some combination of human behaviors, work policies, and personalities, and not on the physical place at all. If on the one hand the use of *environment* to criticize the human atmosphere of a place avoids specific criticism or praise via generalization, on the other it points attention to a central ecological truth: that human emotion *and* behavior are enmeshed in, relative to, and indeed made possible by the physical world and the behavior of other living beings.

Thus, although we tend to assume intellectually that *environment* refers either generally to the nonhuman natural world or to a specific physical locale, in practice the word is used in a wide variety of ways relative to human emotions, needs, movement, and experience, and, accordingly, its implied meaning varies greatly depending on the context. No species, after all, has evolved and lived in unchanging, circumscribed spaces, and while some aspects of the built human environment do have a self-contained quality, humans in general move more fluidly through physical space and social encounters than any other species. (This helps explain why regular assignment to an office space or prison cell is confining and in either or both cases considered punishment, particularly if the place is windowless.) The highly context-dependent usage of *environment*, in effect, provides a kind of cryptic history of our ontology, for the term mutates continuously over the course of a day, a week, a year, inflected differently depending on a variety of factors, including the extent and duration of our movement through physical space, the characteristics of the nonhuman natural environment, the climate and weather and the degree to which they change, and last but hardly least, the level of the subject's participation in a human group.

Momentous experiences (caused by changes in weather, climate, social bonds, and the consequences of all of these), moreover, might result in major shifts in our understanding of the concept of environment. My perceived environment, as I sit and write in my air-conditioned study, is this quiet and enclosed space; but if I go down the steps and out my front door, my environment includes the magnolia tree in my yard rather than simply providing a view of it. Yet because this sense of a safe, secure, undamaged environment is relatively fragile in the context of Hurricane Katrina's impact on New Orleans seven years ago and because I see terrible damage every time I drive to work, it now seems utterly trivial to define my house or my neighborhood as my "environment." Altered awareness readily transforms concepts and words, and in this case the consciousness of a local like myself of what New Orleans is might be compatible with that of a friend calling from another city, if fundamentally unequal. That is, if an out-of-town friend asks me about the environment in New Orleans post-Katrina, I assume that she is asking about the pace of rebuilding and the remaining amount of damage; the increase in crime in poor and still-desolate parts of the city; the general mood of the population; and the status of new business ventures crucial to the city's recovery.

Because change to this environment as a result of the storm has been relatively macroscopic (especially for the lucky minority who lost neither homes nor family members), it is the macroscopic connotation of the term that now predominates. In contrast to this macroscopic view, my study is my "environment" now in only the most trivial sense, reflecting my heightened awareness of the frangible boundaries between proximate places and of an increased identification with New Orleans as, on the one hand, a distinct geographical and conceptual entity and, on the other, a highly vulnerable one. In spite of the apparent simplicity of the term *environment,* then, people understand it quite differently depending on the immediate context. The shift for New Orleanians, which reflects a refocusing of attention away from the static and unchanging aspects of the surround and in the direction of a highly shifting and dynamic definition—*environment* as "what is happening around me"—is an adaptive one.

As I suggested earlier, none of these implied definitions of *environment*—to refer to human attitudes and social relations within a specified milieu; to identify nonhuman nature; to describe the shifting natural and cultural domain outside the individual or group—is, strictly speaking, wrong, since each has utility within a specific context. However, it is inaccurate and certainly unhelpful to think in terms of the first two definitions when we are trying to understand the human relation to nonhuman places and beings. The theory of evolution by natural selection establishes the theoretical ground for a dynamic, perceiver- and context-relative concept of the environment, for the notion that *environment* might be accurately defined as "what is happening around me/us." Environment, from the point of view of any sensate creature, is a context-dependent concept: what defines (or constructs) the environment in an evolutionary perspective depends on the organism's position in space at a given time. The environment is not simply the physical world, or the physical world and the animals in it, but is highly variable and susceptible to change; thus, environment and nature include other members of one's own species as well as other species. In the chapter "Struggle for Existence" in *The Origin of Species,* Darwin, applying Malthusian insight to natural populations, considers why so many members of natural species are born, when so few survive: "The face of Nature may be compared to a yielding surface, with ten thousand sharp wedges packed close together and driven inwards by incessant blows, sometimes one wedge being struck, and then another with greater force" (119). Darwin's metaphor usefully illustrates that all existing species constitute the totality (or the "face") of nature—that species and individuals are in and, from the points of view of other individuals and species, of their given environment at the same time. Just as separate species constitute population groups whose adaptations may enable survival (their fit into "the face of Nature"), so too the individuals of a species are like wedges, either maintaining their place by virtue of selective advantages combined with a suitable environment—including food, safety from predators, parental protection, and the like—or losing that place. For modern humans, who have been resourceful in harnessing the power of non-human nature and in protecting themselves from its most immediate dangers, members of our own species constitute, psychologically speaking, the most significant component of our environment.

Although my examples of the uses of the term *environment* illustrate its highly variable nature, this should not lead us to conclude that the term is semantically unstable or that its meaning is uncertain in any given instance. In each case, our assumptions about the term depend on the context. Discursive context, social situation, and more immediate local (cultural) factors guide interpretation. Anyone with a cultural knowledge of contemporary child care would know immediately that the mother and teacher mentioned above were objecting to human factors, because they would never have agreed at the outset to enrollment or employment at Itsy Bitsy Spider if they had disliked the physical establishment. Additionally, basic human folk psychology will guide the understanding of the conversants. There might be an important difference in perspective between Priscilla's mom and the teacher, but their behavior is guided by larger generalities of human psychology and behavior. Both make judgments about the behavior of others, and both tie their judgments of persons to their perception and reevaluation of place.

Thus, conscious appraisal of our current uses of *environment* prompts us to ask whether its context-dependent semantic variability—referring to persons and behaviors or to physical places—is simply arbitrary or whether it reflects an underlying truth about the human mode of existence. While the recently fashionable concept of *différance* has inclined us to think that such semantic shifts relate only to the language system itself, in the present instance apparent instability may be a symptom of the refusal to look beyond linguistic superficialities. For other words denoting physical locations, such as *place* and *home*, also carry strong connotations of human relationship and feeling. The three words, in fact, might be placed on a continuum of least to most humanly inflected *(environment–place–home)*, revealing that although we want and need to look at the world apart from humanity, it is very difficult to do so.

Why the place-to-person connotations, the insistent merging of locations with social relationships? For humans, the answer is simple: locations realize their significance in the presence of persons, just as persons develop their significance in concrete and specific locations. This is not just a practical matter but a reflection of the evolutionary interdependence of individuals, social groups, and places for the human species. Feelings for people and places are most commonly integrated, operating as parts of a dynamic process of relatedness that assisted survival for our early ancestors and is still, in large measure, functional for our species today. However, the indispensability of group cohesion and coordinated activity suggests that the viability of an environment depends on the existence and strength of human attachments—that, in other words, places are not apt to look very good in the absence of a supportive social group. Human relationships, in short, are a prerequisite to a productive relationship to the larger whole.

Hence, while the nineteenth-century construction *environment* encourages us to cast the nonhuman world as other, the term's varied uses expose the ontological untruthfulness of this construction. In the following section, I explore the existential substrate of the word *place*, a term that will aid in unveiling the developmental and phylogenetic significance of emotional associations with physical locations. In so doing, I build the argument that emotional attachments supply the basis of human sociality and appreciation of nonhuman nature and that feelings for and relationships with other humans are intimately bound up with our attitudes toward physical locations.

Constructing *Place*

Second-wave ecocritics have been increasingly drawn to the concept of place and have begun to exhibit a developing awareness that human considerations, including culture and processes of mind, must be taken into account in analyses of the physical world's representations. Indeed, the growing interest in place suggests that many ecocritics now recognize that human considerations cannot be fundamentally separated from the representation of physical locations.[19] Whereas *environment* so often refers exclusively to the nonhuman natural world, the word *place* rarely has such deceptive neutrality: it is highly charged with human connotations, conjoining perception, affective tone, and cultural factors with physical location. Unlike the word *space*, then, *place* implies value judgment, whether positive or negative. Buell defines the term thus in *Writing for an Endangered World*:

> "Place" . . . is a configuration of highly flexible subjective, social, and material dimensions, not reducible to any of these. In political geographer John Agnew's definition, "place" can be conceived as a matter of (social) "locale," (geographical) "location," and "sense of place." It "combines elements of nature (elemental forces), social relations (class, gender, and so on), and meaning (the mind, ideas, symbols)." Placeness implies physical site, though site alone does not constitute place. It also implies affect, "a deeply personal phenomenon founded on one's life-world and everyday practices," though psychological perception of meaningful place is bound to be constructed in part by collective standards as well as by physical terrain and personal proclivity: places are situated within plural "geographies associated with ethnic, political, economic, informational, cultural and religious formations." But those constructs themselves, in turn, are mediated ecologically by the physical environments that they also mediate.
>
> (60)

In other words, a place is so constructed—that is, designated as a discrete segment of the external surround—because of its humanly determined meaningfulness. But although a given physical location, a place, may be meaningful, perceivers are often unaware of how it has become meaningful to them, because of "the limiting condition of predictable, chronic perceptual underactivation in bringing to awareness, and then to articulation, of all that is to be noticed and expressed," a human condition Buell refers to as the "environmental unconscious" (*Writing*, 60, 22).

Buell's recognition that humans, both as individuals and in social groups, construct places and that place construction submits to a range of shaping factors seems to invite consideration of an evolutionary perspective, but in his ecocritical scholarship Buell repeatedly backs away from naturalistic explanations of place attachment as well as from our unconscious sensitivity to the environment. This refusal to explore the causes of place attachment is disappointing because, after all, why should humans care about physical places? Apparently, Buell fears political incorrectness above all else, and since he erroneously assumes that evolutionary explanations are deterministic (and therefore politically incorrect), he beats a hasty retreat from this most basic question. Thus, in his recent book *The Future of Environmental Criticism* he follows the same pattern of seeming to acknowledge the importance of place attachment as an ecocritical concept, then warning against its potential dangers. After a paragraph noting the contributions of contemporary geography and phenomenology to the study of place, which suggests that being always implies physical situation, and after indicating that the intertwined nature of being and place has positive political implications, Buell cautions that commitment to "place-attachment can easily fall into a sentimental environmental determinism" (*Future*, 66).

Since Buell has positioned himself as a leader among ecocritics, it is worthwhile to quote the paragraph in an effort to understand why he thinks place attachment might be a suspect concept, one that perhaps encourages narrow loyalties to specific types of places (and persons) and thus is aligned with an unsavory politics.

> [One intractable ambiguity in the concept of place] is the fraught relation between environment and emplacement. Devotees of place-attachment can easily fall into a sentimental environmental determinism. Obviously "the trick is to achieve the reintroduction of the environment part while avoiding the determinism part" . . . , but that's no easy matter. Still more slippery is the question of anthropogenic construction. Place-attachment implies *adaptation*, yet in so far as place presumes inhabitance, "transformation of the physical world is inseparable from [its] becoming." . . . Heidegger stresses that "building" worthy of the name demands that "we are capable of dwelling," which in turn presupposes situating oneself responsively within one's environment; but this kind of formulation tends to mystify the fact that dwelling even in his adaptational sense also presupposes building. . . . They are "equiprimordial," to use another Heideggerism. So "the circuit and loops of place tie nature and culture back together."

Although this Rubik's cube of a paragraph, larded with unusual terminology and quotations from diverse and possibly incompatible sources, takes a bit more work than one might wish, it is not as unintelligible as it first appears to be. Once we realize that Buell is not really at all interested in the research theorizing how and why attachments to places exist but instead only in the ethical question whether such attachments help or harm the nonhuman environment, we can formulate a restatement of the "intractable ambiguity" Buell tries to articulate here: Is the value conferred upon a specific location a product of adaptation (meant here in the commonplace, non-Darwinian sense of fitting in or accommodating to the environment), or is it the result of superimposing human values and needs on the nonhuman environment (i.e., "anthropogenic construction")? Following Heidegger, who suggests that the impulses to dwell and to build are equally primordial, the processes of nature and culture are presumed to exist in dynamic relation. But according to Buell, awareness of this relationship between human place-making and the preexisting nonhuman domain seems to drop away in Heidegger's thinking. As Buell clarifies through the example he uses in the next paragraph, romantic primitivism ("sentimental environmental determinism") replaces the awareness that the desire to fit into and the desire to shape a place are simultaneous, "equiprimordial" desires or motivations. In Buell's words, "Heidegger knows that his paradigmatic Black Forest farm was built by peasants two centuries ago; but he is moved to write as if it were the mystical upshot of natural process."

What Buell fears, then, is that the concept of place attachment masks human abuse of natural resources even while it conspires with or justifies an essentialist notion of being and selfhood and is therefore doubly politically unpalatable. What is surprising, however, especially in light of Buell's reliance on Heidegger, is the complete absence of any cultural analysis of the philosopher's sentimentalization of place. Less surprising, simply because it is less conventional in literary criticism, is the absence of a functionalist, evolutionary account of why and by what processes we come to love or despise particular places and the assumption instead that Continental philosophy can supply the answers. While phenomenology brought Continental philosophy closer to considering how people manage bodies amidst concrete environmental demands than it had ever previously been, it still hovered well above the ground; focusing on the notion of being and its situated nature, it nevertheless did not conduct its investigations in light of the developing body of research that specifically describes how various organisms, including humans, manage to exist in nature. Since the insistence on the situated nature of being remained an abstract rather than a specifically demonstrated claim, it facilitated mystifications that a more concrete consideration of situation would not have allowed. The resulting conception of place attachment is exceptionally static; literalizing the second aspect of the term, as though humans are lodged or rooted in the place like rocks or plants, it mischaracterizes the essentially complex and dynamic relationship between human wayfinders and physical domains, including the variety of places through which they have traveled and in which they have sought resources, rest, and refuge for millions of years. In other words, the idealization of nature upon which Heidegger's sentimental construction of place depends, as well as the focus on subjective experience, are themselves artifacts of the limitations of phenomenology rather than inevitable features of place attachment itself. In this respect, phenomenology has been behindhand in its retheorization of ontology and epistemology in light of evolutionary theory; by contrast, pragmatism was spawned by scientific theories premised on a dynamic and changing reality.

Although I suggest below that, first, the capacity to have feelings for places and, second, the capacity for these feelings to change over time are adaptive in the evolutionary sense (i.e., functionally significant in species survival), it is important to distinguish the functionalist explanation from the romantic celebrations of place that give Buell pause. The functionalist explanation I put forward seeks to describe the probable ontogenetic and phylogenetic utility of place attachment. On the other hand, contemporary ambivalence of the kind Buell expresses about place attachment—romantic celebrations of place that coexist with or are facilitated by a disregard for natural ecologies—is perhaps better understood in light of the dramatic impact modernization has wrought on human geographical relatedness. In spite of the distinctive ability of humans as a species to travel through and adapt to varied habitats throughout their evolutionary past, it must be remembered that the range of travel and thus the exposure to varied landscapes was greatly limited for early humans in comparison with their modern counterparts. Balancing between fulfilling basic needs and avoiding threats, "early humans favored acquiring new information about [their] environment while not straying too far from the known."[20] In other words, the ever-present potential of threats to survival acted as a constraint on exploratory, knowledge-seeking activities, and it did so for millions of years. Thus, environmental psychologists such as Stephen Kaplan posit that humans are characterized by a basic ambivalence, one that derives from the inherent tension between understanding and exploration, between "seeking knowledge and avoiding what is new and hard to comprehend" (585). In this ambivalence and in the related, differential valuation of features of the natural world based on the extent to which they present threats or useful resources might be found a key to the ambiguity that so troubles Buell. For it is not so much that "the circuit and loops of place tie nature and culture back together" but that place attachment constitutes a secure and affectionate attachment to the physical world that is, unfortunately, no more or less natural than the exploitative or oppositional attitudes we choose to cordon off as "cultural."

The sentimental attachment to place that Buell cautions against is predicated on the removal of and protections against many threats to survival that make greater mobility viable. Ironically, it is this mobility, along with the security provided by modernization, that causes the phenomena of homesickness and nostalgia, the longing for a lost place and past that, as Bate suggests, attests to the displaced condition of modern humans. If we think for a moment about all of the social, technical, and infrastructural elements necessary for modern humans to travel substantial distances in relative safety—alliance with other human groups; shared knowledge of terrain, climate, resource availability, and local species; means of conveyance; temporary shelters—it becomes clear that modern concepts of travel and corollary conceptions of place depart significantly from the home-based, wayfinding dynamic of early humans. Yet those who have lived in modernized parts of the world torn by disaster know how quickly this sense of security can be stripped away, with loss of electricity (and therefore of nighttime illumination), dispersal of neighborhood social networks, and disruptions to law enforcement providing opportunities for human and other predators.

Remarkably, then—and as counterintuitive as it might seem after being bombarded by the daily news—travel within our communities, cities, and the world is overwhelmingly safe, and this has heightened the exploratory facet of our wayfinding psychology. The ability to pack up a Ryder truck and to drive hundreds or thousands of miles before taking up residence in an entirely different state or country, all without the fear of serious threats to survival, suggests some fundamental differences between ourselves and our hominid ancestors. Nevertheless, over the course of very recent cultural evolution people began to experience ongoing loss and longing as a result of such mobility; often disconnected from the places in their past that have had great personal meaning, people long to return to the landscapes, towns, and houses that constituted *home*. According to Alan McKillop, the first use of the Swiss-German word *Heimweh*, denoting homesickness in exile, was in 1596 and thus attests to a modern sense of rootlessness and longing for place that could not have been felt with such profundity before the existence of homes.[21] (Since settled culture dates roughly from between 12,000 and 10,000 years ago, we might date the concept of home from this point, when permanent dwellings were first established, although earlier hunter-gatherers always had central locations or bases from which they traveled forward and to which they returned.) Whereas both nomadic cultures and early sedentism combine home bases or nesting places with travel over a circumscribed range, modern living, and contemporary living especially, takes to an extreme both dimensions of the human wayfinder's mode of being. Our present-day settlements are complicated and elaborate, making it possible to live entirely within the home if one chooses; yet our systems of transportation and our lifestyles enable and often necessitate travel over vast distances within mere hours.

Suffering from homesickness, from a longing for a place to which one is deeply attached, partakes to some degree in an idealization of that place and of the past; nonetheless, homesickness and the place attachment that cause it are distinct from full-blown nostalgia. According to Svetlana Boym, "Nostalgia (from *nostos*—return home, and *algia*—longing) is a longing for a home that no longer exists or has never existed." Boym suggests that "at first glance, nostalgia is a longing for a place, but actually it is a yearning for a different time—the time of our childhood, the slower rhythms of our dreams. In a broader sense, nostalgia is rebellion against the modern idea of time, the time of history and progress. The nostalgic desires to obliterate history and turn it into private or collective mythology, to revisit time like space, refusing to surrender to the irreversibility of time that plagues the human condition."[22]

Whereas nostalgia is a collective, idealizing, and sentimentalizing phenomenon, providing specifically modern versions of the myth of eternal return, homesickness is in its origin typically private and concrete, based in a love of a physical place and the social and familial life one enjoyed there. Any given instance of homesickness, certainly, may accede to nostalgia, but nostalgic longing is not an inevitable outgrowth of homesickness or place attachment.

Enlightenment rationalists tended to equate love of the native place with folk ignorance and superstition, opposing it to cosmopolitanism, and in Heidegger's mystification of his Black Forest home we are apt to be uncomfortably reminded of the *Volkgeist* that lent so much impetus to fascism. Does place attachment thus inevitably or often justify not only destructiveness toward nonhuman elements in the environment but also a sense of natural or essential superiority over others from locations deemed of less divine sanction? Does the recognition of place attachment encourage what Boym calls "restorative nostalgia"? "This kind of nostalgia characterizes national and nationalist revivals all over the world, which engage in the antimodern myth-making of history by means of a return to national symbols and myths and, occasionally, through swapping conspiracy theories" (41). Interestingly, McKillop suggests that while Enlightenment rationalism posited an opposition between local attachment and cosmopolitanism, the longer philosophical tradition *links* the two. How should we weigh the relative merits of these contrary propositions? Indeed, an evolutionary account of the sources and function of place attachment indicates that the Enlightenment opposition between local attachment and cosmopolitanism might be one in the series of rationalist dichotomies (like *nature* and *culture*) that masks enduring, adaptive continuities across constructed categories. In this case, the dichotomy obscures the fact that cosmopolitan self-assurance requires a sense of security founded on love, care, and protection that early in life becomes associated with the first environment. Thus, while these primary affections for places and persons can be manipulated, as all other affections can, in the service of destructive ideologies, they originate in the need for nodes of support in the individual life and thus are an essential prerequisite for an interest in the larger world.

"If we define place broadly as a focus of value, of nurture and support," claims the geographer Yi-Fu Tuan, "then the mother is the child's primary place. Mother may well be the first enduring and independent object in the infant's world of fleeting impressions. Later she is recognized by the child as his essential shelter and dependable source of physical and psychological comfort."[23] If Tuan's assertion that a person would be *the same as* a place early in human life seems counterintuitive, then we only need to recall that prenatally the statement is literally true, and while the unborn child is unconscious of the identity between place and person, the expectant mother is not. Current developmental psychology stresses the importance of the first relationship between the primary caregiver (usually but not necessarily the mother) and the child. This first relationship is structured to produce a strong attachment between caregiver and child, an emotional bond that motivates the caregiver and infant to stay near each other. The infant's cries and other signals of distress and the caregiver's compulsion to pick up and soothe the baby constitute the dynamic of attachment and caretaking behaviors that, as John Bowlby first theorized in 1969, aid survival in the human species by ensuring protection for highly dependent young.[24] Addressing the evolutionary utility of such behavior, Robert Storey explains that "for the human primate in particular, the establishment and maintenance of strong social bonds were—and are— of the first importance. The human infant is 'altricial,' that is, dependent on nourishment, protection, and care for a period longer than that of any other mammalian newborn, and it is because the period of weaning (and the enculturation that accompanies it) is so long that a fast emotional bond between caretaker and child is crucial" (*Mimesis*, 18).

Whereas our psychoanalytically drenched critical and theoretical culture assumes that the focus of the infant's attention when lying in the mother's arms is the breast, contemporary developmentalists now commonly recognize that this position especially promotes eye contact, a crucial feature of early mother-infant interaction and thus a generative force in the emotional bond. The mother cradles the infant during feeding, and during this time the baby is, given his or her limited perceptual development, perfectly positioned to gaze into the mother's eyes. In the words of Daniel N. Stern, "The arrangement of anatomy, normal positioning, and visual competence dictated by natural design all point to the mother's face as an initial focal point of importance for the infant's early construction of his salient visual world, and a starting point for the formation of his early human relatedness."[25] The maturation of the visual system, which occurs remarkably early in comparison with the human infant's other perceptual and motor systems, promotes the primary attachment and, within the first months of life, stimulates interest in the world beyond the mother. Whereas newborns actively seek contact with the caregiver and perceive her as the source of emotional support, at three to four months babies turn their interests just slightly farther afield, exhibiting interest in hand games and object exploration in lieu of face-to-face interaction.[26] In other words, as a result of the early emotional bond in combination with maturing physical systems, babies' interests grow progressively outward from the mother to the proximate environment, including objects, actions, persons, and nonhuman places, even while fascination with and emotional connection to this larger world never simply replace attachment to the primary caregiver.

Although Freudian and neo-Freudian theory have accustomed us to think that strong attachment to the mother is unhealthy, inhibiting the child's larger social engagement, developmentalists claim that the opposite is the case (Stern, 38–39). Bowlby found that "in the early months of attachment the greater the number of figures to whom a child was attached the more intense was his attachment to mother as his principal figure likely to be" (202). This insight from developmental psychology, that the original emotional bond between the child and the caregiver establishes the basis for a growing constellation of attachments rather than retarding growth, accords with the logic of evolutionary thought. The emotional bonds that motivate and maintain social relationships within a relatively large kinship group were indispensable to early humans, who relied on the interdependent functioning of the group to survive. Although we no longer depend on kinship groups to protect us from the mortal threat of predators—certainly, the development of culture has made that crucial material difference—our affective constitution induces us to develop strong, emotionally rewarding bonds with other humans. Moreover, while modern culture has in some respects decreased our immediate reliance on kinship groups, the complex social and political structures of cities and nation-states could never have emerged without the propensity for strong attachments that, beginning in infancy and normally continuing throughout the life span, fosters social collectivism.

Tuan's invaluable assertion—that "the mother is the child's primary place"—throws into relief the emotional commonality of human attachments, whether they be to aspects of the physical world, other humans, animals, or valued objects. With the growth in his or her perceptual system and the confidence supplied by a nurturing caregiver, the human infant gradually turns his or her attention to the surrounding physical environment, the infant's sense of place evolving beyond the adult's responsive expressions and cradling arms. Although we have long been accustomed to thinking of persons and places as distinct categories with distinct purposes, in many respects they function similarly within our evolved psychology and emotional makeup. Quite simply, a child born into a secure environment will typically love the persons and places associated with that secure environment, for those persons and places function psychologically as nodes of support in the child's life. At the same time, attachments to other humans are normally stronger than attachments to places; most of us experience more intense grief at the loss of a parent than at relocation to a new environment, even though subjective differences in personality and experience can affect and even invert this pattern. Why so? Why are attachments to other humans different in degree, if not in kind? Ontogenetically and phylogenetically, human relationships are primary and prerequisite to love of physical place. While it is true that for all animals the possibility of survival presupposes an environment to survive in, for many mammals, but most especially for humans, the evolution of the species as a terrestrial animal was inextricably bound up with the evolution of strong attachments. As a result, not only does the first relationship of the human infant serve as the foundation for positive interest in the environment of which the mother, family, and friends are a part but one's attitude toward the environment later in life often parallels the health of one's later emotional and social life.

Likewise, to say that human bonds are primary and prerequisite to place attachment does not mean that the physical features of the environment are irrelevant to human feelings for it. Attachment to locations based solely on familial association would have been fatal to our human ancestors, because they would have been unmotivated to leave depleted habitats or dangerous areas. Indeed, the fact that humans respond emotionally to environments at all is a sign that the physical features of locations have evolved significance, since emotions function primarily as behavioral motivators.[27] In other words, in an evolutionary explanation there has to be a reason for caring about water and trees, for taking an interest in large animals, and the like. Yet it is less simple to identify the sources of attraction to an environment than one might expect, partly because of the phenomenon Buell calls the "environmental unconscious"—the limited degree of conscious awareness of our response to the physical surround—but also because of the evolved complexity and variety of human relationship to physical domains. One plausible reason why some of our environmental assessment remains unconscious is that features indicating a viable habitat tend themselves to be indirect.

Over the course of about six million years, humans evolved from arboreal ancestors protected and shaded by trees into a far-ranging, wayfinding, knowledge-seeking species whose cognitive, emotional, and physiological makeup slowly altered as the species sought to meet its needs for food, protection, and mates.[28] Fossil remains of the australopithecines living from 4.5 million years ago to 1.8 million show signs of bipedalism but also adaptations (or vestiges thereof) for climbing trees, but by about 2 million years ago this species appears to have been relatively well adapted to open environments. Living in an open environment presents a species with considerable challenges (unless perhaps it is small and low to the ground); only of moderate size and relatively visible, humans were vulnerable to bigger, faster predators and would have been unable to protect themselves without the aid of a reasonably large social group.

The maintenance of social relations that unify the group and ensure cooperation imposes its own evolutionary imperatives, among them the evolution of higher intelligence. But other features of human evolution connected to a terrestrial lifestyle also demand a bigger brain. Bipedal locomotion—which contemporary theorists speculate may have evolved to reduce heat stress, itself an environmental challenge related to savannah living, or to further promote the sociality conducive to survival—requires a large brain to coordinate many muscle groups. As humans became more far-ranging, they encountered a much greater variety of terrain, flora, and fauna than their tree-dwelling ancestors, and thus the need to process a greater quantity and variety of information created further pressure for increased intelligence. Lacking the internal homing devices that other animals possess, humans were (and are) especially reliant on cognitive abilities to find their way—and to return. Indeed, it may be that internal navigational mechanisms did not evolve in humans precisely because such mechanisms serve generalized action patterns such as migration, whereas human survival required more specific forms of response and orientation. As Helen Ross notes, humans use diverse signs and cues from the environment, recognizing how features of a landscape (e.g., mountain ranges) change in accordance with perspective and easily learning how to orient by the stars and to interpret aerial views.[29] In other words, we are more knowledge-seeking in our relation to the environment than other species because more knowledge-dependent. In the metaphor that Tooby and DeVore employ, humans evolved over a period of about six million years to fit the cognitive niche.

In sum, an animal that by its nature traverses a large domain and assesses what ecological psychologists refer to as its *affordances* (opportunities for action) would be poorly served by a tendency for a narrow range of environmental preferences, as well as by an internal program for getting from place to place. Whereas research on environmental preference in humans (sometimes called environmental aesthetics) of a few decades ago focusing on the content of particular scenes hypothesized a preference for tropical savannah habitats—slightly rolling landscapes broken irregularly by cliffs and bluffs, clumps of trees, and water—recent research in this area takes the more dynamic, processive approach of environmental and ecological psychology. These fields point to the centrality of information-gathering for the organism making its way through the environment, and in keeping with this theoretical perspective researchers find that the disposition of elements in the environment is often of more importance than the presence or absence of a specific feature (e.g., trees or water) to the affective and cognitive response of the organism. As Stephen Kaplan comments in a summary of the research pointing to the preference for savannah scenes,

> The findings across these studies, however, cannot be explained sufficiently on the basis of content alone. Not all nature scenes are highly preferred; even waterscapes show considerable variation in preference. What became apparent is that in their rapid assessment of what they liked, participants were drawing inferences based on the spatial information in the scene. *More specifically, there seemed to be an implicit assessment of how one could function in the space represented by the scene.*
>
> (587, emphasis added)

In other words, preference determinations were relative to where the human subject imagined him- or herself to be situated within the scene. Always already active within the environment, human beings experience the affective-cognitive tension between the immediate perception of coherence (understanding) and the exploratory impulse leading to new knowledge. As a result, test subjects enjoy features of scenes that seem on first consideration contradictory: in terms of immediate features, people like coherence but also complexity; in terms of inferred features, people like legibility but also mystery (587). Of paramount importance to any evolved organism moving through the terrain, however, is the ability to assess the environment quickly, which rests on seeing well without being seen and perhaps on some already existing knowledge of the terrain. A memorable disposition of elements; a perspective that suggests a way forward while providing opportunities for cover and for visual advantage; and evidence or knowledge of resources along the way or at the end point all excite interest. Although subjects in studies of environmental preference are often in the artificial stance of the viewer of paintings or photographs, their responses, as Kaplan here suggests, indicate a projection of self into the scene. Thus, it is not simply the presence of certain features—rolling land, trees, water, cliffs, and animals or other humans—but the relationship of these features to one another in the picture that triggers a specific affective-cognitive response. If a phenomenon such as a clump of trees or the mouth of a cave, correlated with mystery because it suggests hidden features of the environment, is foregrounded in a painting and as a result is perceptually closer to the viewer, it will evoke foreboding; if it is perceptually distanced from the viewer, it is more apt to stimulate curiosity and perhaps to imply potential cover and protection.

The evolutionary advantages of such perceiver-relative preferences, which reveal the correspondingly relative nature of affective and cognitive responses, are not hard to fathom. In our ancestral past, a small grove of trees en route to a hunting ground or foraging area, approached with caution and proving to be uninhabited by predators, might have offered welcome respite from direct sunlight and the watchfulness and apprehension of traveling on open land. Curiosity having been rewarded by the opportunity for protection and rest, this grove might become a *place,* a location stored or mapped in the memory of some group members because of its usefulness. Similarly, exactly because no one can live without water, ponds or streams along the route would almost inevitably become features of interest, but always, I suspect, charged with a sense of danger since no one, including large cats and other predators, can live without water. Thus a watering hole, as a vital or indispensable resource but also a potentially fatal location, might become a *place* highly charged with contradictory emotions. And what if a member of the group is killed here? As I suggested in my discussion of *environment* in pre- and post-Katrina New Orleans, memory and experience continually modify the perception and assessment of geographical locations, and the making and remaking of specific spots into *places* with a cognitive history has been a regular part of the wayfinding, knowledge-seeking mind of humans for millions of years.

While our constructions of *environment* and of *place* have altered significantly as a result of the transition to sedentism and then the emergence of modernity, the larger picture suggests that human place-making is not only an ongoing process but also a multifaceted one, engaged with the full range of human emotions.

Typically, feelings of attachment to a birthplace or original habitat result from the care given and thus the sense of security developed there; nevertheless, it would not have been adaptive for such feelings to result in an essential and entrenched place attachment, because for nearly all of our evolutionary history we have been on the move. Thus, the romantic primitivism of Heidegger's attachment to his Black Forest farm, which compels him to write, as Buell puts it, as though that dwelling "were the mystical upshot of natural process," is a symptom of his modernity, as are Wordsworth's images of churches and monasteries grown out of or merging back into the natural scene. It is our consciousness of separation from nature and our yearning to belong in it again that make us desire a fixed and self-sufficient place that never existed in our nomadic, ancestral past. Buell claims that the contemporary person has an "archipelago" of place attachments as a product of the capacity to travel and explore facilitated by modern living, and he imagines that this ability to attach to multiple places cures us of the worrisome idealizations that permit totalizing myths to obscure the realities of nonhuman nature (72). But in reality it is such mythic constructions and their pervasiveness that are new, whereas the capacity for multiple attachments, part of an ongoing, affective-cognitive evaluation of place, has always been vital to our species. It hardly seems accidental that the emergence of nostalgia is connected with the history of modern warfare, an activity that offers travel under what I imagine are the least pleasant environmental circumstances (Boym, 3–5).

Since the development of feelings for and knowledge about persons and physical places is a complex process of interdependent elements, and since a person's sense of relatedness does not simply unfold over the developmental span but requires active engagement on the part of an individual who is physically and cognitively immature, one might well ask what supplies the purposiveness necessary for the baby to grow well in the world. Again, the answer parts ways with Freudian and neo-Freudian theorizing. As environmental and ecological psychology point out, organisms are always actively engaged in their environment, and the case is no different for babies as they face, from their very first moments, the series of adaptive tasks that life presents. According to Stern, the central organizing principle in the infant's psychological, emotional, and cognitive development, which, under adequate circumstances, results in fondness for persons and places beyond the mother and stimulates enthusiasm for the larger world, is the sense of self. From the moment of birth, Stern claims, infants possess an emergent sense of self, not a concept, of course, but "an invariant pattern of awareness" that includes physical cohesion, continuity in time, agency, and mental intentions.[30] Whereas Freud claimed that experiences of union with the mother constituted regression, Stern asserts that such experiences are the successful result of organizing the interaction of self and other. At two to six months, with the consolidation of a core sense of self, infants first achieve such experiences, and between nine and eighteen months, with the emergence of a sense of subjective self, infants are devoted to creating such experiences as much as (or more than) they are to establishing autonomy. Since the experience of union requires consciousness of self as an independent entity, it is more likely secondary rather than primary, and its emergence contemporaneously with the growing physical abilities of the child most certainly attests to its adaptive centrality. That is, without these extremely pleasurable experiences of shared emotional well-being (what humans call love) and without their counterpart—anxiety at being left alone and helpless on the infant's part and fear and concern about a helpless dependent on the caregiver's—parents and children would, disastrously, part ways at the toddler stage.

For humans, then, the sense of self provides a means of relating the organism to everything external to it, and since those features of the external environment are frequently in flux, the self is correspondingly a dynamic, ongoing construction. Thus, developmental psychology and contemporary neurobiology part ways with both psychoanalysis, which construes the child as an undifferentiated entity for the first year and a half of life, and poststructuralist historicisms claiming that the self is a recent invention, a product of capitalism or modern culture. Whereas the emergence of democratic individualism has most certainly transformed our self-concept, the self itself—a core notion in the organism of subjective agency, purpose, and physical integrity—is a basic requirement of human life. In Damasio's words, "When we talk of the molding of a person by education and culture, we are referring to the combined contributions 1) of genetically transmitted 'traits' and 'dispositions,' 2) of 'dispositions' acquired early in development under the dual influences of genes and environment, and 3) of unique personal episodes, lived under the shadow of the former two, sedimented and continuously reclassified in autobiographical memory" (222–23). Furthermore, because the self orients the subject relationally, the integrity and strength of the self depends on the stability of the environment. When a child wins an award or moves to a new town, the sense of self undergoes modification in relationally specific ways. In other words, the sense of self is bound up with the environment, and changes to the self will affect perception of the environment.

Just as the sense of self is altered, transformed, or fractured over the course of one's lifetime, Stern insists that matters such as orality, trust, attachment, and the like, do not resolve themselves in stages, as Piaget theorized, but are issues for the life span, and they are likewise bound up with the sense of self. This view, I believe, is in accord with commonplace observation. Thus, positive experiences of attachment to persons and places during the developmental span do not determine that relationships later in life to friends, lovers, and new places will be either easy or successful. In one's relationships with new persons, the personalities, senses of self, and varied experiences of those persons will also have an effect on the nature and quality of the attachments. The ability to develop positive feelings for new places will also depend on a range of factors but will probably be inhibited in any case by feelings of alienation. Such feelings of alienation are, I would argue, the counterpart of place attachment, and they frequently draw on the strong association of places and persons. Most people find it difficult to move great distances and adjust to new landscapes, but often their feelings depend largely on the presence or absence of a network of social support—on human attachments—in the new place.

Literary Constructions of *Nature, Place,* and *Environment*

Our constructions of *nature, place,* and *environment* are a product of the interaction between our relationships with other people, our sense of self, our past experiences, our cultural context, and our subconscious responsiveness to nonhuman nature and human beings. Moreover, the quality of our experiences originating in one of these factors may well affect the emotional and cognitive connection to and perception of the rest. When, for instance, a child grows up in a nurturing family amidst natural beauty, he may develop a special love of place and appreciation of nature. On the other hand, when human relationships connected with a specific place have failed, the place itself is often seen through the lens of that failure or, alternatively, human relationships are rejected and an immersion in the nonhuman natural world takes the place of human social relations.[31] Literature is a rich repository of dynamic constructions of *nature, place,* and *environment,* and as ecocritics begin to acknowledge our evolved and unavoidably human-centered perspective, they will see the value in studying literary works that highlight the dramatic relationship between mind and world. The ever-expanding canon of literature provides, indeed, innumerable points of entry into such constructions, and the purpose of what follows here is to demonstrate, on the basis of just a few examples, the relevance of psychological literature to our understanding of how humans construct the nonhuman environment.

As the developmental research I presented in the previous section insists, positive feelings for the home and one's native locale grow out of the infant's bond with the primary caregiver. Literature abounds in representations of the successful result of this process—family security that coincides with a feeling of general well-being in the natural world—but I am not aware of many attempts, aside from Wordsworth's, to describe the normative process itself. Writing nearly two hundred years before the experimental insights of contemporary psychology, Wordsworth, in the passage about the infant babe in book 2 of *The Prelude*, renders a remarkably accurate description of the process by which love of the caregiver stimulates interest in and attachment to the external environment:

> Blessed the infant babe—
> For with my best conjectures I would trace
> The progress of our being—blest the babe,
> Nursed in his mother's arms, the babe who sleeps
> Upon his mother's breast, who, when his soul
> Claims manifest kindred with an earthly soul,
> Doth gather passion from his mother's eye!
> Such feelings pass into his torpid life
> Like an awakening breeze, and hence his mind
> Even in the first trial of its powers,
> Is prompt and watchful, eager to combine
> In one appearance all the elements
> And parts of the same object, else detached
> And loth to coalesce. (ll. 237–50)

The child who is nursed in his mothers arms and "gather[s] passion from his mother's eye" is "blessed" because the exchange of feeling triggers his interest in the world around him. From the safety of his "first place," to use Tuan's phrase, the baby develops an eager interest in the world, and the governing security stemming from mutual attachment and parental care "irradiates and exalts / All objects through all intercourse of sense" (ll. 259–60). In the figure Wordsworth adopts here, loving feelings project a benign light on the world, illuminating a totality that would otherwise seem a random assortment of objects. Thus, Wordsworth not only explicitly draws the connection between parental nurture and a developing, positive awareness of the physical surround but furthermore suggests that the continuous, expanding pattern of the child's interest in the proximate environment is a *natural* process:

> No outcast he, bewildered and depressed;
> Along his infant veins are interfused

The gravitation and the filial bond
Of Nature that connect him with the world.   (ll. 261–64)

In the first part of the passage, Wordsworth insists on both the naturalness of this process and the causal structure of the newborn's developing love and awareness: mother love precedes and establishes the condition for enthusiastic engagement with the larger environment. Furthermore, part of the very naturalness of the process involves, not replacing the mother with other love objects, but extending feeling toward the now perceptibly beautiful objects of the world. Typically, we equate gravity with material process, and filial feeling with human life, but here the poet insists on the commonality of sensate humans and physical world by a natural bond of force and feeling that emanates, as suggested by the passive construction ("Along his infant veins are interfused"), from multiple points in a holistically perceived world.[32]

Containing so little in the way of nature imagery or description, this passage nonetheless offers something of central value to environmentalists: a theory of how human beings begin to love the nonhuman natural world, one that establishes the ground for ongoing, benign communion with nature. A common complaint against Wordsworth's poetry, stemming probably from the joy and spiritual healing that nineteenth-century writers such as Matthew Arnold, John Stuart Mill, and William James found in him, is that he offers a rather simple romantic primitivism, projecting a will onto the world for the beauties he would find there. Certainly, extracted from the totality of Wordsworth's poetic output, the infant-babe passage and others might seem to support an overwhelmingly idealistic, transcendentalizing picture of the natural world. But to take this view is to ignore both how fully Wordsworth articulates the difficulty of sustaining belief in "The gravitation and the filial bond" that subserves holism and how impossible that vision became for him personally after his brother John's death in 1805. Before that traumatic event, the poet's different means of presenting nature indeed dramatize our fundamental human ambivalence toward the nonhuman, and as ecocritics, including Bryson, Hitt, and Brooke Libby, point out, there is much to be gained from studying ambivalent representations of the nonhuman natural world.[33]

By turns cautiously seeking coherence, enthusiastically exploratory, angry, and mystically overwhelmed, Wordsworth's great poetry is all the more relevant to ecocriticism for the sometimes restless uncertainty with which it generates alternative constructions of nature, for underlying these shifting conceptualizations is one large, unanswerable question that should concern us all: What does it mean for a conscious being to love the insensate world? If "Tintern Abbey" dramatizes the hard-earned recovery of previous experiences of nature mysticism—"a sense sublime / Of something far more deeply interfused / Whose dwelling is the light of setting suns"—its psychological victory is counterbalanced by the shifting conceptions of nature not only in the Tintern lines but more obviously throughout the larger body of the poet's work.[34] For instance, the five lyrics typically grouped together as the Lucy poems enact the speaker's perceptual, affective, and cognitive displacement from the natural place he loves after the death of his sweetheart.[35] Seen through the lens of grief, the natural landscape Lucy inhabited renders back, actually, what his mind and emotions select out of it. Because the living Lucy, in the speaker's eyes, was always a natural yet human thing, and because the speaker defines himself in relation to Lucy and the nonhuman natural world, her death disrupts not only his sense of self but his love and conceptual understanding both of Lucy and of the nonhuman world with which she is identified. Thus, it is fitting that Wordsworth's representations of nature shift dramatically across the poems as the speaker moves through various phases of grief, in the process continuously reconstructing his concepts of self, lover, and natural environment.

Since the sense of self is relational, and since in Wordsworth's poems the affective bond with the deceased Lucy is especially connected to the physical world, these poems offer a vivid example of how disruption in human relations inevitably redounds upon the natural world. In fact, the speaker's identification of Lucy with nonhuman nature renders the impact of her death on his perception of the latter unusually direct. The second of the five poems, "She dwelt among the untrodden ways," reflects the thoroughgoing loneliness of grief, its logic suggesting that because Lucy was known by so few, she is not simply dead but, having been apparently cancelled out, nonexistent:

> She dwelt among th' untrodden ways
>   Beside the springs of Dove,
> A Maid whom there were none to praise
>   And very few to love.
>
> A Violet by a mossy Stone
>   Half-hidden from the Eye!
> —Fair as a star when only one
>   Is shining in the sky!
>
> She *liv'd* unknown, and few could know
>   When Lucy *ceas'd* to be;

But she is in her Grave, and oh!
   The difference to me.   (ll. 1–12)

The dominant natural images in this short lyric, most especially the violet "Half-hidden from the Eye" and the solitary star to which Lucy is compared, reflect the speaker's perception that he has been the only witness to her existence. Thus, for the time being at least, nature does not console but disturbingly confirms the excruciating isolation he feels, because he is only able to see the small, obscured, and remote objects, as though Lucy lived and was valued in his consciousness alone. Each of these entities—self, Lucy, nature—becomes for him small, isolate, and precious. Psychologically speaking, the ever-present fullness and variety of the natural world, and the connection of the violet and star to the larger whole, is invisible.

In "She dwelt among th' untrodden ways," then, the first poem to mourn Lucy's death, the conceptual diminution of the nonhuman natural world is a direct result of the loss of affectional bonds that are central to a positive sense of place. For the speaker, alienation from his lover transmutes into alienation from place and nature, even while the specialness of the objects expresses the speaker's crushing desire to grasp his beloved, his world, and himself again. In the subsequent poem, "Three years she grew in sun and shower," Wordsworth brings to the fore the undertone of ambivalence in the first poem by associating distrust of nature with an elemental source of our mixed feelings: I mean, of course, the inextricability of that observed nonhuman natural world with the process of death. From the first stanza of the poem, Wordsworth illustrates this ambivalence by personifying nature as a mother whose selfishness is in direct proportion to and necessarily bound up with her lovingness:

Three years she grew in sun and shower,
Then Nature said, "A lovelier flower
On earth was never sown:
This Child I to myself will take,
She shall be mine, and I will make
A Lady of my own.   (ll. 1–6)

Mother Nature's already unsavory possessiveness—her acquisition, ownership, and reshaping of the growing Lucy into some not quite human type of lady—is elaborated but simultaneously complicated by the five subsequent stanzas, in which "she" alone speaks, concretely depicting aspects of the girl's growth under her tutelage. Thus, maternal Nature's voice, which Wordsworth frames within the poem itself as an imaginative projection of the grieving speaker, dominates the poem for five of its seven stanzas. In nearly equal parts seductive and disturbing, this voice expresses the speaker's not quite manifest awareness that the pull toward insensibility, toward the merger of living girl with flora, fauna, and inert matter, necessarily involves the loss of one's humanity:

> She shall be sportive as the fawn
> That wild with glee across the lawn
> Or up the mountain springs,
> And hers shall be the breathing balm
> And hers the silence and the calm
> Of mute insensate things.   (ll. 13–18)

Wordsworth expresses the ambivalence underscoring the pull toward insensibility with subtle complexity here, as he does in other poems outside the Lucy group, including "Old Man travelling" and "Resolution and Independence," but two things differentiate these poems from Nature's announced intention to systematically dehumanize Lucy as she develops toward adulthood.[36] First, the subjects of these other poems are both extremely aged men, and thus the apparent process of ontological change, that is, the perception that the human subject of the poem is drawing close to the status of an insensate natural object, is more readily accepted by speaker and reader than in "Three years she grew." Second, however, Wordsworth complicates matters in "Resolution and Independence" and "Old Man travelling" by revealing the perspectival limits of his speakers, who specifically desire the compensations against loss provided by the processive naturalization of persons in these poems. Wordsworth is ambivalent about whether the naturalization of the old men in these poems is largely a consoling lie issuing from the perspectives of middle-class speakers, who thus mask the pain of physical deterioration and poverty, or a productive means of coping with the perception of suffering and of graciously redeeming the inevitability of death. As readers of "Resolution and Independence" and "Old Man travelling," then, we are asked to both identify with and judge the speakers, acknowledging the inevitability of our own objectifications of common folk viewed from the standpoint of the educated middle class, and we are invited to find our own consolations for the difficult fact of death. But in "Three years she grew," by contrast, Lucy's death at the hands of Nature just as she reaches physical maturity seems, viewed developmentally, perverse in its decided unnaturalness.

In the conclusion of the poem, Nature's articulation of Lucy's development becomes synonymous with the process itself, for as soon as her voice falls silent, the speaker implies, Lucy dies:

> Thus Nature spake—The work was done—
> How soon my Lucy's race was run!
> She died and left to me
> This heath, this calm and quiet scene,
> The memory of what has been,
> And never more will be.——
>
> (ll. 37–42)

In spite of the accepting tone of this last stanza, Wordsworth does not resolve the speaker's ambivalence toward nature in the poem's conclusion. Indeed, Lucy herself, acted upon by Nature for most of the poem, becomes complicit with her in the end, as the speaker perceives his lover's death and bequest of the scene as intentional actions. Casting himself as a passive observer, the speaker personifies Nature, and in thus attributing agency and intention to material process he augments the sense of human subjection to natural forces by depicting them as purposive. At the same time, the expanded identification of Lucy with the physical surround suggests a step forward in the grief process, wherein the healing self tentatively associates the deceased lover with the beloved natural place, an affective home located in both Lucy and the inhabited land. But while the depiction of nature in this final stanza suggests that the speaker has progressed beyond the isolation expressed in "She dwelt among th' untrodden ways," the powerful personification that dominates two-thirds of the poem casts a long shadow over this brief moment of reconciliation and acceptance.

The ambiguities of the fourth and most famous poem in the cycle, "A slumber did my spirit seal," confirm that the healing process—the unification of a renewed self with place and nature through the emergent transformation of the beloved into a memorialized object—is not yet complete. Reflecting with mournful irony on the human capacity to idealize the living, breathing objects of our loves, the speaker ponders the apparent conundrum presented by death:

> A slumber did my spirit seal,
>   I had no human fears:
> She seem'd a thing that could not feel
>   The touch of earthly years.
>
> No motion has she now, no force;
>   She neither feels nor sees;

Roll'd round in earth's diurnal course,

With rocks and stones and trees!   (ll. 1–8)

The second of the two stanzas equally implies that the completion of the process of objectification entails, on the one hand, Lucy's final dehumanization and, on the other, her complete assimilation into the holistically perceived processes of nature and life. Does decomposition in the world of matter transform the beloved into a larger part of the greater whole or merely reduce her to nothingness via an anonymous and amoral process? Perhaps the poem only appears to present intractable ambiguities because humans are prone to attribute intention and purposive action to insensate aspects of reality. Having just illuminated that tendency by personifying nature in "Three years she grew," Wordsworth now depicts the speaker in the midst of accepting the fact that the material reality of death is the very ground of Lucy's inclusion in a larger whole. What especially distinguishes this poem from the preceding one is the absence of the submerged feelings that are the source of his ambivalence, a distressing compound of love, devotion, and anger, projected onto the personification of nature in the preceding poem. In "A slumber did my spirit seal," Wordsworth replaces these muted but potent feelings with the speaker's sense of abiding wonderment at his own past idealization of Lucy as well as at the overpowering fact of natural process.

Wordsworth wrote the first four Lucy poems in 1798–1800, then added another lyric, "I travell'd among unknown Men," about two years later.[37] This addition suggests the poet's intuitive recognition that the suspension of the grieving speaker's ambivalence in "A slumber did my spirit seal" did not represent a final phase in the interdependent reconstruction of self, lover, and place. Notably, the speaker is finally able to reconstruct nonhuman nature as a cherished *living place*, not an image of the past (as in the conclusion to "Three years she grew"), by temporal and geographical distance. Whereas there is only a troubled sense of nature as a constituent of valued place in one of the first four poems ("Three years she grew"), in "I travell'd among unknown Men" travel abroad after the early phases of grief have run their course precipitates the speaker's reaffirmation and transformation of his old attachments, unified by a renewed sense of place. Addressing England, he proclaims:

Among thy mountains did I feel

The joy of my desire;

And She I cherish'd turn'd her wheel

Beside an English fire.

Thy mornings shew'd—thy nights conceal'd
  The bowers where Lucy play'd;
And thine is, too, the last green field
  Which Lucy's eyes survey'd!

(ll. 9–16)

Travelling physically (away from England) and psychologically (away from grief), the speaker arrives at a new place, where Lucy is memorialized as *humanly* natural and the speaker's identification with her, as he sees through her eyes, supersedes his ambivalence about the dehumanization to which a maternal Nature subjects us. The imaginative capacity to reconstruct *place* as England—which combines a loved locale, the speaker's memory, and Lucy's life—supplants his earlier conflicting feelings toward an unreconstructed nature. What does it mean for a conscious being to love the natural world? Applying this central question to one specific instance in which nature has apparently violated that love, Wordsworth locates the answer in the psychic and cognitive process of transformation and regeneration. As in so much of his poetry, Wordsworth suggests that the capacity to see nature properly, as one of our interrelated and essential attachments, is a product of mind and imaginative effort.

As far as a multitude of Wordsworth scholars have been able to discern, the Lucy poems are not based, as is much of the poet's best poetry, on a biographically verifiable circumstance. Nonetheless, running through the imaginative constructions of these poems is the characteristically shifting conception of nature and an attendant ambivalence about this difficult-to-grasp entity or process that threads through the poet's most biographically based works. Wordsworth knew from his own experience that our love of the world, extending and developing from the first environment of the mother, invites us to misconstrue the terms of that relationship. In fact, our constitutional tendency to envision nature as a purposive agent—the very claim, in Wordsworth's famous phrase, that nature never would betray the heart that loves her—sets the stage for that betrayal, for nature, understood as the nonhuman natural world, of course, cannot be *anyone's* mother. Wordsworth poetry is the best literary record available of the effort of a struggling human to reconcile himself to an amoral process with which our most profound feelings are bound up; in the end, the poet seems to have recognized that in his greatest nature poetry, almost entirely written before he turned thirty-five, he perhaps asked too much. In "Elegiac Stanzas, Suggested by a Picture of Peele Castle in a Storm," written in the summer of 1806, about a year and a half after John Wordsworth drowned on the same seacoast and six months after

Wordsworth first saw his friend Beaumont's painting, the poet praises human stoicism over and above the contrasting conceptions of nature the mind conjures.[38] Comparing his memory of an idyllic, youthful sojourn on the coast near Peele Castle to Beaumont's storm-wracked painting, the autobiographical speaker declares that his youthful perception of the rugged monument "Beside a sea that could not cease to smile" is shallow and misguided, a "fond delusion of my heart" (ll. 19, 29). When Wordsworth addresses Beaumont from the vantage point of irreconcilable loss, he declares, "This Work of thine I blame not, but commend / This sea in anger, and that dismal shore" (ll. 43–44). Hardly ambivalent about the fact that the image of nature to which his psyche currently responds is that of sublime terror and incredible destructiveness, Wordsworth nonetheless focuses on the immediate psychic efficacy of alternative constructions of nature. For, in contrast to the picture drawn from a distant memory and that based on a recent viewing of Beaumont's painting, Wordsworth's construct, his picture, is the poem "Elegiac Stanzas" itself, which contains the opposed images of the castle and sea in a single representation. Thus, while his final assertion of man's strife against nonhuman nature and the imperative of stoicism have a special psychological and emotional legitimacy at the time of writing, the value of human endurance as the dominant stance toward the erosions of nature and time is contingent upon present circumstances.

"Elegiac Stanzas" develops out of the conviction that nonhuman nature is of central importance to human functioning but inspects the problem of a youthful, pastoral communion with nature that seems invalidated by adult grief. Many other romantic-era poems express how human failures or failed relationships color or even determine how the speaker sees nature. Charlotte Turner Smith, who had a great influence on Wordsworth and who was a remarkable poet in her own right, also addresses the interrelationship of the self and nature and explores particularly the contrast between memories of an idyllic, pastoral childhood and distressing adult circumstances in *Elegiac Sonnets,* especially in the first thirty-five of these poems. Like Mary Darby Robinson, Smith was married as a teenager to a husband ill-equipped to take on the responsibilities of a wife and family, and many of her sonnets are frankly autobiographical laments for the happiness destroyed by her marriage. Writing before Wordsworth and Coleridge pursued the same subject, Smith concludes that her personal quest for restoration in nature results only in the distressing realization that the pastoral idyll of childhood is a cruel delusion. Watching young children at play ultimately prompts not joy but sorrow for these children, who in time will "feel the thorns that lurking lay / To wound the wretched pilgrims of the earth." Similarly, memory of her own bucolic childhood intensifies rather than alleviates her current despair, reinforcing the conviction that only death will bring release. Gazing on the "hills belov'd" of her happy childhood, Smith asks, "But can they peace to this sad breast restore / For one poor moment soothe the sense of pain / And teach a breaking heart to throb no more?"[39] The answer, in this sonnet, "To the South Downs," is no. Although the love of nature and the youthful experience of its pleasures are real, the anxieties and cares of adulthood not only disable nature's salutary effect but exacerbate present misery, as memory throws into relief the divide between past happiness and present despair. Smith's insistence in the sonnets that nature cannot restore suffering humans is akin to Coleridge's argument against the Wordsworthian creed in "Dejection": "Oh Lady! we receive but what we give / And in our life alone does Nature live / Ours is her wedding garment, ours her shroud!"[40] For Coleridge as for Smith, the veil of despair—the web of thought, feeling, and experience through which they perceive—is too thick for nature's healing rays to penetrate.

The emphasis romantic-era writers put on the human mind has made them relatively unpopular in recent decades, for the ascendance of postmodern theory was propelled in part by a Marxian-inflected ideology that construed psychological literature as a flight from the world of matter. But if we recognize that the world of matter can only be known via the human affective, perceptual, and cognitive apparatus—the orienting machinery of human survival, an inherently self-interested project, if you will—we might be more inclined to appreciate the profound importance of romantic psychologism and less inclined to make ideologically committed but intellectually inadvisable value judgments. Only then can we begin to ask the questions that will enable us to understand our complex relationship with nonhuman nature, questions such as, Why and how is it that that particular mind has come to know the world in this specific way? What can we learn about either this individual or the general ways that humans come to know their environments, the species-typical patterns? How and when do literary representations provide the opportunity to analyze the psychological relationship of humans to nonhuman nature?[41] Wordsworth and other romantic-era poets were the first to explore the complexities of the evolved but distinctively modern human mind in its efforts to fit self and nature into a fruitful conception of *place*.

No Place: *Wide Sargasso Sea* and Psychic Displacement

In the readings of romantic-era poetry above, I offered a glimpse of how literary depictions of the mutual dependency of self, human others, and nonhuman natural environment illuminate our evolved feelings for environments as well as our habitually modern tendency to contemplate or reflect on nature, to turn it into an object of consciousness rather than to live immersed in it. I have primarily focused on poetry, all of it lyric with the exception of the *Prelude* passage, for the lyric mode characteristically explores subjective emotion, consciousness, and cognition, often, as in the cases above, in a meditative relationship to the nonhuman environment. Conceived of as pure modes, lyric and narrative are polar opposites that emanate from the opposition within human experience between inward self-organization and practical social, physical, and temporal outward-directed functioning. Literary works range between these two poles, mixing lyric and narrative in different degrees, just as a blend of the two modes defines the ecology of human living. Since its focus favors inwardness, the lyric mode does not emphasize the importance of social community to a stable sense of self, others, and environment, nor does it represent the challenges to an organism moving through the environment. In narratives, by contrast, the primary impulse is toward actions unfolding over time, and thus both the general emphasis and the typically greater length of stories enable the depiction of a larger social world and a wealth of interpersonal and social behaviors played out in scenes set in geographically dispersed locations.

Narrative literature depicts the relationship between characters' social lives and the physical environment in considerable variety. Nevertheless, over and over again, fiction illustrates the alignment of stable interpersonal and social relationships with natural communion and a positive sense of place; and over and over again (though perhaps with greater frequency since fiction is about problems), the same literature associates social instability and personal isolation with dangerous environments. Perhaps nineteenth-century English fiction writers most exploited this relationship: the lonely Pip, of marginal family and social associations, wandering the marsh encounters the desperate and starving Magwitch; the vilified child Jane Eyre, finding comfort in pictures of forbidding seascapes amidst the isolating and censorious environment of Gateshead, because they reflect her desolation.

If in many respects eighteenth- and nineteenth-century writers exploit this alignment of natural and social circumstances in their constructions, some twentieth-century writers have chosen to invert ironically the truistic pattern. Thus, in Katherine Mansfield's New Zealand stories, including "Prelude" and "At the Bay," the shimmering beauty of the natural world parallels and seems to support the superficial stability of conventional social and familial life, masking individual isolation and unhappiness. Likewise, in several stories in John Fowles's

Ebony Tower, nature offers authentic sites of renewal to which the human characters are by and large unequal. For readers of these stories, the natural world stands apart from and highlights the failings of the characters, itself undiscoverably authentic yet serving as a backdrop for the lesser lives and unsatisfying relationships they have chosen. In contrast to this English tradition, American literature has evoked a far more dichotomous vision of nature wherein wildness and Edenic perfection serve as the proving ground of the rugged (male) individual; still, even the most romantic invocations of this myth require a network of social relations, though it is typically configured as male and homosocial. Where women are the focal characters of American and other wilderness stories, they fare considerably less well; isolation and the hardships of frontier life, unendurable without the support of a minimal social network, drive Ole Edvart Rølvaag's Beret mad. The New Zealander Mansfield and the Canadian Alice Munro tell similar stories of women driven to psychological extremes when simultaneously confronted with the physical violence and lack of social support characteristic of the frontier.

Although writers offer quite varied depictions of the natural world's relationship to the social world, then, relative constraints upon representation reveal the mutual interdependence of the perceived environment, social relationships, and the sense of self from the species perspective. Isolated and vulnerable characters typically suffer *placelessness*—perceived or real threats from a potentially inimical environment that are the counterpart to psychic vulnerability. While strong social relations can result in attachment to places with rather harsh climates or limited resources, extreme threats emanating from the environment always put pressure on human relationships and on self-coherence. In representational narrative as in real life, no one is happy when the environment turns violent, because everyone responds viscerally to individual or collective threats to survival. Thus, whereas the lyric poetry of writers like Smith and Coleridge represents the subjective extreme in our relationship with nature, showing how personal misery makes one immune to natural beauty, stories like Wallace Stegner's "Genesis"— the tale of a cattle roundup during a brutal snowstorm in Saskatchewan— sometimes depict the opposite condition, the objective extreme wherein threats from the environment strain social relationships, sanity, and self-coherence. In such circumstances—blizzards, hurricanes, earthquakes, fires—*place* cannot be located, because weather and cataclysm obliterate all other dimensions of the nature construct. To be without places is to lose one's bearings, to be an inherently orienting organism bereft of orientation.

The loneliness of Smith and Coleridge had personal sources, but the intertwined relationship among crises of self, social relations, and place can have sociopolitical causes as well, and postcolonial literature provides some of the most dramatic depictions of the deformative effects of a dysfunctional social order on the constructions of self, others, and physical environment. In the novels and stories of Jean Rhys, distorted perceptions of the physical environment coincide with varying degrees of social marginality and psychic malaise, and among these works *Wide Sargasso Sea* in particular exhibits how human perception of all things external to the self, including nonhuman nature, can be deformed by the psychological impact of a dysfunctional social order. Whereas Rhys's four earlier novels, nearly all of which employ modern European settings while exploring related psychological and social situations, also illustrate an impoverished sense of place, *Wide Sargasso Sea* stands out for its attention to physical place and to nonhuman nature specifically, thus demonstrating one circumstance under which nature is viewed inimically.[42]

Primarily a prequel to Charlotte Brontë's *Jane Eyre*, *Wide Sargasso Sea* takes as its central character Antoinette Cosway Mason, who is based on the deranged wife of Edward Fairfax Rochester, imprisoned in the attic in Brontë's Victorian novel. A Caribbean native, Rhys saw *Jane Eyre* as the English side of the story, and she wanted to show the interrelationship of social and psychological chaos after the emancipation, the conditions to which a character like Bertha, unsympathetically portrayed in Brontë's novel, would have been subject. Unlike *Jane Eyre*, *Wide Sargasso Sea,* published in 1966, is a twentieth-century psychological novel, and as such it focuses particularly on how the inability to trust one's perceptions results in a psychological disorder in which boundaries between self and other— both human others and the physical environment—collapse, disabling the cognitive constructive processes required for normal human functioning. Notably, this mental instability, which afflicts both Antoinette and her unnamed husband (the Rochester character of Brontë's novel), finds its first cause in the untrustworthiness of human others.

Over the course of her writing career, Rhys's technique developed from the naturalistic realism of *Voyage in the Dark* to the psychological realism of *Good Morning, Midnight* and *Wide Sargasso Sea.* The human implications of psychologically realistic works depend on the specific focus and technique of the author; in Rhys's case, the inward view typically correlates with mental disorder and the loss of a sense of self as a purposive agent. Because the fragmented self is incapable of acting in a goal-directed fashion, this psychologically mimetic novel dramatizes the collapse of our most basic human mode of living in reality by disabling narrative movement. The formal and stylistic features of *Wide Sargasso Sea,* a novel written and rewritten over several decades, mimic the simultaneous disin-

tegration of narrative agency and individual identity and thus dramatize the ero-
sion of the ecology and ontology of effective human life.

Throughout the evolution of our wayfinding, far-ranging but home-based
species, narrativity has remained robust because of its agentive force: structuring
both thought and social exchange, it has served to bind the members of human
groups and help them plot their movements through time and space. To repeat
Michael Carrithers's apt description: "By means of stories humans cognize not
just thoughts and not just situations, but *the metamorphosis of thoughts and situations in a flow of action*" (311–12, emphasis added). Integrating the actions and
purposes of human groups within their prescribed domain, narrative brings
into relation and coordinates sequence, causality, physical place, knowledge of
interaction with human others, and self-concept. In other words, because narrative is in the most fundamental evolutionary sense a central aspect of the pragmatic process of human living, it has in day-to-day life an agentive force. Furthermore, that sense of agency enables the adaptive negotiation of physical locations
and the construction of areas as *places* to be sought or avoided in the interests of
survival.

In contrast to our cognitive-social narrativizing, literary narrative frequently
asks us to reflect on instances in which actor, action, goal, scene, and agent no
longer appear to function in an effective sequence. In chapter 2 I discussed how
Wordsworth's violation of narrative structure in "Simon Lee" disrupts the action
orientation of comic narrative, causing the focus to shift away from Simon as an
agent in a humorous tale and toward his subjective experience of poverty and
aging. Whereas Wordsworth thus subverts narrative sequence to highlight the
moral and ideological limits of the comic tale, Rhys dismantles it to dramatize the
psychic and social destructiveness of the failed colonial enterprise. Employing
a style that modulates from discursively coherent homodiegetic narration into a
fragmented stream of consciousness, Rhys enacts the process of mental breakdown as both a permanent phenomenon in Antoinette and a temporary one in
her husband. As Kathy Mezei points out, Rhys's technique in *Wide Sargasso Sea*
differs from true stream of consciousness, because Antoinette is trying to structure a narrative, but the line between the experiencing child and the present consciousness of part 1 is blurred.[43] Furthermore, Rhys underscores the blurring of
selves effected stylistically in part 1 by delivering most of part 2, by far the longest
section of the novel, from the husband's perspective. Formally, then, Antoinette's
attempted narrative envelops her husband's, conceptually entangling his thoughts
and actions within her progressive deterioration and comprehensively imploding
the romance narrative structure for which both characters yearn, a structure that

is realized, furthermore, however painfully and slowly, in the precursor Bildungs-roman *Jane Eyre*, against which readers assess the differences in Rhys's text.

While many Rhys scholars have recognized that the author's style and narrative descriptions mimic mental deterioration in the two main characters, some second-wave feminist readings have interpreted mental disorder as "the colonial subject's resistance to British domination."[44] Such readings point welcome attention to one aspect of the environment, the sociopolitical context. However, in flattening psychic life into the concept of subjectivity and in correspondingly overemphasizing matrices of power in their notion of context and environment, these scholars focus on the conceptual dimension of the text to the exclusion of the mimetic dimension. On the conceptual level, certainly, madness is disruptive and destructive to the colonial order, a fact vividly symbolized in the burning of Thornfield; on the psychological (and in this case the material) level, however, madness destroys the person as well. Individual tragedy, in other words, is inseparable from resistance to colonial control.

Thus, while Rhys intends the final conflagration at Thornfield to mirror and be folded within that at Coulibri in part 1 and thereby suggests that the empire brings about its own destruction, she is equally determined to show the human cost of cultural incoherence. Almost always, in representational fiction and in life, some degree of social and cultural coherence is prerequisite to psychic stability and individual agency. As the environmental psychologists Stephen and Rachel Kaplan explain, culture, defined as a set of consistent patterns for functioning, offers a coherent understanding and a pattern of relationships to people, place, and world.[45] In defining problems and shaping their solutions, then, culture extends cognitive power by lending perspective and providing a "map" for healthy functioning. In thus extending cognitive power, culture weakens the hold of the immediate environment on human groups and individuals. Cultures are generated over time by human groups, and as Kaplan and Kaplan explain, any crisis that threatens those groups with the loss of their interpretive structures is traumatic. Since West Indian colonies were founded on slavery, their cultures probably never provided a very robust or coherent interpretive structure.[46] From a naturalistic perspective, institutional slavery may weaken sociopolitical structures for a species that has lived, over the course of its evolution, in relatively egalitarian social groups. From a historical perspective, at the time that the European colonial enterprises instituted slavery, the colonizing nations themselves were already on a course toward more democratic sociopolitical forms, resulting in internal contradictions in values and systems.

By the time of Jamaican emancipation in 1847, the sugar trade had long been in decline, and the cultural guides, patterns, or interpretations for functioning were either nonexistent or ill-suited to the chaos of postemancipation life.[47] It is just this loss of viable cultural patterns of conduct and guides to understanding that provides the context for *Wide Sargasso Sea*. Even the young Antoinette, put in the convent after her family flees from the burning estate, finds the doctrines preached there frankly unbelievable because so out of keeping with what she has already experienced. Antoinette reports that after an obligatory comment on kindness to the unfortunate, Mother St. Justine "slides on to order and chastity, that flawless crystal that, once broken, can never be mended" (32). Her mentally handicapped brother dead from smoke inhalation, her mother driven mad, and her home burned to the ground, it is little wonder that she finds such catechizing ridiculous. Unconvinced by Old World understanding, her colonial culture torn by endemic hatreds, Antoinette has no new understanding or set of patterns to shape her relations with her environment.

For Antoinette and her husband, the loss of temporality and sequence, and hence the loss of narrative agency, governs the perceptions of persons and places outside the self. In the wayfinding mind, the sense of place is always *relative to,* and without a functional set of relations physical domains cannot be constructed as places and integrated into experience perceived by the self. The sense of place is relative not only to selfhood, social relations, and sociopolitical context but also to a larger sense of the physical environment, traversed on the ground and perceived through the senses, patterning and reinforcing the interrelated sense of time and meaning. The antipathy to nonhuman nature and formerly loved places in *Wide Sargasso Sea* thus signals a generalized breakdown of the wayfinding mind and its ecological behavior. Whereas at times the presentation of physical place operates symbolically in the novel—most notably, as critics have widely recognized, in the early presentation of Coulibri as a fallen Eden, signaling the loss of innocence—it is a mistake to thus limit its meaning, for Rhys intuited that place and its negotiation are part of an integrated process and system of sense-making.

Ultimately, Antoinette's husband suffers only temporary psychic disorder, because he is able to leave behind the chaos of postemancipation Jamaica and Dominica and return to the familiar cultural-interpretive context of Victorian England. As Carinne Melkom Mardorossian notes, "England is the landmark against which he measures the Caribbean place and its people. . . . [He is unable] to look at the Caribbean without framing it" ("[De]Colonization," 82). Strictly speaking, however, the problem is not that he frames the place according to his own cultural assumptions—as Kaplan and Kaplan suggest, all humans do this— but that his cultural assumptions, based on his primary environment, are so mismatched with the new reality he confronts. His temporary descent into madness mirrors Antoinette's more inexorable decline, wherein the instability of social relationships renders individuals incapable of distinguishing falsehood from truth, reality from dream, and self from other.

Rhys enacts the breakdown of the husband's wayfinding abilities—the everyday capacity to negotiate and map the self through social relations and physical locations—in a scene almost exactly halfway through the novel, where he stumbles through the woods at Granbois, the honeymoon house in Dominica. As Coral Ann Howells points out, this scene mirrors Antoinette's dream of being lost in the woods in part 1; in so doing, it actualizes the unconscious mental activity of one character in the physical actions of the other and in the process asserts their shared identity. As the husband loses his way in the forest, his perception of nonhuman nature is not simply colored by his dependence on new acquaintances in an alien social reality where no one trusts anyone else; it is overdetermined by that social reality, that is, overdetermined by his interactions with the *human* aspect of the environment. In fact, he has been rendered distrustful and psychologically vulnerable by the arranged marriage that brought him to Jamaica in the first place. As the younger son in an aristocratic English family, he has grudgingly agreed to marry a wealthy Creole planter's daughter, for all intents and purposes accepting exile from England and upper-class English culture in exchange for a planter's fortune and an inferior (because not natively English) wife. Thus severed from his established cultural and familial context, new to Jamaica and Dominica, he is vulnerable to the insinuations of Daniel Cosway, a mixed-race islander who claims to be Antoinette's half-brother. Although repulsed by Daniel's hatefulness and his bald attempt at blackmail, the husband is nevertheless deeply affected by Daniel's remarks, because he lacks a shared understanding and set of relationships to guide him in the unfamiliar Caribbean environment. Prejudiced against blacks and former slave owners alike and shocked by the social and physical disorder of the islands and the familiar relations between blacks and whites, he is nonetheless profoundly attracted to the sensuality of the place and its persons. All this consorts to overwhelm his perceptions and judgments, destabilizing the self and impeding its relation to the environment.

After reading Daniel's letter insinuating the impurities and outrages of Antoinette and her family—"You have been shamefully deceived by the Mason family. They tell you perhaps that your wife's name is Cosway, the English gentleman Mr. Mason being her stepfather only, but they don't tell you what sort of people were these Cosways . . ." (56–57)—he eats alone, naps, then walks out of the house in the afternoon heat. He recollects:

I went out following the path I could see from my window. It must have rained heavily during the night for the red clay was very muddy. I passed a sparse plantation of coffee trees, then straggly guava bushes. As I walked I remembered my father's face and his thin lips, my brother's round conceited eyes. They knew. And Richard the fool, he knew too. And the girl with her blank smiling face. They all knew.

I began to walk very quickly, then stopped because the light was different. A green light. I had reached the forest and you cannot mistake the forest. It is hostile. The path was overgrown but it was possible to follow it. I went on without looking at the tall trees on either side. Once I stepped over a fallen log swarming with white ants. How can one discover truth I thought and that thought led me nowhere. No one would tell me the truth. Not my father nor Richard Mason, certainly not the girl I had married. I stood still, so sure I was being watched that I looked over my shoulder. Nothing but the trees and the green light under the trees. A track was visible and I went on, glancing from side to side. . . . The track led to a large clear space. Here were the ruins of a stone house and round the ruins rose trees that had grown to an incredible height. At the back of the ruins a wild orange tree covered with fruit, the leaves a dark green. A beautiful place. And calm—so calm that it seemed foolish to think or plan. What had I to think about and how could I plan? Under the orange tree I noticed little bunches of flowers tied with grass.

I don't know how long it was before I began to feel chilly. The light had changed and the shadows were long. I had better get back before dark, I thought. Then I saw a little girl carrying a large basket on her head. I met her eyes and to my astonishment she screamed loudly, threw up her arms and ran. The basket fell off, I called after her, but she screamed again and ran faster. She sobbed as she ran, a small frightened sound. Then she disappeared. I must be within a few minutes of the path I thought, but after I had walked for what seemed like a long time I found that the undergrowth and creepers caught at my legs and the trees closed over my head. I decided to go back to the clearing and start again, with the same result. It was getting dark. It was useless to tell myself that I was not far from the house. I was lost and afraid among these enemy trees, so certain of danger that when I heard footsteps and a shout I did not answer. The footsteps and the voice came nearer. Then I shouted back. I did not recognize Baptiste at first. He was wearing blue cotton trousers pulled up above his knees and a broad ornamented belt round his slim waist. His machete was in his hand and the light caught the razor-sharp blue-white edge. He did not smile when he saw me.

(62–63)

These three paragraphs interweave description of the physical environment, thoughts about others, and encounters with other people as the husband walks into the forest without apparent purpose, losing his way on an overgrown, disappearing path. Rhys thus illustrates the interconnection between social and cultural relations and the spatial and psychic breakdown of wayfinding. One dimension of psychic disorientation is perceptual, and Rhys depicts this through the husband's inability to assimilate visual aspects of the environment and judgments about them to any context of understanding. Although he calls the clearing with the stone ruin "a beautiful place," this assertion of beauty stands apart from and appears to contradict his central preoccupation in this section of the novel: discovering the truth. (Indeed, his perception of beauty throughout the novel is persistently at odds with other perceptions and his judgment of the culture.) His inability to trust his father, his brother, Richard, Antoinette, and Daniel leaves him without a context for understanding this new place and its people, and this carries over into his distorted perception of physical place. As Helen Ross explains in *Behavior and Perception in Strange Environments*, moderate arousal improves functioning in stressful situations, but anxiety impedes it, causing perceptual narrowing, loss of peripheral vision, and distortions of size and distance. Already susceptible to such sensory distortion because of the anxiety produced by the loss of his interpretive context and his pervasive distrust, the husband characterizes the forest as a beautiful yet hostile medium where "the light is different." Conceptually, the image of descending into a green place of increased perceptual confusion pervades the novel and, combined with the Sargasso Sea of the title, establishes a metaphor of submersion and entanglement. In this episode, the husband begins to see as if he were underwater, where visual perception is poor because the refractive power of the cornea is lost and advancing and retreating colors are reversed.

Once he is in the forest (the central paragraph), he is especially preoccupied with two things: the green light and the looming and enclosing "trees that had grown to an incredible height." As night begins to fall and the green light gives way to darkness, he is "lost and afraid among these enemy trees, so certain of danger that when I heard footsteps and a shout I did not answer." That he hesitates to reply in spite of his fear of the forest is not surprising, for Rhys frames his entrance into the forest by highlighting his suspicions that Richard, his father, his brother, and Antoinette are all savoring a truth of which he is the victim. His anxiety-driven perception of the environment, itself a product of his alienation from a network of social support, feeds back into his thoughts when the only sensate creatures he sees as he loses his way, the swarming white ants on the log, trigger thoughts of those he fears have tricked him into marriage.

Moreover, Rhys accentuates the atmosphere of human social and psychic dysfunction by suggesting that fear and distrust have altered his appearance—that emptied by psychic desperation, he has come to resemble a zombi. His anxiety, like that of the other people who enter the forest, is of social origin, but it colors his perception of the whole environment. When the little girl carrying the basket reacts with extreme fear, she both exhibits the pervasive breakdown of human trust and serves as a projection of his own increasing fear. Likewise, although Baptiste has come to find him, the overseer is perceptibly changed—wearing different clothes, wielding a machete, unsmiling. While these changes reflect Baptiste's own anxieties and the practical need to clear away undergrowth, to Antoinette's husband they are further signs of the unknown and unknowable that presently control his life. When the two men reach the red clay path that leads directly to Grandbois, he imagines Baptiste's smile as the "service mask on the savage reproachful face I had seen," even though it is equally possible that the overseer is expressing genuine relief.

The exchange with Baptiste as they make their way out of the forest exacerbates the breakdown of environmental perception, social relations, and psychic functioning, because Baptiste rejects the husband's interpretations of his own experience, both of the presumed physical evidence of paving and of the little girl's fearful response. He asks Baptiste, "There was a road here once, where did it lead to?" And Baptiste answers, "No road." When he insists, "But I saw it. A *pavé* road like the French made in the islands," Baptiste repeats his response. The husband is convinced that his interpretation is correct—"The stone I had tripped on was not a boulder but part of a paved road. There had once been a paved road through this forest"—but Baptiste claims this is untrue. Convinced of what he has seen but lacking confirmation from other observers, the husband is unable to construct a coherent sense of this place, an overgrown hut in a clearing somewhere near a deteriorating trail. As a result, his judgments have the hallucinatory quality of auditory and visual perception of people isolated for too long in dangerous environments, a feature that Rhys takes to a technical extreme toward the end of part 2, where his thoughts truly fragment (H. Ross, 161–62).

Similarly, when he inquires about the little girl's fear in the clearing near the house, "Is there a ghost, a zombi there?," Baptiste replies, "Don't know nothing about all that foolishness." Yet the pervasiveness of obeah in the islands and the evidence of the offering under the orange tree make it improbable that Baptiste does not know what the other local inhabitants believed. The husband reads after returning to the house that "negroes as a rule refuse to discuss the black magic in which so many believe" (64). If the husband interprets Baptiste's denials as evasions, he may once again be misjudging the depth of the overseer's fear. As Judith Raiskin points out, the priest who lived in the hut evokes the historical figure Père Jean-Baptiste Labat, who justified slavery and tortured blacks for practicing obeah and for this became a mythologized force in their beliefs. These facts strongly suggest that Baptiste shares the local belief that denial and silence are the only means of containing monstrous evil—a belief that Antoinette shares and acts on when, for instance, she tells her husband that the town name "Massacre" must refer to something that happened long ago (38n4). (Antoinette's reasons for denial, however, are not the same as Baptiste's; Mardorossian identifies this response as an instance of planter-class amnesia ["Subaltern," 1075].) Because the husband's interpretive structure and experience render him incapable of fathoming the history of fear and violence that prompts such evasive behavior, he sees a plot and a plan in what is very probably a tacit cultural consent to repress the terrors of the past and the disorder those terrors perpetuate. But at the same time, in highlighting the dysfunction of the failed colonial order wherein the deepest beliefs are unexpressed and truth is habitually evaded, Rhys demonstrates that a greater openness to new interpretive structures would not solve the problem. The discrepancy between what is believed and what is articulated attests to the cognitive and social impoverishment of postemancipation culture, for if, as Kaplan and Kaplan claim, culture extends cognitive power by lending perspective and providing a map for healthy functioning, there is no *culture* to speak of—and thus great cognitive disempowerment—here.

Furthermore, because physical locations are rendered manageable by the network of social support, including beliefs, the dearth of support renders such places treacherous. In the source that informs him about obeah, the husband learns that the word *zombi* has a rather elastic definition: "A zombi is a dead person who seems to be alive or a living person who is dead. A zombi can also be the spirit of a place, usually malignant but sometimes to be propitiated with sacrifices or offerings of flowers and fruit" (64). Driven by a sense of how a cultural legacy of fear, distrust, and violence leads to a pervasive living deadness, Rhys elevates the term *zombi* to an overriding metaphor for the inextricable states of the novel's characters and the places they inhabit. The priest's abandoned hut, epitomizing the larger geographical areas of the West Indian islands, evokes a terrifying spirit, but since Antoinette's husband cannot contextualize conflicting feelings and perceptions within a valid interpretive context, it is *no place* to him.

Granbois remains no place for him, its spirit a zombi, because human relationships fail. Unable to trust what he is told and left to infer what is unspoken, encouraged to distrust the evidence of his senses, Antoinette's husband cannot construct a solid and productive sense of Dominica's reality. Instead, the logic of his feelings governs his final assessment of Dominica:

> I hated the mountains and the hills, the rivers and the rain. I hated the sunsets of whatever colour, I hated its beauty and its magic and the secret I would never know. I hated its indifference and the cruelty which was part of its loveliness. Above all I hated her. For she belonged to the magic and the loveliness. She had left me thirsty and all my life would be thirst and longing for what I had lost before I found it. (103)

If Wordsworth's infant-babe passage depicts the seminal process by which the nonhuman world becomes loved via the first place of the mother, this passage illustrates its negative counterpart, wherein the husband's feelings for the nonhuman natural environment of Dominica and for Antoinette are indissolubly linked. Importantly, his objective and constant recognition of natural beauty does not alter his negative judgment, further suggesting that the safety and coherence of human relations is often more fundamental than physical features of the environment to the positive construction of place. If anything, his continued perception of natural beauty increases his hatred of both Dominica and Antoinette. His decision to take Antoinette with him when he leaves for England, which he overtly credits to his sense of responsibility, is at least in part malicious, as the passage above shows. Forced to recognize his own limitations, he vengefully removes Antoinette from the environment to which, as he so well knows, she belongs.

Whereas the husband can control his hatred of place and person (the Caribbean and Antoinette) through dissociation and destructiveness (to thus destroy Antoinette is to trivialize her and reduce her power) and by reestablishing his sense of self and reaffirming cultural coherence by returning to England, familial and social dysfunction and danger characterize Antoinette's girlhood during the early postemancipation years. From childhood, Antoinette experiences insecure emotional attachments that affect her sense of self and of place. Her mother, Annette, doubly ostracized in Jamaica (for her whiteness and for her Frenchness— "a Martinique girl" on an English island) and further isolated by her lack of resources, becomes preoccupied with her own grief and with her mentally disabled son Pierre. Annette dissociates herself from Antoinette, and Antoinette knows it: "I was old enough to look after myself. 'Oh, let me alone,' she would say, 'let me alone,' and after I knew that she talked aloud to herself I was a little afraid of her" (11). After Annette rejects again her daughter's attempts to comfort her several times, Antoinette says, "Once I would have gone back quietly to watch her asleep on the blue sofa—once I made excuses to be near her when she brushed her hair . . . But not any longer. Not any more" (13). At about the age of eight, Antoinette must accept her mother's emotional withdrawal and must hide the grief she feels as a result. Although Christophine, a former slave and loyal servant, acts as something of a mother substitute from this point on, she is powerless to give Antoinette the self-integrity she lacks.[48]

Antoinette's early sense of rejection and weak emotional bonds are confirmed by her one childhood friendship, rooted as much in shared hatred as in developmental commonalities. She makes close friends with Tia a day after, the narrative obliquely suggests, this girl followed her, taunting, "White cockroach, go away, go away. Nobody want you. Go away" (13). Tia and Antoinette bathe in the natural pools, eat bananas, and rest in the afternoon heat, then trade racial insults. Rhys graphically depicts the impact on the self of such conflicted emotional attachments when Coulibri Estate is burned by rioting ex-slaves. Tia throws a stone at Antoinette, who says, "I looked at her and I saw her face crumple up as she began to cry. We stared at each other, blood on my face, tears on hers. It was as if I saw myself. Like in a looking-glass" (27).

The mirror image simultaneously suggests self-fragmentation—as each girl sees in the other an externalized portion of herself—and overidentification of self and other, a breakdown of boundaries between the two. Nor does Antoinette wish to identify with Tia in a moment of hatred directed at herself, yet Tia's tears express the grief and confusion that Antoinette has long kept hidden. Through this oblique, concise early portion of the narrative, then, Rhys establishes that the deformation of loving relationships by hatred and distrust results in an unstable, fragmented sense of self. This is, in sum, the most significant component of Antoinette's early *environment;* it will shape her reactions both to other people and to nonhuman nature throughout the remainder of her life.

As Stern explains, self-integrity is prerequisite to union experiences with others; equipped as she is with an unstable sense of self and with a learned distrust of other people, it is no wonder that Antoinette does not seek out social relationships. From the time she is quite young, in fact, Antoinette associates safety with "evasion, burial, escape," as Mezei comments, and thus with physical and psychic withdrawal (204). In the brief period when her mother is courted by Mr. Mason before marrying him, Antoinette, like her mother, leaves the house and stays

away all day. The solace she seeks in nonhuman nature, however, also seems
rather bitter:

> I took another road, past the old sugar works and the water wheel that had not
> turned for years. I went to parts of Coulibri that I had not seen, where there was
> no road, no path, no track. And if the razor grass cut my legs and arms I would
> think, 'It's better than people.' Black ants or red ones, tall nests swarming with
> white ants, rain that soaked me to the skin—once I saw a snake. All better than
> people.
>
> Better. Better, better than people.
>
> Watching the red and yellow flowers in the sun thinking of nothing, it was
> as if a door opened and I was somewhere else, something else. Not myself any
> longer.
>
> I knew the time of day when though it is hot and blue and there are no
> clouds, the sky can have a very black look.   (16)

Along with the recurring dream that Antoinette has as a child, the passage foreshadows her husband's walk in the forest at Granbois, and in equating dream
with waking experience and overlapping the experiences of two different people,
these episodes together reproduce the dissolution of boundaries necessary for a
clear perception of reality, of an environment external to the self. For Antoinette
as for her husband later, the promised peace of retreat from human life is an illusion. In the first part of this passage, her very need to compare the razor grass and
ants to human beings indicates simultaneously her preoccupation with the failure of human relationships and her desire to negate human emotional and social
needs through nonhuman nature. In apparent contrast to this, the next portion
of the passage suggests, possibly, a moment of benign contact with nature, un-
encumbered by the affective distortions of her human relationships—although
the flat language, so distinct from the rhetoric of mystics describing their out-of-
body experiences, gives cause for concern.[49] Yet the final portion of the passage
undercuts this moment of release: the sky can be black when what she sees is a
cloudless blue. Antoinette has learned early what her husband will learn later: in
this place the evidence of the senses does not count. The feeling of release and
escape, of genuine contact with nonhuman nature, cannot be a source of tranquil
restoration for Antoinette, who lacks emotional and cognitive contexts for assimi-
lating such an experience. Such emotional and cognitive contexts develop and are
sustained in human social relationships; for Antoinette, the emotional context
would have been provided by a sustained, loving relationship with a nurturing

parent and by progressive development of friendships with children and other adults uncomplicated by racial hatred. The capacity to respond to nonhuman nature, to experience one's participation in it without a threat to the dissolution of self, is an interaction built upon productive, lifelong relationships with other people. The dysfunctional emotional and social world Antoinette inhabits makes communion with nonhuman nature impossible.

Having been taught to distrust her perceptions by the unreliability of human relationships, Antoinette cannot really love the material world; nonetheless, she tries to cling to physical places and things as substitutes for human relationships. When she and her new husband arrive at Granbois, she acknowledges the loneliness of the place but tells him, "I love it more than anywhere in the world. As if it were a person. More than a person" (53). But her love of Granbois goes back to the time before her father's death, before the emancipation and the family's decline into poverty, and thus before her mother's rejection of her. By contrast, toward the end of part 2, when they have lost hope of salvaging their relationship, Antoinette tells her husband, "I loved this place and you have made it into a place I hate. I used to think that if everything else went out of my life I would still have this, and now you have spoilt it. It's just somewhere else where I have been unhappy, and all the other things are nothing to what has happened here. I hate it now like I hate you and before I die I will show you how much I hate you" (88–89). Although she clings to the belief that physical places and objects have a permanence and reliability not available in human relationships, she also understands that in psychological terms they do not, for every place that she goes becomes profoundly associated with the emotional relationships experienced there and hence becomes, for Antoinette, "somewhere else I have been unhappy" (89). Grandbois has become for her what it is for her husband—a zombi, drained of any potential value by their mutual hatred and the history of destructive relations out of which those hatreds have grown. The spirit of the place mirrors the self-deprived Antoinette, a zombi without a basic sense of identity and agency and thus devoid of the ability to orient in physical space.

In keeping with this, the husband's thoughts as he looks back at the house at the end of part 2 might be somewhat different in tone from Antoinette's, but they are similar in the degree to which psychological disorder affects the perception of place. On the verge of leaving Granbois, he says that "the sadness I felt looking at the shabby white house—I wasn't prepared for that. More than ever before it strained away from the black snake-like forest. Louder and more desperately it called: Save me from destruction, ruin and desolation. Save me from the long slow death by ants. But what are you doing here you folly? So near the forest. Don't you know that this is a dangerous place? And that the dark forest always wins?" (100). The forest at Granbois, in which he temporarily saw a peaceful haven, is now hateful and threatening to him in his psychologically vulnerable state, just as it is to Antoinette. In such states of psychic disorder everything external to the unstable self is potentially threatening, and no relatively objective understanding of its true dangers can be reached. In psychological terms, there is virtually nothing outside the self, because there is no cohesive sense of self to serve as the orientational center.

"Landscape is personal and tribal history made visible," claims the geographer Yi-Fu Tuan. Although mimetic in its presentation of mind-independent objects, landscape painting is a subjective presentation that illuminates the individual and sociocultural values of the artist, resulting in his or her individualized construction of place. Using words rather than paint, realistic literature also makes personal and tribal history visible, often depicting the interdependent relationship between social community, viable selfhood, and physical place. In the psychological realism of *Wide Sargasso Sea*, Rhys demonstrates the far-ranging effects of an inherently unstable social structure wherein pervasive distrust, eroding the self, interpersonal relations, and any sense of reliable knowledge, undermines faith in perception and the capacity to locate places of value in the physical world.

Ecocriticism has the opportunity to become perhaps the most far-ranging, theoretically cohesive, sophisticated, creative, and relevant area of literary scholarship, because humans are natural organisms that just happen, from time to time, to write books. This fact alone suggests that studies in literature and the environment can become a multifaceted endeavor that explores the relationship between literary texts and aspects of nature from one vantage point or another, though all of them should be informed by a basic understanding of evolution by natural selection.[50] I have chosen to emphasize evolved psychology and psychological literature in this chapter because ecocritics tend to view the human mind as a regrettable phenomenon, one whose influence should be acknowledged but then put aside. But if ecocritics begin to engage in a more forthright investigation of our way of knowing and being, and if they begin to relate that knowledge to their analyses of literary texts, they will illuminate how values, relationships, social networks, and traumatic events affect our positive constructions and terrible devaluations of natural and built locales. In this respect, I suspect, literature will be a profound resource, showing that the capacity to trust and love other humans makes it possible to love the world.

CHAPTER FOUR

Remembering the Body

Feelings, Concepts, Process

Sometimes we use our minds not to discover facts but to hide them. We use part of the mind as a screen to prevent another part of it from sensing what goes on elsewhere. The screening is not necessarily intentional—we are not deliberate obfuscators all of the time—but deliberate or not, the screen does hide.

One of the things the screen hides most effectively is the body, our own body, by which I mean the ins of it, its interiors.

Antonio Damasio

Cognitivism in the Matrix of Experience

Like ecocriticism, the field of cognitive approaches to literature has emerged as a recognizable subdiscipline of literary studies only within the last two decades, and also like that other recent area of study, its beginnings predate its recent ascendance by at least another ten years. Yet whereas the area of studies in literature and the environment overtly shares the postmodern political orientation and the Theory-dominated notion of interdisciplinarity that informed the subdisciplines that emerged in the seventies, neither the original momentum of cognitive literary studies nor its recent elaboration into a variety of practices has been primarily motivated by political or ideological concerns. Cognitive literary theorists share the intellectual and theoretical view that contemporary science can describe at least some aspects of the human mind and that these descriptions will illuminate in one way or another the features of literary works and the processes with which they are engaged.

Yet while the scholarly rationale for cognitive approaches seems virtually unassailable, the logical and intellectual impulse behind the field has hardly been a guarantee of a cohesive program (or, for that matter, an integrated set of approaches) for future study. Whatever its origins, any academic field faces the challenging question of its value and relevance as its practices proliferate even while the area is organizing and defining itself. In the introduction to an anthology of essays on cognitive approaches, Alan Richardson acknowledges this somewhat confusing state of affairs:

> One might object at the outset that "cognitive" is too broad, too vague, or too unstable a term to characterize in any meaningful way the varied body of work discussed below. Used to distinguish cognitive *psychology* from the behaviorist approaches it largely displaced, "cognitive" generally refers to an overriding interest in the active (and largely unconscious) mental processing that makes behavior understandable. Used in conjunction with *linguistics,* "cognitive" sometimes distinguishes the work of George Lakoff from that of Noam Chomsky, although Chomsky appears as a founding figure in accounts of cognitive *science.* "Cognitivism" will sometimes also be used to distinguish first-generation cognitive science, heavily influenced by artificial intelligence theory and prone to consider the mind as software running independently of its bodily or mechanical hardware, from later theories insisting on the special character of an "embodied" or "wet" mind. Nevertheless, "cognitive science" and "cognitive neuroscience" have remained useful if unwieldy terms, signifying (rather like "feminist studies" or "cultural studies") interdisciplinary ventures loosely held together by a set of common interests, allegiances, and reference points rather than a coherent discipline unified by shared paradigms and methodologies. Perhaps the most accurate definition of cognitive literary studies, then, would be the work of literary critics and theorists vitally interested in cognitive science and neuroscience, and therefore with a good deal to say to one another, whatever their differences.[1]

Richardson's characterization of cognitive science and cognitive neuroscience—"interdisciplinary ventures loosely held together by a set of common interests, allegiances, and reference points rather than a coherent discipline unified by shared paradigms and methodologies"—provides a good part of the answer to why literary scholars with an interest in the human mind might have quite diverse views about how to utilize psychological findings in literature. If, as Antonio Damasio puts it, "the traditional worlds of philosophy and psychology have gradually joined forces with the world of biology and created an odd but productive alliance," it is nevertheless the case that cognitive neuroscience is quite young (13). Indeed, the experimental study of the human mind alone is of recent origin, and newer still are the technologies that can link neural patterns to cognitive processes. What we know about the human brain-mind at this point in time, as neuroscientists like Damasio take pains to point out, is comparatively little. The goal of neuroscience, to unite the insights and findings of several fields to augment our understanding of brain-mind processes, is as admirable as it is ambitious. At the same time, we are in the early phases of this venture.

Among literary scholars, opponents of research projects that marry science and the humanities are not hard to find, and many of these are apt to point to the youth of neuroscience and the inferential nature of experimental psychology to confirm the prejudice that science has nothing of interest to offer the student of literature. But drawing such a hasty conclusion is unwarranted in light of the pragmatic process whereby ideas are tested, gain or lose force, and are rejected as invalid or accepted as legitimate knowledge by communities of learning. The more intellectually defensible conclusion to draw, given the experimental and provisional nature of so many psychological findings, is that our own uses of ideas from this new field will themselves be provisional and experimental. Such a stance should hardly seem controversial in literary studies, in which practices have never been unified and standards of accountability have never been systematically, much less rigorously, applied.

That said, the increasingly various names and labels applied to subgroups within the field of cognitive literary approaches can prove bewildering to practitioners and the uninitiated alike, and it might be useful to distinguish some of these areas before I narrow my focus to two related developments that have had considerable appeal among American scholars. Within psychology itself, as Richardson points out, scholars typically distinguish first-generation from second-generation cognitive science. As Bruner explains, the cognitive revolution of the 1950s was spurred by the desire to move away from behaviorist objectivism and place meaning and interpretation at the heart of psychology. The aim of cognitivism was thus not only to supersede the fragmentation of psychology that was itself the result of a too-stringent adherence to the positivist ideal of reduction, causal explanation, and prediction but also to catalyze interdisciplinary efforts between the humanities and social sciences. Yet the presumably revolutionary movement shifted focus early in its development from meaning construction to information processing, reinstituting a new reductionism that reabsorbed stimulus-response theory via the computational metaphor. The net result was a model of cognition that left no room for the study of intentional states such as believing or desiring or for a theory of agency (Bruner, 1–11). In sum, a movement intended to move psychology away from a dehumanizing and mechanistic theory of mind soon capitulated to a new permutation of those assumptions.

In contrast to first-generation cognitive scientists, those in the second generation emphasize the "embodied" nature of mental experience, drawing on a tradition in philosophy, psychology, and biology that descends from Charles Darwin and the American pragmatists through the ecological psychologist J. J. Gibson and his followers, including Edward Reed.[2] In keeping with their attunement to process and to the relational significance of entities and events, a philosophical perspective in large part indebted to a grasp of the implications of evolutionary theory, the pragmatists recognized the fallacy of subject-object dualism, which subtends the conception of a passive mind; the continuous and indispensable centrality of feeling in all human action, including abstract thought; and the characteristic wholeness of experience. We do not perceive in bits and pieces, through a mind collecting inputs separately through eyes, ears, nose, and fingertips; instead, our orientation and coordination in an activity affect and shape the quality of what is experienced, as Dewey makes clear in the following example of an unanticipated sound: "If one is reading a book, if one is hunting, if one is watching in a dark place on a lovely night . . . in each case, the noise has a very different psychical value; it is a different experience. . . . What provides the 'stimulus' is a whole act, a sensorimotor co-ordination, it is born from it as its matrix . . . the 'stimulus' arises out of this co-ordination; it is born from it as a matrix, it represents as it were an escape from it. . . . We do not have first a sound and then activity of attention, unless sound is taken as mere neuron shock or physical event, not as conscious value."[3] Stop for a moment and give Dewey's words the pragmatic test by applying them to an experience of your own. If I were running on the Mississippi River levee and spotted an unleashed, unattended dog somewhere nearby, the matrix of feeling-perceiving-thinking-acting would organize my response to the animal and would differ considerably from the response I would have if I were to see the same free-roaming mammal from my study window. I have learned that unleashed dogs attended by their owners at this location are all well trained and heel when a runner approaches. About strays I am far less certain. Thus, my response (accompanying emotions and thoughts that everything is OK or, alternatively, that I need to buy pepper spray) would be, not to seeing a dog, but to seeing the animal in what Dewey calls the matrix of experience, my ongoing activity under a specific set of conditions.

As Reed points out, organisms are fundamentally unlike mechanical systems in that they do not need to be put in motion; they are instead, to use Dewey's word, engaged in the matrix (feeling-perception-cognition-action) of an experience in the service of regulated, ongoing activity. In this process of self-regulation, feeling guides continuous action (which should be construed broadly to include the action of thought). Says James, "Our own bodily position, attitude, condition, is one of the things of which *some* awareness, however inattentive, invariably accompanies the knowledge of whatever else we know. We think; and as we think we feel our bodily selves as the seat of the thinking. If the thinking be *our* thinking, it must be suffused through all its parts with that peculiar warmth and intimacy that make it come as ours."[4] Feeling is not only necessary and prior to all action, including mental action, but the basis of reasoned decisions, according to Damasio. Furthermore, the "awareness" of which James speaks attests to the relationship between feeling and consciousness. If consciousness originates, as Damasio claims, in the feeling of knowing, James's final words in this passage reveal the adaptive value of the continuous link between feeling and the special sort of awareness we call "consciousness." Consciousness and self-consciousness—not only the awareness that we know but also the added awareness that the knowing is specifically one's own—are warm and intimate. Knowledge, in short, feels *good*. And when knowledge feels good, organisms are apt to seek it actively, to want as much of the thought and feeling of mastery as possible. For humans, apparently, such pronounced epistemic motivations improved "the art of life" (Damasio, 31).

Taking the long view, then, from an evolutionary, ecological, and embodied perspective, organisms are not, as cognitivism would have had it, analogous to machines, no matter how wonderful those machines may be. Far from it. As Humberto Maturana asserts, "Living systems are units of interactions; they exist in an environment. From a purely biological view, they cannot be understood independently of the part of the environment with which they interact, the niche; nor can the niche be defined independently of the living system that occupies it" (qtd. in Gibbs, 42). In essence, Maturana is making the same point that I made about environment in chapter 3, but from the point of view of the organism. Since an organism is already active in its environment, its sensory assessment and action are relative to the experiential matrix, and thus, writes Gibbs, "perception does not take place in the brain of the perceiver, but rather is an act of the whole animal, the act of perceptually guided exploration of the environment" (Gibbs, 43). Such perceptually guided exploration is the stuff of the ongoing regulation of activity whereby the animal assesses the aspects and features of an environment that will serve or hinder its survival. In keeping with this, ecological psychology has replaced the concept of *resources,* which tends to suggest useful material aspects of the environment, with that of *affordances,* defined as opportunities for action, which more accurately reflects the holistic epistemic perspective that is required for an organism engaged concurrently in monitoring safety, seeking food, finding a mate, protecting offspring, and the like. Since natural environments are subject to the contingencies of climate change, fluctuations in the population, and movement of other species, it would be extremely maladaptive for even simple species to run according to a program. Reed points out that Darwin's earthworm experiments, wherein the animals altered their behavior to adjust to the displacement of leaves and soil in their environment, provide empirical verification that the worms self-regulate rather than act according to mechanistic instinct (20–24). And this from an animal without a brain!

It appears that this total picture of evolved organisms, including human organisms, has finally put to rest mechanistic conceptions of the behavior and mental processes of life forms, and we might confidently assume that cognitivism's computational metaphor is well behind us. Perhaps cognitivism was an inevitable victim of that great invention of the late twentieth century, the computer—but I think we trivialize the tenacity of the mechanical attitude toward mind if we see it as nothing more than an accident of historical timing. After all, although the limitations of the Enlightenment model of the mind were criticized before the turn of the nineteenth century, the temptation to recast this model in ever-newer forms is alive and well. "The desires & perceptions of man untaught by any thing but organs of sense, must be limited to objects of sense": why is it that when psychology recognizes the fallacy of a passive, mechanistic mind, which William Blake thus denounced in 1789, mind as machine continues to exert an irresistible pull?[5]

As the following survey of some current areas in the field of cognitive literary approaches suggests, literary scholars have been reluctant to absorb the full implications of the "embodied" perspective for a variety of reasons. Notable among these are the continuing dominance of linguistics in interdisciplinary approaches; the persistence of an ideological ethos stemming from structuralist and poststructuralist theory; the innate tendency to "hide the body"; and the knowledge-seeking orientation itself.

In what follows, after a brief survey of some of the many theories and practices that currently fall under the heading of cognitive literary studies, I focus on the theory of conceptual metaphor, the cornerstone of cognitive linguistics and perhaps the most influential idea in cognitive approaches to literature as practiced in the United States. Addressing specifically the theoretical developments in the career of Mark Turner, the scholar who deserves credit for introducing the theory of conceptual metaphor to literary studies, I indicate the value of a broader evolutionary-ecological perspective for those practitioners of conceptual-metaphor analysis. In the process, I offer an assessment of conceptual blending, the theory of cognition that draws on and attempts to refine the theory of conceptual metaphor, on whose development Turner and Gilles Fauconnier have collaborated since the late nineties. Ultimately, I suggest that a more synthetic approach to modeling cognition, one that keeps sight of the ecological need for behavioral flexibility and the evolutionary emergence of cognitive fluidity in humans and does not rely exclusively on features of language to produce evidence of cognition, can prevent the dryness and abstraction that ironically has resulted from the application of cognitive theories to literary interpretation. For instance, in particular those literary works that dramatize cognitive process are not well served by an emphasis on metaphor or conceptual structures alone. In readings of Coleridge's "Dejection: An Ode" and Raymond Carver's "I Could See the Smallest Things," I suggest that along with the conceptual metaphors, the impulse toward narrativity and the feelings evoked by the narrative process are part of the epistemic matrices highlighted and experienced in these works.[6]

Multiple Cognitions

Among the current research areas in language, literature, and cognition, Richardson identifies the following in his introduction to *The Work of Fiction*: cognitive poetics, cognitive linguistics, cognitive semantics, cognitive rhetoric, conceptual blending, evolutionary literary theory, cognitive historicism, cognitive narratology, and cognitive aesthetics of reception. Although this list in itself constitutes an abundance of approaches, it hardly completes the map of contemporary practices in the area. Peter Stockwell's 2002 student-oriented text, *Cognitive Poetics: An Introduction*, overlaps in some respects with Richardson's discussion of the field but also includes separate chapters on topics such as prototype analysis, diexis, and cognitive grammar, which do not figure largely in either Richardson's description or the sampling of scholarship in the field that he and Spolsky provide in *The Work of Fiction*. As Stockwell explains in his introduction,

> The different approaches in the field have placed their emphases in stylistic and persuasive patterns (rhetoric) on the one hand, or in the grammatical representation of conceptual structures (grammar and logic) on the other. . . . The understanding of cognitive poetics in America has centred very closely around cognitive linguistics, which for institutional reasons has become a major means by which linguists can engage in language study that does not follow the Chomskyan generative tradition. The American model has been highly influential around the world [and is mainly concerned] with metaphor, conceptual structures and issues of reference.
>
> Traditionally, the discipline of stylistics has flourished in Europe and Australia, and has had limited appeal so far in America. (9)

As Stockwell points out, some influences and practices in America differ from those in Europe and Australia, and this accounts for the differences between his overview and Richardson's. However, while quite distinct approaches have developed in various parts of the world, there is an overriding similarity: cognitive approaches on the whole have been dominated by the discipline and evolution of theories in linguistics. Thus, although the governing theories drawn from that discipline differ markedly regarding the aspect of language they analyze, and although the field of cognitive approaches, particularly in the United States, has begun to address nonlinguistic aspects of cognition, the overall attention to linguistics as the source of valued theories and, moreover, the presumption that attention to language alone will reveal all we wish to know about mental processes in the text evince strong continuity with structuralism and poststructuralism.[7] Even though the generative force for cognitive approaches was not the impulse to social consciousness that fueled feminism, Marxism, postcolonialism, and ecocriticism, the subdiscipline is nevertheless continuous with these schools in the choice of linguistics as the extraliterary discipline of primary importance. Since literature is made out of words (and blank spaces), an emphasis on the operations of language hardly seems misplaced; however, as I suggest in the rest of this chapter, too great a focus on language curtails attention to many aspects of cognition that are relevant to literary expression—just as too great an emphasis on discourse in some Foucauldian-inspired readings discouraged attention to cultural and historical developments and practices.

It is perhaps inevitable that the term *cognitive poetics* lends itself, over time, to signifying an array of cognitively oriented practices, since the term *poetics* has traditionally referred broadly to theory within literary studies. But *cognitive poetics* originally applied to the practice of Reuven Tsur, probably the first to turn to cognitive science in the service of literary understanding. An intellectual descendant of Russian formalism, Tsur has sought to explain the distinctive features of literary language by extending and further developing the concept of defamiliarization and establishing its mental dynamics. In Stockwell's usage, however, *cognitive poetics* refers to the considerably varied practices of all researchers employing some aspect of cognitive theory to literary study; in his sense, it is a synonym for *cognitive approaches.*

Stockwell explains that in Britain and Australia the chief influence has been from a specific branch of linguistics, *linguistic stylistics* (sometimes called *literary linguistics*), which focuses on describing the surface language features of the text and sees literature as a particular set of data among a plethora of written artifacts. Influenced by structuralism as well as by Noam Chomsky's generative grammar, this branch of linguistics concentrates on the structures and organization of language. The shortcomings of a theory that emphasizes language structures at the expense of the broader implications of embodiment are readily apparent in Stockwell's discussions. For example, while he notes in passing that "all forms of expression and forms of conscious perception are bound, more closely than previously realised, in our biological circumstances" (4), there is no substantive discussion of how biological circumstances factor into the literary worlds and works briefly addressed in the text. Indeed, in some cases, such as that of deictic shift theory, a model intended to explain how a reader gets inside a text and understands shifts in perspective, it is hard to imagine a way of speaking about literature that is less consistent with the ecology of human experience. Commenting on the narrative technique in the beginning of *Wuthering Heights*, for instance, Stockwell states, "This part of the narrative pushes and pops from the deictic centres of child Catherine (within the textual deixis of the Bible notes) almost twenty years previously and Lockwood reading in the same location in the narrative present" (50). The idiosyncratic terminology here—*pop* and *push*—is, instructively, drawn from computer science and thus reflects the cognitivist inheritance that is far removed from the inferential, meaning-making process envisioned by the embodied theory of mind.

Taken together, the related fields that have enjoyed popularity in the United States—cognitive linguistics, cognitive semantics, and cognitive rhetoric—demonstrate the interplay between language theory, philosophy, and literature, allied areas that developed initially in the work of the linguist George Lakoff and the philosopher Mark Johnson and in the first phase of the literary theorist and critic Mark Turner's career. With the publication of *Metaphors We Live By* in 1980, Lakoff and Johnson inaugurated a paradigm shift in the understanding of both metaphor and the processes of human cognition. Claiming that the human conceptual system is fundamentally metaphorical, Lakoff and Johnson point to the pervasiveness of metaphor within everyday speech. Most of our concepts are typically organized around spatialized metaphors that are not randomly assigned but have an experiential basis derived from bodily experience. Although everyday metaphors may vary from culture to culture, some common metaphors are consistent across cultures, and in some cases it is hard to distinguish a physical from a cultural basis for the metaphor. In many cases, conceptual metaphors present the abstract in terms of the concrete and provide conceptual limits.

For instance, common figurative uses of *up* and *down* predictably correlate elevation with emotions and actions: "I'm feeling down (or up)," "He rises early," "He fell asleep." These orientational metaphors are consistent with our bodily orientation in space and its coherence with physical and psychic states (upright posture indicating purpose and resolve, downward droop signaling depression or exhaustion, prone position consistent with rest or sleep).

Just as one set of metaphorical uses of *up* and *down* remains reliably consistent, ontological metaphors reveal a pervasive tendency to see emotions, events, and ideas as entities and substances. Lakoff and Johnson comment that "human purposes typically require us to impose artificial boundaries that make physical phenomena discrete just as we are: entities bounded by a surface" (25). Conceptualizing in this fashion enables identification, quantification, action, assignment of causality, and belief that we understand, and Lakoff and Johnson suggest that in some cases it is based in the territorial instinct. The statement "He's out of sight right now," for instance, draws on the conceptual structure VISUAL FIELDS ARE CONTAINERS, because the perceptual modality of sight is not a physical space in which a person is or is not located. Likewise, container metaphors pervasively represent phenomenal and emotional states—"he's in love," "he's in trouble," "she's in a funk," "she thinks outside the box," "she's in her glory," and so on.

Separately, Johnson has developed a theory of the experiential dynamics underlying everyday conceptual metaphors. In *The Body in the Mind: The Bodily Basis of Meaning, Imagination, and Reason* Johnson argues that the human experience of reality is shaped by the contours of bodily movement and that common forms of bodily movement result in gestalt structures that confer order upon and help humans reason about experience. These gestalt structures, which Johnson calls *image schemata,* are nonpropositional and analog in nature and figurative in character. In Johnson's formulation, image schemata are abstract analogs to physical processes that transcend any specific sense modality and operate at a level between abstract propositional structures and images. They are dynamic, fluid patterns rather than mental pictures. Some of the most basic image schemata include container, path, links, cycles, scale, and center-periphery.

In Johnson's account, then, it is these image schemata that provide the phenomenological awareness that serves as the basis for the conceptual metaphors that he and Lakoff have identified in language. As a philosopher, Johnson is much concerned with the implications of his theory for the longstanding tradition that has separated rational from imaginative capacities and that has based accounts of meaning on the former. Whereas objectivist accounts claim that meaning is a relationship between abstract symbolic representations and mind-independent reality, and whereas the field of semantics has seen truth and meaning fundamentally as a matter of the satisfaction of propositions, Johnson claims that meaning is based *fundamentally* on nonpropositional structures. In selecting the word *schemata* for these structures, Johnson places himself consciously in the tradition of Kant, who applied the term *schema* to nonpropositional structures for the imagination.

Johnson mounts a strong argument against cloistered conceptions of rationality, suggesting instead that all knowing derives from phenomenal experience and that objectivist accounts of truth and meaning are therefore essentially misguided. At the same time, the exact nature of image schemata is something of a puzzle. In his most recent book, *The Meaning of the Body,* Johnson claims that an image schema "is a dynamic, recurring pattern of organism-environment interactions. As such, it will reveal itself in the contours of our basic sensorimotor experience." Further, "image schemas appear to be realized as activation patterns (or 'contours') in human topological neural maps" (136, 142). But as Gibbs asks in his overview of this theory,

> how are image schemas represented, given their cross-modal character? Where might image schemas be represented in the brain, given that they arise from recurring bodily experiences that cut across vision, audition, kinesthetic movement, and so on (i.e., are the SOURCE-PATH-GOAL and MOMENTUM schemas encoded in the visual cortex or some other part of the brain)? The abstract, yet still definable, character of image schemas does not provide easy answers to these questions. At this point, linguists and psychologists should be cautious in making concrete claims about how and where image schemas might be mentally represented. *Image schemas may best be understood as experiential gestalts that do not necessarily get encoded as explicit mental representations.*
>
> (114, emphasis added)

For his part, Johnson is at pains to clarify that image schemata are not representations in the conventional sense of mental images and that such terminology is only acceptable if we understand it as a reference to neural maps. The evolving conception of image schemata and the attendant questions about their exact nature points, perhaps, to the unsuitability of the terminology, for since both the adjective *image* and the noun *schema* encourage the notion of mental picture, the phrase itself suggests internal representation, as perhaps Gibbs's repeated recourse to the concept of representation in this passage indicates. Since single-cell organisms and earthworms both behave in habitual ways and adjust their behavior to changes in the environment, image schemata are not necessary for functional motor competence or behavioral flexibility. The question then becomes whether the image-schema concept appropriately characterizes an intermediary phase in the process of consciousness emerging from bodily experience in higher animals, that is, the feeling of knowing, of making an image.

Johnson's theory brings to the fore a matter that bedevils cognitive science as well as all those who hope to use its findings and theories to further other pursuits: what is the precise nature of mental images, and what is the total process by which they are produced? For although image schemata as currently theorized do not have a feel of mental concreteness, they are proposed as a vital link in the process of producing the neurobiological processes and/or mental representations upon which we base our actions. With respect to image schemata, mental images, and representation, we are brought up against the limitations of human knowledge in linking discernibly bodily experience to mental experience. If, as Damasio suggests, we are naturally adaptively inclined to "hide the body," then the gaps in our knowledge about what makes the mind and body a continuous whole must surely encourage that hiding of the physical ground from which the mind emerges. Johnson's whole career has been devoted to articulating the physical basis of mental activity; nonetheless, that is no guarantee that theorists building on his ideas will not, wittingly or unwittingly, lose the body in the pursuit of words.

From Cognitive Rhetoric to Conceptual Blending

In *More Than Cool Reason: A Field Guide to Poetic Metaphor* (1989), coauthored with Lakoff, and *Reading Minds: The Study of English in the Age of Cognitive Science* (1991), Mark Turner introduced the theory of conceptual metaphor to literary scholars and recommended a program further exploring conceptual connections via their linguistic expression, a program he calls *cognitive rhetoric*. In *More Than Cool Reason* Lakoff and Turner extend the linguist's theory of conceptual metaphor by providing an overview of some common metaphorical constructions that pervade everyday expression and by demonstrating their prevalence in literary works throughout the English-language tradition. Among the salient constructions are LIFE IS A JOURNEY, PEOPLE ARE PLANTS, DEATH IS DEPARTURE, A LIFETIME IS A DAY, DEATH IS SLEEP, LIFE IS FLUID, LIFE IS A PLAY, TIME IS A CHANGER, TIME MOVES, and TIME IS A PURSUER. Some very general metaphors include PURPOSES ARE DESTINATIONS, STATES ARE LOCATIONS, and EVENTS ARE ACTIONS (52). Lakoff and Turner explain that understanding these metaphors rests on knowing, usually unconsciously, a set of correspondences between two domains. For example, Lakoff and Turner point out that a reader's comprehension of Robert Frost's "The Road Not Taken" depends on our everyday comprehension of the LIFE IS A JOURNEY metaphor. While understanding this poem appears to be a rather simple matter for any speaker of English, doing so depends on recognizing these correspondences between the domain of life and that of journey: the person leading a life is a traveler; his purposes are destinations; the means for achieving purposes are routes; difficulties in life are impediments to travel; counselors are guides; progress is the distance traveled; landmarks are gauges of travel; a crossroads is a life choice; resources and talents are provisions. In the language of cognitive linguistics, features from the source domain of *journey* or *travel* are mapped onto the target domain of *life* (3–4).

Since Lakoff and Turner's basic thesis is that the same common metaphors that people employ unconsciously in everyday speech also provide conceptual structure in literature, the theory raises questions about both the distinctiveness and the difficulty of literary works. As the authors themselves ask, "If we often have the same conceptual metaphors in ordinary language as in poetry, why is it that the poetry should seem so much harder?" To which they answer: "First, poetic uses are often conscious extensions of the ordinary conventionalized metaphors; for example, 'Time hath a wallet' is in part an extension of TIME MOVES. Because they are conscious, they can draw upon different cognitive resources than the automatic and effortless use of fully conventionalized modes of metaphorical expression. Second, authors may call upon our knowledge of basic conceptual metaphors in order to manipulate them in unusual ways. The unusual use of a normally automatic and unconscious metaphor takes effort" (53–54). While Lakoff and Turner thus explain why literary metaphors require some decoding, their answer begs the underlying question why writers and readers construct and labor over difficult figures whose source concepts are commonplace. But in this first foray into conceptual metaphor, as well as in his subsequent scholarship, Turner is more interested in the conceptual grounding and processing of linguistic expressions than in developing a theory of literature. As Richardson notes, "Turner has described his project not as erecting a 'theory of literature' but as establishing a 'common ground' that might support a number of different theories. . . . Along with his emphasis on rhetoric and corresponding interest in extraliterary texts, this has made it hard to gauge the adequacy of cognitive rhetoric to support a theory of literature per se" (5).

As Richardson's remarks, published eleven years after *Reading Minds*, indicate, Turner has not elaborated on the contribution of cognitive rhetoric to literary theory since his important first efforts, nor has he done so with conceptual blending, his more recent effort to refine cognitive dynamics beyond the insights of cognitive rhetoric. Notwithstanding his abilities as a sensitive reader of literature,

Turner has become, in essence, more intrigued with analyzing the processes of cognition as he understands them than with the application of psychological findings to literary theory and interpretation. In retrospect, Turner's evolution from literary scholar to cognitive theorist is not particularly surprising given his conception of cognitive rhetoric as a break with poststructuralism whereby a new understanding of the everyday mind will lead back to a classical conception of rhetoric's contribution to science and philosophy. Noting that Turner and other cognitivists share with Jonathan Culler the view that literary scholars should not simply interpret texts but also take an interest in the process that makes interpretation possible, Joseph Bizup and Eugene Kintgen point out that Turner's conception of literary study "differs from Culler's in its insistence on the continuity between understanding literary language and understanding natural language."[8] For Culler, special conventions for reading poetry result in distinct interpretive operations; for Turner, the interpretive processes for understanding poetry are fundamentally the same as those for comprehending common utterances.[9] The crux of the matter is that for Turner "the common and ordinary features of language are the most interesting, most complex, and most in need of explanation" (Bizup and Kintgen, 854). Since he began his engagement with conceptual metaphor, Turner has been interested primarily in demonstrating how the study of language contributes to our knowledge of cognition, thereby illustrating the significance of rhetorical inquiry in all academic disciplines.

Far from eschewing the practice of literary interpretation, however, Turner sees literary study trivialized and ghettoized by the two-cultures assumption. "Under the default concept of literary criticism, the project of this book is extrinsic since it declines to see literature as a special world to be treated with special tools designed exclusively for the investigation of literature" (*Minds*, 239). Hoping to reinvigorate literary study by paving the way toward interdisciplinary exchange, Turner maintains in *Reading Minds* that cognitive rhetoric can inform literary criticism at three levels, and he provides brief examples of each. He includes the level of individual expression, such as "I am a parcel of vain strivings tied"; that of controlling conceptual connection, such as that between journey and self-discovery in *The Odyssey* or between conversational wit and sex in *Much Ado about Nothing*; and that of genre definition, such as the connection between conversation and lyric (148–50). Among these, he suggests that "the first level [of local phrasing] is the most important and most pervasive" (240). Recognizing that literary critics, who generally focus on complete works, are unlikely to be convinced that individual expressions merit close, isolated scrutiny, Turner insists that the conceptual connections expressed at macrocosmic and microcosmic levels are similar, and thus local phrases are "windows on conceptual activity in general" (241). Turner's subsequent scholarship has remained remarkably consistent with the view expressed here in two respects: he has remained committed to analyzing and explaining the normative conceptual patterns underlying linguistic expression, and on balance, he has devoted himself especially to the analysis of local expression in both his early work on cognitive rhetoric and his later work on conceptual blending.

Thus, while Turner clearly envisions a two-way exchange between cognitive science and literary studies, his emphasis in *Reading Minds* on the prototypical patterns of conceptualization that can be gleaned in language inevitably recruits literary works as illustrative instances of the theory of conceptual metaphor. And indeed, different as his theoretical perspective is from that of Gottschall, the Darwinian literary critic who espouses a reorientation of literary studies in line with scientific methodology, both draw on science to emphasize specific normative or typical features of literary phenomena. If scholars choose to emphasize the common features of literary works, it is hard to imagine a justification for literary studies as a field in its own right, since such a method does not seem to be aligned with the nature of the object. To a significant degree, then, interdisciplinary scholars should take to heart the warnings of reductionism issuing from the two-culturists and be advised that some aspects of the scientific perspective, such as the focus on the typical case and the tendency toward literalism, may be ill-suited to the literary studies.

Even though Turner originally envisioned the resuscitation of literary studies through interdisciplinary exchange, the shape of his own career and the emphasis of his scholarship ironically suggest that literature is increasingly irrelevant to contemporary intellectual pursuits. Some literary scholars have fruitfully combined the insights of cognitive rhetoric with other techniques to enhance pedagogy and scholarship, but its viability as the ground for a theory or theories of literature is questionable.[10] Cognitive rhetoric, whether premised on conceptual metaphor or conceptual blending, relies exclusively on the evidence of cognition revealed in language and thus strictly limits its understanding of cognitive activity and of the evolutionary-embodied explanation of the complex structures of human thought. Notwithstanding the fact that since the publication of *Reading Minds* Turner has increasingly relied on neuroscience, cognitive archaeology, and other aspects of evolutionary theory to assert that conceptual processes lie on an evolutionary foundation, his increasingly schematic analyses of conceptualization are at odds with the flexibly responsive species that cognitivists such as Mithen, Donald, and Gibbs depict.

In collaboration with the linguist Gilles Fauconnier, Turner has elaborated conceptual blending (also known as conceptual integration), a theory that extends the insights of cognitive linguistics to concepts that are drawn from different domains but are based, unlike metaphor, on disanalogies.[11] Conceptual blending thus provides a broader umbrella for the fundamentally creative view of cognition proposed in the earlier joint efforts of Lakoff, Johnson, and Turner, and it likewise extends the critique of analytic philosophy that is at the heart of cognitive linguistics and semantics. Moving beyond the terminology of source and target domains developed in cognitive linguistics, Fauconnier and Turner construct a new terminology and elaborate schematic diagrams to elucidate their theory and to demonstrate how varied conceptual inputs combine to produce new conceptual structure. *Mental spaces* are "small conceptual packets constructed as we think and talk"; when such spaces contribute to a conceptual blend, they are referred to as *input spaces*. Mental spaces are connected to *frames*, which consist of long-term schematic knowledge, "such as the frame of *walking along a path*, and to long-term specific knowledge" (40). Combining the elements from the distinct input spaces and frames results in *emergent structure* and enables one to " 'run the blend'—that is, operate cognitively within it, developing new structure and manipulating the various events as an integrated unit" (60).

Fauconnier and Turner distinguish four main kinds of integration—simplex, mirror, single-scope, and double-scope—which differ with respect to the number of frames and input spaces they engage. The last of these, double-scope blending, which entails two different input spaces with different frames, both of which contribute partially to the blend, has the distinctive capacity to create emergent structure, and it is this capacity for double-scope blending that Fauconnier and Turner see as the crowning achievement of humankind. To illustrate, Fauconnier and Turner present as one of their many examples of double-scope blending a scenario in which a parent whose adult child is investing in the stock market chides the child with the warning that he is "digging [his] own grave" (131–35). According to the authors, this is an example of a double-scope network that draws on clashing inputs: on one hand a frame related to death and burial and on the other an "unwitting failure" frame. In the blend, the event structure, which includes causality, intentionality, participant roles, temporal sequence, and identity, comes from the "unwitting failure" input, because the causal and social dynamics of gravedigging clash with the structure mapped onto the blend. Furthermore, Fauconnier and Turner "emphasize that in the construction of the blend, a single shift in causal structure—*The existence of a grave* causes *death*, instead of *Death* causes *the existence of a grave*—is enough to produce emergent structure, specific to the blend: undesirability of digging one's own grave, exceptional foolishness in being unaware of such undesirability, correlation of depth of grave with probability of death" (133). With this example and others, Fauconnier and Turner demonstrate how some apparently rather simple statements draw on a complex set of linguistic associations, and they infer that the cognitive processes underlying expressions are structurally similar to their linguistic analyses.

In the view of Fauconnier and Turner, the emergence of double-scope integration stands as the major cognitive achievement in human evolution. Drawing on Steven Mithen's analysis of the evolution of cognitive fluidity in modern humans, which proposes that humans underwent a cognitive explosion between sixty thousand and thirty thousand years ago that enabled them to associate previously compartmentalized knowledge from three discrete domains (social, natural, and technological), Fauconnier and Turner claim that the emergence of double-scope integration propelled the evolution of language. They insist that the capacity for conceptual blending preceded language:

> Continuous improvement of blending capacity reached the critical level of double-scope blending, and language precipitated as a singularity. But why should double-scope blending have been the critical level of blending that made language possible? The central problem of expression is that we and perhaps other mammals have a vast, open-ended number of frames and provisional conceptual assemblies that we manipulate. Even if we had only one word per frame, the result would be too many words to manage. Double-scope integration, however, permits us to use vocabulary and grammar from one frame or domain or conceptual assembly to say things about others. It brings a level of efficiency and generality that suddenly makes the challenging mental logistics of expression tractable. The forms of language work not because we have managed to encode in them these vast and open-ended ranges of meaning, but because they make it possible to prompt for high-level integrations over conceptual arrays we already command. Neither the conceptual operations nor the conceptual arrays are encoded, carried, contained, or otherwise captured by the forms of language. The forms need not and indeed cannot carry the full construal of the specific situation but, instead, consist of prompts for thinking about situations in the appropriate way to arrive at a construal.   (182–83)

Although Fauconnier and Turner maintain that Mithen incorrectly places the evolution of language before that of cognitive fluidity, it is not clear that there is substantive disagreement between these theorists, especially given Mithen's developed discussion of the evolution of language in his most recent book, *The*

Singing Neanderthals. Defining language as "a communication system consisting of a lexicon—a collection of words with agreed meanings—and a grammar—a set of rules for how words are combined to form utterances," Mithen distinguishes between such advanced compositional structures and formulaic, holistic utterances of much earlier origin that serve as the basis of both music and language (12). Adopting the theory of the linguist Alison Wray, Mithen proposes that early human communication was composed of multimodel messages that constituted meaningful wholes that could not be broken down into semantic units. Over the course of human evolution, in Wray's conception, holistic phrases underwent a gradual process of segmentation that ultimately resulted in grammatical structure and words as semantic units. Thus, Wray's theory challenges that of the current dominant theorist, Derek Bickerton, whose compositional theory suggests that protolanguage was characterized by words (semantic units) without grammar. Furthermore, Mithen follows the anthropologists Leslie Aiello and Robin Dunbar in proposing that language evolved primarily to promote social grooming and thus aid in the maintenance of social relationships once group size became too large for physical grooming to serve this function. However, Mithen modifies Aiello and Dunbar's claim to suggest that "early hominid social vocalizations" had perhaps more in common with music than with language as we know it, constituted by "elaborations of the type of rhythmic and melodic utterances used by gelada monkeys" (*Neanderthals*, 136). According to this view, then, in the course of evolution music and language came to occupy separate behavioral-cognitive domains, just as holistic messages became segmented into discrete elements related to an overarching grammatical structure.

What is striking about the difference between Mithen's account of language and that of Fauconnier and Turner is not the matter of when exactly compositional language arose but how protolanguage and then language emerged in relation to other human capacities and what the functional utility of each was at the relevant stages of evolution. According to Mithen, pressure to develop holistic communicative patterns with vocal and gestural components rendering them emotionally and informationally expressive (and thus socially manipulative or persuasive) would have increased with the emergence of a terrestrial lifestyle. According to this view, protolanguage is one among several major adaptations—bipedalism is another—that enhanced human sociality and whose evolution may have been driven primarily by its increasing contribution to sociality. Mithen acknowledges that one significant limitation of the holistic communication system that Wray posits is that since each message is a unified whole, there is a distinct limit to the number of messages that can be remembered. Yet the result is the conservatism in human thought and behavior between 1.8 million and 250,000 years ago consistent with the patterns of living suggested by the archaeological record. Mithen points to evidence of symbolic capabilities, a necessary precursor to language, dating from about 70,000 years ago, evident in the Blombos Cave painting in South Africa, and he furthermore claims that the brain circuitry enabling cognitive fluidity underlies the capacity for metaphor—that is, association across domains of knowledge—which seems crucial to compositional language. Viewed from such a functionalist perspective, it is hard to see what use humans would have had for a compositional language before they developed the capacity to associate knowledge across domains.

Since Fauconnier and Turner do not offer a functional rationale for the emergence of language, they do not address the possibility of protolanguage and the needs it might have served. They are preoccupied instead with the relatively local and specific problem of when language arose in relation to cognitive fluidity (or, in their terms, the capacity for double-scope integration). When Mithen says, in a phrase that Fauconnier and Turner home in on, that recent anthropological evidence suggests that "both archaic *H. sapiens* and Neanderthals had the brain capacity, neural structure and vocal apparatus for an advanced form of vocalization, that should be called language" (qtd. in *Way*, 186), it is not at all clear that he means the advanced compositional rather than the proto form of language. Rather, Mithen's concern throughout all his work is with the consistency of anthropological, archaeological, geological, and other forms of evidence that make certain behaviors and capacities possible. Thus, when Fauconnier and Turner insist that Mithen "assumes that language falls out of a combination of big brains and modern vocal apparatus" (186), they forward a claim that runs counter to Mithen's fine-grained, extended evolutionary analyses. Most fundamentally, evolutionists recognize that adaptations such as bipedalism and language are extremely "expensive"; that is, they require great amounts of energy and the gradual emergence via natural selection of anatomical structures and systems that can support such capacities. According to this logic, something as elaborate as human language could not simply "fall out" of other developments but must have precursors with a long history of functional utility.

By contrast, Fauconnier and Turner assert that once double-scope integration was in place, "language precipitated as a singularity," without positing any preliminary forms of communication. On the one hand, it is not their purpose to offer a developed account of the evolution of language; on the other, their account of its emergence is extremely cursory, particularly given their reliance on linguistic expression as the key to cognition. In their view, there had to be thought before compositional language emerged—the theory of the development of double-scope blending relies on the presumption of earlier stages of cognition—but according to their practice, there are no aspects of cognition lying outside of (and quite possibly far more ancient than) language that are worthy of consideration.

In addition, their explanation of the emergence of language participates in a way of speaking about the mind that is more consistent with cognitivism than with an embodied, ecological, dynamical systems perspective. In the passage quoted above, Fauconnier and Turner summarize their explanation for the necessity of double-scope integration as the cognitive prerequisite to language. First, note that no aspect of this passage suggests that cognition is part of an interaction with the environment. Rather, the problem of language and cognition is an internal, subjective one: "[humans] and perhaps other mammals have a vast, open-ended number of frames and provisional conceptual assemblies that we manipulate." The terminology here suggests that cognition is primarily a matter of mental or intellectual problems for which the right logistical solution must be selected. If one game plan does not work, then we experiment with another "frame" or "assembly." The picture of cognition as constituted primarily by sets of solutions and action plans violates the rather broadly accepted view that plasticity of response has been crucial in human evolution. Theories of frames, scripts, and scenes present the same problem as does Johnson's theory of image schemata: to what extent are these cognitively instantiated? If cognitively instantiated, to what extent are they culturally informed or produced? To what extent, if any, are they the product of genetic evolution? Second, understanding cognition may be an intellectual puzzle, but much in human cogitating is not. Far from manipulating assemblies, much of cognition, as Fauconnier and Turner themselves assert, is unconscious and therefore below the level of intentional choice suggested by the word *manipulate*. Probably more importantly, neuroscience today generally accepts the view that feelings and emotions generate and direct thought processes, but *The Way We Think* offers no account of affect in the conceptual process. It follows, then, that Fauconnier and Turner see language principally as a matter of the articulation and expression of cognitive blends.

In short, the theory of conceptual blending or integration has a number of shortcomings as a comprehensive theory of cognition, and these limitations subserve an understanding of thought that has more in common with cognitivism (first-generation cognitive science) than it does with an embodied theory of mind (second-generation cognitive science). First, although developed in light of evolutionary principles, it is abstract and schematic, implicitly suggesting that once having evolved, high-level cognition appears to have divorced itself from bodily states and emotion. Second, Fauconnier and Turner's metaphorical language (e.g., *input spaces* and *mental packets*) clashes with neurobiological terminology and thus obfuscates rather than clarifies the contemporary understanding of mental process. Third, the model is based only on linguistic analysis and thus presumes that unconscious and lower levels of cognition operate according to the conceptual and logical patterns of linguistically expressed thought. Fourth, just as the emphasis on language and conceptual processes limits a full understanding of cognition, it results in a restricted and impoverished notion of meaning. Fifth, the ubiquity of blending as proposed by the model is cognitively impractical, implying complex processes underlying apparently simple phrases. Sixth, the inattention to the natural or cultural grounding of specific conceptual structures results, ultimately, in the picture of an inefficient, scattershot mind that thinks without priorities or distinctive motivations.

In the assessment of L. David Ritchie, Fauconnier and Turner's metametaphors of "spaces," "packets," "assemblies," and so on, as well as the schematic correlates, present a problematic depiction of cognition.[12] As Ritchie points out, although Fauconnier and Turner claim that their model coheres with a connectionist account, they do not explain how their account plays out in neuronal assemblies; in fact, the governing conception of compartmentalized units and spaces conflicts with connectionist understanding. The uses of circles and boxes in schematic representations reinforces the sense of boundaries separating conceptual elements; so many separate spaces and representations, which seem to indicate neurologically distinct units, suggest an extraordinarily high cognitive load for processing rather simple expressions or phrases, such as "digging your own grave." Whereas blending theory posits the construction of a new space for each blend, in neurological terms, activation levels or new linkages between neuronal groups would have to be established. Echoing a repeated criticism, Ritchie further points out that metaphors of "space" and "blending," whose reference to actual neuronal processes is unclear, inhibit testability.

Clearly, because of the gap between what we know of neurological processes and what we experience at the level of language, cognition, behavior, and social exchange, descriptions and representations of cognition are of necessity metaphorical and schematic. Yet when the gap between heuristic devices and the apparent phenomena they are intended to elucidate widens, those devices are of questionable epistemic value. Advances in brain research have made faculty psychology an artifact of the nineteenth century; localist arguments about language centers, for instance, have been amended, as neurophysiology and neuroanatomy have revealed that while certain parts of the brain are central to particular aspects of language, capacities for oral and written communication are widely distributed across brain areas. If this is true of language, then surely the cognitive capacities of modern humans entail widely distributed and varied processes that are not well served by a model that envisions cognition as a matter of conceptually structured input spaces that contribute to and help create other linguistically mediated conceptual spaces.

Human knowledge is not primarily contained in spaces or packets, and it is probably not very helpful to think about or visualize it this way. Among other things, thinking about cognitive process in terms of spaces and packets encourages a view of cognition as, first, entirely conceptual and, second, language-governed. Fauconnier correctly asserts that "although language data, a richly structured signal emanating from the mind/brain, is in plentiful supply, it is often under-estimated scientifically and socially as a source of deeper insight into the human mind," and he claims further that "if language data is a signal operating on less accessible cognitive constructions, then it is fair to say that linguistic research has focused on the structure of the signal itself rather than on the nonlinguistic constructions to which the signal is connected."[13] Until Lakoff and Johnson introduced cognitive linguistics and the theory of conceptual metaphor, researchers did not explore language for evidence of cognitive structures. Cognitive linguistics forcefully suggests that cognition is relative to bodily understanding and orientation, that language reveals a deeper understanding of how we know. Conceptual blending likewise claims to reveal cognitive constructions below the level of language, yet analyses of integration impart a languagelike organization to conceptual inputs that quite likely misrepresents the elements in the blend.

For instance, let us return to the example of double-scope blending that I cited earlier from *The Way We Think*, "digging your own grave." Fauconnier and Turner assume that there are two input spaces, one related to death and burial and one related to unwitting failure, and that each has a separate event structure: in the first, death is the cause of the grave being dug and the body being buried, and in the second, the agent is the cause of his own failure. But it is not necessary to activate the event structures of burial rituals to comprehend "digging your own grave." More parsimoniously, a series of general associations contribute to comprehension, as does the explicit causal structure of the statement. Death and graves have negative connotations that are highlighted by the context, since Fauconnier and Turner present the statement as that of "a conservative parent who keeps his money in his mattress [expressing] disapproval of an adult child's investing in the stock market by saying 'You are digging your own grave'" (131). Given this scenario, and assuming that some discussion of the investments serves as a preamble to the parent's judgment or warning, the child might well process the message based on tone of voice and context alone, that is, without even listening to the words. Since this is a grown child, the dynamics of the relationship have a great deal to do with whether he or she is even listening. Any adult who stopped and thought about the sentence would be able to analyze its elements as do Fauconnier and Turner, but that does not mean that those conceptual packets are active in the comprehension or, for that matter, construction of such a phrase. Moreover, since this particular blend is a common expression in English-language culture, it probably does not involve more complex cognition on the speaker's part than the more literal "you're only hurting yourself."

Thus, while Fauconnier and Turner reasonably suggest that language can tell us some things about cognition, their method assumes that interpretive operations performed on language will reveal all of the elements and elucidate all of the processes of cognition. Without an adequate testing procedure, however, there is no way to prove that cognitive processes are isomorphic to the linguistic blends that are the subject of analysis. The lack of a testing procedure is problematic given the counterintuitive assumption that the brain must process, at varying levels of consciousness, the specific components of a conventional phrase or metaphor. Common sense suggests that so much cognitive effort devoted to decoding language in lieu of more holistic attention to the total situation would result in semantic impoverishment, for, quite simply, linguistic expression is, in some contexts, inexact or limited in importance. In fact, in a study of the extent to which root metaphors and conceptual mapping occur in everyday language use, Yeshayahu Shen and Noga Balaban found that "the fact that conventional metaphorical instantiations of a given metaphor appear in a given discourse does not seem to reflect a corresponding activation (in the producer's mind) of the root metaphor. . . . The conventional expressions we use in ordinary language may have acquired a conventional meaning of their own and do not necessarily rely on the activation of the complex mapping of what are assumed to be their corresponding root metaphors."[14] Rather, "the use of metaphors in unplanned discourse appears more like free, uncontrolled 'navigation' between a large number of root metaphors than a consistent elaboration of any unifying root metaphors. Indeed, special planning seems to be required to make discourse metaphorically coherent" (151).

Well before the emergence of cognitive linguistics, in fact, commentators, including George Orwell and Morse Peckham, pointed out that writers and speakers often use conventional phrases and metaphors to mask sloppy thinking or to mislead intentionally. As Orwell explains, "A newly invented metaphor assists thought by evoking a visual image, while on the other hand a metaphor which is technically 'dead' (e.g., *iron resolution*) has in effect reverted to being an ordinary word and can generally be used without loss of vividness. But in between these two classes there is a huge dump of worn-out metaphors which have lost all evocative power and are merely used because they save people the trouble of inventing phrases for themselves. . . . Incompatible metaphors are frequently mixed, a sure sign that the writer is not interested in what he is saying."[15] Politicians often use metaphor and overgeneralization to avoid specifics, but almost all of us use them now and then when it is hard to articulate a literal meaning. In the example discussed here, it may be emotionally easier and certainly more succinct to say "You're digging your own grave" than to state what the conservative parent imagines: "You will end up impoverished, homeless, and lonely, living in shelters and probably victimized by others in want." In using the conventional phrase, the parent expresses his fears without having to imagine them in the concrete detail that more literal expression requires. Among literary writers, Flannery O'Connor often overloads her characters' speech with clichés as a means of characterizing them dramatically. In the first pages of "Everything That Rises Must Converge," Mrs. Chestny has misgivings about her new hat but then affirms, "Well . . . you only live once and paying a little more for it, I at least won't meet myself coming and going," and then, trying to console Julian about his material prospects, she asserts, "I think you're doing fine. . . . You've only been out of school a year. Rome wasn't built in a day."[16]

Since Fauconnier and Turner state that the blending process is both commonplace and predominantly unconscious, I suspect that they would insist that even the most intellectually unimpressive mind is constructing such blends all the time. But it is not true that people have to respond to or comprehend the denotative meaning of an utterance to use it appropriately. Children who enter language-immersion programs between the ages of four and six can respond appropriately based on context, gesture, tone, and repetition without understanding a single word of the second language. Guided by context and motivated by the social desire to participate, they learn a second language with relative ease, because their experience is holistic. In fact, developmentally, all of us are exposed to language before we can understand a single word of any language. As we mature, our understanding of language becomes more sophisticated, varied, and exact, and we use it to sharpen distinctions and concepts, but our thinking is not then reducible to all that language enables us to do.

What level or specificity of perceived meaning is sufficient for the adequate comprehension of a phrase in any given situation? Responses to this question will differ according to the operant definition of *meaning*. Fauconnier defines *meaning construction* as "high-level, complex mental operations that apply within and across domains when we think, act, or communicate" (1). In other words, meaning is an intellectual, or even an intellectual's, activity. By contrast, the embodied view of mind assumes that "if we reduce meaning to words and sentences (or concepts and propositions), we miss or leave out where meaning really comes from" (Johnson, *Meaning*, 11). Rather than being confined to "high-level, complex mental operations," a pragmatic account claims, meaning is relative to its value in experience. As Johnson explains, "Sometimes our meanings are conceptually and propositionally coded, but that is merely the more conscious, selective dimension of a vast, continuous process of immanent meanings that involve structures, patterns, qualities, feelings, and emotions. An embodied view is naturalistic, insofar as it situates meaning within a flow of experience that cannot exist without a biological organism engaging its environment. Meanings emerge 'from the bottom up' through increasingly complex levels of organic activity; they are not the constructions of a disembodied mind" (10). In this embodied or ecological perspective, according to which "perception is the ability to derive meaning from sensory experience in order to guide adaptive behavior" (Gibbs, 42), meaning is an emergent property of the interaction between an organism's sensory and cognitive apparatus and the environment; it is inherent in the survival-oriented biases of perception and not a product of cognition acting on perception. The pursuit of meaning, then, is a basic function of survival and a continuous property throughout human experience; as such, it is a contributing feature to all acts of cognition, irrespective of their simplicity or complexity.

This pragmatic, embodied, and ecological definition of *meaning* seems to me consistent with the view that evolved organisms are purposefully engaged in their worlds and oriented in species-typical ways. Notwithstanding the extraordinary nature of human cultural evolution, much of what we find consciously meaningful and that we can conceptualize and articulate in a sophisticated fashion is co-extensive with ancient feelings, needs, and desires. For the parent and child engaged in the discussion about how to make the most of one's life savings, meanings are in play before the discussion begins. Indeed, this specific, personal history of the father and son emerges from our general evolutionary substrate of parent-child conflict. If the parent habitually criticizes the child, a history of bad feelings and perhaps a poor self-image have much to do with the situational meaning of "You're digging your own grave." Meaning in this instance, as in most, has little to do with the "high-level, complex mental operations" proposed by blending theory, and it is not hard to imagine a scenario in which the linguistic components of the phrase are not processed by either father or son.

As Dewey points out in his elucidation of the relational significance of an external event to a perceiver, "What provides the 'stimulus' is a whole act, a sensorimotor co-ordination; it is born from it as its matrix." And I would add that even though language often carries denotative content, the matrix always serves to structure meaning to one degree or another. In the "You're digging your own grave" scenario, the matrix is especially important to the determination of meaning because the relationship between the two participants has a particularly long and intimate history. If, driven by the desire to earn his father's love and approval, the son has worked long and hard putting himself through law school and earning a partnership in a respected law firm, he may respond, "That's the last straw." Emotion and habit form a crucial part of the matrix in this scene, in which incomprehension and mounting frustration on the one hand and desire for approval, mounting frustration, and, ultimately, rejection on the other largely structure meaning. Whereas the figures of speech themselves do have a complex conceptual origin, my suspicion is that none of the conceptual processing during or after this exchange has anything to do with graves, camels, or straw or how these concrete realities have come to be blended with unwitting failure, limited patience, and the like. Guided by emotion, father and son arrive at their respective conceptual understandings in this moment relative to their ongoing relationship, and the actual words (in the scenario as I have imagined it) are relatively unimportant.

Taken together, the specific emphases and omissions of conceptual blending have resulted in a theory of cognition that has much more in common with cognitivism than with second-generation cognitive science. In conceptual blend theory, the mind sorts and recombines conceptual inputs, and meaning is the result of this generally self-contained process.[17] Certainly, when Fauconnier and Turner assert that "language prompts for meaning," they are not incorrect; combining concepts and expressing them in language does indeed result in cues for new meanings. In fact, as I suggested in chapter 2, the specificity and sophistication of many or all high-level concepts is probably dependent upon language to one degree or another. The problem is that Fauconnier and Turner take the pattern of high-level, linguistically governed operations as characteristic of all cognition. One perhaps paradoxical result of this method of theorizing cognition is that mental processes appear enormously complex and simultaneously rather random, because the theorists have not articulated any constraints on, parameters for, or biases in mental processes.

In spite of strong disagreements about the evolved structure of the human mind, all evolutionary psychologists and most cognitive psychologists accept that mental operations, like behavior, have a species-typical orientation and that that orientation is the result of cognitive and behavioral biases that are conducive to survival. Whereas the theory of conceptual metaphor, which was the foundation of Turner's earlier project in cognitive rhetoric, asserted that meaning and metaphor had a bodily basis, conceptual blend theory does not posit any links between cognitive structures and bodily imperatives. As the evolutionary critic Joseph Carroll noted in 1999, criticizing the first of these two programs, "The central problem the cognitive rhetoricians have failed to solve is that of grounding the concept of 'domains' within some larger concept of human experience and cognition. In the work of Lakoff, Johnson, and Turner, the concept of domains remains nebulous and variable. . . . The closest Turner gets to a systematic order is an apparently random list of categories that he calls 'conceptual domains': eating, dress, learning, buildings, travel, combat, and plants."[18] As Turner has put aside the project of cognitive rhetoric in the pursuit of conceptual blend theory, the possibility of a behavioral-cognitive species logic underpinning conceptual domains has receded further into the background. This is in spite of the fact that he and Fauconnier provide a list of fifteen types and subtypes of vital relations in *The Way We Think,* including identity, change, time, space, and cause and effect. The resulting description of mind operating in an ecological vacuum does not put any limits on conceptual domains, much less posit their relative salience, because it provides no theoretical explanation for why certain domains or vital relations exist.

All in all, blending's supposition that structured concepts underlie all mentation conflicts with the notion of a situated, evolved organism motivated to survive in the matrix of experience. As Merlin Donald points out in his critique of Chomskyan linguistics, "The innovative, incomplete, ungrammatical, intuitive language of the streets, the trademark of humanity, so effortless and subtle, seems to violate all of [the] rules in one way or another. The average human is the exact opposite of an AI algorithm: full of knowledge, short on rules and exact denotations, harnessing language to the pragmatic end of expressing and expanding underlying knowledge" (24). In Donald's view, the minds, behaviors, and communication systems of modern humans are primarily pragmatic and intuitive; unlike computers, they are directed by "context and meaning" rather than by rules and concepts (23). Whereas the cognitive explosion that occurred between sixty thousand and thirty thousand years ago and resulted in the evolution of compositional language enabled humans to blend knowledge from previously compartmentalized social, technological, and natural domains, the species surely had the capacity well before that phase to make associations and inferences at lower levels of consciousness as it managed life in its changing environment. As the ecological psychologist Reed argues, thinking about a variety of things at different levels of consciousness simultaneously is probably a basic characteristic of human thought, whereas the capacity to channel cognition and to focus on one thing at a time is most likely learned through educational systems. It is unlikely that the loosely associative mode of cognition that precedes the evolution of extended consciousness and cognitive fluidity is a thing of the past. By contrast, the structured concepts that Fauconnier and Turner identify as the substrate of cognition upon which language acts in the construction of blends are, I would argue, largely a product of language itself.

Cognition, Consciousness, and the Modern Mind

Contemporary evolutionary accounts of the human mind all describe a complex organ whose structures and processes are the result, not of some preordained design or logic, but of adaptations and systems that evolved to solve environmental problems as they arose. In Donald's words, the highly differentiated and specialized architecture of the human brain-mind is "a mosaic structure of cognitive vestiges from earlier stages" of human evolution (3). Donald hypothesizes three major stages in the emergence of the modern mind from the primate mind and claims that a new representational system emerges with each stage. Although as it arises each stage subsumes the representational system of the previous stage, all three representational systems contribute to human cognition and behavior at our current evolutionary juncture.

Of central significance in the divergence of humans from primates was the evolution of expanded consciousness. With the exception of chimpanzees, most primates lack self-consciousness, which is the highest level of consciousness and a requirement for modeling the self in the environment. Without self-consciousness, creatures are limited to episodic culture and memory—bound to the present, the concrete immediacy of time and place, and capable of only a limited degree of conscious awareness. In the first transition away from primate culture, according to Donald, humans developed the capacity for mimesis. Donald defines pure mimetic skill or mimesis as "the ability to produce conscious, self-initiated, representational acts that are intentional but not linguistic" and includes among its constituents "tones of voice, facial expressions, eye movements, manual signs and gestures, postural attitudes, pattern whole-body movements [that can be used] to express many aspects of the perceived world."[19] Whereas the culture of *Homo afarensis*, of four million years ago, appears episodic, that of *Homo erectus* (1.8 million years ago) shows clear signs of mimetic skill. Anthropological evidence of toolmaking, fire use, coordinated seasonal hunting, rapid adaptation to new climates or ecologies, an intricate social structure, and primitive ritual all suggest mimetic skill and cultural developments far superseding those of episodic culture. These cultural achievements rely on the capacities for intentional representations; a generative, recursive capacity for mime; a voluntary, public communicative system; differentiation of reference; unlimited modeling of episodic events; and voluntary, auto-cued rehearsal. Mimetic skill is primarily visuomotor, supramodular, and unencapsulated; mimetic representation replaced episodic memory and became the governing system until the evolution of language. Today, the vestiges of mimetic mind and culture remain embedded in the modern mind.

With the evolution of language, humans made the transition from mimetic culture to mythic culture. Whereas a common hypothesis has been that the onset of the last ice age was the source of the selection pressure responsible for the evolution of *Homo sapiens sapiens* and the capacity for language, Donald points out that earlier migrations out of Africa, which took place under arduous conditions, did not result in selection pressure for language. Neanderthalers survived for hundreds of thousands of years, some in very harsh climates, before they either interbred with the ancestors of modern humans or were wiped out by them. Donald argues that the primary selection pressure was competition from rival hominids, which led, ultimately, to the survival of a single subspecies of humans, a unique feature of our species among mammals. Language evolved within an already existing human culture and was therefore grafted onto a functioning system. Although major anatomical changes in the vocal apparatus provide the means of a new communication system, they were not, in Donald's view, its cause: "Like bipedalism in the australopithecines, [the vocal apparatus] is probably only the tip of the iceberg, anatomical testimony to a more complex pattern of adaptation" (212). Like Fauconnier and Turner, Donald maintains that the cognitive changes are more basic than language. Moreover, he argues that "the primary human adaptation was not language *qua* language but rather integrative, initially mythical, thought" (215). Basing his argument on the considerable evidence for myth in Upper Paleolithic culture as well as in contemporary tribal cultures, Donald claims that "the myth is the prototypal, fundamental, integrative mind tool. It tries to integrate a variety of events in a temporal and causal framework. It is inherently a modeling device, whose *primary* level of representation is thematic" (215).

What functional explanation justifies the theory that language evolved for the purposes of myth? After all, mythic capability may well enable "the grand unifying synthesis of formerly disconnected, time-bound snippets of information," but it provides such syntheses by constructing narrative accounts of questionable validity. Yet Donald claims that the driving force behind language evolution was the capacity for such accounts, rather than the need for enhanced social and political organization or collective technology, even though language certainly improved these features of human society. Among the various causes of language emergence, it is myth, not the functional organization or system within which humans live, that augments sociality itself. In offering an account of origins tied to the ecological features of a group's existence, myth provides shared context and meaning for the way of life of a people. And as long as the mythic explanations provided do not contradict ecological conditions, their imaginative components are not harmful and simply contribute to the sense of group solidarity and emotional attachment among members. If one takes a long-term evolutionary view, then, Donald's proposal makes sense, for the enhancement of affiliative feeling throughout human evolution has been a profound mechanism of survival. The creation of collective technologies and refined sociopolitical structures may in fact depend on the enhanced sense of mutual attachment and meaning provided by myth. Furthermore, if myth was not of primary importance in the development of language, its ubiquity and perseverance are difficult to explain.

Myths always take narrative form, and whether or not one accepts that the drive toward integrative story was the chief cause of the evolution of language, it is hard to deny that myths emerge with language. This returns us to a point that I made in chapters 1 and 2: narrativity (narrative thinking) emerged in human evolution from the basic perception of causality, and in enhancing social and ecological understanding, narrativity provided the opportunity for goal-oriented thinking and action. The evolution of language set the stage for formalized, shared stories in addition to conversation and day-to-day narrativity, and these myths themselves, in articulating shared meaning, established the context for elaborated and coordinated action plans. Thus, narrative skill not only is very basic to human thinking but also permeates human life in all its facets. All of this further supports the view that narrativity operates at a general level of cognition rather than being structured within various inputs and packets, as Fauconnier and Turner claim. Following Donald, I would suggest that more ancient aspects of mind still operate within the modern mind and that dominant epistemic biases such as narrativity, which have remained pragmatically useful throughout evolution, operate within the holistic, embodied orientation of the organism in a loosely associative fashion. Recalling Hume's "three principles of connexion among ideas . . . *Resemblance, Contiguity* in time or place, and *Cause* or *Effect*" (*Enquiry,* 17)—a summary of the associationist psychological-philosophical tradition that, as I noted in chapter 2, clearly converges with current research positing strong causal and narrative cognitive predispositions—I surmise that all three are probably interdependent cognitive tools that served as the inferential basis for negotiating the environment long before they came to connect ideas.

In Donald's hypothesis, the final manifestation of the modern mind emerges with the transition to theoretic culture and the capacity for analytic, logicoscientific cognition. Unlike the first two stages in the evolution of human mind, this one is not premised on major biological change; in fact, this shift in human thinking has occurred too rapidly to be the product of biological evolution. Central to the development of analytic, logicoscientific culture is the development of external memory devices, which are preceded by three major cognitive innovations. First, pictorial cave paintings dating from about forty thousand years ago constitute visuographic invention, which is linked to both episodic and mimetic memory. These provide the initial evidence of the construction of a new visuographic path to external memory stores. Second, writing, which originated in trade about fifteen thousand years ago, is a distinctive development in which graphic symbols bearing no relationship to what they represent are employed to represent ideas directly. Cuneiform developed slowly from pictorial representations to symbols by about 8500 BC, gradually becoming phonetic and taking on linear, grammatical structure about 2800 BC (285–89). The emergence of accounting systems, lists, and syllabaries facilitated such skills as sorting and the identification of similarities, which previously had not been possible because of constraints on biological memory. While these external symbol systems greatly augmented human cognition, they required the memorization of a great many symbols and thus constituted a sizable burden on human memory. In time, however, "the invention of the phonetic alphabet reduced the memory load imposed by reading skill and allowed a much wider diffusion of literacy" (297). Phonetic alphabets not only reduced the number of visual symbols but linked written language to speech, and "the act of reading is thus directly plugged in to a specific auditory complement of the visual record" (299). Although this development might seem to suggest a biological linkage between writing and speech, Donald convincingly argues from the neuroscientific evidence that this is probably not the case. The refinement of symbolic codes and the consequent dissemination of their use went hand in hand with the development of the external symbolic storage system, which includes all written and symbolic artifacts and the institutions and technologies, such as libraries and computers, that maintain them and facilitate their use.

Donald's revolutionary claim is that the symbol systems and storage devices of theoretic culture inaugurate "a *hardware* change, albeit a nonbiological hardware change" in human memory. Reviewing the psychological research on working memory, Donald notes how troublesome the concept has been, because all evidence suggests that people can retain a quite limited amount of material in current memory at any give time. The development of the ESS therefore constitutes an entirely new form of memory that revolutionizes cognition, enabling extended mind. My work on this chapter is an obvious example of engagement in the ESS. I develop an argument that would be impossible without external memory stores, and I devise a further contribution to those stores as I draw on and use the symbols of the external symbolic storage system: phonetic writing, handwritten notes and copies of books, a computer, electronic databases, a word-processing program, and so on. Less obviously, almost everything in our day-to-day mode of modern life requires the ESS. The organization of items in a grocery store is enormously dependent on alphabetic, numeric, and pictoral symbols. Driving rests on proficient use of street and highway signs, traffic signals, directional signals, and the like, and all modern modes of travel depend on these. As Donald points out, formal education is largely devoted to teaching the use patterns of the ESS. "External memory," which includes "culturally transmitted memories that reside in other individuals," as well as external memory media, "is best defined in functional terms: it is the *exact* external analog of internal, or biological memory, namely, a storage and retrieval system that allows humans to accumulate experience and knowledge" (308, 309).

Donald's proposal that the development of visuosymbolic systems and the ESS constitute a major transition in cognition might at first seem compatible with Fauconnier and Turner's conceptual blend theory, which defines cognition as the blending of structured concepts deduced from language and other types of symbols. But Donald is insistent that "each of the three transitions [in human cognition] has involved the construction of an entirely novel, relatively self-contained representational adaptation—that is, a way of representing the human world that could support a certain level of culture and a survival strategy of the human race. Each style of representation acquired along the way has been retained, in an increasingly larger circle of representational thought. The result is, quite literally, a system of parallel representational channels of mind that can process the world concurrently" (357). People shift effortlessly between representational modes, and modern activities and cultural forms adopt aspects of all three systems. In "symposia or public lectures," for example, "all the elements of human cognitive evolution come into play":

> The symposium or lecture will take place in an established mimetic framework; the audience, lecturer, and outside world all understand the unwritten mimetic rules of behavior governing their roles in the event. The lecture proper usually combines a spoken narrative with pictorial, ideographic, and phonological visual devices, using all three visuographic channels. . . . The lecturer is also embedded in a social framework, replete with symbols and signs of status, credibility, and power. The audience and lecturer alternate between various media and cognitive levels. The lecturer says one thing while illustrating another, while the audience registers yet a third message, embedded in a complex fabric of communication surrounding the event. Other players in the symposium may use gestures, ideograms, analog models or logograms; logic might dominate, then induction. The minds of the participants harness every symbolic device the human race has painstakingly invented over the last 200,000 years, to the common end of modeling, in the external arena, some idea. (357)

The human mind that Donald describes, "a mosaic structure of cognitive vestiges from earlier stages," draws on the resources of its representational systems as they suit immediate circumstances. This is true of personal interactions as well as socially structured events. This is true of the "digging your own grave" scenario, for instance. The implied rules governing the conversation between father and son, as well as gestural communication, constitute its mimetic dimension, and the utterance itself is an extension of the narrative or mythic dimension constituted by the mutual story of their relationship. These two levels probably dominate the interaction, though perhaps the phrase itself and documents or facts related to investment transactions are keyed to the ESS and thus constitute the theoretic dimension of a logicocentric style of thought.

Donald presents a comprehensive proposal of the evolution of cognition that manages to account for its most significant, technically advanced components while simultaneously illustrating its continuity with biological evolution. His account of the human mind is far more pragmatically likely than that proposed by Fauconnier and Turner. First, at the level of symbolically coded information, the level of exclusive importance to Fauconnier and Turner, Donald maintains that much information is stored in external memory, the ESS, rather than in biological memory. Thus, because information and concepts can be stored externally, thinking need not impose the excessive cognitive load demanded by conceptual blend theory. Second, Donald describes cognition functionally and pragmatically, so that each representational system has an evolutionary and social utility. Prelinguistic, mimetic representation, which includes the voluntary modulation of vocal and facial expression, may have evolved "as part of a general adaptation for bringing emotional responses under the control of the voluntary movement systems" and enables the supplementation of emotional expressions, as well as their instrumental manipulation (183). Supersignaling one's emotional state or, indeed, feigning distress, anger, sorrow, and the like, has a cognitive component that is not, however, informationally or conceptually dense. Third, and perhaps most importantly for literary scholars, who tend to overstate the contribution of language to literary representation, Donald not only places language in the context of the evolution of cognition but distinguishes between the cognitive functions subserved by oral skills and those subserved by written skills. Donald's theory of cognitive evolution thus proposes that three forms of representation—mimetic, mythic, and theoretic—are successively grafted onto the episodic foundation that our earliest ancestors shared with primates. Although compositional language emerges in the second stage, it becomes virtually a new force in human cognition with the emergence of material symbolic systems.

Overall, while one might reasonably expect that the emergence of language would result in a more cohesive cognitive system, language has had instead a paradoxical role in human epistemology. The cultivation of reasoned discourse and the attainment of ever-higher levels of education inclines us—especially those of us who spend our professional lives in an arena in which linguistically driven conceptualization dominates—to sympathize with the model of cognition provided by conceptual blend theory, but the research of evolutionists and embodiment theorists suggests that cognition is far more multifaceted than that theory claims. Even though the entire impulse of an organism is to orient itself in a way that perceptual, somatic, and cognitive information can be combined to provide unified insight and action, the process involved appears rather piecemeal, dependent upon a jerry-rigged brain, whose more recent biological structures and neurological processes function in conjunction with far older parts. Extended mind—our mind—of which all literature is product and portion, results from all these structures and processes. Given this complexity—three simultaneously engaged representational systems, various levels of consciousness, and the central role of feeling in cognition—how can we understand a single act of cognition, much less analyze the cognitive process of an individual literary text?

Rather than applying a single model of conceptual processing, attending to the situational context of cognition should provide relevant keys to the interpretation of the mental act. Acts of cognition have very different motivational sources and thus vary in accordance with the motivation. For instance, Fauconnier and Turner posit a familial relationship as the occasion for the use of the truism "digging your own grave," which leads me to claim that because of the emotionally laden situation and the conventionalism of the phrase, the words themselves have relatively little importance in the emergent meaning for either speaker. But "digging your own grave" is in many respects an atypical example for Fauconnier and Turner, who draw on riddles, newspaper editorials, visually blended symbols, and logical problems to illustrate their points. Thus, many of their examples are the products of recent, ESS-governed cognition, and nearly all are contextualized by an ESS-governed process low on emotion rather than an affectively loaded, familial one. This is true of the "Iron Lady and the Rust Belt" example, which analyzes the blends underlying the response, in the 1990s, to the claim that the United States needed its own Margaret Thatcher: "But Margaret Thatcher would never get elected here because the labor unions can't stand her" (18–19). In this case, the sentence cannot serve its purpose without the auditor's or reader's having knowledge of Thatcher and capacity to understand a hypothetical situation in which she ran for president of the United States. Emotion might be a factor in processing the response, depending on the political commitments of the conversationalists and the total context of their exchange, but the nature of the emotional involvement would be different in kind from that in the "digging your own grave" scenario. Because written language is crucial to drawing precise distinctions, creating precise and stable categories, and specifying concepts, double-scope blending may provide a very accurate explanation of the Iron Lady blend. This blend arises in and is primarily understood in relation to the modern culture made possible by external storage systems, and it does not seek to express nonlinguistic levels of cognition and emotion. Double-scope blending may well provide an accurate description of how novel concepts that depend on language emerge for thinkers versed in the relevant cultural context.

Every action must be understood within the matrix of experience, as Dewey suggests, and cognition is a form of action and thus a reminder that the body and the external world are the condition of all thought and therefore integral to it. But we tend to hide the body and the visceral responses that are the precondition and motivation for the lowest to highest levels of consciousness. Why? As Damasio explains, "I could describe the hiding of the body as a distraction, but I would have to add that it is a very adaptive distraction. In most circumstances, rather than concentrating resources on our inner states, it is perhaps more advantageous to concentrate one's resources on the images that describe problems out in the world or on the premises of those problems or on the options for their solution and their possible outcomes" (29). Hiding the body is apparently endemic and systematic: "One of the chief ways the body hides from our conscious awareness," claims Johnson, "is a result of what Michael Polanyi (1969) called the 'from-to' character of perception. All our acts of perception are directed *to* or *at* what is experienced and *away from* the body doing the perceiving. This is what phenomenologists call the *intentionality* of the mind. In Polanyi's words, 'Our body is the only assembly of things known almost exclusively by relying on our awareness of them for attending to something else. . . . Every time we make sense of the world, we rely on our tacit knowledge of impacts made by the world on our body and the complex responses of our body to these impacts'" (*Meaning*, 4–5). Although, as Damasio claims, current neurobiology suggests that some parts of the brain are free to roam over and map the world, while others are "stuck" on internal states, a simple evolutionary logic dictates the concentration of perception, cognition, and consciousness on external phenomena. Simply put, because the great challenges to survival come overwhelmingly from outside the individual organism, directing attention outward serves organismic fitness, as the evolution of perceptual systems and cognitive predispositions for environmental exploration attests.

The construction of meaning takes place in the matrix of experience, as the organism already active in the environment processes information under the direction of species-typical and individual biases and directives, orienting intentionally toward affordances (opportunities for action) of perceived significance to the organism. Damasio's conception of the emergence of consciousness and the self provides a phenomenological account grounded in neuropsychology that harmonizes with Donald's account of increasingly complex cognition supported by several representational systems. For humans, feelings and emotions direct attention to external and internal situations, and consciousness originates in the feeling of knowing, of making an image, which Damasio defines as "a mental pattern in any of the sensory modalities, e.g., a sound image, a tactile image, the image of a state of well-being" (9). Like other animals, humans are motivated first and foremost by feelings: hunger directs us to the acquisition of food, exhaustion to sleep, sadness to withdrawal, and so on. Like these, the feeling of knowing or image-making serves the interest of higher organisms, but unlike these, it has the capacity, over evolutionary time, to propel the evolution of three necessarily intertwined features of human mind: higher consciousness, cognitive complexity, and the autobiographical self. The feeling of knowing, I want to suggest, is in some respects different in kind from many other feelings, for even that first glim-mering awareness of internal processes directed toward regulating interaction with the environment must have felt good, betokening potential release from time-bound episodic memory and heralding the mastery and independence that come with placing the self and present circumstances within a larger trajectory of events.

Ontogenetically and phylogenetically, then, the first somatic response to know-ing constitutes the initial stage in a causal process from which consciousness emerges in successive levels of complexity. The most basic form of consciousness enables the connection of image-making and life-regulating processes, leading in evolutionary time and over the individual life span to the capacity for a far more sophisticated level of life regulation that includes "complex, flexible, and custom-ized plans of response [that] are formulated in conscious images and may be executed as behavior"—a far cry from the "relatively simple, stereotyped patterns of response [that constitute the most basic level of life regulation, including] metabolic regulation, reflexes, [and] the biological machinery behind what will become pain and pleasure, drives and motivations" (Damasio, 55). Reaching this level of life regulation depends upon a complex sense of self, for if "consciousness is knowledge, knowledge consciousness," then the protoself (a nonconscious en-semble of brain activities that maintain a state conducive to survival) is not suf-ficient as a knower, nor is the transient core self, which is endlessly re-created in the interaction with external objects and corresponds to core consciousness, awareness of the here and now. Because the sense of self provides continuity of reference, an orienting point for all that consciousness encompasses, the autobio-graphical self is a necessary correlate to extended consciousness. Extended con-sciousness, with its entailment of a complex, autobiographical self, enables a sense of the self in historical time and a keen sense of the world around it.

One cognitive predisposition is especially important to the function of con-sciousness and the constitution of an autobiographical self. As Damasio asks,

How do we ever begin to be conscious? Specifically, how do we ever have a sense of self in the act of knowing? We begin with a first trick. The trick con-sists of constructing an account of what happens within the organism when the organism interacts with an object, be it actually perceived or recalled, be it within body boundaries (e.g., pain) or outside them (e.g., landscape). This account is a simple narrative without words. It does have characters (the or-ganism, the object). It unfolds in time. And it has a beginning, a middle, and an end. The beginning corresponds to the initial state of the organism. The middle is the arrival of the object. The end is made up of reactions that result in a modified state of the organism.

We become conscious, then, when our organisms internally construct and internally exhibit a specific kind of wordless knowledge—that our organism has been changed by an object—and when such knowledge occurs along with the salient internal exhibit of an object. The simplest form in which this knowledge emerges is the feeling of knowing. (168–69)

Damasio's hypothesis, that core consciousness is the result of "an imaged, nonverbal account" (169), suggests that the causal rule—a predisposition to constructing a linear sequence of causally related events—is a necessary precondition for "the feeling of knowing" and thus for consciousness itself. This "simple narrative without words" is the prelinguistic emergence into consciousness of narrativity (narrative thinking). Of course, with the evolution of language, this "simple narrative without words" becomes the basis of a story or, more likely, bits of several stories, processed linguistically at a higher level of consciousness. While our inclination to hide or minimize the importance of the body tempts us to think that basic human epistemology and consciousness might have transcended their bodily basis with the potent, abstract medium of language, research in language and communication suggests that the structures and meanings of language are tied to perception and action. With respect to the immediate point, numerous studies indicate that language adheres to the basic causal, storylike nature of thought. Gibbs observes that "people translate words and sentences into a flow of events comparable to normal perceptual experiences. For instance, researchers argue that the words in which events are represented in language reflect their chronological order" (Gibbs, 178). The fact that we might see such a point as self-evident further underscores how deeply engrained bodily experience is in language.

In keeping with this, although Donald is surely correct to suggest that the evolution of writing inaugurates a new phase in human cognition, propelling the development of theoretic culture, he never claims that structured concepts and logic have come to dominate cognitive processes. Much to the contrary, contending that the transition to theoretic culture, whose first stage is demythologization, is still in process, Donald describes the modern mind thus: "The introduction of the new visual mechanisms of the third transition, which constitute a variety of access routes to external memory, changed cognitive architecture completely, since there were now mental vehicles not only for externalizing working memory but also for pooling the outputs of the three innate representational systems. The governing *biological* system was still the oral-narrative system; but it was embedded in a larger, partly external, structure" (306–7).

Keeping in mind that the last two phases in human cognition (mythic and theoretic) have occurred within the last sixty thousand to thirty thousand years, and assuming for the moment that humans will survive for many millions of years (a large assumption, admittedly), it is theoretically possible that the biological system itself will take on a logicoscientific structure. But I think this is unlikely. Narrative knowing is so fundamental to pragmatic negotiation of the nonhuman world and the social world because it works to make sense of things and to provide social cohesion. Oral and written narratives augment the sense-making capacity and social-bonding functions of narrative thinking and holistic, mimetic communication many times over, because they constitute refined and specific mechanisms for establishing the content of stories and disseminating them and as a consequence enable a detailed account of the basis of group identity. If the sociality of primitive humans and animals results from feelings that motivate cooperative behaviors, then myth might be said to provide a cognitive component and complement to those behaviors. While our governing narratives many become more secular and fact based than those of past cultures, cultural narratives are, in effect, a basic element of modern social cohesion. Without that sense of cohesion, theoretic culture has no purpose.

Given this complexity, how do we make sense of a single act of cognition? First, humans are knowledge-seeking organisms, as Kaplan says, and because knowing became adaptively crucial millions of years ago, motivating them to sustain a coherent, autobiographical self, a higher consciousness, and cognitive complexity, knowledge feels particularly good to humans. Second, the self creates meaning as it brings together perception, somatic response, memory, and inference, and the cognitive predisposition most basic to this process of meaning-making is narrativity. Narrativity itself is not necessarily a conscious phenomenon, but frequently basic narrativity, the construction of "what happens within the organism when the organism interacts with an object," pushes toward a higher level of consciousness. For instance, whereas a walk to the end of the driveway to retrieve the morning paper does not usually entail encounters that prompt conscious narrativizing, walkers and runners who observe stray dogs on the river levee are likely to construct brief internal, linguistic narratives that include an action plan for coping with a potentially dangerous situation. Third, in the process of constructing the account, the person engages in a broadly associative process, attempting to bring all input into satisfactory relation. Again, at the higher levels of consciousness, bodily based metaphors and conceptual blends emerge within the larger narrative context.

As Turner puts it in *The Literary Mind*, "Narrative imagining—story—is the fundamental instrument of thought. Rational capacities depend upon it. It is our chief means of looking into the future, of predicting, of planning, and of explaining."[20] But in this book, written after *Reading Minds* and before his joint endeavor with Fauconnier, *The Way We Think*, Turner does not explain how these claims about narrative square with his earlier work on the fundamentally bodily based nature of metaphors. Maintaining that the mind constructs and projects small, spatial stories (parables), Turner describes story as a local, immediate process rather than a governing predisposition. While we do indeed construct small narratives all the time, and sometimes project these narratives from one situation to another, the human mind is engaged in a continuous, narrativizing process that incorporates smaller observations and associations. It is this propensity to organize causally related sequences of events that most fundamentally guides us through the matrix of experience.

But at the same time, as Dewey's metaphor of the matrix perhaps implicitly suggests, moments of existence are not only varied and textured but comprehended in the context of past experience and the operant sense of self. Thus, even though the mind operates selectively on perceptions, facts, and memories from all that is available to it, the narrative construction of experience, which in a functional system must be aligned with the thinker's self-narrative (i.e., the internally accepted autobiographical account of the self), requires not only the assimilation of many disparate facts but the alignment of the self-narrative with external sequences of events and stories. Particularly for modern humans, who think within the structures of extended cognition, the available wealth of information and of varied narrative accounts often lends complexity but also enables coherence in the construction of linear accounts and action plans. In instances where there is too much conflict among narrative sequences and disparate facts, that very wealth of information and of conflicting accounts can destabilize the autobiographical self, requiring a reconstruction of the self-narrative in keeping with the present situation. Since the autobiographical self—the organism's constructed account of its essence and history—is the fundamental point of reference for acts of higher cognition, its re-regulation or reformulation in moments of crisis is a necessary starting point for cognitively coherent, ongoing accounts and thus for high-level life regulation. With the development of theoretic culture and the extended cognition it facilitates, refined and sometimes recorded accounts of the autobiographical self become not only possible but perhaps even necessary. The consequences of the Enlightenment—including the rise of democratic individualism, the movement toward mandatory public education, and the emergence of psychology as an independent discipline—provided additional impetus for a complex story of the human self, because a modern, autobiographical self generates the personal structures of meaning that enable self-determination and promote the fulfillment of individual responsibilities. If on the one hand extended consciousness has enabled reflection on, and creative depiction of, the process of self-orientation and the construction of cognitive coherence, on the other the social changes of the past several hundred years have made such cognitive and creative activities inevitable.

In the Literary Matrix: Cognitive Ecological Process

A work of literature is never simply a linguistic account of experience; it is an intentional act of communication, and thus it entails the construction or refashioning of experience for some communicative purpose. While of the two works I analyze in the remainder of this chapter, Coleridge's "Dejection: An Ode" and Raymond Carver's "I Could See the Smallest Things," one is an autobiographically based poem and the other is a fictional story, both nevertheless trace the epistemic process of a developing consciousness or awareness that has consequences for the self-narratives of the first-person narrators. These works are, in other words, aesthetically organized imitations of the process of life regulation, and as such they draw on formal and thematic aspects of language that reflect perceived actuality, but they do so in a highly selective fashion. For whereas "people will experience only those aspects of the world to which they are attending" and "often fail to notice changes in the environment that are quite large and in full view" (Gibbs, 66), any linguistic event is, by contrast, the product of prior attentional selection. That is, language is a humanly evolved phenomenon, and thus human priorities organize its structures and the contexts of its use. Far from being a mirror held up to reality, then, a linguistic utterance or written document cannot depend on the selective habits or intentions of the speaker or writer. Even if the goal of many works of art is to trigger responses that are similar to actual somatic and emotional responses, with the ultimate aim of producing conscious, cognitive insight, as I am claiming is the case with the literary texts I discuss here, authors must select and arrange those features carefully, because readers tracking experiences in language are not prepared to filter out extraneous features.

In spite of the significant differences between oral and written communication, the considerable expansion of cognition with the development of symbolic systems, and the selective processes of authorial invention, our basic cognitive mode of approaching literature or any potential object of knowledge is that of the wayfinder, and thus isomorphic to that of real-world negotiation. In other words, readers seek knowledge within the ecologies they inhabit.[21] Moreover, in works that dramatize the process of consciousness specifically, such as Coleridge's poem and Carver's story, the textual structures themselves mimic the movement of minds toward knowledge, which coheres with the epistemic process of a person's moving through a geographical domain. Humans narrativize in time and space, certainly, but only then in an environment rich in affordances, the objects, substances, and beings in relation to which knowing is necessary and action is possible. Literature mimics this feature of experience as well: all aspects of the text that refer to the concrete dimension of perceived reality, whether they be descriptive, imagistic, metaphoric, or symbolic, serve a crucial function, providing opportunities for (cognitive) action, because they are aspects of the domain within which the narrators, characters, and readers map the ongoing story. Just as Kaplan concludes that people appear to project themselves into pictures when they are determining environmental preference, making judgments based on how they could function in the visually perceived environment, I am claiming that readers perform a like projection into a text and that objects or objectlike elements are both part of the necessary basis of that projection and a prerequisite to knowledge in literature.[22]

In both works under discussion here, the authors direct the epistemic process of the reader via identification with a first-person speaker.[23] In both, something outside the speaker triggers a bodily change or adjustment that results in feelings that focus attention and, in consequence, motivate and guide reasoning processes. Like most literature that takes as its subject the epistemic process (the emergence into higher consciousness of something to be known), these works begin by directing the narrative impulse, which initially operates below the level of consciousness, toward a problem in consciousness. This happens in both the dramatic situation of each work as well as in the cognitive process of the reader. But although the reader's process is parallel to and largely tracks those of the first-person speakers, it is artificial (in comparison with everyday cognition) in that the intentionally structured literary environment constrains and guides the epistemic process. Furthermore, while narrativity and concrete objects or places are root dimensions of most imaginative literature that derive from a knowledge-seeking, wayfinding epistemology, they have the capacity to operate with enhanced epistemic viability in literature, for several reasons: they have been intentionally selected by the author; they are purely cognitive and thus divorced from direct practical consequences; and they are dynamically integrated with the ESS, which expands memory capacity through symbolic support and thus facilitates knowledge of depth and complexity. Added to the necessarily selective nature of linguistic expression, the literary result is carefully arranged verbal environments that not only permit the violation of physical and temporal rules of real-world experience but also exploit such violations to enhance the epistemic process and affect higher consciousness.[24]

The great insight of cognitive linguistics and semantics is that humans are constitutionally inclined to think in terms of bodily relations in a concrete reality and that they do not let go of bodily based cognition even when matters under consideration seem purely internal, that is, psychological or intellectual. I am suggesting that not only the contents of literate thought but also its structures and processes cohere with bodily based experience. Space and time are key, integral requirements for narrativity, and the sense of place, of the bodily relationship, provided by concrete elements consequently assists the feeling of "something to be known." These operate as affordances (opportunities for action) within the text, as the narrativizing reader, working in a broadly associative manner on all aspects of the textual environment, processes and assimilates them in the act of constructing meaning.[25] Like many of the conceptual blends that Fauconnier and Turner discuss, the complex conceptual associations and transformations—the cognitive action, as it were—of many literary works typically depend on a level of thinking and memory capacity that is only possible in literate culture.

Vines and Vipers: Re-regulation in Coleridge's "Dejection"

As Charles S. Bouslog commented in 1963, Coleridge's "Dejection: An Ode" is "one of the least self-contained of famous poems," since the source of the feeling that is its subject lies in the background narratives of Coleridge's relationship with Wordsworth's family circle, as well as in his personal past, and since the poem's form, imagery, and narrative by turns derive from, allude to, and comment upon the same dimensions of Wordsworth's first four stanzas of the Immortality ode.[26] The fact that "Dejection" is a drastic revision of an earlier, semiprivate verse letter and a response to an ode the majority of which would not be completed until two years later makes it especially uncontained in some respects. Put in terms of pragmatic, embodied cognition, the matrix of experience from which the poem emerges and that it simulates is particularly complex, and this accords with the multi-faceted cognitive process Coleridge refashions for his reader's participation.

At the time that Coleridge wrote "Dejection," in 1802, he was in daily contact with Wordsworth and his family circle, which included Mary Hutchinson, soon to be married to William, and Mary's sister Sara. Coleridge himself had married another woman, Sara Fricker, in 1795, the consequence of the ill-begotten scheme between himself and Robert Southey to found a "pantisocracy," an ideal community, along the banks of the Susquehanna River in Pennsylvania. Yet by 1802 Coleridge was in love with Sara Hutchinson, Wordsworth's future sister-in-law. In the private verse letter written probably on the nights of April 4–5, 1802, Coleridge addresses Sara directly, expressing his love for her, his frustration over and guilt about his own domestic woes, and his philosophical differences with Wordsworth. This unequivocal source poem for "Dejection," "A Letter to Sara Hutchinson," lay in the Dove Cottage archives undiscovered and unpublished until the mid-twentieth century.[27]

The existence of "A Letter" makes it possible to infer some of Coleridge's intentions in turning a private communication into a publishable poem. Although "A Letter" apparently was never meant for Sara's eyes only—Mary Hutchinson had copied it in April 1802, and Coleridge shared it with Wordsworth and other close friends in the several weeks after writing it—its lack of focus and level of personal revelation clearly suggest that it is addressed to a restricted audience of intimate acquaintances. By contrast, "Dejection: An Ode," published in the *Morning Post* on October 4, 1802, is 139 lines long, less than half the length of the original verse letter. Coleridge eliminated all the material in the original that was either too self-pitying or too private to engage the reader, while retaining and adding concrete description and figurative language, including the descriptions of the storm and the evening sky and the metaphors of the luminous cloud and mist, the twining vine, and the viper thoughts. These features operate as affordances in the text, that is, opportunities for action, which in this case means cognitive action directed toward insight and critical to establishing the somatic basis of the reader's response. In effect, through careful selection Coleridge strengthens the cognitive dimensions of the poem and in so doing simulates the matrix of his experience for the reader.

Coleridge's transformation of "A Letter" into "Dejection" illustrates how literature simultaneously requires enough dimensions of evolved cognition for the reader to enter an imagined sense of spatiotemporal reality and relies on aspects of cognition not possible in a natural, prelinguistic environment. Of course, the degree to which a work of literature depends on theoretic culture varies widely, but once a text is written, rather than simply transcribed, it will exhibit signs of its connection to extended cognitive structures. Throughout the poem, Coleridge employs the resources of extended cognition to dramatize conscious reflection on and creative depiction of the process of re-regulation of the self and the construction of cognitive coherence. Since the poem begins in a moment of foreboding that foreshadows both external and internal crisis, it arouses a vicarious anxiety in the reader that motivates interest in the plight of the speaker. As David Miall and Don Kuiken conclude based on empirical studies of reader processing, "Enactive readers progressively transform an affective theme across striking or evocative passages, becoming implicated in the existential concerns embodied in those passages."[28] So, too, the autobiographical speaker Coleridge depicts longs for a way forward. First and foremost, then, in this literary depiction of a mind in the process of reassembling the self, feeling guides reasoning processes, pushing toward the construction of an account, that is, a narrative about what has happened and what will occur in the future.

The title, epigraph, and first stanza of Coleridge's poem introduce the perceptive reader to three different but interrelated narrative strands that, in combination, suggest the difficulty of straightforward story, that is, of a linear sequence of causally related events progressing toward a realizable goal. (The reader who knows something of the biographical and literary background of the poem will have an even keener sense of the contextual dimensions that confound sequential story.) Immediately following the title of the poem, the epigraph from "Sir Patrick Spence" recounts the ill omen's being reported to Sir Patrick by one of the sailors:

Late, late yestreen I saw the new Moon,
With the old Moon in her arms;
And I fear, I fear, my Master dear!
We shall have a deadly storm.

The contrast between Coleridge's title ("Dejection: An Ode") and the epigraph—the one suggesting a lyric meditation on sadness, the other forecasting violent weather—signals the contrast between the speaker's perception of external reality and his emotional state, a contrast Coleridge makes explicit in the first stanza:

Well! If the Bard was weather-wise, who made
    The grand old ballad of Sir Patrick Spence,
    This night, so tranquil now, will not go hence
Unroused by winds, that ply a busier trade
Than those which mold yon cloud in lazy flakes,
Or the dull sobbing draft, that moans and rakes

Upon the strings of this Æolian lute,
   Which better far were mute.
  For lo! The New-moon winter-bright!
  And overspread with phantom light,
  (With swimming phantom light o'erspread
  But rimmed and circled by a silver thread)
I see the old Moon in her lap, foretelling
  The coming-on of rain and squally blast.
And oh! That even now the gust were swelling,
  And the slant night-shower driving loud and fast!
Those sounds which oft have raised me, whilst they awed,
  And sent my soul abroad,
Might now perhaps their wonted impulse give,
Might startle this dull pain, and make it move and live!   (ll. 1–20)

Here Coleridge establishes a relationship between three possibly connected stories: that of his dejection, that of the apparently impending storm outside the window, and that of Sir Patrick Spence. From among the various strands of story, the reader likely selects the speaker's dilemma as the primary narrative, for reasons of innate predisposition and convention. The title, of course, announces a state of feeling as the poem's focus and theme, thus directing attention to the speaker; moreover, while the epigraph alludes to another narrative, convention indicates that epigraphs serve a range of functions with varying degrees of importance. However, even without these signposts to the primary strand of the narrative, readers would focus on the plight of the speaker simply because the self is the essential point of reference for perception and action. Thus, in his or her projection of self into the text, the reader identifies with the speaker's distress, for it is only in relation to this particular self within the poem that the reader can navigate and construct meaning within the textual environment.

The ballad stanza evokes the story of Sir Patrick, who reads the portent correctly and meets his end along with the Scots lords in the violent storm. The relevance of this narrative to Coleridge's poem is ambiguous at the outset, but in the long run the ballad's simple, externalized progression acts as a foil to the problematic progression in "Dejection." In the ballad, the "old Moon in [the new Moon's] arms" is an unequivocal affordance for Sir Patrick, and the meaning he derives from it is correct, but unfortunately, his culture does not allow the sailor to act on the meaning he forbodes, bound as he is to his king's command. Because of the externalized nature of ballad narrative and its related psychological flatness, the experience of the reader or hearer of "Sir Patrick Spence" fundamentally parallels that of the characters in the poem. As the point of departure for "Dejection," the ballad functions in ironic contrast to the story of Coleridge's speaker, who cannot identify or make use of legitimate affordances outside himself. However, *Coleridge's reader* has a different experience from that of *the poem's speaker.* That experience of the poem's potential affordances is twofold until stanza 6. Whereas in the first five stanzas descriptions and metaphors that are possible opportunities for cognitive action become, instead, obstacles to joy and comprehension for the speaker, the reader experiences both the positive mood and insight that these features elicit and the speaker's frustration and failure.

Just as the fatalistic story of "Sir Patrick Spence" bears an ambiguous relationship to the poem's present situation, in the first stanza the implications of the actual weather for the speaker's emotional crisis are uncertain. Even as the speaker reports the current atmospheric tranquility, he colors the scene with his own anxiety and restlessness, injecting signs of the anticipated storm into the present moment of calm. For instance, in foreseeing winds that "ply a busier trade," he seems to conflate the mild winds of early evening with the tumultuous ones that will, presumably, follow. The "dull sobbing draft," which is grammatically parallel to "winds" and thus placed in the future, nevertheless takes present-tense verbs, as it "moans and rakes / Upon the strings of this Æolian lute, / Which better far were mute." Ideally, the secondary narratives of the ballad and the developing weather would be subordinated and assimilated to the primary story, that of the speaker's dejection. The troubling emotional state and the problematically related narrative elements that Coleridge introduces in the first stanza provide the basis of "something to be known," motivating the reader to comprehend the speaker's "dull pain" and to see it resolved via a cohesive narrative account resulting in a re-regulation of the self.

It is clear, then, by the end of the first stanza, that the narrative focus is an internal and subjective one, for the primary story the reader pursues is the cause of dejection, the reason for its persistence, and its ultimate outcome. In the course of the narrative, both the perceived physical reality outside the window and the poet's metaphorical constructions operate as affordances—in this case opportunities for internal action, a change in the state of the self resulting from the ongoing process of meaning-making. One of the considerable ironies of this quest is that while it seems dependent upon a belief in natural and social realities outside the self, those realities cannot act on the speaker independent of his perception and self-understanding. Because the speaker distrusts internal representations of external objects, they lack the power to change him in the way that he wishes.

Whereas the speaker's ability to imagine the storm while the night is yet serene hints that the imagination itself will produce the objects effecting transformation—as, in fact, is eventually the case—the concrete elements in the poem repeatedly fail to rouse the poet from inertia and hopelessness.

Stanzas 1 and 2 perhaps most vividly illustrate the twofold experience of the reader, for whom the imagery evokes emotional effects that the speaker himself denies. In these stanzas, Coleridge further elaborates the imbalance between inner and outer, wherein the most vividly described beauty of the evening affords no opportunity for change in the speaker's emotional state. In contrast to the first stanza, where his imagination rushes out to fill the calm evening with the specter of the storm to come, the description of the evening sky in stanza 2 is apparently precise and uncomplicated by fevered anticipation:

> All this long eve, so balmy and serene,
> Have I been gazing on the western sky,
>   And its peculiar tint of yellow green:
> And still I gaze—and with how blank an eye!
> And those thin clouds above, in flakes and bars,
> That give away their motion to the stars;
> Those stars, that glide behind them or between,
> Now sparkling, now bedimmed, but always seen:
> Yon crescent Moon, as fixed as if it grew
> In its own cloudless, starless lake of blue;
> I see them all so excellently fair,
> I see, not feel, how beautiful they are!
>
> (ll. 27–38)

As A. Harris Fairbanks observes, the poem takes place over the course of an entire evening, a fact that readers are likely to overlook given that moments of perception and insight are selected out for attention in Coleridge's psychological narrative.[29] Nevertheless, the lapse of time marked by the break between stanzas 1 and 2 helps account for the increased calm that accedes to the resigned conclusion of stanza 3, where the hope of emotional revitalization through nature is futile, since, the autobiographical speaker says, "I may not hope from outward forms to win / The passion and the life, whose fountains are within" (ll. 45–46). Because he has become, as he will finally demonstrate, too cut off from mind-independent reality to make use of its affordances, his perceptions cannot help reorganize the self. Although that is exactly how the story develops, the narrative seems arrested, I think, because visualizing the image of moving stars (as a competent reading of the poem requires) will typically evoke awe and pleasure, because it conjures up the phenomenon of induced movement, resulting from the expectation that the main part of the visual field will remain stable.[30] In the end, the reader will simultaneously experience the capacity for traveling stars to mitigate despair and the speaker's inability to feel what he so affectingly describes.

The first stanzas, then, illustrate the speaker's difficulty in availing himself of affordances and subsequently deriving meaning from the matrix of experience that would precipitate the re-regulation of the self. But although the speaker makes no progress through his psychological terrain, the reader has begun to construct a story through causal inferences and the speaker's assertion that his lack of psychological resources prevents progress. In stanzas 4 and 5 Coleridge deepens this sense of obstruction through a series of interrelated metaphors that draw on the autobiographical context of the poem and, in so doing, expands the poem's experiential matrix. Unlike the first two stanzas, where the speaker's anticipated image of the storm and the stars in the calm night sky are vividly evoked for the reader, the intertwined metaphors of stanzas 4 and 5 reveal the speaker's overactive imagination. These new metaphors are introduced as he directly addresses Sara for the first time in stanza 4:

> O Lady! we receive but what we give,
> And in our life alone does Nature live:
> Ours is her wedding garment, ours her shroud!
> And would we aught behold, of higher worth,
> Than that inanimate cold world allowed
> To the poor loveless ever-anxious crowd,
> Ah! from the soul itself must issue forth
> A light, a glory, a fair luminous cloud
> Enveloping the Earth—
> And from the soul itself must there be sent
> A sweet and potent voice, of its own birth,
> Of all sweet sounds the life and element!   (ll. 47–58)

Coleridge first and foremost complicates the experiential matrix through his allusions to both Wordsworth's work and his life. The basic idea of the stanza develops the assertion of the preceding one, that "genial spirits" (meaning both *good* and *creative* spirits) or "joy" is not bestowed by nature but must issue from the self. The marriage of a mind that, in Wordsworth's phrase, is "creator and receiver both" to the natural world is premised, Coleridge insists, on the psychological resources of the individual (*Prelude,* bk. 2, l. 273). But here the conventional metaphors of wedding garment and shroud, betokening the character of different minds' unions with nature, points attention to facts outside the text, for the publication date in 1802 is that of both Wordsworth's wedding and Coleridge's wedding anniversary.[31] Following this, the wedding garment—a metaphor for what the speaker cannot project onto the world to effect a happy marriage—gives way to that of "A light, a glory, a fair luminous cloud / Enveloping the Earth—."[32] This image alludes unambiguously to the opening lines of Wordsworth's Immortality ode, which Coleridge had read only days before writing "A Letter," the source poem for "Dejection":

> There was a time when meadow, grove, and stream,
> The earth, and every common sight,
>   To me did seem
>   Apparell'd in celestial light,
> The glory and the freshness of a dream.[33]

In stanza 6 of "Dejection" Coleridge argues via a countermetaphor that the divine light shed on the natural world is not only a product of individual psychological resources but also salutary because it potentially obscures more than it reveals. The clarity suggested by Wordsworth's "celestial light" mutates into "a fair luminous cloud / Enveloping the Earth" in Coleridge's hands, a light that is beautiful because it veils the contours of mind-independent reality. Finally, in the last lines of the stanza, Coleridge refigures this "luminous cloud" as "a sweet and potent voice." Lest there be any doubt about the interrelated nature of these metaphors, stanza 5 weaves them all together again and identifies "Joy"—"Life, and Life's effluence, cloud at once and shower" (l. 66)—as their referent.

This series of metaphoric substitutions has a variety of implications for the epistemic processes of reader and speaker. First, it throws into relief the extent to which the speaker's imaginative projections overshadow and outpace his perceptual-cognitive apprehension of mind-independent reality, a feature of his psychology that is clearly indicated in stanza 1. Despite the rather breathless pace of metaphoric generation, the speaker himself seems to have no qualms about what he is saying and how he has chosen to say it. The borrowed nature of the metaphors, their very multiplicity, and their tacit focus (William Wordsworth) deceptively suggest that they have no power to operate as affordances for the speaker, that is, to pave the way toward conscious insight, relief from dejection, and re-regulation of the self. The entire two stanzas, in fact, are both an elaboration of line 46 and an apparent digression from the true matter at hand, defining as they do the speaker's psychic life entirely as the negation of his friend's simultaneously life-giving and obfuscatory capacity for joy. In this sense, they have their own rather precise logic: felicitous union (to nature or woman) is the product of internal well-being and gladness that, no matter what it may obscure, showers light and song (read: Wordsworthian poetry) on the world.

In the source poem, this interrelated series of metaphors appears in the opening of the twentieth and final stanza, 295 lines into the 339-line verse letter. Whereas the figures of speech thus stood as something of an afterthought to numerous lines of complaint and self-recrimination in the original poem, here they replace that portion of the text and, in so doing, presume to take on a central epistemic and dramatic function. Yet whether or not the reader grasps the implied critique of Wordsworth's doctrine of the healing powers of nature, these stanzas exacerbate the already frustrated sense of forward progression and the striving after "something to be known." The three types of inferences readers generate—backward-looking (explanation), concurrent (association), and forward-looking (prediction)—have all been sharply constrained by the speaker's inability to navigate through his psychic dilemma.[34] And because the logic of the metaphors of marriage, light, and musical voices only serves to define the speaker according to an emptiness or inertia reminiscent of that which precipitated the poem, the narrative seems fatally stalled.

Furthermore, the unsettling manner in which the figurative elements transmute into or replace one another inhibits the reader's effort at visualization and implies that imagination will not supply the opportunities for knowledge and re-regulation of the self that, we already know, cannot be supplied through engagement with the object world. Although philosophers and psychologists are hesitant to discuss representational processes in the mind because of the dualistic metaphysics underlying traditional theories of representation and the current gap in knowledge between activity in neural networks and its mental products, some process evidently enables us to "see" what is not perceptually present.[35] This process is central to literature, which is materially constituted by nothing more than abstract symbols. Some recent language research on perceptual and conceptual priming effects "generally suggest that the perceptual characteristics of objects, including those that objects afford, might be automatically activated in memory, but perhaps not for all cases, when concrete nouns are read" (Gibbs, 178). All in all, this research in psycholinguistics indicates that such perceptual response is context sensitive. Considered in this light, Coleridge's overabundance of metaphors likely inhibits such priming functions, interfering with coherent visualization and thus obstructing the route to bodily based meaning. The effect is rather the reverse of the account of emergent structure in conceptual blending.

Whereas conceptual blend theory suggests that new structure is created when double-scope capacities merge aspects from different domains, Coleridge's metaphoric substitutions undermine the sense of a coherent semantic whole and as a consequence emphasize the fragmented nature of experience and feeling.

This juncture in the poem, however, after Coleridge has repeatedly frustrated the reader's desire for narrative-epistemic progress, marks a major transition. For the transformation and redeployment of Wordsworth's "celestial light" imagery consolidates the speaker's specifically Coleridgean sense of self, defined by the negation of feeling, joyous communion, and, presumably, vital creativity. In defining what he lacks—joy that has perhaps a problematic relationship to the real—the speaker recuperates a sense of authenticity and effects a reorientation toward his present crisis. Having already demonstrably failed, in stanzas 1–3, at the productive interaction with nature that forms the core of his friend's poetry, Coleridge has articulated through contrast the core of his own identity—not-Wordsworth—in stanzas 4 and 5. The autobiographical speaker, previously stymied by the effort to find resolution through the methods of another's self, now provides an account in words that signal the emergence of knowledge into consciousness. In stanzas 6 and 7 Coleridge brings together feeling and thought, inward and outward experience, through a remarkable assimilation of narrative to metaphoric elements that, in their visual and progressive logical clarity, are the obverse of the frustrated narrative and metaphoric confusion preceding them.

There was a time when, though my path was rough,
   This joy within me dallied with distress,
And all misfortunes were but as the stuff
   Whence Fancy made me dreams of happiness:
For hope grew round me, like the twining vine,
And fruits, and foliage, not my own, seemed mine.
But now afflictions bow me down to earth:
Nor care I that they rob me of my mirth;
   But oh! each visitation
Suspends what nature gave me at my birth,
   My shaping spirit of Imagination.
For not to think of what I needs must feel,
   But to be still and patient, all I can;
And haply by abstruse research to steal
   From my own nature all the natural man—

This was my sole resource, my only plan:
Till that which suits a part infects the whole,
And now is almost grown the habit of my soul.

Hence, viper thoughts, that coil around my mind,
    Reality's dark dream!
I turn from you, and listen to the wind,
    Which long has raved unnoticed. . . .   (ll. 76–97)

In these climactic stanzas of the poem, Coleridge ultimately transforms a narrative impasse into a culminating series of metaphors of constriction, vividly depicting the failure of forward-moving story through the transmutation of its root metaphor, the path, into twining vines and snakes. Up to this point in the poem, the speaker's attempt at narrative has been a matter of unconscious process, and while both speaker and reader understand that it has not been a success, *story itself* has not been the subject of the poem. With the reconstitution of the speaker's distinct identity, however, Coleridge dramatizes a conscious awareness of story as subject. That story can now be told, because the matrix of experience includes Wordsworth's philosophy and family circle, which enable the speaker to establish a starting point for his story but simultaneously differentiate his poetry and identity from those of his friend. Coleridge underscores the extent to which Wordsworth and his poetry provide the context and causal trajectory for the speaker's story by the clear echo of the opening clause of the Immortality ode: "There was a time when . . ." In mimicking the ode's rhetoric, Coleridge places the speaker's psychobiography unequivocally in the context of Wordsworth's, because the poet's revision of the first line of stanza 6, originally "E're I was wedded, tho' my path was rough," indicates an incontrovertible intention to echo Wordsworth's ode. In their structure too both lines signal a distinctly narrative trajectory, looking back and offering explanation and thus laying the groundwork for concurrent and forward-looking inferences. As he begins to construct his account, the speaker employs the most commonplace of everyday metaphors, life as a path or a journey. Both this and the echo of Wordsworth indicate a heightened consciousness of storytelling and life as story.

In the literature on cognitive metaphor and embodiment, theorists posit that the source-path-goal image schema, which is first learned developmentally in tracking objects and is one of about two dozen image schemata employed in everyday thinking, underlies the metaphor "life is a path or journey." Additionally, research on representational momentum, the internalized representation of physical momentum that involves the ability to follow imaginatively the path of a moving object and then focus on the resting point, suggests that humans expect objects to keep traveling even if they encounter an obstacle (Gibbs, 91, 139). Along with the pervasive evidence for narrativity, these findings highlight the degree to which humans are strongly biased toward causality and forward movement. Whereas Coleridge frustrates this bias in the beginning of "Dejection," in stanza 6 he invokes it both structurally and conceptually. Since, according to Gibbs, studies show that people do not understand figurative expressions as conventions, but as actions, readers of "Dejection" probably construct a limited simulation of movement along a path. Coleridge furthermore exploits a bodily based, visual response by extending the path metaphor: false "joy" and "dreams of happiness" result in hope, figuratively rendered as objects along the path, "the twining vine" and "fruits, and foliage." However, this natural path is, presumably, a false path along which joy and Fancy meretriciously promise to transform suffering into "dreams of happiness." Of course, Coleridge offers a fairly direct statement of all this, as well as of the ensuing attempt to escape feeling through abstruse research, thus filling out the narrative of the "dull pain" he complains of in stanza 1.[36] Nevertheless, the real emotional and cognitive action occurs through conceptual transformations that facilitate an increasingly coherent and bodily based understanding of the speaker's dilemma. With the emergence of the path metaphor, the course of the narrative itself has become an object of consciousness and thus an affordance for both speaker and reader, whose experiences are closely aligned in this climactic portion of the poem. That path, along which readers travel imaginatively, is linked via visual association with the twining vine, which transforms linear progress into entanglement. Just as an untamed vine chokes the life from a host tree or bush, the speaker is bowed down to earth by his sufferings, Wordsworthian hope, and thus the narrative path he has tried to pursue, among the entangling afflictions.

The final transformation of the path metaphor into "viper thoughts" in the opening lines of stanza 7 completes the associative action of this climactic portion of the poem, for it refigures the deceptively beautiful but actually destructive image of the vine into another kind of tangled line, the repulsive and deadly coiling action of poisonous snakes. Although Coleridge has explained the cause of his emotional dilemma in the last ten lines of stanza 6, the image of viper thoughts erupts with epiphanic clarity in the beginning of stanza 7. In the same manner that Coleridge depicts the mind turned in on itself through conceptual processes that turn in on and shut down narrative, the poem itself coils in accord with the cruel narrative irony it produces, that the speaker has, in fact, cultivated the "dull pain" he wishes to escape at the beginning of the poem. The sublime Pindaric ode, with its irregular line and stanza lengths, becomes the embodied image of the processes of a mind under duress, and the fact that the "viper thoughts" image does not appear in the source poem strongly suggests that in revising the private verse letter for a public audience Coleridge intended to prompt and extend the associations between path, vines, snakes, and the form of the poem as a whole.[37]

Because the visually related metaphors of stanzas 6 and 7 successively embody linear progress, entanglement, and constriction, they afford emotional and conscious knowledge that *feels good* in spite of the unhappy nature of the message. Miall and Kuiken suggest that defamiliarization ("putting in question prior concepts or feelings") appears to result in uncertainty, which is itself a control condition for literary understanding. Uncertainty "heralds the transformations in understanding that occur during the reader's thematization of the literary text. . . . As the vehicle of interpretation, . . . feeling initiates a process in which existing schemata become recontextualized, leading to new insights for the reader" (133–34).[38] Although the route to insight and its content are highly individualized, the literary features that trigger this process appear relatively stable. In this case, I surmise that the defamiliarization of the bodily based metaphor "life is a path" provides the somatic-affective basis for new insight, because from the evolutionary-ecological point of view, paths that transmute into vines and thoughts that are snakes are unknown entities, and thus their apprehension evokes uncertainty, an adaptive emotional response that, in turn, redoubles the epistemic process. But even though response to these metaphors has a bodily basis, the capacity to track their functions and construe meaning within the text depends on its written nature, that is, its coextensiveness with the ESS. The abilities to cognize metaphoric associations; to recognize them as an inversion of the figures for Wordsworthian joy; to apply the insight of stanzas 6 and 7 to the initial problem posed by the poem; and to expand the matrix of experience to include Wordsworth's family and philosophy depend upon the expanded memory capacity provided by symbolic systems and the many likely retracings of the narrative path that those systems enable. The same is true, of course, of the ability to create a cognitive artifact of such unimaginable complexity in the first place.

The remainder of stanza 7 and stanza 8 provide a denouement to the culminating moment of insight. Finally looking outside the window again, the speaker returns to the framing narrative of the incipient storm with its dim promise of release and its stronger overtones of doom. But since he has already shut down the narrative by consciously recognizing the self-destructiveness of his earlier plan for psychic renovation, it is logically fitting that the storm has "raved unnoticed" for some time and that, once he notices it, he responds with terrified imaginings rather than a sense of release. In stanza 7, the longest stanza of the poem, the speaker, addressing the wind, vents his overheated imagination. His "genial spirits" suffer no lapse here, and emotional deadness hardly seems at issue, reconfirming that the "dull pain" and creative depletion of the poem's opening attest to the shadow of Wordsworth's presence there. Without joy and the capacity to draw sustenance from the nonhuman natural world, the speaker nonetheless commands a powerful imagination and is far from emotionally dead.

Addressing the wind, the speaker gleans a succession of vivid and frightening images in its song, including a witches' home on a desolate mountaintop and a bloody battlefield. During a lull in the storm he hopes for a story different in tone than the foregoing, and the course of his thoughts diverges into a narrative no less frightening than those that preceded it. The wind

> tells another tale, with sounds less deep and loud!
> A tale of less affright,
> And tempered with delight,
> As Otway's self had framed the tender lay,—
> 'Tis of a little child
> Upon a lonesome wild,
> Not far from home, but she hath lost her way:
> And now moans loud in bitter grief and fear,
> And now screams loud, and hopes to make her mother hear.   (ll. 117–25)

The distressing vision of a child out of her mind with fear, following on those of a malign and destructive humanity complicit with violent nature, might be taken to indicate the final futility of the speaker's attempt at re-regulation. But self-narratives need not be happy, and re-regulation of the self is not synonymous with restoration and healing. If the speaker is defined only as the negation of the Wordsworthian self by the end of stanza 5, stanza 6 explains how and why he is different, and stanza 7 fills out the concrete dimensions of his difference. Since criticism generally agrees that the lost child in these lines alludes to Wordsworth's Lucy Gray, there is even, perhaps, a note of triumph in the speaker's realignment of his self with his own past accounts. Following the logic established in stanza 5, which implies that joyous communion shrouds the harsher aspects of reality, Coleridge's depiction of the terrified child likewise suggests that Wordsworth veils inconsolable sorrow in self-serving imagination. For in "Lucy Gray" the child who disappears without a trace, like her footsteps in the snow, never quite dies:

> Yet some maintain that to this day
> She is a living Child,

That you may see sweet Lucy Gray
Upon the lonesome Wild.[39]

On the whole, a mind that indulges in terrifying fantasies is no more or less projective than one that sees the world through the mists of joy, but when it comes to the experience of loss, abandonment, and helplessness, Coleridge implies, it might actually see more clearly. In depicting the sensational excess of a mind dominated by its own fearful visions, Coleridge constructs an authentic counterpart to the Wordsworthian "philosophic mind" that can redeem the most troubling facts and experiences. The self re-regulated in this poem is, incontrovertibly, one that lives under the threat of periodic siege from its own fantasies, as it has in the past, but this is better than living according to another's story. What has emerged into consciousness for both speaker and reader is knowledge of the cause and persistence of dejection, and with it a broader conception of the meaning of a regulated self.

In turning attention away from the self and toward Sara and her future in the final stanza of the poem, Coleridge follows the pattern of the greater romantic lyric, whereby the resolution of self-crisis precipitates imaginative human communion. Having affirmed that his own life is governed by rhythms that are different from those of the sustaining joy of the Wordsworths, he offers a blessing for future happiness:

> Joy lift her spirit, joy attune her voice;
> To her may all things live, from pole to pole,
> Their life the eddying of her living soul!
>   O simple spirit, guided from above,
> Dear Lady! Friend devoutest of my choice,
> Thus mayest thou ever, evermore rejoice.   (ll. 134–39)

The lines seem to concede that joyful living when divinely sanctioned may be, at least sometimes, an authentic merger of internal characteristics with the qualities of the universe. Joy "guided from above"—divine joy—lifts up the soul and imparts visionary power and song, because it does not erroneously emphasize the human relationship with the natural world. Although Coleridge has performed what Walter Jackson Bate calls his characteristic usherlike gesture in the closing of the poem, wishing for his addressee what he has denied himself, the conclusion, far from being a pathetic wish that another might have a happier life than his, finalizes the re-regulation of the self by bringing imagination under the control of powerful belief. Having rejected the beliefs that govern the Wordsworthian imagination, he has returned, via his earnest desire for Sara's happiness, to his own form of authentic joy. The poem ends in a chorus of joy for Sara, as the repetitions of *joy* and *rejoice* blend with the rhyming words *voice, choice,* and *rejoice*. These repetitions and rhymes in turn echo those of stanza 5 and thus retrospectively qualify the claim that the speaker is barred from the experience of joy. Shorn of the imagery that connected it to the Wordsworthian notion of benign exchange with nature, the song lifts the speaker as he sings it into imaginative communion with Sara, dramatically demonstrating that his form of joy, sporadic and punctuated by self-doubt though it is, is no less authentic than his friend's.

Shrinking the Self: "I Could See the Smallest Things"

The matrix of experience in "Dejection" is dynamical and expansive, illustrating the capacity of consciousness to enlarge the domain of inquiry to resolve the problem of the self. For the speaker in that poem, placing the current crisis in the context of past experience and ongoing relationships enables a fully contextualized and relational sense of the self, one defined and governed by a Coleridgean imagination and capable of its own peculiar form of joyful relation to others. By contrast, Raymond Carver's "I Could See the Smallest Things," like the other stories in the stylistically and formally austere collection *What We Talk about When We Talk about Love,* operates through a willed exclusion of experiential context. Since the publication of this collection in 1974, scholars have debated the merits of the so-called minimalist technique that Carver practiced therein, one that, in leaving so much unsaid, heightens the sense of trapped and uncomprehending characters.[40] In addition to focusing on the surface of events and using as few words as possible to delimit that surface, Carver curtails action in his fiction, pointing out himself that "most of my stories start pretty near the end of the arc of the dramatic conflict."[41] Michael Trussler comments that "Carver's approach to narrative stresses the radical temporality of experience" (35), but it might be more accurate to say that Carver depicts the radically temporary nature of experience for his characters, an effect he achieves through the constraints he places on narrativity and thus on both internal and external action.

Since Carver's critics find minimalism both morally and aesthetically objectionable, it is worth asking what a cognitive-evolutionary approach, one that embraces a scientifically informed humanism, can add to the discussion. In terms of embodied, pragmatic psychology, Carver refuses to furnish his fictive environments with fully human matrices of experience and, correspondingly, to grant his characters satisfactory autobiographical selfhood, a feature particularly apparent in his first-person stories. This is especially so in "Smallest Things," a story whose focus is more specifically epistemic than that of perhaps any other Carver story. In "Smallest Things" the story's contracted experiential matrix is mirrored in its carefully delimited time frame and domain, both physical and psychical. Unlike in the case of "Dejection," moreover, the author's own life is not a central context for comprehension, even if the ubiquitous themes of communication, domestic strife, and alcoholism play their part. And unlike in "Dejection," in "Smallest Things" the narrator, Nancy, is not intellectual or prone to self-analysis. Nor is Nancy aware of great psychological pressure to comprehend something about herself or her emotional state, although she has the opportunity to do so. And yet, even while it is so different from Coleridge's poem in its emotional, psychological, and conceptual containment, "I Could See the Smallest Things" exhibits the impulse toward something to be known, the narrative process of the way-finding cognition that directs itself toward conscious knowledge in the pursuit of self-regulation.

Just under five pages long and divided into four short sections, "I Could See the Smallest Things" is a lyric story built on a slim narrative: Nancy, awake or awakening in the middle of the night, hears the yard gate unlatching. Her husband, Cliff, lies passed out beside her in bed; a full moon illuminates the yard. Unable to sleep, Nancy gets out of bed, looks out the window, tries to sleep again, then goes down to the kitchen, where she smokes one of Cliff's cigarettes. When she goes outside to shut the gate, she finds her neighbor, Sam Lawton, with whom Cliff had had a falling out years before, standing by the fence. She goes around the fences to the two yards to see what Sam is doing (killing slugs), has a brief conversation with him, then goes back inside. Realizing then she has forgotten to shut the gate, she looks at her husband, thinks about the slugs, and tries hard to sleep.

Carver distributes the potential for insight—both Nancy's and the reader's—in a handful of carefully selected affordances in the contained environment that Nancy traverses (bedroom to kitchen to yard to neighbor's yard and back) and in her conversation with Sam. Although the limitations on territory, temporal span, and retrospect signal constraints on knowledge seeking, the actual potential for meaning resides in Nancy's sudden sense of receptivity and the capacity for association that her susceptibility triggers. Unlike Coleridge's speaker, Carver's character narrator is, for the moment, hyper-attuned to the physical environment and, in the beginning of the story at least, compelled to construe potential significance within the contours of her experience. Yet as critics such as G. P. Lainsbury, Gunter Leypoldt, and Jon Powell point out, Carver's minimalist technique, manifest in limitations on linguistic expression and a lack of sentence-level hierarchy, results in language that hides and leaves out information, putting the onus of understanding on the reader.[42] In "Smallest Things," this is largely because the evolved desire to know stands in tension with Nancy's self-protective disposition to avoid meaning, a disposition that, sadly, proves justified in light of the probable content of the knowledge available to her. While this tension between a universal (and definingly human) proclivity toward sense-making and a resolute reticence is characteristic of much of Carver's fiction, "Smallest Things" differs from most of the author's work in its concentrated focus on the epistemic process. "Smallest Things" is—oddly, given its minimalist technique—an interior story, intimate and painful because the reader shares Nancy's immediate experience intensely yet diverges from her in understanding.

Over the course of the story, the ambiguities emerging through a network of associations and the progressive negativity of images belie the apparent simplicity and relative felicity of meaning construal at the story's outset. The very first paragraph introduces several of the most important elements:

> I was in bed when I heard the gate. I listened carefully. I didn't hear anything else. But I heard that. I tried to wake Cliff. He was passed out. So I got up and went to the window. A big moon was laid over the mountains that went around the city. It was a white moon and covered with scars. Any damn fool could imagine a face there. (31)

Throughout the first short section, Carver builds on the central images he introduces in this first paragraph, the gate and the moon. Nancy mentions the gate five times, thinking about it "standing open . . . like a dare" (32), and she comments on the clarity of the yard under the full moon: "There were no scary shadows. . . . I could see the smallest things" (31). Because of the emphasis on the moon and the opened gate, the experienced reader readily recognizes their symbolic function, illuminating and opening out onto a terrain of knowledge that stands in contrast to Nancy's circumscribed domain. For Nancy, the sense of enhanced visual perception accompanied by security draws her toward a heightened consciousness that she would not normally pursue and that stands in contrast to, and draws her away from, Cliff's unconsciousness, his awful breathing and his gaping mouth. Thus, in spite of Nancy's jaded tone, Carver triggers powerful, positive conceptual priming effects through objects that embody exploration and insight.

In themselves, the gate and the moonlight are rather obvious symbols, but the pattern of associations that Carver weaves throughout the story undermines the sense of security and the desirability of illuminating knowledge, rendering the initial invitation to insight all too easy. Indeed, if readers typically generate three types of inferences—explanation, association, and prediction—Carver's decision to constrain the opportunity for backward- and forward-looking cognition puts a premium on the associative process. As a result, when meanings are changed or modified during the concurrent processing of associations, there is no larger context within which to gauge their significance; consequently, the implication of these associations is abnormally magnified for both the character narrator and the reader.

Moreover, the moment Nancy expands the domain of her inquiry by stepping outside the house, the increased opportunity for knowledge immediately provides distressing results. Although from the bedroom window "there are no scary shadows," when Nancy enters the yard she is startled to see Sam near his fence, and the first thing she says is, "Sam, you scared me," thus turning Sam into a formerly unperceived "scary shadow" (32). Nancy's description of Sam connects him with the moon: "His hair was silvery in the moonlight and stood up on his head. I could see his long nose, the lines in his big sad face" (33). In this manner, Sam is linked with potentially illuminating knowledge, but since his is a *real* face, implicitly exhausted by experience or knowledge, the association of vision with Sam now carries a sense of burden. Sam is "chewing something," an unattractive detail that acquires several associations in the next section and that is in direct contrast to the image of Sam as an illuminating presence.

In the penultimate paragraph of section 2, Carver offers us a brief insight into Nancy's consciousness that simultaneously reinforces the desire for expanded insight and experience and develops the suggestion of threat or uncertainty. As Nancy walks around the fence into Sam's yard to see what he is doing, she says, "I let myself out and went along the walk. It felt funny walking around outside in my nightgown and my robe. I thought to myself that I should try to remember this, walking around outside like this" (33). These two sentences epitomize Nancy's ambivalence about potential insight, because while self-consciousness about her nightwear expresses her sense of vulnerability, she uncharacteristically wants to enshrine the moment in memory. Moreover, the repetitions of *out, outside,* and *walking around outside* suggest to the reader that in some senses Nancy has never been outside. These narrative elements build on the initial image of the gate in section 1, which is "like a dare," enticing but somewhat frightening.

In the third section, Carver injects a sense of menace into the story through the association of the object of Sam's obsession, the garden slug, with Sam and alcoholism. The section's narrative elements, in turn, associate Sam and drinking with Nancy's husband, Cliff. As Powell notes, "Carver achieved a sense of menace by leaving out, or by providing only clues to, crucial aspects of [his stories]. Both character and reader sense that something dangerous or menacing is 'imminent' or 'submerged,' but both character and reader, unable to find *the* meaning of the given clues, must battle *between* readings of those clues. Menace develops as meaning itself becomes elusive" (647). At this juncture in "Smallest Things," meaning becomes elusive for two reasons: the network of associations suddenly becomes more complex, and the slugs, introduced as a new affordance, give these associations a negative cast. As part of the domain Nancy traverses, the slugs are quite different from the objects that first command her attention, the gate and the moon. These first images carry the suggestion of mobility, freedom, and vision, because the removal of barriers and better lighting are isomorphically related to physical liberty and perceptual advantage. Slugs, of course, have none of these inherent positive associations; though not in themselves menacing, they are re-pugnant. They are primitive organisms, and like things that, according to evolu-tionary psychology, humans find universally disgusting—rotten meat, decaying flesh, blood, pus, soft tissue—slugs are slimy and, to human perception, poorly formed; and although unlike "rotten meat and decaying flesh," they probably are not dangerous, they suitably embody a sense of uncleanliness.[43] In section 3, Carver creates a sense of menace by tying the disgust engendered by the slugs—slimy, subhuman, unclean—with Sam and Cliff.

Instructively, although Nancy affirms in the beginning of her narrative, after just getting up, that aided by a brilliant moon that seems, for the moment, like the greatest possible light, she could see "the smallest things," this turns out not to be true, as she was only seeing from inside. Whereas she was initially able to see "the clothespins on the line" in the moonlight (31), now Sam uses a flashlight to direct her attention to the slugs, smaller things, or, as he later says, "slimy things" (35). Just as *small* mutates lexically into *slime,* Sam, with his sad moon face, becomes inextricably linked to ugliness. He is obsessed with the slugs, explaining to Nancy that he puts out bait, as well as showering them with Ajax in the middle of the night. Nancy reports that as he says this, "He [turns] his head to one side and [spits] what could have been tobacco" (34). Now invited to see in a different way, Nancy fixates visually on two things, the death of a slug paralyzed by the flash-light beam ("The thing stopped moving and turned its head from side to side") and "whatever it was" he was chewing (34). The ambiguity about what Sam is chewing, the spitting, and the emphasis on the action itself tie Sam to the primi-tivism, sliminess, and implied uncleanliness of the slugs. As Sam shows her how he kills the slugs, he asks about Cliff, confesses that he wishes they were still friends, and mentions that he has stopped drinking. Since this section, section 3, opens with Nancy explaining that Cliff and Sam had "[gotten] to drinking" on the night of their falling out, Sam's story ties back in to Cliff's lying "passed out" in the bed. As the implication of seeing focuses on extreme smallness and repulsiveness in this section, the invitations to insight embodied by moonlight and the opened gate have receded into the story's background.

Nancy has had no conscious revelation at this point in the story, but the narrative account in the last short section suggests that her perceptions have been unsettling even before she makes an overt connection between her husband and the slugs. First, the short paragraph that begins this section emphasizes order-making and withdrawal: "In the bedroom, I took off the robe, folded it, put it within reach. Without looking at the time, I checked to make sure the stem was out on the clock. Then I got into the bed, pulled the covers up, and closed my eyes" (35–36). This paragraph clearly conveys a desire for a ritual conclusion to her nighttime adventure, a conscientious contraction of the domain of the story to the confines, ideally, of her own unconscious body. But Carver has foreshadowed the notion that such a withdrawal to an inward world does not correlate with safety. In the brief retrospective narration that begins the previous section, section 3, Nancy recounts the death of Millie, her friend and Sam's wife, before Sam and Cliff had had their falling out: "She was only forty-five when she did it. Heart failure. It hit her just as she was coming into their drive. The car kept going and went on through the back of the carport" (33). Heart failure and disease serve as metaphors for the failed relationships throughout the story collection, and here Carver combines the metaphor with literal damage to the domain of such relationships, the home. Just as Millie was not safe from death in her place of greatest security, Nancy is not safe from the information she is processing as she tries again to sleep. Instructively, the moment she realizes she has not closed the gate, she is wide awake.

Criticism is divided on the extent of Nancy's revelation in the last short paragraphs of the story, but I think it is safe to say that her disturbing insight will not be suppressed easily:

> I opened my eyes and lay there. I gave Cliff a little shake. He cleared his throat. He swallowed. Something caught and dribbled in his chest.
>
> I don't know. It made me think of those things that Sam Lawton was dumping powder on.
>
> I thought for a minute of the world outside my house, and then I didn't have any more thoughts except the thought that I had to hurry up and sleep. (36)

Ernest Fontana asserts that "Nancy is awakened, against her will, to the painful realization that she is alone like her fenced-in neighbor in a world of sleeping slugs, one of whom is her husband."[44] But how awakened is she? Fontana's reading is supported by the emphasis on thinking in the last sentence, where the character narrator uses the verb *thought* and the nouns *thoughts* and *thought*. For someone who is not prone to analysis, Nancy conveys an urgent need to shut down thinking, willing unconsciousness as a means to suppress permanently the ugliness that has been revealed to her.

Whereas Coleridge's speaker works through his own mental processes to arrive at a new, albeit painful, degree of self-understanding, knowledge for Nancy, Carver implies, is simply counterproductive. The many small things of the story, its circumscribed physical spaces, commonplace objects and creatures, and minimal human interactions, are nonetheless too large for a mind primed to seek adaptive benefits from knowledge seeking and meaning-making. Nancy's response to her unwelcome insight is to try to shrink down to the smallest possible thing under the covers, eyes closed, mind stopped. In the minimalist technique of this collection, which some of Carver's critics find too extreme, the author's exposure of the sometimes dehumanizing conditions of life is arguably more rather than less humane than stories that offer more traditional forms of closure and insight in their conclusions. As Leypoldt says, "Faced with Nancy's arrested epiphany, the reader's hermeneutical efforts may lead a few tentative interpretive steps further than Nancy's stage of awareness. Thus while the epiphany neither effects the solid closure of those [in other Carver stories], . . . it has subtly slid from the arrested epiphany to what I would like to call an 'ironized epiphany'" (539).[45] Yet I question how ironized the epiphany is here, since Nancy has only just stopped short of articulating what the correspondence between the slugs and Cliff—inert, snoring, and an obstacle to her sleep—is. Nancy has, after all, told this story to someone, or to herself.

If in the human evolutionary past the feeling of knowing was a special feeling that betokened the possibility of greater mastery for our species and in so doing motivated the evolution of higher consciousness, cognitive complexity, and autobiographical selfhood, the limited domain of Carver's fiction and the inefficacy of even slight opportunities for knowledge within that domain require readers to confront situations that deny characters their functional humanity. Although Nancy is not linked to the drinking and physical repulsiveness that constitute the sluglike characteristics of Cliff and Sam earlier in the story, her final desire for smallness and unconsciousness ultimately ties her to the subhuman imagery associated with the men. To make oneself less than human in these circumstances, Carver implies, may be the preferred option, for human consciousness only traps the character with her ultimately useless insights. But to opt for something like the cancellation of self-consciousness and a return to the cognitive limits imposed by the eternal present of episodic memory is, to say the least, profoundly counterintuitive. Carver's characters typically function in a world of severely constrained possibilities, and their frequent ambivalence about the knowledge they nevertheless pursue demonstrates a resistance to, or lack of faith in, a fully articulated human life. In their ambivalence about the knowledge-seeking disposition and the possibility of mastery and freedom it provides, Carver's characters struggle with a fundamental aspect of human nature, and I believe it is this struggle that so offends some of Carver's critics. However, the truth of life is that circumstances are not always conducive to the exploratory intelligence of humans, and the writer who depicts the difficulty of functioning in a reduced territory should not be castigated for failing to offer false consolations. Although scholars have differed about the content of Nancy's epiphany and the degree to which she grasps it at the end of "Smallest Things," it is certain that *the reader* recognizes the sad implication of her willed turn away from knowledge, sympathizing with her yet being left to ponder what it means to make oneself small.

Through the development of symbolic systems and external memory stores, humans have, in tandem with the development of logicoscientific thought, greatly expanded their capacity for reflection and conscious awareness, and the literary record attests to the human eagerness to engage in enhanced reflective processes. Yet ironically, the abstract nature of that process and its technological mechanisms lure us away from the source of our need to think at all, the time-bound and vulnerable bodies we would rather forget. In this chapter, I have tried to demonstrate that our typical cognitive patterns are coextensive with evolved bodily experience and that those patterns not only establish rudimentary features of literature but also emerge in the dynamical action of many literary works. To the extent that I have been successful in doing what I have heretofore avoided, employing a model for interpretation, I would insist that that success depends on the model's suitability for literary works focused on showing consciousness in action. The varied implications of our linearizing, associative, affectively motivated, domain- and object-sensitive cognition for different kinds of literature remain to be elucidated by other scholars. At this point, though, I hope that cognitive approaches to literature can put aside computer models of mentation and look past the structures of language to an evolved mind whose epistemic orientation has made those later achievements possible.

CHAPTER FIVE

Endangered Daughters

Sex, Mating, and Power in Darwinian Feminist Perspective

In *her* world, men loved women as the fox loves the hare.
And women loved men as the tapeworm loves the gut.

Pat Barker

Now here we see the beauty and the great value of the novel. Philosophy, religion, science, they are all of them busy nailing things
down, to get a stable equilibrium. . . .

But the novel, no. The novel is the highest complex of subtle
interrelatedness that man has discovered. Everything is true in its
own time, place, circumstance. . . . If you try to nail anything down,
in the novel, either it kills the novel, or the novel gets up and walks
away with the nail.

D. H. Lawrence

The Emergence of Darwinian Literary Criticism

Evolutionary literary criticism has a rather different recent history from ecocriticism or cognitive approaches to literature. Whereas studies in literature and the
environment grew out of the ecology movement initially, and whereas, over several decades, cognitive approaches developed out of the commitment to bring
together cognitive research and literary study, evolutionary literary criticism was
at first a response to the pervasive antihumanism of the poststructuralist hegemony. Once assertions grounded in French philosophical, sociological, and psychoanalytic thought—about the instability of language and meaning and about
the constructed nature of nearly everything, including identity, sexuality, gender,
and human nature—had become commonplace in the 1980s, humanists generally inhabited the discursive subjectivities that Michel Foucault still held in re-
serve for the deliquesced individual.[1] The other option, responding to the heart of
poststructuralist claims, not just its radically skeptical epistemology but its strong

constructionist impact, was a rather taller order than most literary scholars were willing to take on, and it is hardly surprising that many so readily succumbed to the suddenly unyielding power of the institutional state apparatuses.[2]

Like all repressive ideologies, however, poststructuralist constructionism, born of "a mood of antinomian rebellion and self-indulgence" though it most assuredly was, had sown the seeds of vigorous discontent.[3] Thus, in 1993 and 1996, respectively, Joseph Carroll and Robert Storey published two books that sought to rebut Theory's reigning skepticism and constructionism by demonstrating that many of its claims were no longer supportable in light of contemporary evolutionary social science, cognitive neuroscience, and related fields. Although Carroll's *Evolution and Literary Theory* and Storey's *Mimesis and the Human Animal: On the Biogenetic Foundations of Literary Representation* ultimately make very different sorts of connections between our evolved nature and literature, the fundamental thrust of these two seminal texts is the same. Both seek to demonstrate (as Storey's title makes explicit) that literary representation rests on biogenetic foundations, and both scholars go about this task by presenting evidence that certain features of what we commonly refer to as human nature have a biologically defined character and are not subject to choice or cultural construction. In their wide-ranging use of research across scientific subdisciplines, Carroll and Storey were the first scholars in the literary humanities to display a mastery of current research on human evolution, and in so doing they broke new ground for interdisciplinary research in literary studies. Nevertheless, because of both authors' unabashed criticism of poststructuralism, and because of the general misconceptions about Darwinian evolution prevailing in the humanities well into the mid-nineties, evolutionary approaches to literature were poorly received until at least the turn of the twenty-first century. (Earlier attempts to establish the evolutionary foundations of the arts, of course, extend back to Darwin's time.) Now evolutionary approaches are growing in number, although the field's diversity at present is somewhat masked by the still-predominant thematic emphasis on sex-differential mating strategies and pair bonding. Even though in this chapter I focus on this very topic (as well as the generally ignored, but intimately related, issue of power struggles that arise from differential strategies), it should be clear at the outset that in my view, an evolutionary literary theory approaching *Darwinian* comprehensiveness would include all of the topics covered in this book and many others besides. In sum, while in this chapter I acknowledges sex and mating as central topics for evolutionary approaches, in the book as a whole I stake a claim for the broader scope and significance of the field.

Because Carroll's goal was to transmute his extended, erudite challenge to

Theory into a transformational program for literary studies, and because of his prodigious productivity since publication of his first book, he and several others associated with the approach in the early years established the identity of Darwinian literary criticism (or, as Carroll sometimes alternatively prefers, and as I shall henceforth refer to his approach in this chapter, adaptationist literary criticism) as an approach initially identified with the so-called Santa Barbara school of evolutionary psychology of Leda Cosmides, John Tooby, Steven Pinker, and others. Evolutionary psychology, in this narrow use of the term, holds that the human mind is made up of many specialized adaptations that were formed during a period of major species evolution in the Pleistocene. In keeping with this, Carroll's adaptationist approach to literary criticism originally leaned toward finding correspondences between hypothesized psychological adaptations, presumably acquired in the environment of evolutionary adaptation (EEA), and aspects of literature.

As Cosmides and Tooby admit, the EEA refers not to an actual time and place but to a statistical composite that represents abstractly the temporal and physical conditions under which the bulk of human cognitive evolution occurred. Although many evolutionary theorists still regard the EEA concept as valid, in recent years Carroll has become an outspoken critic of Santa Barbara evolutionary psychology's commitment to cognitive modularity (also referred to as domain specificity or, most colorfully, the Swiss army knife model of the mind), according to which discrete adaptations evolved to solve environmental problems as they arose in the EEA.[4] As he notes in his review of *Consilience,* making a distinction between Santa Barbara evolutionary psychology and its parent field, human sociobiology, E. O. Wilson's list of aspects of human nature "is an apparent hodgepodge: dreaming, fear of snakes, taste, mother-infant bonding, facial expressions corresponding to the basic emotions, cognitive tendencies toward conceptual reification and dichotomization, and color vision. . . . As evolutionary psychology moves away from the sociobiological emphasis on inclusive fitness [the replication of one's genes in future generations] as a direct and proximate motive, it approaches more closely to cognitive psychology as a matrix discipline, and in this move it tends to eliminate the underlying motivational principles that would provide structure to randomly assorted lists of cognitive mechanisms."[5] In his repeated criticisms of evolutionary psychology since publication of this review, Carroll has sometimes been unduly harsh, for as Kevin Laland and Gillian Brown point out, Santa Barbara evolutionary psychology is not theoretically incompatible with other evolutionary approaches. Nonetheless, the central importance of Carroll's point here should not be overlooked. However jerry-rigged or random the human mind may appear (and in some respects may be), organisms seek, not just survival and reproduction, but maximization of inclusive fitness. Santa Barbara evolutionary psychology tends to sidestep discussion of ultimate causes (original evolutionary causes still operant at the motivational level) that contribute to proximate (i.e., current) motivation and behavior.

Carroll's 2005 essay "Human Nature and Literary Meaning: A Theoretical Model Illustrated with a Critique of *Pride and Prejudice*" is perhaps the first essay in which he distances adaptationist literary criticism theoretically from a domain-specific or modular approach to the evolved human mind, and his goal there is to replace the mechanistic, computer-inspired conception of the human being with that of a thinking animal whose predominant life motives grow out of its fitness priorities. Carroll argues that evolutionary psychologists should heed the findings of cognitive archaeologists like Mithen and the evidence of the cultural explosion connected to the evolution of language from sixty thousand to thirty thousand years ago, and he refocuses his literary adaptationist program through the lenses of life-history analysis and Darwinian psychiatry. By subordinating the Santa Barbara school's modular, one-adaptation-per-problem (adaptation executioner) concept of the mind to a more extensive vision of human evolution, Carroll claims,

> we can formulate a better, more comprehensive account of the human motivational system by integrating two concepts: (a) the concept of human life history as a cycle organized around the distribution of effort between "somatic" and "reproductive" activities, and (b) the concept of "behavioral systems."
>
> The central categories of life history analysis are birth, growth, death, and reproduction. The organisms of all species engage in two fundamental forms of effort—the acquisition of resources (somatic effort) and the expenditure of resources in reproduction. Birth, growth, and death are somatic activities. Mating and parenting are reproductive activities. . . . All the main activities in the life history of an organism are integrated and interdependent.   (194)

In Carroll's view, then, "the central challenge for a specifically Darwinian form of literary criticism is to connect the highest levels in the organization of human nature with the most detailed and subtle aspects of literary meaning. Can we connect the basic life history goals—survival, growth, and reproduction—with the finest nuances of theme, tone, and style in the organization of literary meaning in specific works? The answer to this question will determine the success or failure of Darwinian literary criticism, and the answer is 'yes, we can.' *The elementary principles of life history analysis enter into the organization of all literary representations, and the manner in which any given author manages those principles is a defining feature in the character and quality of that author's work"* (189, emphasis added). Thus, according to the model of adaptationist literary criticism, which he currently practices and promotes, Carroll explicitly links qualitative assessment of the literary work with the organization of the elements of life history (survival, growth, and reproduction) in it, a move that seems to suggest that those works representing life history at the thematic level might fare best in adaptationist criticism, a point to which I shall return.

In spite of the avowed theoretical shift away from the Santa Barbara school of evolutionary psychology and toward life-history analysis and behavioral systems, which has at least the appearance of casting a broader net in terms of the literary content the field addresses, adaptationist literary criticism continues to exhibit a predominant focus on sexual psychology and mate selection. This is true of both the analysis of *Pride and Prejudice* in the article cited above and a more recent article on *Wuthering Heights,* which I discuss at length in the next section. In general, Carroll's usual focus since the mid-nineties on realistic nineteenth-century novels tends to preselect this segment of life history and, given his stature in the field, establishes it as a paradigm for evolutionary analyses.

It is far from self-evident that the "central task" of an evolutionary approach to literature is to focus on features of mate selection specifically or life history in general, as opposed to epistemic processes, ecological relations, or any number of evolutionarily informed and inflected topics. Nor is it self-evident that any or indeed all of these could establish the success or failure of the entire approach in short order. That is likely to take some time. Without question, sex and mate choice are central concerns in human evolution and culture, not to mention big favorites of literary critics, but they do not form the single important topic of biological evolution and cultural production. As Carroll acknowledges in the introduction to *Literary Darwinism: Evolution, Human Nature, and Literature* and in the recent *Style* essay "An Evolutionary Paradigm for Literary Study," his most fair-minded descriptions of the field of Darwinian literary criticism to date, the work now being conducted is increasingly diverse.

For instance, Marcus Nordlund's 2007 *Shakespeare and the Nature of Love: Literature, Culture, Evolution* follows my appeal to develop a more biocultural orientation in evolutionary criticism, and it does so, interestingly, with a particularly life-history approach to Shakespeare's works, although Nordlund conceptualized and wrote his study of Shakespeare before Carroll championed life history as a model for adaptationist literary criticism.[6] In his book, Nordlund brings together evolutionary social science, cultural analysis, Shakespeare criticism, and knowledge of the plays to interpret four kinds of love—parental, filial, romantic, and sexually proprietary—represented in Shakespeare's plays. Also suggestive of the varied inflections an evolutionary criticism can have, Brett Cooke's *Human Nature in Utopia: Zamyatin's "We"* takes an eclectic and inventive approach to evolutionary content analysis in literature. In his introductory chapter, Cooke hypothesizes that human nature clarifies why life in utopia is dull and why the related body of literature tends to be boring. According to Cooke, what stands out about Zamyatin's novel is the basic struggle between social engineering and an innate nature. In the body of his study, Cooke explores diverse topics, such as meals, food distribution, and their relation to communal organization; reason as a "hothouse plant," an ideal of utopian schemes but a recent addition to human nature; and child's play as irrelevant to the state even while the novel itself is Zamyatin's child.[7]

Just as significant are theories focused less on content than on evolved form. Narrative is a central topic under consideration these days, and William Flesch proposes a novel thesis in *Comeuppance: Costly Signaling, Altruistic Punishment, and Other Biological Components of Fiction*. Stressing the importance for social animals of detecting cheaters, Flesch asserts that tracking or monitoring others is more important than imitation in literary fiction, because it enables the detection of those who do not cooperate socially, also known as cheaters or free riders. In Flesch's view, narrative takes advantage of our predisposition to monitor and reciprocate in kind. In *On the Origin of Stories,* the most ambitious recent book to propose a general evolutionary theory of literary art, Brian Boyd moves from a general theory of the evolution of the arts to a specific explication of the function of narrative literature. Proposing that the arts begin in both solitary and shared patterned cognitive play that reshapes the mind, raises the status of individual artists, and stimulates the general human willingness to cooperate, Boyd claims that all these functions developing together "*evolved* art to *create creativity*" (119); in other words, creativity evolved as a later adaptation of the dynamical features already existing in the artistic process. Fictional representation constitutes a special case of patterning that enables us to extend and refine our capacity to process social information.[8]

While Carroll has on occasion applauded the diversity of approach and subject within Darwinian literary studies, by his own recent accounting, it does not all conform to the field's "central task." This is troubling, because Darwinian critics look to Carroll as their authority, and he has embraced his role as a leader and mentor. Yet it is unclear why he has chosen to define the field so narrowly. Moreover, even as Carroll has developed new, significantly refined interpretive models since 1993, he has been insufficiently attentive to the culturally situated nature of human behavior, the aesthetic complexities of the literary text, and the dynamics of textual production and consumption, all Darwinian features of art behaviors. Although he continuously refines his interpretive models, he never explains revisions to his previous models or interpretations. I explore below, as a case in point, both his first, very brief commentary on *Wuthering Heights* in *Evolution and Literary Theory* and his recent article-length analysis of the same novel, "The Cuckoo's History: Human Nature in *Wuthering Heights*," which illustrates Carroll's reconsideration of adaptationist methodology but also demonstrates the need for further theoretical and methodological refinement. Ironically, the literalism that emerged in Carroll's first efforts at evolutionary literary theory has been exacerbated by his very genuine recent efforts to broaden the scope of his conception of adaptationist criticism. For in turning to life-history analysis as the core area of current evolutionary social science of value to adaptationist literary criticism and in connecting the ordered goals of life history with the genre of romantic comedy, Carroll takes two steps that are questionable on Darwinian grounds. First, in extracting the normative pattern of typical surviving organisms (life history) as the feature of interest for literary theory and criticism in all evolutionary social science, he idealizes evolution. And second, in establishing this normative pattern of actual life history as a standard of aesthetic and generic evaluation, he literalizes the function of art, misconstruing the social, psychological, and aesthetic value of a range of genres and modes.

Whose Life History?

Carroll's goal in "Cuckoo's History," as in his other recent essays on nineteenth-century fiction, is to provide sensible constraints on interpretation and to mediate the critical traditions that have either subordinated conflicting impulses to "a superordinate set of norms" or dehumanized *Wuthering Heights* by placing unresolved conflicts in a postmodernist theoretical context (241). *Wuthering Heights* is a particularly appropriate choice for analysis, since the novel has been a source of great critical debate. Carroll's claim is that by reintroducing and "foregrounding the idea of human nature, Darwinian literary theory provides a framework within which we can assimilate previous insights about *Wuthering Heights,* delineate the norms Brontë shares with her projected audience, *analyze her divided impulses,* and explain the generic forms in which those impulses manifest themselves" (242, emphasis added). In the case of *Wuthering Heights,* Carroll's interpretive claim about what he refers to as the novel's "total structure of meaning" is that the psychologies and behaviors of the two generations basically fall into patterns corresponding to tragedy (or a subcategory thereof that Carroll, more problematically, denominates "pathological supernaturalism") and comedy, which upholds social patterns and community and corresponds, in Carroll's view, to the normative patterns of evolved human life history. Thus, at the outset of this recent essay, he describes his aim to account for the two major plot strands (Heathcliff-Catherine and Hareton-Cathy), and he gives a sketch of the components of his model of analysis.

The new essay is therefore much broader in scope than the brief discussion from his first book, which I summarize here. Early in *Evolution and Literary Theory*, just before he offers his cryptic gloss on the Heathcliff-Catherine relationship, Carroll provides a theoretical statement that tellingly reveals his enduring interest in authorial psychology, although this interest is couched in language that obscures it somewhat: "We can say that literature gains access to primal forces, that it assimilates these forces to figurative structures, and that such structures constitute an intuitive imaginative synthesis—sensory, affective, and conceptual—that often outruns scientific understanding" (43). Now, psychological critics of all stripes agree with the notion that all persons, including writers, are motivated in part by psychic forces beyond their conscious awareness, but given Carroll's understandable and comprehensively expressed animus toward poststructuralist textualism, his phrasing here is odd.[9] Strictly speaking, it is not "literature [that] gains access to primal forces," because "literature" is constructed by intending human authors, who are persons with a limited yet crucial degree of insight into their goal-directed activities. But it is just these persons, the evolved human authors, intentional producers of texts with necessarily limited self-awareness, who make only sporadic appearances in Carroll's theory. Throughout the development of Carroll's evolutionary literary criticism since 1993, in fact, the absence of a consistent, pragmatic concept of authorial intention and the habitual substitution of an evolutionarily informed version of depth-psychological analysis of the author as a component of critical interpretation (rather than, for instance, as a component of evaluative criticism or literary biography, whose aims it more legitimately serves) frequently obfuscates Carroll's interpretive claims.[10] This not only conflicts with some of the other protocols Carroll establishes for his interpretive model but selectively psychologizes away aspects of literary works that seem in his view less meritorious than others. Carroll's two separate analyses of the Heathcliff-Catherine relationship serve as cases in point, ultimately suggesting that the psychopathology that disables normative adult sexuality and reproductivity is not of great literary—and, perhaps, human—consequence.

It is worth considering, then, how Carroll views this relationship and how in the recent essay that relationship fits into his full-scale interpretation of the novel. In his original reading of the Heathcliff-Catherine relationship, he first glosses the Westermarck effect, the incest-avoidance phenomenon first observed by the Finnish anthropologist Edward A. Westermarck in 1891 and reported in *The History of Human Marriage*.[11] Based on Westermarck's still-robust empirically grounded theory that boys and girls raised together from a very young age will avoid sexual relations later in life, Carroll insists that "the central conflict in the [Heathcliff-Catherine story] would not be, as is commonly thought, a conflict between unregulated, demonic sexual passion and tamely civilized behavior but rather between regressive childishness and responsible adult behavior" (*Evolution*, 45). In the recent essay, his commentary on the Heathcliff-Catherine relationship forms only a small part of his total reading of the novel. Without acknowledging this original interpretation from *Evolution and Literary Theory*, Carroll alters his view of the relationship considerably in the new essay, making no reference to Westermarck's theory of incest avoidance or to incestuous overtones at all. Instead he says:

> As children, Heathcliff and Catherine have entered into a passional identification in which each is a visible manifestation of the personal identity of the other. Each identifies the other as his or her own "soul." Each is a living embodiment of the sense of the other's self. This is a very peculiar kind of bond—a bond that paradoxically combines attachment to another with the narcissistic love of one's self. Self-love and affiliative sociality have fused into a single motive that transforms the unique integrity of the individual identity into a dyadic relation. Dorothy Van Ghent astutely characterizes the sexually dysfunctional character of this dyadic bond. The relationship is not of "sexual love, naturalistically considered," for "one does not 'mate' with one's self." (251)

Whereas this recent psychological analysis of the relationship is similar to the first in its brevity and in its focus on the inadequate self-development of both Catherine and Heathcliff, which inhibits mature adult attachments, Carroll adopts a less condemnatory, more purely descriptive language than in the first analysis. In both cases, however, the analysis seems to have the function of explaining character psychology as a means of minimizing the relationship's importance insofar as the novel will permit, and in both cases the assumption seems to be that a relationship devoid of normatively functional mating psychology cannot have major literary significance. This is extremely puzzling unless one assumes that for Carroll the criteria for significance are external to the aesthetic object.

The only way that I can make sense of Carroll's attributions of significance and, more especially, his notion of a text as a "structure of meanings" is to assume that we are not talking about literary meaning or significance in the usual sense at all, but about what is normatively significant or meaningful in terms of the elementary goals of life history. In this light, the novelistic facts that account for the peculiar bond that emerges between the two children have great importance for an interpretive critic attuned to the construction of meaning within the textual environment but perhaps not to the life-history normativist.

Nonetheless, Carroll knows that readers and critics alike have treated the Heathcliff-Catherine relationship as *a*, if not *the*, major component of the novel, and as a consequence he wants to account for its central role in what he terms the text's "total structure of meaning." To this end, he demonstrates the fully psychopathological nature of the Heathcliff-Catherine relationship by summarizing Heathcliff's "necrophiliac excursion" at the time of Catherine's interment, when Heathcliff reclines in the grave beside Catherine's corpse. In Carroll's view, Brontë's

> empathic evocation of the feelings of Heathcliff and Catherine . . . indicates that her own emotional energies, like theirs, *seek a release from the constraints of human life history.* Some of the most intense moments of imaginative realization in the novel are those in which violent emotions assert themselves as autonomous and transcendent forms of force—moments like that in which Catherine's ghost cries to be let in at the window and like that in which she haunts Heathcliff and lures him into the other world. *For both Catherine and Heathcliff, dying is a form of spiritual triumph. The transmutation of violent passion into supernatural agency enables them to escape from the world of social interaction and sexual reproduction.* In the sphere occupied by Hareton and the younger Cathy, males and females successfully negotiate their competing interests, form a dyadic sexual bond, and take their place within the reproductive cycle. In the separate sphere occupied by Heathcliff and Catherine, the difference of sex dissolves into a single individual identity, and that individual identity is absorbed into an animistic natural world.   (253, emphasis added)

Thus, Carroll acknowledges the force of the Heathcliff-Catherine relationship while explicitly suggesting that it appeals, if not to like pathologies in the lives of readers, then to a combination of unhealthy, regressive, and destructive inclinations that the audience shares with the author, a point he makes explicit in the immediately subsequent passage: "The fascination Heathcliff and Catherine exercise over readers has multiple sources: a nostalgia for childhood, sympathy with the anguish of childhood griefs, a heightened sensation of the bonding specific to siblings, the attraction of an exclusive passional bond that doubles as a narcissistic fixation on the self, an appetite for violent self-assertion, the lust for domination, the gratification of impulses of vindictive hatred and revenge, the sense of release from conventional social constraints, the pleasure of naturalistic physicality, the animistic excitement of an identification with nature, and the appeal of supernatural fantasies of survival after death" (253). In Carroll's final assessment, the romantic comedy resolution never fully resolves the energies of pathological supernaturalism, because of "a restless discontent with the common satisfactions available to ordinary human life" (254). While many readers do not suffer from Brontë's sexual and social disturbances, that is, we do share the commonplace griefs and frustrations that Carroll lists, we are alert to "discords within the adaptively functional system in which we live" (254).

In his analysis of *Wuthering Heights,* then, Carroll gives the genre of romantic comedy, which aestheticizes and conventionalizes the adaptively functional system of human life described by life-history analysis, pride of place. Of course, we do not live in literary works, and Carroll's habitual tendency to treat literary works as though they are social systems and, as an extension of this, to treat character dysfunction as though it were evidence of the character's marginal place within the social system, conflates humans and their social arrangements with aesthetic artifacts. I noted in chapter 3 that politically motivated literary criticism in particular tends to confer preferential status on certain modes, genres, or techniques, but the undercurrent of a similarly didactic strain in adaptationist literary criticism is unexpected, at least in that Carroll does not begin from the liberationist paradigm of poststructuralists. But evolution is just a process, not itself inherently storylike, as H. Porter Abbott notes, and in our inevitably human narrativizing of it we risk distortion, reduction, and reification.[12] Indeed, evolution is so vast a process that it is ultimately impossible not to recast it in one's own image to some extent. In the case of Carroll's adaptationist literary criticism, the equation of human life history with the genre of comedy militates against impartiality in the analysis of other literary modes and, in this specific instance, encourages the derogation of tragedy and, with it, thoughtful analysis of the Heathcliff-Catherine relationship. In so doing, it strangely suggests, as does the strain of ecocriticism that champions literary realism, discussed in chapter 3, that some modes of literature are not only more aesthetically valid but also more natural than others. To the contrary, since Charles Darwin was inspired by Thomas Malthus's writings on population, his recognition that many more members of a species die than live on to propagate or, in the terms applied here, fulfill the course of life history, would at least suggest that tragedy is no less natural than comedy.

Wuthering Heights and the Social Emotions

Wuthering Heights does not offer very pure versions of tragedy or romantic comedy, but genre criticism is never an exact science in any case. Carroll notes, of course, Northrop Frye's seminal work on genre, *Anatomy of Criticism,* but he overlooks the individual chapters Storey devotes to tragedy and comedy in *Mimesis and the Human Animal,* and these discussions together provide the necessary context for any current evolutionary consideration of the genres. Storey's assessments suggest that, on the whole, the genres have quite different adaptive functions. At the outset of his chapter on comedy, which follows his chapter on tragedy, Storey surmises that the genre exhibits a normative bias toward male wish-fulfillment:

> Certainly the *resolution,* at least of romantic comedy, translates the action to a conceptual plane, since that resolution seems born of an insistent male wish (and a wish, significantly, of the usurper): that the hero of New Comedy should get his girl, often irrespective of what that girl should want or think or feel. Roman theatrical convention tended to ensure that she had little say in the matter. . . . Later comic dramatists (Shakespeare, most familiarly) will smite both partners with a passion, but how fundamentally superfluous is such motivic scrupulosity is suggested by modern successes in the older vein—Mike Nichols's film *The Graduate,* for example, whose Elaine has the tractability of doll or dream. Such pieces work because comedy has, I think, precisely the opposite of that appeal described epigrammatically by Horace Walpole: The world is a comedy, not to those that think, but in fact to those that feel. Unlike tragedy, which encourages scenario-spinning, exercises of consciousness that its Creons neglect, comedy forestalls the thoughtful response. "Comedy usually moves toward a happy ending, and the normal response of the audience to a happy ending is," as Frye writes, "'this should be.'" . . . The affiliative spectacles that conclude most comedies [arouse] a pleasure that recoils at analysis. Unions in comedy can be flimsily motivated; they're sufficiently justified by the feeling they excite. (154)

Storey notes as well the seductive power of the conclusions in romantic comedy, which lead the most sophisticated of critics to overemphasize the element of communal exuberance. Expanding his discussion beyond the parameters of generic romantic comedy, Storey proceeds to link the evolution of all forms of comedy and wit to the audience's perception of mastery. Unlike tragedy, which has at its human center the problem of power and from that source derives its seriousness, its empathic force, and its conflicts, comedy is based on the audience's emotional distance from the characters and on a sense of masterable discrepancies. Comedy encourages the audience's detachment and confirms "self-ratifying intuition" (175), whereas tragedy deepens and refines the social emotions and encourages scenario-spinning.

With Storey's analysis in our sights, we can go back to Carroll's important introductory observation that *Wuthering Heights* has long puzzled readers because of the way it blends these genres, one of which (if we put Carroll's and Storey's insights together) has the objective of affirming life history (comedy) and one of which has the objective of fine-tuning the social emotions (tragedy). Hence, while Brontë's enmeshed relationship with her alcoholic brother Branwell, as Carroll indicates, is undoubtedly a psychological source for some of the tragic elements of *Wuthering Heights,* the author seems to have cast a knowing eye on rationalist Enlightenment and romantic norms and intentionally integrated tragedy and comedy, furthermore consciously leaving some of the tragic energies unresolved in the romantic-comedy conclusion. Much criticism on the novel in the past several decades is in keeping with my own view that Brontë purposely depicts Heathcliff and Catherine, the two characters at the heart of the tragic plot, as self-justifying, psychologically damaged, and emotionally stunted individuals. Pointing to the pronounced degree to which the novel's principal characters attribute their own psychological and behavioral failings to one another, for instance, Marianne Thormählen concludes that the author expects readers to note the extent to which characters not only overestimate their reasoning abilities but attribute their own characteristics to others.[13] Indeed, her ultimate aim, given the story's gaps in knowledge, ambiguous relationships, and resultingly prolonged conflicts of power, appears closer to that claimed by Storey for tragedy—fine-tuning the social emotions—than to the strong communal consolidation of normative comedy, but in the long run Brontë evinces ambivalence toward pure generic norms just as she does about philosophies, ideals, and social attitudes such as rationalism and romanticism (not to mention Victorian cultural hegemony). Whereas Carroll's reading implies that the two generic elements are incompletely assimilated (and perhaps therein implies that the novel is aesthetically flawed), I believe that Brontë ultimately integrates the two in a way that also fully brings together the realistic and conceptual levels of the story.

The general distinction that Storey makes between tragedy and comedy has some deeper implications for the rest of this analysis. If comedy draws on our sense of mastery—our sense of superiority to characters and the situations they encounter—and if romantic comedy in particular reasserts the social order and the functionally adaptive system (sanitized in its purer manifestations of its ever-embedded, ever-humanly natural aberrations), it provides primarily psychological and emotional rewards for the audience. If tragedy, on the other hand, is about power, it speaks to our species-typical ambivalence toward one another and, in contrast to comedy, to what seems beyond our control, and it therefore exerts psychological, emotional, and cognitive demands.[14] Unlike the bastard mingled drama that Sir Phillip Sidney eschewed, the tragicomedy, wherein tragic possibility and its challenges accede to the logic of romantic comedy and its rewards, *Wuthering Heights* is saturated in the tragic ethos, the problem of power and its abuse. It is not just that the abuse of power is protracted in the novel; the sphere of action—the domestic, familial sphere—intensifies and prolongs the reader's psychological pain and magnifies the sense of inexplicable, unmasterable cruelty. The truth is, however, that the cruelties in the novel are readily explicable once readers are willing to admit what they are and once readers begin to think about how scenario-spinning comes to function in tragedy in general and in this novel in particular.

For scenarios to be spun, and for any literary work or dramatic production to incite analysis and "the thoughtful response," things have to be missing, because it is these holes and gaps that undermine the feeling of mastery and control. In *Wuthering Heights,* informational deficits focus attention on two features of the story and their ability to unsettle all other human relationships (and, therefore, power dynamics): first, the character of Heathcliff, and second, the Heathcliff-Catherine relationship. Certainly, Heathcliff, who fits the morally ambiguous type of the Byronic hero rather than that of the classical tragic hero, evokes, in the long run, a complex blend of feelings that cannot be resolved easily and that would tend to encourage narrativizing. Frye compares him to other villains of low mimetic tragedy (39), but the beginning and end of his story offer a far more complex profile than is provided for the typical villain. At first (it seems), through no cause of his own, he is the center and source of the novel's problems of power and relationship. Introduced unceremoniously into the household by Mr. Earnshaw after a trip to London and given the name of a dead Earnshaw child, has he been adopted, or is he, in fact, Mr. Earnshaw's illegitimate son? Although evolutionary theory still struggles to explain altruism toward nonkin, literature and perhaps life itself abound in examples in which the benefits to the giver are obscure.[15] But whatever the reason for Heathcliff's introduction into the household, there is no balance of power thereafter, and it is the problematic nature of familial power relations, not the cause of their disruption, that is the focus of the story. Whereas it is impossible to surmise the feelings of Mrs. Earnshaw, who before her death early in the novel must raise an adopted or illegitimate child in the place of her deceased child, not so those of Hindley, formerly sure, as the eldest son, of his entitlement. The main narrator, Nelly Dean, does indeed tell Lockwood that Heathcliff's is a "cuckoo's history" (28),[16] but the fact remains that Heathcliff is not analogous to the cuckoo's egg left in another bird's nest; Heathcliff is adopted (in however odd a fashion), not left on the doorstep by a band of gypsies. Catherine's and Mr. Earnshaw's early favoritism toward Heathcliff, the deaths within two years of both parents, and displaced Hindley's bitterness and tyranny all provide the conditions under which the unusually intense bond forms between Heathcliff and Catherine. In the sudden absence of parental care and, in this case, the substitution of a perhaps too-indulgent parent (Mr. Earnshaw) by an abusive guardian (Hindley), a bond between children that conflates attachment to another with loving the self seems a psychologically predictable phenomenon.

Cruelty is a negative means of expressing power, and whereas there seems nothing inexplicable in the fact that Heathcliff, who knew no love other than Catherine's after Mr. Earnshaw's death, would seek revenge on those who had humiliated and abused him and strive to dominate over weakness (a psychology lesson Brontë may have imbibed from Percy Shelley), what seems hard to fathom is the extent to which cruelty comes to dominate the microcosm of the novel.[17] For while Heathcliff waxes monstrous, the narrators, Nelly and Lockwood, occupying vastly different social spheres, combine with the Lintons, Heathcliff, Catherine, Hindley, Joseph, and Linton Heathcliff to articulate the novel's abuses of power both large and small. On the one hand, it is, as Carroll points out, part of our evolved psychology to understand the disruption that ensues when Heathcliff is introduced into the household, for this causes "a parasitic appropriation of resources that belong to the offspring of another organism" (249). Carroll goes partway toward explaining the natural impact of the introduction of Heathcliff into the household, its deformation of human sociality and power, and its related working-through in the genres of tragedy and comedy. For it is at this point, when Heathcliff is just a small boy, that cruelty and incivility take precedence in Brontë's story. Indeed, the cruelty and incivility that emerge in the early pages of *Wuthering Heights* are as demonstrably a part of human nature as the principles of life history at the core of Carroll's theory.

Ultimately, Brontë's point is that none of these characters occupy separate spheres or are coded into separate genres or discourses. Whereas Carroll sees the tragic and comedic elements stay on separate paths, I would suggest that Brontë effects a merger of the two at the end of the novel that has the fine-tuning function for the reader that Storey surmises is typical of tragedy. Heathcliff's realization that Catherine lives in Hareton and Cathy suddenly dissipates his will for revenge and effects a dramatic resolution. It is imperative that Brontë effect this assimilation through Heathcliff, who, as both monster and victim, most occupies the ambivalent center of the reader's efforts to construct an emotional, moral, and social order to the novelistic world:

> Five minutes ago, Hareton seemed a personification of my youth, not a human being. I felt to him in such a variety of ways, that it would have been impossible to have accosted him rationally.
>
> In the first place, his startling likeness to Catherine connected him fearfully with her. That, however, which you may suppose the most potent to arrest my imagination, is actually the least, for what is not connected with her to me? and what does not recall her? I cannot look down to this floor, but her features are shaped on the flags! In every cloud, in every tree—filling the air at night. . . . The entire world is a dreadful collection of memoranda that she did exist, and that I have lost her!
>
> Well, Hareton's aspect was the ghost of my immortal love, of my wild endeavours to hold my right, my degradation, my pride, my happiness, and my anguish— (247)

In effect, through especially the perception that Hareton is the incarnation of Catherine, the ghost with whom Heathcliff has long been obsessed, now literally materialized, becomes an obliterating presence. While perhaps for Catherine "dying is a form of spiritual triumph," as Carroll claims for both characters of the major tragic plot, this is hardly true of Heathcliff, who has not sought or expected death but has been highly motivated by a thirst for revenge against those who have abandoned him and, indeed, as Eric P. Levy notes, against life itself.[18] Indeed, revenge has been Heathcliff's lifeblood.[19] From this point on, however, Heathcliff cannot stand to be in the presence of Hareton and Cathy. He tells Nelly, "Those two, who have left the room, are the only objects which retain a distinct material appearance to me; and that appearance causes me pain, amounting to agony" (247). At the level of psychological realism that is Carroll's focus of analysis, Heathcliff is not well suited, given what readers know of his psychologically formative experiences (compared with his later material successes), to entering "the world of social interaction and sexual reproduction," and his overestimation of the love object since childhood, as well as the narcissistic pattern of attachment to Catherine, is symptomatic of the inadequate care, abandonment, and abuse to which he was subject as a child. Furthermore, the fact that Heathcliff identifies with Hareton ("the personification of my youth"), whom he has debased as an act of revenge but cannot help loving in his own fashion, merges with Hareton's uncanny resemblance to the elder Catherine to create an obliterating sense of Catherine and Hareton's nascent love. Heathcliff dimly recognizes that their union will be the final outgrowth of his love for Catherine (young Cathy is literally Catherine Earnshaw's daughter and Hareton is figuratively Heathcliff's adoptive son), and thus their love logically countermands the revenge motive and, in effect, provides no psychological justification for him to continue living. Since they are the living evidence of Catherine's omnipresence and thus the cause of his joy but also the longtime objects of his revenge, he understandably finds their presence intolerable. In sum, although Heathcliff is just beginning to perceive that he must leave this world, he also recognizes that he and Catherine remain inevitably, materially within it.

Conceptually, of course, this means that at the realistic level the story (the accomplishment of life-history goals in the romantic plot) is inextricably linked with the conclusion of the tragic plot and the purgation of feelings aroused by cruelty and revenge as the dominant modes of power. Brontë's *reader* escapes nothing with Heathcliff's death, but closes the book with a consciousness more attuned to the manifold ways humans choose to exert power through the exercise of cruelties great and small. We are reminded of the smaller ways in many of the scenes involving the Lintons, such as the memorable first scene at Thrushcross Grange, when Edgar and Isabella nearly pull apart their pet dog. Edgar is quick to establish his sense of social superiority over Heathcliff when he makes Catherine's acquaintance, and it does not seem wonderful that Heathcliff would seek revenge. Is this the fault of Mr. Earnshaw's misguided kindness, or is there another cause? Is Heathcliff Mr. Earnshaw's illegitimate child? *Conceptually*, it does not matter, ultimately, what Heathcliff's origins are: he is, in this sense, related to the Earnshaws, the natural, unknowable, and eternal thing his name names him, the dead child come back to disrupt and so finally to tame the world of the Heights by exposing the cruelties we so liberally license within our adaptively functional systems.

Inbreeding Depression and Romantic Incest

In developing his recent analysis of the novel, Carroll put aside his earlier discussion of the incestuous overtones in the Heathcliff-Catherine relationship. But the novel *does* have incestuous overtones, and a biocultural interpretation of the novel needs to consider how they might apply to the conceptual level of the novel if they do not quite fit the factual level. Among other things, it is certainly odd that the incestuous overtones are most pronounced in the relationship of the two characters who are not ostensibly biologically related, whereas Hareton and young Cathy are as closely related as Charles Darwin and his own wife. Thus, there is an apparent misalignment of the actual and the conceptual levels of the novel with respect to the incest motif (though this is untrue if, in fact, Heathcliff is the illegitimate offspring of Mr. Earnshaw). In his first analysis, Carroll employs the theory of incest avoidance to claim that critics have erroneously imputed a sexual component to the Heathcliff-Catherine relationship. To my mind, this is another instance of treating literary artifacts as though they were adaptively functional systems. Literature does not have to play by the rules of the actual, simply because readers do not require that it does. As Alan Richardson puts it, "Fictive works can bear a number of different relations to the rules and regularities of daily experience, often giving us the inverse of the lived world."[20] Events that adhere to conditions of probability within the literary world and motifs that are compatible with such conditions but are impossible in the observable, actual world have long been acceptable to readers and theater audiences. As Aristotle recognized, the conditions of probability are determined by the work itself, not the laws of the physical or social universe. One serious challenge for those engaged in interdisciplinary approaches that bring the scientific realm to bear on the imaginative is to confront and acknowledge the willing suspension of disbelief that empowers fictive representation, for our legitimate awareness that biopsychological factors inform literature inadvertently pushes us toward a literalization of aesthetic material. And yet we know that, properly contextualized within the total artwork, asexual reproduction, routine cannibalism, incest, and many other literally unlikely behaviors are often fully plausible. *Facts*, furthermore, cannot answer to what readers feel, and any reading of *Wuthering Heights* must contend with the fact that most readers will necessarily infer that mutual sexual interest explains the intensity of the feelings in such an obsessive relationship. I believe that the relationship *is* incestuous, metaphorically if not literally so, because the bond between Heathcliff and Catherine represents the psychological equivalent of inbreeding depression. That is, deprived of the healthy, distributed, and varied forms of human attachment that typify the life-history pattern, Heathcliff and Catherine, lacking normal relationships with parents, siblings, and an extended social community, become so pathologically overidentified with each other that they are not properly individuated. Because they do not recognize and develop their own autonomy, of course, they are unable to grasp the autonomy and individuality of others.

In her depiction of Heathcliff and Catherine's incestuous, psychological entanglement, Brontë knowingly engages a common motif of her time. Richardson places her use of the motif in the context of a literary historical overview of the romantic-era literary pattern and describes social trends that frame it. The literary motif of romantic incest was influenced by associationist psychology and sympathy theory, which suggested that those raised together from an early age would share the same basic nature and would have gathered impressions from the same environment, experiences that could not be reproduced in later life. Romantic incest, thus conceived, was an intensification and extension of the normal sibling relationship. However, as Richardson points out, in all its literary representations it ends in tragedy, even in the works of Byron and Shelley, who both idealized it. In Richardson's view, changing conceptions of the family and women, including trends toward tighter nuclear-family units and the emphasis on childhood as a playful, protected, developmental phase; warmer sibling relationships before brothers went to school; and idealization of women all had an enduring impact on sibling relationships and provided the social background against which the literary motif of romantic incest developed.

To my mind, moreover, the forces of modernity propelled by the industrial revolution fostered the need for close relationships, which, in effect, healed and legitimated fragmented and dispersed selves. Disease, separation, and untimely death were common in the lives of these writers, but so were the values of sympathy, education, and self-development, and it is hardly a wonder that the cherished sense of family would, under the strain of repeated loss, become an image of the sibling mirrored as the self. In the backgrounds of these authors, certainly, the intensity of sibling relationships that resulted in the incest motif seem to have been the result of two things: absent parents, particularly mothers, who tended to succumb to disease after giving birth for five or six years in rapid succession, and either under- or overexposure to one's own siblings. When Emily Brontë's mother died in 1821, her aunt Elizabeth came to live with the family in Haworth; in 1824 Emily, aged five, left home to attend the Cowan Bridge School for clergymen's daughters, but she left in 1825 after the death there of two of her sisters, Maria and Elizabeth. Sometimes families were divided, however. When William Wordsworth was eight, his mother died, and his sister Dorothy, to whom he was especially attached, was sent to live with their cousin Mary Hutchinson. William went to live with his uncle Christopher. William and Dorothy did not see each other again for nine years, after which she lived with her brother as a member of his household for her entire adult life. Donald Reiman persuasively argues that while there is no evidence of an incestuous relationship between the brother and sister, there is evidence of conflicting and confused feelings.[21]

Nonetheless, by the time Brontë employed the incest motif, as well as that of the Byronic hero, it was fairly well worn, and the Victorian temper held sway. If the incest motif in its original manifestations is problematic, signifying a much-desired unity that has suicidal consequences, Brontë's employment of it in *Wuthering Heights* is, at the outset, hopelessly darker because informed by the manipulations of the unstable personality. As an operant feature of the novel, the incest motif draws powerfully on the sense of the illicit and forbidden; readers respond to a sense of basic wrongness in the kinship between Heathcliff and Catherine, which is like that of actual incest but actually "purely" psychological, rather than biologically based, in its nature (the overidentification stressed by Carroll and many others).

Thus, although first cousins, Hareton and Cathy are generous, kind-hearted, and socially different *enough* to repair the wreck of the Lintons and the Earnshaws into a system that functions again. Sadder and wiser children than the young Edgar and Isabella, they also, like that earlier generation, however, live without one salient feature of comedy: a settled and established human community. The sense of isolated families in this novel is extreme for narratives of the mid-Victorian era. Although many nineteenth-century novels feature individuals or families temporarily severed from larger communal structures, within the narrative none are so chronically disconnected as the characters in *Wuthering Heights*. The narrators and the characters seem to live in their own worlds and those of the two dysfunctional families, with infrequent contact with the communities and cities beyond. As a result, Wuthering Heights, and eventually Thrushcross Grange, draws no social and moral sustenance from the larger human community.

As I have stressed throughout this book, humans are perhaps the most social of species because the protection of the group has been necessary to the survival of individuals in the course of species evolution. Attachment to place often becomes the image of human security, but this image, like the "rainy night" representative of Catherine and Heathcliff's love, can also be deceptive. As Levy notes, theirs is a love founded on rejection and a shared state of exclusion, so the "scamper on the moors" that symbolizes their bond also marks their isolation from the larger community (164). In so doing, it underscores the fragility of their relationship, because it marks the patterns of that relationship as wholly disconnected from communal order. What makes them feel united, in sum, marks their essential instability; indeed, it marks the social and natural instability of the world of *Wuthering Heights*. The vulnerability of that world to disruption seems, in all likelihood, a function of its too-minimal social order.

In the view of the anthropologist Robin Dunbar, "the lack of social contact, the lack of a sense of community, may be the most pressing social problem of the new millennium."[22] As my analysis suggests (and as Dunbar would likely agree), the problem of deficient community emerged well before the twenty-first century, and it marks literature in a variety of ways. Turning my attention now to sex-differential mating strategies, power dynamics, and individuality and equality within relationships, I ultimately suggest that in D. H. Lawrence's novella *The Fox* the lack of community removes a check on the power dynamic in the human pair bond, as well as eliminating an advising system in the process of mate choice to the main characters. The socialization of the central male character, Henry Grenfel, combined with his youth and a number of other factors, exacerbates some key features of male reproductive behavior. After providing an overview of the literature on sex-differential mating strategies in the next section, I explore the sociohistorical, individual, and social factors that lead to Henry's need to control Nellie March to supersede his desire for a viable, productive relationship with her. Especially because evolutionary psychology posits a conflict between the reproductive priorities of women and those of men, we might expect that women's interests are likely to be compromised under ecological conditions in which communal and other forms of support are lacking. Mimetic literature provides a rich and varied picture of life on the margins, and a Darwinian feminist perspective can illuminate male-female power dynamics in such lonely places.

Mating Strategies, Monogamy, and Sexual Equality

In *Madame Bovary's Ovaries: A Darwinian Look at Literature,* written in 2005 for a popular audience, David P. Barash and Nanelle R. Barash present the following evolutionary explanation for the core of Jane Austen's work:

> Jane Austen's domain . . . is the female-oriented realm of sexual selection: choosing a mate and getting chosen. Just as males have largely cornered the market on violent same-sex competition, females occupy the spotlight when it comes to the choosy component of sexual selection. Why this difference? Essentially, it's because females have something that males want. Since males are comparatively eager and more or less sexually undiscriminating ("easy come, easy go" is a biologically accurate account of male sexuality, on several levels), females are often in the driver's seat: mate choice is largely their province.[23]

Or as Kathleen Turner once steamily inquired of William Hurt, "You're not smart, are you? I like that in a man."[24] There are more contagious clichés in the Barashes' book than you can shake the proverbial stick at, but the bare bones of what they say about the differential mate-selection strategies of men and women and about

Jane Austen's preeminent exemplification of it is textbook evolutionary psychology, and they are hardly the first to use Austen as an example. As the Barashes do here, literary commentators such as Brian Boyd, Carroll, and Kathryn Duncan and Michael Stasio, who pitch their analyses toward a scholarly audience, all emphasize the role of female choice in Austen's universe of monogamous mate selection.[25] But the disproportionate emphasis on the matchmaking talents of this spinster novelist both instructively reflects the baseline norms with which adaptationist criticism connects her work and simultaneously misses the opportunity to emphasize not only that the operation of choice is ecologically sensitive but that the operation of *female choice* has nothing to do with *sexual equality*. The purpose of this section, then, is to explain how recent evolutionary psychology has modified our conception of human mating dynamics; to illustrate how that picture of the differential mating and survival strategies of men and women has been employed in adaptationist criticism; and to claim that the somewhat disproportionate attention to the single feature of female choice in Austen's world casts a rather rosy light on the dynamics of human mating. While evolutionary social science has taken enormous strides toward correcting male bias, we need always to keep in mind that correction in one context hardly amounts to complete and permanent remediation.

Compared with the early thinking about female sexual behavior from an evolutionary perspective, the notion that females actually exercise reproductive choices appears wildly revolutionary. As the biological anthropologist Sarah Blaffer Hrdy explains in *Mother Nature: A History of Mothers, Infants, and Natural Selection,* hypotheses about male and female abilities and behavior in nineteenth-century evolutionary thought and in early sociobiology and ethology in the mid-twentieth century suffered from male bias. According to Hrdy, the Victorian-era social theorist Herbert Spencer, whose particular notion of evolution strongly reflected his culture's positivism, also held that

> the supreme function of women . . . was childbearing, and toward that great
> eugenic end women should be beautiful so as to keep the species physically
> up to snuff. Because mammalian females are the ones that ovulate, gestate, bear
> young, and lactate . . . Spencer assumed that the diversion of so much energy
> into reproduction had inevitably to lead to "an earlier arrest of individual evo-
> lution in women than in men," . . . Not only were men and women different,
> but Spencer's females were mired in maternity.
>
> [Spencer argued that] the costs of reproduction constrained mental devel-
> opment in women and imposed narrow bounds on how much any one female

could vary from another in terms of intellect. Since variation between individuals is essential for natural selection to take place (which is true), Spencer
reasoned (wrongly) that there was too little variation among females for proper
selection to occur, precluding the evolution in women of higher "intellectual
and emotional" faculties, which are the "latest products of human evolution."

(14)

In short, Spencer and other evolutionists of his day imported many of their
culture's attitudes about men and women—that the cultural division of labor
was preordained by physiology, that women had not evolved "the power of abstract reasoning and that most abstract of emotions, the sentiment of justice"
(Hrdy, 15), that smaller-than-average brain mass correlated with lower intelligence for women—into evolutionary theory and used evolution to validate those
attitudes.[26]

Hindsight reveals that many of these attitudes were still robust nearly a hundred years later. In the 1960s, many animal researchers studied maternal behavior out of its natural context, focusing on the dyadic mother-infant unit without
observing that relations with the larger group and features of the physical environment were fundamental to a mother's *decision* to nurture. One thing these
empirical research programs reveal is a failure to grasp the implications of Darwinian thinking that fluctuating and, over time, changing features of the environment are central to evolution, which in turn implies that behavior gauged
to promote survival will vary significantly depending on environmental conditions. Recognition that researchers needed to look at a more complicated picture
emerged with a growing awareness that natural selection does not function primarily at the level of the group: individual behavior must promote *inclusive fitness,* the survival of that individual's genes. Mothers who focus solely on producing and nurturing young without taking account of changes in the social group
and of the viability of the natural environment—in other words, mothers who are
essentially passive except with respect to their young—are unlikely to survive for
very long, much less produce viable offspring. In short, animal researchers became aware that a picture in which males competed for access to females and
females reproduced and nurtured young was highly simplified, and research in the
past forty-five years has focused on *female choice* concerning when conditions
are favorable for raising young to maturity.

Hrdy's lucid gloss on the ethological context clarifies why Jane Austen's work
stands as such a fine textbook example for adaptationist literary critics. The opportunity to make positive reproductive choices depends on ecological conditions,

including resource availability, parental and social support, and adequate shelter, and this generally holds true for humans as well as for other mammalian species. When conditions are adverse, however, females choose not to mate (if possible) or choose not to invest in offspring unlikely to survive under harsh conditions. The ecological conditions of Austen's novels are, all things considered, enormously stable, since each reflects a well-established, hierarchically ordered social community whose operative principles have not been fundamentally challenged or eroded at the outset or during the course of the narrative by war, environmental catastrophe, or some other disabling force.

"What do Jane's young ladies look for in a mate?" ask the Barashes. "The same traits that female animals generally look for in their swains. Call them the three goods: good genes, good behavior, and good stuff" (43). In fact, the discriminating attention that modern human females pay to the availability of these three goods in their suitors drives the phenomenon of *hypergamy,* or marrying up, a specialty of women. But the picture as so far described, wherein men compete with one another and women, with their hypergamous hopes, vie for the attention of higher-status males is, in truth, rather simplified. As David Geary explains in his overview of sexual selection in contemporary humans, there are four central factors to the dynamics of human mating: female-female competition; male choice; male-male competition; and female choice.[27] In any given case, sociopolitical contexts and environmental conditions affect the expression of all four of these factors, and not least of these contexts would be the type of marriage system operating within the existing social system. Monogamous marriage systems have been established in one in six societies worldwide; nearly all others are polygamous. Polyandrous societies are extremely rare, accounting for less than 1 percent of marriage systems, and typically exist in conditions of great privation and scarcity.

In the passage from *Madame Bovary's Ovaries* quoted above, the Barashes suggest that because men are preoccupied with competing with one another to establish sociopolitical power and acquire resources, they leave the women to sort out the sexual arrangements for them. Of course, film noir notwithstanding, none of us has ever seen a world so rich in undiscriminating men, and the reality of the matter is that male choice is, to one degree or another, an operant factor in the dynamics of mating. However, how large or what kind of role male choice plays may depend on that of the other three factors, not least of all male-male competition.

The ultimate (evolved or original) cause of male-male competition is reproductive access to women. If a man successfully acquires resources and power, he maintains his high status by *controlling lower-status males and women*. One-on-one and coalition-based aggression are more common in societies in which there is greater variation in male reproductive success than in Western monogamous societies, because such variation is a product of allowing a few men to disproportionately control women and material resources. In such societies, in other words, some men, because of their status, are able to attract many wives and therefore have many children, and thus men of low status have a comparatively difficult time finding mates. Male-male competition takes four basic forms: blood revenge; economic gain; female capture; and personal prestige. Clearly, the first and third of these forms of competition are in conflict with female choice, since they oppose the inclusive fitness and, indeed, direct psychological needs of a woman, who cannot count on resource provision from a deceased spouse or provide nurture to her infant once she has been captured. Although the second and fourth forms of competition are far more common in modern industrial society than the first and third, even laws prohibiting blood revenge and capture have not entirely relegated them to our ancestral past.

This brief account of male-male aggression is by way of a reminder that half of the methods that promote inclusive fitness for men are not only deleterious to the inclusive fitness of women but also a primary source of societal violence. While adaptationist literary scholars directly acknowledge and discuss conflict in male and female reproductive strategies, their literary analyses emphasize that Western monogamous society has been a valuable compromise, depressing the more violent forms of male-male competition both by serving the need of lower-status males for reproductive access and by facilitating female choice for social stability. Yet monogamy's overall functional utility for the individuals who make fitness decisions within the monogamous system depends significantly on their place in the social hierarchy as well as on the overall health of the social communities to which they are connected. In Jane Austen's novels, that social world is quite robust, and its general strength results in perhaps artificially vigorous representations of Regency and Victorian England. Moreover, no fringe-dwelling character, no Mrs. Bates in danger of falling through the social net, ever moves to the center of the action. I will return to the topic of monogamy in a moment, but for now we should recognize that from an evolutionary point of view, evidence suggests that the reproductive interests of men and women will never be aligned.

In nearly all species, including humans, males and females have distinct reproductive strategies, because the two sexes have different roles in the reproductive process. For women, as for most mammalian females, reproduction is expensive; fertilization of an egg entails a long and physically taxing pregnancy. Not only is the human infant notoriously helpless, demanding a great deal of attention, but the developmental span of a human being is extremely long compared with that of other species. Since all evidence drawn from traditional as well as modern societies and ethology indicates that women are overwhelmingly responsible for the nurture and protection of the young, they have a very high degree of parental investment. By contrast, for men, sex and reproduction are not particularly costly: compared with women, who have a limited supply of eggs, men have abundant sperm; men do not have physiological costs associated with pregnancy; and men's parental investment in young is typically a fraction of women's. Given this scenario, Darwinians argue that males will seek out sex more often than females and will compete with other males for access to females, whereas females will be more selective in mate choice, prizing males who can provide protection and resources, the counterpart to their high parental investment in young.

It is these different roles in the reproductive process that cause the differential approaches to mating in the interests of inclusive fitness, and the relatively high emphasis in men on intersex competition and in women on selectiveness are a reflection of this.[28] Cross-culturally, studies of female choice identify a preference for dominant males, resource provision, and monogamy. Women are, as evolutionary social scientists repeatedly point out, the "choosy" sex, expressing a preference for kindness and intelligence in their mates. Notably, then, women may assess prospective mates according to qualities that may not be readily available in a single candidate: although dominance and strong resource provision are highly desirable, a man with superior intellectual, emotional, and social characteristics may often be preferable to a rich, arrogant provider. In Geary's view, this is especially so in contemporary nucleated, mobile Western families, which frequently lack connection to a larger kinship or communal group. Since the everyday emotional satisfactions that are, in effect, a fundamental part of being human are quite hard to come by in our society, the derivation of such satisfaction from the marital relationship itself becomes emotionally crucial for many women.

Unlike women, who generally exhibit a preference for dominant, resource-holding males, men pursue a mixed reproductive strategy overall, seeking short-term partners requiring low investment as well as long-term marital partners requiring high investment. Not surprisingly, the criteria for the types of partners vary greatly, and it is this mixed strategy that earns men the reputation for being less "choosy" than women. Men prefer the same personal and behavioral attributes in long-term partners that women do: they want friendly wives with a sense of humor who are intelligent, kind, and understanding. Like women, they put a high priority on attractiveness; in fact, as it will surprise no one to learn, sexual attractiveness is an even greater priority for men than it is for women. In cross-cultural studies of thirty-seven countries, men consistently preferred partners younger than themselves, a finding explained in evolutionary terms by the fact that fecundity peaks at about age twenty-five, then steadily declines to zero at age forty-five. However, when seeking short-term partners, men are not so selective, especially with regard to intelligence (Geary, 147).

To the extent that men invest parentally, their choices will align more with women's, and this is indeed what happens in monogamous marriage systems, as Geary explains. Whether socially imposed or ecologically produced, monogamy restricts the power of elite men and constrains male-male competition by eliminating the advantages of its more violent forms and aggressive expressions. In monogamous systems, men of lower status generally enjoy a higher degree of reproductive access to women than in societies governed by male coalitions, where high-status males, by virtue of having many wives, deprive lower-status men of sexual access. In this manner, monogamy greatly reduces male-on-male violence and indeed reduces social violence overall. Monogamy enables fuller expression of female choice at the same time that it intensifies male choice and female-female competition. As Geary remarks,

Male-male competition in these societies essentially shifts from the use of physical violence to control the behavior of other people to the accumulation of indicators of cultural success. . . . Achieving cultural success is simply another means of achieving control and increasing one's ability to exercise one's reproductive preferences, but this influence is not achieved by force.

Rather, for men, cultural success increases the ability to exercise one's reproductive preferences, but the exercise of these preferences is moderated more by female choice than by direct male-on-male aggression. . . . Female choice, in turn, is largely influenced by the social, material, and perhaps the genetic benefits that a marriage or mating partner can provide to a woman and her children. Moreover, with a relatively monogamous mating system, marriage restricts the man's parental investment to one woman, or at least one woman at a time, and her children. Relatively high levels of paternal investment, in turn, appear to result in men being rather more choosy than might otherwise be the case, with male choice largely focused on compatibility with a potential marriage partner and on indicators of the women's likely fecundity. . . . The other side of this coin is that as men become more selective in their choice of marriage partners, competition among women for preferable marriage partners increases. Such competition involves enhancing indicators of fecundity (e.g., the use of makeup to produce a more youthful appearance) and derogating and socially excluding competitors.   (156)

Geary's summary of the impact of monogamy highlights the complexity of human mating dynamics, for characteristic differences between male and female choice are significantly altered by the marriage system alone. However, we must avoid interpreting Geary's assessment too optimistically. While it is undoubtedly true that distinct social institutions, legal codes, and legal enforcement tend to bring the reproductive strategies of men and women into greater alignment, this does not presuppose that any marriage system is inherently more egalitarian than another. Reproductive interests can be brought into relative alignment without addressing the question of equal rights at all, as Jane Austen's novels, written well before the advent of married women's property rights in either Britain or America, so well illustrate. Equal rights and opportunities for women as autonomous social beings is a quite separate matter from situations that might be conducive to *female choice,* a term referring to fitness decisions. In fact, Geary's concluding sentences, which point to the increased intensity in the fourth central factor in mating dynamics, *female-female competition,* imply that women actually face a new mating challenge and a new obstacle to women's rights under institutional monogamy: increased competition among themselves.

Whereas men compete to acquire resources and thus gain status and reproductive access to women, women compete with one another for the attention of resource-holding males. Female-on-female aggression is almost never as intense or direct as male-on-male aggression, and research indicating sex differences in relational aggression from the preschool years onward shows that girls favor relational aggression and demonstrate an increase in its use about the time of puberty. In addition to directly enhancing their looks to attract desirable men, "social gossiping and social exclusion might be an implicit tactic designed to increase social stress" (137). Gossip against competitors is often focused on sexual fidelity. Furthermore, evolutionists view dowry traditions in societies that have them as forms of female-female competition, because payment to the groom's family occurs primarily in highly stratified societies with socially imposed monogamy. Since wealthy men in such societies are investing in a single wife, the mate value of these men is extremely high.

In short, if monogamy increases aggression between women, who are not predisposed to organize as men are in same-sex coalitions, we should not assume that the lot of all women is necessarily in every way improved by it. Although women in polygynous as well as monogamous societies all state a preference for monogamy (in other words, not sharing the husband and resources), it seems crucial to acknowledge that the institutionalization of this form of marriage, which appears to provide some fitness benefit for women, nonetheless increases other challenges that women face in the area of mating dynamics. Since increased aggression between women in a monogamous society translates, for many women, into greater difficulty in both finding and retaining husbands, the assumptions about stable support that likely stand behind the preference for monogamy may be partly illusory, unless women's property rights and strong child-support laws are in place and consistently upheld in societies where divorce has become available. Ironically, however, the tendency of monogamy to work against female alliances (because it increases female-female competition) probably delayed the institutionalization of these protective measures at the very time when divorce was becoming more common in the West.

If evolutionary psychologists are correct in suggesting that mild polygyny is, on average, the typical reproductive strategy of the human male, and if we live in a patriarchal culture, the obvious question, then, is this: How did monogamy come about? Robert Wright summarizes the conclusion of the biologist Richard Alexander, proposed in 1975 and still considered the major explanation for the spread of state-imposed universal monogamy (SIUM): "Polygyny has tended to disappear in response to egalitarian values—not values of equality between the sexes, but of equality among men. And maybe 'egalitarian values' is too polite a way of putting it. As political power became distributed more evenly, the hoarding of women by upper-class men simply became untenable. Few things are more anxiety-producing for an elite governing class than gobs of sex-starved and childless men with at least a modicum of political power" (98). Why so untenable? Because sex-starved men are, simply put, dangerous. Wright suggests that monogamy is, effectively, a sociopolitical bargain among men that provides reproductive access to a greater number of men by limiting each man to a single wife; this bargain has the larger social benefit of reducing violence. Although Westerners are inclined to think of polygyny as backward, Wright points out that a lower-class woman and her children might well be better off if she were the third or fourth wife of an affluent man than if she were the only wife of a poor one.

Walter Scheidel's current research on the purportedly monogamous systems of ancient cultures lends support to Alexander's analysis by providing a more thorough historical account while, importantly, rebutting the suggestion that monogamy necessarily institutes sexual equality between men and women.[29] In Scheidel's words, "The traditional dichotomy of 'polygamy' and 'monogamy' fails to capture real-world differentiation among marriage and mating practices" (3).

Noting that "in the Greco-Roman world, elite polygyny looms large in the Homeric tradition," Scheidel reports that "it was not until the sixth century CE, after centuries of Christian influence, that the emperor Justinian claimed that 'ancient law' prohibited husbands from keeping wives and concubines at the same time" (4). The key to this apparent puzzle is the importation of captured women:

> The institution of chattel slavery helped facilitate as well as mask effective polygyny in the context of SIUM. . . . It is therefore misleading to suggest that SIUM permitted "a paradoxical combination of principles, sexual equality and social inequality." Instead, SIUM coupled with chattel slavery served to maintain strict (serial) monogamy—ensuring access to legitimate wives for low-resource men and preserving an appearance of sexual equality that chimed with concurrent ideals of judicial and sometimes political equality—whilst simultaneously enabling the translation of resource inequality into effective polygyny, i.e., sexual *in*equality. It is only in a closed population with a balanced sex ratio that these features could not possibly be reconciled: Greeks and Romans solved this problem by importing disfranchised women from outside their own in-groups.   (9)

Clearly, a substantial portion of the female population of ancient Greece and Rome under these nominally monogamous systems had neither choice nor the other forms of autonomy and rights associated with sexual or any other kind of equality.

As Scheidel's analysis of early "monogamous" systems makes explicit, then, you may call your marriage system one thing while leaving some women without rights or freedom. Yet the extent to which men seek to control, and even successfully control, the behavior of women is a matter apart from where control appropriately lies for the organism motivated to preserve its inclusive fitness. Given the opportunity, women will tend, on the whole, to organize their behavior and experience in ways that differ from the ways men organize theirs. As Geary explains, the human mind serves as a functional system that controls individual experience and reproductive opportunity under all conditions. Although unconscious, the ultimate (evolved) motives that constrain individual decisions and orient the organism in the interests of inclusive fitness affect a broad range of behaviors and decisions. Because men and women have different roles in reproduction and correspondingly differing mating strategies, they typically differ in many of their motivational, emotional, cognitive, and developmental patterns. The individual functional system will seek to control experience at various levels in keeping with what the environment, which includes members of other species as well as one's own, allows. Unsurprisingly, then, women and men vary in the values that manifest and express their efforts to control reproductive opportunity and inclusive fitness. On the whole, women orient toward altruism, reciprocity, and social stability, whereas men orient toward aggression, power, and political activities. In particular, men attempt to control both resources and women, but perhaps most significantly, they seek to garner and control the former as a means of access to and control over the latter.

These peculiarly human dynamics may help to explain why the marriage system of a culture in and of itself does not tell us much about women's rights or autonomy within it. Controlling resources is, in effect, a species-specific means of controlling women: "Unlike men, the males of most other primate species cannot easily control the food sources that females need to support their offspring. As a result, male-male competition in these species is not typically focused on the control of biological resources (i.e., food) but rather on the control of social and sometimes physical (e.g., territory) resources" (Geary, 162–63). With the increased mobility that came with the development of modern culture, the control of resources may have become, for a time, a more critical element in controlling women than it had been. What is notable across species is that males exert some form of control over resources that females require to promote their inclusive fitness. Not to put too fine a point on it, males of all species control resources either directly or indirectly so that they can gain access to and control the reproductive resource they require—females.

But crucially, since individuals seek to control their individual experience, and since, as Geary puts it, "the desire to control is the fundamental motivation underlying the behavioral and psychological development of human beings" (161), the above gloss highlights that a central, indeed urgent focus of attention for the Darwinian feminist is male control and power that are the outgrowth of treating women as reproductive resources. Stated bluntly, the ultimate cause of men's efforts to dominate and control women is the drive to corral women's energies toward the end of the men's inclusive fitness, and this evolved motive is typically in conflict with the needs of women, but also of men, as autonomous individuals. As Geary's overview makes clear, the reproductive priorities of men alone or women alone are not in themselves, in any case, a neat list of logically integrated, much less conscious, motives. Young women may be drawn simultaneously to highly dominant, successful providers and less dominant, more sensitive men. Men who are faithful to longtime wives and advocate greater equality for girls and women may also seek to control the behavior of women with whom they live and work. Literature provides abundant evidence of these unconscious motivations and conflicts, and it focuses attention on the aspects of sexual psychology that threaten to undermine a woman's autonomy. Works of literature are so often an ideal resource for looking at this multilevel psychological conflict between the differential, impersonal motivations of inclusive fitness, the problem of individual psychology and autonomy, and the shared emotional and psychological needs of pair-bonding humans. What is glaringly absent thus far from Darwinian analyses of literature is any discussion of sexual control and power, both of which are implicated in the conflicting dynamics of men and women, who must pool their fitness motives in the service of their life-history goals. In the analysis that follows, then, my focus is on how the need to control and "master" the woman often overrides an apparently mutual desire for achieved pair bonding.

Quarry or Wife? The Proprietary Male and Relational Possibility in *The Fox*

During his lifetime, D. H. Lawrence produced a substantial body of discursive prose alongside his novels, stories, poems, plays, and travel writing. These philosophical texts, at once freewheeling, ironic, didactic, and self-contradictory, have been frequently used to interpret the author's fiction, although critics have become increasingly aware in the past several decades that such a practice may tend to obscure or oversimplify the author's best creative productions. Nevertheless, in the most recent Cambridge edition of Lawrence's *Psychoanalysis and the Unconscious and Fantasia of the Unconscious* (2004), Bruce Steele suggests that these texts are useful for precisely this purpose, that is, as guides to the interpretation of Lawrence's contemporaneous fiction. In the nine-year period from 1914 to 1923, when the revised, novella version of *The Fox* was published, Lawrence also produced four major discursive texts—*Study of Thomas Hardy* (1914), *Psychoanalysis and the Unconscious* (1921), *Fantasia of the Unconscious* (1922), and *Studies in Classic American Literature* (1923)—that reflect his shifting ideas on such topics as the location of the unconscious and its relation to ratiocinative consciousness, the proper relationship of men to women, the primacy of the individual and the difficulty of self-development, and the current system of education and the necessity of educational reform. Not only did Lawrence's ideas shift over this nine-year time frame but sometimes even within the same text the pronouncements he makes about one topic seem to conflict with those he makes about another. For instance, Lawrence's overt insistence on a subordinate and passive role for women has been especially problematic for feminist critics. When, in chapter 9 of *Fantasia of the Unconscious*, the novelist claims that boys and girls should be kept apart because the sexes are absolutely different and need to retain their "sex polarity," he clearly contradicts his earlier assertions that well-balanced persons contain both male and female elements.[30]

Yet the problem of how well the author's postwar discursive pronouncements accord with the evidence in the creative work of the same period remains. As Duane Edwards notes, it seems strange that Lawrence, who disliked bullies of any kind, who gave individual women individualized advice, and who believed in the *value* of sexual difference, should be called a chauvinist.[31] Edwards focuses on passages extrapolated from works such as *Aaron's Rod* that insist that the woman must submit and argues that Lawrence is insisting on acquiescence during love-making, not blind subservience, and he claims that Lawrence fully recognizes the threat of domination that men represent to women. Those female characters who acquiesce, Edwards maintains, are ultimately "less ambivalent, more self-assured and more intense than the man" (214). Edwards's analysis is consistent with Lawrence's repeated assertion that the integrity of the individual is of primary value but that individuals only exist and develop relationally. Nevertheless, Edwards's analysis does not speak to the reactionary pronouncement in *Fantasia*, which frankly relegates women to a servile role. Too busy around the campfire with cast-iron pots and stew meats, women would not experience any form of relational development, whether through sexual intercourse or any other medium.

However, this image of women by the campfire not only is incongruous with respect to Lawrence's earlier discursive writings, his characterizations of women, and his personal relationships with them (including his mother, his wife, and his many educated and independent female friends) but contradicts his insistence on the integrity of all individuals. Lawrence remains absolutely consistent on this point throughout his writing, and thus Peggy Brayfield follows the author's lead when, drawing on the 1925 essay "Morality and the Novel," she asserts that at the conclusion of *The Fox* Henry has failed by "demanding a sacrifice from [March, whereas she] has been more inclined to seek a 'true relatedness.'"[32] In a similar vein, and drawing on a personal correspondence of later date, Judith Ruderman suggests—correctly, in my view—that a letter Lawrence wrote in 1919 to Rosalind Baynes's husband helps explain how we should interpret the ambiguous ending of the second version of *The Fox*. This letter, written when Baynes and her husband were considering divorce, insists on the primacy of one's individual integrity and one's regard for the integrity of the other:

One has to learn that love is a secondary thing in itself. The first thing is to be a free, proud, single being by oneself: to be oneself free, and to let the other be free: to force nothing and not to be forced oneself into anything. . . . I believe if you . . . would each of you [be] self-sufficient & to a degree indifferent or reckless, you and Rosalind would keep a lasting relationship. . . . One should keep one's soul proud and integral, that's all.[33]

If for Lawrence submission ever meant giving up individual consciousness, his discursive writing and his fiction from the difficult period of his life and writing between 1918 and 1922 seem to be in conflict on this matter. Ultimately, however, the fiction keeps an ambivalent but clear faith with the statement he made to Baynes about the primacy of the individual.

In fact, one reason why *The Fox* is especially rewarding for evolutionary analysis is that the impulses of the writer *as a writer* probably undermined his original intentions (summarily executed in the 1918 short story), and with them his didactic, philosophical claims.[34] Furthermore, the tension between these two aspects of Lawrence's writings—a reactionary impulse demanding the submission of women on the one hand and an enduring recognition of the integrity and autonomy of all individuals on the other—corresponds to the conflict between the impulse to control women and the drive to grant them autonomy that Darwinian feminists especially should address. Whatever Lawrence's original intentions in light of the doctrine propounded in *Fantasia,* the author must have been aware that the perspective of the story had altered dramatically with its expansion into a novella. One indication of this is that the symbols and dreams in the revised story have since become the stuff of fabulous critical conjecture; another is that in the novella Lawrence suddenly focuses attention on the contradiction inherent in Henry's pursuit of March. The young man's persistent, sly, seductive talk and his persistent, dramatic, erotically charged use of indirect force, all of which he enlists without much conscious awareness, suggest a major shift in writerly conception. Lawrence's narrator uses direct language to convey Henry's conflicting motives: "And it was as a young hunter, that he wanted to bring down March as his quarry, to make her his wife" (24). In many respects, this sentence becomes the thesis of Henry's psyche. Attuned to the tensions in Henry's conflicted pursuit of March, the alert reader will ask, Will Henry be able to figure out that a dead animal is not a desirable spouse? In evolutionary terms, the sentence embodies the conflict between the view of woman as reproductive resource and the impulse to grant her autonomy, allowing, along with it, progressive mutual individuation within the relational structure of the human pair bond.

More complex on the realistic level than the short story in its portrayal of character psychology and behavior, particularly with respect to Henry, the novella

The Fox is also far more complex in its use of animal symbolism, which actively incorporates the author's knowledge not only of animal fable and of the literature drawing on it but also of Freudian psychoanalysis, Frazer's anthropology, and, most significantly, early Jungian analytic psychology. As Marijane Osborn notes, Lawrence inverts the traditional fable structure in this story, representing people as animals rather than vice versa.[35] But while the animal imagery in the original 1918 short story "The Fox," which is itself fablelike in structure, can be glossed as a simple transposition of animal types onto persons, in the novella the symbolism of the animal is dynamical and tied in particular to the potential for Jungian relational interdependence and individuation.

Lawrence read Beatrice Hinkle's translation of Carl Jung's *Psychology of the Unconscious* in 1918, and it was in Jung, and Jung's American disciple Trigant Burrow, that Lawrence found a depth psychology harmonious with his own mythic mode of thought. For Jung, the archetypes of the collective unconscious are formal in essence; their particular content is filled in by the individual. In *The Fox*, the characters' conceptions of the animal reflect their divergent attitudes toward nature, themselves, and sexual relationships. Particularly in the case of Henry and March, the differences between their conceptions of the fox delineate a psychic distance that must be bridged if they are to find all levels of fulfillment— a satisfaction that includes both a sexual and an emotional component and complements a simultaneous and ongoing process of individual development. The challenge of integration and relationship that Lawrence poses, moreover, is not just March and Henry's, but the reader's as well. As Ronald Granofsky astutely observes, Lawrence is a more metafictional writer than most commentators recognize, and he spoke of the revisions to *The Fox* in just such terms:

> In a letter to Earl Brewster, Lawrence refers to his story "The Fox" as if it were itself an animal. He has, he writes, "put a long tail" to what was "a bobbed short story. Now he careers with a strange and fiery brush." . . . Lawrence identifies his own endangered career with the careering of the fox that is hedged in by English fences and faced with extinction, much as he had felt himself to be in Cornwall during the war. . . . What is at risk, in the end, is Lawrence's own conception of reality and, thus, the kind of fiction he is capable of producing. He feels it necessary in 1921 to add a "fiery brush" to "The Fox" so that, unlike the animal *of* the story, the fox that *is* the story itself can survive his new norms.[36]

Although, as Granofsky insists, Lawrence ultimately did great damage to his art by trying to suppress the female element in his aesthetics and his personality,

The Fox eludes this willed effort to discipline his art in accord with a dogma of leadership.

"A Study of Human Mating"

In *D. H. Lawrence: Novelist*, F. R. Leavis's early influential study of the writer, the critic wrote of *The Fox* that "its strength lies—and it is one of the supreme things among the major tales—in the fulness, depth, and unambiguous clarity with which it presents its theme."[37] Comparing the novella favorably to Lawrence's *You Touched Me*, Leavis asserts that *The Fox* is "much more fully and unequivocally a study of love. For that is what *The Fox* is, even if it doesn't answer to the ordinary notion of a love-story. It is a study of human mating; of the attraction between a man and a woman that expresses the profound needs of each and has its meaning in a permanent union" (272). Many subsequent critics have not found *The Fox* deserving of such high praise, insisting that it is inconsistent and even dishonest to one degree or another in its symbolism, its character portrayal, and its attitude toward women. At the same time, a number of critics who regard the story highly generally follow the lead of Ruderman's pre-Oedipal analysis.[38] Osborn, for instance, astonishingly claims that "the friction at the end of the story, rather than occurring between representatives of sexual genders as such, is between the one partner who in order to dominate strives to 'take away [the] consciousness' of the other, and the other who strives rebelliously to stay awake. It reflects, as several people have pointed out, not so much sexual strife as a mother-child relationship" (93). In a similar vein, Granofsky suggests that Henry fails to succeed with March because he inverts the parent-child hierarchy (58–59). In the analysis that follows, I hope to demonstrate that evolutionary psychology renders analytically explicit what is, in many respects, evident in the manifest content of the tale: that the power dynamics are directly tied to evolved, sex-differential strategies of mating. Along the way, I suggest that both pre-Oedipal readings, rather absurdly casting Henry in the role of a mother, and readings like Stanley Renner's[39] and Leavis's, which acknowledge the force of mating and sexual difference, ignore the degree to which Lawrence presents Henry's extreme but nevertheless prototypically male desire to dominate March in a negative light. Again, the psychological literature helps clarify the pattern in Lawrence's tale, wherein the wish to dominate and control inheres in sexual attraction and the male proprietary impulse. In the final analysis, the need to dominate and control appears to take precedence over efforts toward a mutually satisfying, loving, sexually fulfilling marriage.

In *The Fox*, two thirty-year-old women, Jill Banford and Nellie March, have established themselves on a small farm with the financial assistance of Banford's father during World War I. The story begins at the end of the war; the farming enterprise is not going well, and the fox has been making off with chickens. March, the land girl who does the farm chores, takes the gun and tries to kill the fox, but when she comes face to face with him, she cannot shoot him. Soon Henry Grenfel, a young soldier, appears at the farmhouse, where he had lived formerly with his grandfather. When Henry, who had run away from his grandfather's home and joined the army in Canada, learns that his grandfather is dead, he manages to solicit an invitation to stay for the evening, and thereafter he reestablishes himself on the farm. He decides the next day that he will propose to March, to whom he felt immediately attracted. Attracted as well to Henry but feeling ambivalent and pressured by him, March nevertheless agrees to marry him, much to Banford's dismay. After Henry listens on the other side of the bedroom door to Banford telling March how worthless he is, he takes the gun and goes outside; he then decides to search for the fox, which he finds and kills. However, when Henry leaves in a few days to join his regiment in Salisbury Plain, March writes to him asking to call the marriage off. Desperate and enraged, Henry requests a twenty-four-hour leave from his commanding officer. When he arrives at the farm, March is in the process of chopping down a tree. She hands the axe to Henry, who strikes the tree, allowing it to fall in such a way that one of the branches hits Banford and kills her. At the end of the story, March and Henry, now married, are in Cornwall waiting to leave for Canada.

Some critics have reasonably argued that Nellie March is the main character of *The Fox,* for the story opens with her perspective and emerging sexual desire and concludes with the disappointing result of her union with Henry. But it is primarily through Henry's actions and perceptions that the reader judges the potential viability of the relationship, because once he enters the story, it is his pursuit of March that primarily directs the course of action. As Lawrence himself acknowledges, he is interested in chemistry and interactions, not old-fashioned notions of character, and this is consistent with his not establishing a single main character. Nevertheless, since Henry's decisions and, especially, his inability to change personally determine the outcome of the story, the initial part of my analysis stresses his psychology and actions. The second part stresses how the symbolic use of the fox dramatizes both the psychic disparities and the possibility of a psychic change that can serve as the foundation of a mutually gratifying sexual and emotional relationship between the characters.

The isolated setting and the dramatic situation in *The Fox* do not highlight the evolutionary advantages of the discharged soldier at the end of World War I.

Certain cultural and demographic conditions, as Geary points out, tend to favor female choice, while others favor male choice. In general, female choice is improved by an oversupply of men and usually exhibits a trend toward more conservative social patterns and values. On the other hand, male choice is improved by an oversupply of women and witnesses the liberalization of mores, an increase in out-of-wedlock births, an increase in women in the workforce, and lower paternal investment. If in the aftermath of World War I the reduced population of young men enjoyed itself amid a much larger population of equally sex-deprived young and not-so-young women, perhaps willing to accommodate itself to a freer morality, there is no *direct* evidence of these sociohistorical facts in Lawrence's novella. Yet these form part of the setting of the story and as such have a general relevance to Henry's psychology. If men tend under balanced conditions to view women as reproductive resources, then the implication is that an oversupply of women would predictably exacerbate the tendency. As the ensuing analysis certainly acknowledges, many individual factors help account for Henry's blunt pursuit of March, but the historical-ecological context also informs his assumption that March is his for the taking.

Although Banford's parents make an appearance at the end of the story, the mating game in *The Fox* is notably devoid of the social relations and rituals that typically structure courtship and marriage, and in this sense the tale functions in striking contrast to those of Austen's novels, for instance, where mating dynamics play out against a backdrop of other characters and within a regulated series of conventional social activities. Lawrence had long interpreted the sexually repressive attitudes fostered by and inherited from the Victorian era as a product of female control, especially of the domestic sphere, and one of the few advantages he saw in the war was that it relaxed this hold women had over the sexual arena. One way of dramatizing that situation fictionally is by simply eliminating the old arena, and in many respects that is what Lawrence does in the novella.

Given the isolated environment and particular historical circumstances, many of the general features of human mating dynamics—female-female competition, male choice, male-male competition, female choice—are not directly relevant in the dramatic situation of the story but are instructive in their absence. Undoubtedly, the unconscious and elemental nature of the attraction between March and Henry, coupled with the isolated environment, is part of the tale's appeal, but it is also the source of difficulties that ultimately surface in the relationship between this woman and this very young man. Whereas an environment allowing for the balanced and socially organized operation of male and female choice and, significantly, an emerging consciousness of choice may guide a man and a woman toward some shared values within the pair bond, an environment without such competitive elements eliminates pressure toward mutuality and compromise. It is a mistake, however, to think that there is no competition at all in the story; as the tradition of pre-Oedipal criticism has pointed out, Banford is a "devouring mother" and thus a competitor to whom March is tied emotionally and economically. Ultimately, whether Banford herself is a sexual competitor is of no real importance, since her emotional and social needs effectively block Henry's sexual interests in March.

At least as significantly, because of the factors that have shaped Henry's character and psychology, male-male competition and male coalitional behavior linger in the background of this story and arguably have a strong impact on the outcome. In many respects, Henry seems to have enjoyed the sort of upbringing Lawrence recommends in *Fantasia of the Unconscious,* according to which girls should "learn the domestic arts in their perfection" and avoid reading and the self-consciousness it brings, while boys should be raised in a separate sphere in small cadres of soldiers under a "proud, harsh, manly rule" (119). In both cases, Lawrence eschews the mechanization of training and production. Within these groups of ten men, the soldiers must be willing to choose a leader and pledge absolute obedience. The small cadres feed into higher levels of increasing size organized along the same principle. Much of Henry's upbringing has taken place outside of the standard institutions that Lawrence disparages. At age twelve he left Cornwall with his grandfather to go live at Bailey Farm, but three years later he ran off to Canada, eventually joining the army there. Since Henry is therefore about twenty at the time of the story, this means that his adolescence has been spent almost exclusively under the influence of men; "he has developed to young manhood without a mother and therefore free of the socialization of male sexuality that has traditionally been largely the responsibility of women" (Renner, 254). In many respects, this is the sort of formative upbringing and training that Lawrence seems to envision in *Fantasia.* Although Lawrence deplored the mechanization of modern culture in general and World War I as an outgrowth of that culture, and although he likewise deplored the spurious ideals for which the war was fought, he admired some of the soldiers he knew, such as William Henry Hocking, the Cornishman upon whom the character of Henry is to some extent based. Like Captain Hepburn in *The Captain's Doll,* the second of the three Ladybird novellas (*The Fox* is the first of the three), Henry acquires his independence through his army service but does not sacrifice his individuality for his country or cause. It is surprising, then, that a character matching rather well the author's new educational proposal for young men does not succeed better in the task set for him.

All told, the information about Henry's background suggests that his weak socialization, his professional training within male coalitions for armed combat, and even, perhaps, a trace of antisocial personality disorder fuel his attitude toward mating. The homosocial world that has shaped him as a young man contributes to, but is not fully responsible for, his proprietary approach to March and the rapidity with which his aggression escalates into violence.[40] As Granofsky points out, Henry is a variant of Lawrence's gamekeeper figures, who occupy a place between classes.[41] Himself not hemmed in by divided class loyalties and therefore more independent in some respects than the genuine gamekeeper, Henry faces, from the perspective of Darwinian feminism, the special challenge of overcoming a socialization experience that has exacerbated prototypical male tendencies toward aggression, violence, and control of reproductive resources. These militate against kindness and intelligence, the personal values that Geary claims both men and women rate highly and that no doubt usually contribute to mutuality in the marriage bond. In his earlier criticism on the novel, Granofsky surmises that March is a humanizing influence on Henry and that Banford is a brutalizing one; while the judgment is to some extent true, it suffers from a veneer of residual sentiment that Darwinian feminism strips away by inspecting the novelist's own descriptions of sexual attraction, manipulation, and pursuit. Although Lawrence hints that Henry could become a kind husband, Henry is almost preternaturally inclined to view March as a resource and to demonize Banford as a dangerous competitor who must be lethally exterminated.

The feminist critic Hilary Simpson claims that Henry "is cast in the role of the homecoming master,"[42] but it is important to look closely at the following passage, which relates the young man's first cogitations regarding his desire to acquire both March and the farm. Henry has been staying at the farm for several days, and as he returns from hunting,

> the dusk was falling as he came home, and with the dusk, a fine, late-November rain. He saw the fire-light leaping in the window of the sitting-room, a leaping light in the little cluster of dark buildings. And he thought to himself, it would be a good thing to have this place for his own. And then the thought entered him shrewdly: why not marry March? He stood still in the middle of the field for some moments, the dead rabbit hanging still in his hand, arrested by this thought. His mind waited in amazement—it seemed to calculate—and then he smiled curiously to himself in acquiescence. Why not? Why not indeed? It was a good idea. What if it was rather ridiculous? What did it matter? What if she was older than he? It didn't matter. When he thought of her dark, startled,

vulnerable eyes he smiled subtly to himself. He was older than she, really. He was master of her.

He scarcely admitted his intention even to himself. He kept it as a secret even from himself. It was all too uncertain as yet. He would have to see how things went.

(23)

If this passage is analyzed in light of the evolutionary psychology of mating, existing criticism, and, not least of all, the outcome of the story, it becomes quite clear that *Henry* has cast himself as "the homecoming master," not the author, and a crucial question at this juncture is the extent to which he is even master of his own motives. Whereas Renner maintains that Henry is, unlike March, sexually experienced, the paragraph immediately preceding the passage above belies such an inference: "[March's] figure, like a graceful young man's, piqued him. Her dark eyes made something rise in his soul, with a curious elate excitement, when he looked into them, an excitement he was afraid to let be seen, it was so keen and secret" (23). As Peter Balbert observes astutely, "Henry [feels] sexually drawn to [March] in the subtle ways that his timidity cannot acknowledge as erotic. . . . He emanates a calm virginity in his temperament and demeanor even as he functions as a practiced killer with a gun."[43] Henry exhibits the same temperamental virginity a few days later in his sudden conscious awareness that March is indeed physically vulnerable to him when he first sees her in a dress.[44] His sexual naiveté is especially relevant to the long passage quoted above, because he seems not to recognize that his real motive for hanging around the farm is to acquire March as a mate. As Henry stands in the field, he thinks first that he would like the farm, yet a mere page later his identity as "a huntsman in spirit, not a farmer" is affirmed by the narrator from within Henry's point of view. Clearly, although Henry is keenly aware of wanting things at Bailey Farm, he has little sense of how to fit these to his identity and even less of what his own motives and desires might be.

The literature on male reproductive strategies therefore brings the passage into striking focus, for Henry (who has just been out hunting, and thus provisioning the two women with far better food than they had been consuming when he arrived) unconsciously associates the acquisition of material resources (the farm) with reproductive resources (the woman he desires). Since the text preceding the passage is about his attraction to March and the text following it concerns his need to proceed with caution in courting her, it is clear that she, not the farm, is the object of interest, which logically coheres with the propositions of evolutionary psychology, as does the evidence that none of this is self-evident to Henry. In other words, he has made the unconscious connection that acquiring the farm will improve his chances of winning March over, even though he does not want to be a farmer. In short, if it has seemed illogical to previous critics that he has wanted first one thing, then another, the evolutionary rationale clarifies why his motives might seem to shift so disconcertingly. In fact, there is no real shift in priorities, just a lack of conscious awareness about what they are. Additionally, the initial attraction to resources as a means of controlling March soon falls by the wayside, for two reasons: they do not seem important in influencing her decision; and the conflict with Banford moves to center stage.

A third aspect of this passage, the hint of sadism comingled with Henry's naïve belief in his dominance—that he is "master of her"—raises the question whether he cares, or indeed has the capacity to care, for March, or for that matter, more disturbingly, anyone else. While there is no question that he is erotically attracted to March, his capacity to feel is frankly at issue in the story. Having just hinted at Henry's sense of vulnerability should his "keen and secret" desire for March be gleaned, Lawrence now places the young man in a field, dead rabbit in hand, reflecting cynically on how he might coax March into marriage. (Only a page later the narrator, in Henry's point of view, reports that he would have to proceed cautiously because "March was suspicious as a hare" [24], thus directly identifying the object of Henry's desire with the evening meal.) The troubling psychological perspective according to which marriage becomes a net or trap to prevent the desired woman's access to the man's vulnerable self—the "timidity" that Balbert astutely notes in this hale, inexperienced boy—fits with an antisocial tendency evident in Henry's background and behavior. Although the narrative does not provide details about his parents or clarify at what age Henry's grandfather became his guardian, it does explicitly state that he had never gotten along with the grandfather. Furthermore, there is no suggestion that he has friends in Cornwall, near Bailey Farm, or from his years in the army. Likewise, there is great erotic charge, but perhaps no love, in the soft, seductive voice he uses to persuade March to marry him. Finally and most importantly, in his battle with Banford, a small and sickly woman, he is incapable of considering the broader consequences of destroying her, consequences that utterly undermine the "mastery" that he rather preposterously assumes at the outset. For in severing Banford from March, he inevitably plunges his wife-to-be into the solitude of grief while simultaneously shredding a whole series of human bonds. Henry is naïve in his assumption that he is "older" than March and "master of her," because the only legitimate interpretation of his thinking, based on his subsequent actions, is that greater physical strength and masculine aggression correspond to *mastery* and that aggression pitted against passivity constitutes *age*. Yet Lawrence himself rejects this notion of dominance and mastery in the conclusion to the story, which leaves the two locked in a battle of wills. Henry's rival is no doubt dead and his marriage consummated, but as the narrator reports from within Henry's perspective, "If he had won her, he had not yet got her" (66).

All in all, the implication that Henry lacks social and emotional bonds and cannot understand their meaning for others hints at the possibility of an actual dysfunction—antisocial personality disorder—which is tied in important ways to lower than normal fear responses and males' riskier behavior than females'. As Ann Campbell explains in *A Mind of Her Own: The Evolutionary Psychology of Women*, "Antisocial personality disorder is a syndrome characterized by an indifference to the well-being of others, an absence of remorse or guilt and a failure to learn from experience which can often result in persistent lawbreaking."[45] Although Henry's behavior is within the bounds of the law, it is noteworthy that in his own mind he imagines that he wills Banford's death: "In his heart he had decided her death. A terrible still force seemed in him, and a power that was just his," and he never feels a moment's remorse (64–65). Whereas recent research in neurochemistry suggests that certain aggressive reactions are responses to fear triggered by increases in noradrenaline, antisocial personality disorder is characterized by a subnormal fear response perhaps resulting from malfunctions in the noradrenaline system. "Men who behaved this way," reports Campbell, "may have been more cold-bloodedly instrumental than others in their fight for dominance despite the risks of self-destruction that it carried" (82).[46]

There is no question that Henry exhibits a cold-blooded instrumentality in his battle with Banford over March, and Lawrence's pointed use of the word *heart* in the story's grotesque denouement reverberates, for the attentive reader, with Henry's question to March only a week earlier, when she was reluctant to leave Banford, who was "sobbing her heart out," inside. As Henry observes, Banford is sobbing out three hearts at once.

"Your heart?" said March. He still gripped her and detained her.

"Isn't it as good as her heart?" he said. "Or do you think it's not?"

"Your heart?" she said again, incredulous.

"Yes mine! Mine! Do you think I haven't *got* a heart?"—And with his hot grasp he took her hand and pressed it under his left breast. "There's my heart," he said, "if you don't believe in it."

It was wonder which made her attend. And then she felt the deep, heavy, powerful stroke of his heart, terrible, like something from beyond. It was like something from beyond, something awful from outside, signalling to her. And the signal paralysed her.   (52)

Wanting to confirm the promise of marriage and share a few minutes of intimacy with March before leaving for Salisbury Plain, Henry appears sympathetic in this scene even as Lawrence directs attention to his use of force. Lawrence succinctly establishes the different notions of the heart, one associated with sentiment, the other with ardent and powerful physiological processes and physical acts. The question "Isn't it as good as her heart?" hangs over the story unanswered until the tree branch fells Banford in the denouement. It is possible that the answer to Henry's question is yes, that his heart is as good as Banford's, but, psychologically and ethically considered, neither of these antithetically defined hearts is much good at all. One heart figures relationship to the other as brute physicality, the other as conventionalized sentiment, and both characters use these modes of engagement manipulatively, as means of establishing dominance over March. Importantly, March recognizes that Banford has been using her, a point that Lawrence makes clear earlier in the story when Banford, shifting her tactics, directs her insults at her friend instead of at Henry. Soon after the killing of the fox, she expresses surprise that March would let herself be treated "so cheaply." March replies, " 'Don't you worry yourself, nobody's going to treat me cheaply. And even you aren't, either.' She had a tender defiance, and a certain fire in her voice" (47). Although March loves Banford and wishes to protect her, she is relieved at the end of the story that her friend is dead, knowing that she had not been able to make her happy. On the one hand, March is tired of trying to satisfy this manipulatively sentimental woman, who would have her take all the responsibility and expend all the care. On the other, she is incapable of the inertia Henry's brute masculinity demands, imagining as they wait in Cornwall that she should be "submerged under the surface of love" like so much seaweed (67). Ironically, Henry's desire "to make her submit, yield, blindly pass away out of all her strenuous consciousness" (70) has resulted in unhappiness and extreme self-consciousness for March: "Everything around her seemed to watch her, seemed to press on her" (67). As the fiction writer and the didact D. H. Lawrence teases out the implications of *Fantasia* in these final pages of *The Fox*, the new philosophical insistence on psychosexual difference and female submission emergent in his discursive writing loses credence as a fictionally represented woman tries to maintain autonomous individuality while hoping for shared fulfillment with her spouse in marriage. Yet demonstrably, that fulfillment is not represented in Henry's heart, but perhaps by the fox that lies too far beyond Henry's ken.

The suggestion that Henry may be socially and affectively dysfunctional helps to explain why he undermines himself and why dominance is a losing proposition for him. In turn, of course, this helps to explain his obsession with dominance. In evolutionary psychology, discussions of males and dominance traditionally focus on status in male coalitions, but recent research on dominance hierarchies is more sensitive to the fact that all relationships of power and status depend critically on the general social skills of the participants. Thus, some current studies revise somewhat the literature on male dominance, suggesting first that it tends to be short-term and second that the prosocial and affiliative behaviors favored by females often lead to dominance for males. Discussing the results of a recent study of nonhuman primates, Campbell explains "that a male's relationships with females is [*sic*] vitally important in determining his rank" (67). Whereas previous research assumed that reproductive success was a result of high status, some studies now suggest that the causality might be reversed, with high status a result of reproductive success. What, then, leads to reproductive success? The affiliative, prosocial—or "act nice"—behaviors favored by females apparently affect reproductive success and rank among nonhuman primate males. Given the complexity of human culture, as well as the long-term, sexually segregated functioning of its patriarchal institutions, it is likely that matters are somewhat different among humans, there being many areas in which women have long had little or no influence on rank among men.

Yet in addition to the aspects of Lawrence's story that suggest an actual antisocial aspect to Henry's personality, his direct interactions with the two women suggest strict limits to his social skills (or "act nice" behaviors) that enforce his position as a low-status male and thus perhaps fuel his preoccupation with dominating March. Both his charm and his social limitations are to some extent attributable to his immaturity as well as to his sexually segregated development. The narrator describes him as both puppyish and catlike, both qualities of domestic animals associated with foxes that overlap with Banford's early suppression of her own fear because "He was such a boy" (16), and these youthful characteristics help him befriend the women. At the same time, his impetuosity overrules his judgment that if he does not proceed with caution in courting March, "she would turn round on him with savage, sardonic ridicule, and dismiss him from the farm and from her own mind, forever" (23). In spite of his revealing fear, which speaks to the timidity and sexual immaturity Balbert notes, Henry not only proposes to

March that evening when they are outside chopping logs but presses her once he senses that as soon as he dismisses the argument against the age difference, "his voice seemed to sound in her somewhere where she was helpless against it" (25). Filled with a sense of victory, Henry draws close to her and repetitively insists that she accept his proposal:

> "Say then," he said. "Say then you'll marry me. Say—say?" He was softly insistent.
>
> "What?" she asked, faint, from a distance, *like one in pain*. His voice was now unthinkably near and soft. He drew very near to her.
>
> "Say yes."
>
> "Oh I can't," she wailed helplessly, half articulate, as if semi-conscious, and *as if in pain*, like one who dies. "How can I?"
>
> "You can," he said softly, laying his hand gently on her shoulder as she stood with her head averted and dropped, dazed. "You can. Yes, you can. What makes you say you can't? You can. You can." And with an *awful softness* he bent forward and just touched her neck with his mouth and his chin.
>
> "Don't!" she cried, with a faint mad cry like hysteria, starting away and facing round on him. "What do you mean?" But she had no breath to speak with. It was as if she was killed.
>
> "I mean what I say," he persisted *softly and cruelly*. "I want you to marry me. I want you to marry me. You know that, now, don't you? You know that, now? Don't you? Don't you?"   (26, emphasis added)

As in the later scene when Henry and March go out to the shed after he insists on the efficacy of his heart, Henry here uses his overwhelming physical presence to gain an advantage over her and extract a commitment. (In the later scene, in spite of having been sensitized to her female vulnerability, he literally corners her in the shed [53].) Critics such as Osborn, who deny the centrality of gender dynamics in the conclusion of the story, ignore the fact that the terminal power dynamics derive directly from the palpable erotic tension of these earlier scenes, which carry subtle but characteristically Lawrentian overtones of sadism because of the exploitation of advantages of sexual and physical power. March's sexual attraction to Henry renders her helpless, and Lawrence manages the narration to highlight Henry's manipulation of his immediate advantage. His harassing insistence that she "say yes"—assent to his proposal—is, as the narrator overtly notes, cruel even if the two characters love as well as desire each other, because her acceptance is exacted through the exertion of a masculine force that foregrounds March as a sexual resource without considering her individual needs and desires.

There is, in fact, no narrative reason why the proposal or the marriage must take place quickly, and Henry's haste speaks again to his youth, his desire for mastery, his antisociality and indifference to others (here March, the woman he presumably loves), and his perhaps impulsive conclusion that, as he later tells her, "when I think of my life, and of you, then the two things go together" (53). Ambiguity thus arises concerning the degree to which his own sexual arousal is contingent upon the perception of March's helplessness, for it is he, after all, who has thought of her as "his quarry."

Whether Lawrence intended it or not, then, the last line of the novella echoes March's muted replies as Henry calls her from her numbed trance in the proposal scene: " 'If only we could go soon!' he said, *with pain in his voice*" (71, emphasis added). Together, the lines represent a negation of what the two might have achieved and constitute Henry's anxious befuddlement that what seemed so easily "won" a short time before—mastery, sexual fulfillment, love, or all three—has so utterly eluded him. As I suggested above in the section on mating strategies and sexual equality, we should expect conflicts of motives between and within individuals, and often motivations that seem to subserve inclusive fitness in the short term may offer little satisfaction to autonomous individuals. Henry's pursuit of March in *The Fox* provides a striking example of how a behavior "designed" to serve evolutionary ends is finally dysfunctional for the specific psychological and relational needs of the individuals involved.

"A Study of Love"

Leavis calls the novella "fully and unequivocally a study of love, . . . a study of human mating," and while he acknowledges that *The Fox* is not a typical love story, his refusal to make any distinction between "human mating" and "love" is either radical or just slightly strange. Lawrence is the writer in English best suited to pointing to the distinction between mating and love, for he understood that the sensual satisfaction humans take in sex for its own sake is something different from the emotional engagements and processes of selfhood entailed in the yearning toward a long-term pair bond. Evolutionary psychology gives us some of the reasons why love may be a curiously elusive phenomenon for a species predisposed to intimacy, and in *The Fox* Lawrence invites his readers to explore the difference between mating and love. Crafting a symbolism that merges his understanding of the natural world with the formulations of Jungian analytic psychology, Lawrence expresses the foxlike elusiveness of that achieved and satisfying pair bond through the complex animal imagery of the story.

Critics have offered a bewildering array of interpretations of the significance of the fox and, in connection with this, the portions of the text in which the animal figures most prominently, the two dreams and his death. Jan Good, for instance, suggests that the fox represents the masculine element in Henry, as well as the masculine part of March, which must die for the relationship to succeed.[47] Arguing along similar lines but specifically about the shooting of the fox, Renner claims that this act signifies a suppression of the instinctive male sexual drive, which Henry must learn to control if he is to successfully court March. Balbert argues that Henry must kill the fox to destroy the false identity that March has imposed on him. In contrast to these readings, others suggest that the symbolic implications of the killing of the fox are negative. Somewhat tentatively, Granofsky suggests that Lawrence's text may be consciously Jungian and that the death of the fox represents Henry's failure to integrate antithetical aspects, specifically his shadow, or female, elements, into the self (56–57). Differing from most critics in that she focuses on what the fox represents to March, Brayfield points out that although the animal first represents Henry, the fox's meanings increase over the course of the story, and later it stands for all the realms of experience March craves.

One of the responses among critics to the perceived failure to nail down the fox's significance has been to assume (contra Leavis) that the story is flawed, rather than that Lawrence intentionally structured the text so that quite divergent readings of the symbolism seem credible. For the novella transforms the original short story into a tale about perception and its relation to interpersonal growth and fulfillment. If, as Granofsky suggests—and I believe he correctly follows Lawrence's lead—the tale itself is truly the fox, this provides a hint that any quest for fixed valuations of the symbols are bound to come up short. Rather, we should expect that the tale's major symbol will be dynamical, like a living creature, and exhibit some of the characteristics of the particular animal in question. Actual foxes, as Lawrence himself was surely aware, are difficult to categorize simply and thus lend themselves to symbolic ambiguity.

However, the animal symbolism is, at the outset of the narrative, strikingly static in comparison with that of the central portion of the story, because retaining this feature of the original short story enables Lawrence to establish a challenge for both his characters and his readers. In the beginning, each character is identified with a particular animal or animals: Henry with the fox, March with hares and rabbits, and Banford with fowls (chickens and ducks). As Osborn notes, the attribution of animal characteristics to humans inverts the fable technique of adopting animal characters. The purpose of this technique in fables is to provide immediate, one-dimensional characterization; arguably, in the short story version of "The Fox," which is identical to the text of the novella through March's first dream, animal symbolism functions similarly. In the final, novella version of *The Fox*, by contrast, animal symbolism often reflects the extent to which characters conform to and embrace limited perceptions of themselves and others.

The opening of the story, for example, exploits animal imagery to reflect the self-imposed limitations under which March and Banford live. Banford and March have narrowed their failing farming enterprise down to fowls, but even these domesticated birds fail to thrive (as does Banford, with whom they will soon be identified). It is in an ironical description of this farming endeavor that Lawrence first introduces the fox:

> One evil there was greater than any other. Bailey Farm was a little homestead, with ancient wooden barn and two-gabled farm-house, lying just one field removed from the edge of the wood. Since the war the fox was a demon. He carried off the hens under the very noses of March and Banford. Banford would start and stare through her big spectacles with all her eyes, as another squawk and flutter took place at her heels. Too late! Another white leg-horn gone. It was disheartening. (9)

In depicting Banford as a chicken amid the flock, particularly in a context that highlights the incompetence of the women as farmers, Lawrence necessarily undercuts the demonic nature of the fox. Slinking boldly up behind Banford, the fox might *seem* like a demon to a chicken or to a particularly bad farmer, but what stands out in this passage is his relative competence. As it turns out, recent studies of bird mortality on chicken farms suggest that levels of fox predation are strongly correlated with the quality of the farming. One study reported that "in general, bird mortality was higher on farms where overall bird mortality was high, suggesting that poor overall standards of bird husbandry may be associated with levels of fox predation."[48] Such studies suggest that in a very real sense bad bird husbandry shapes Banford's perception of the fox as "a demon." To be blunt, it is her incompetence as a farmer that makes him into the evil she sees.

As an observer of nature, Lawrence is apt to have known some things about foxes that recent studies, such as those mentioned above, confirm. For instance, he probably knew that the farmer who grew crops and also raised livestock was far better off letting foxes live and risking the loss of an occasional bird to fox predation. In England, not foxes but rabbits cause the lion's share of agricultural damage; because the former prey on the latter, foxes are an indirect benefit to agriculture rather than pests. Lawrence did not have to go back to his Beatrix Potter to figure this out, and even though March and Banford have not planted so much as a vegetable garden, the identification of Nellie March with the rabbit or March hare suggests that she is a greater liability to Bailey Farm than the fox who is making off with the chickens.[49] In suggesting that Henry is the fox come to rid Bailey Farm of its languid chickens and destructive rabbits, Lawrence reproduces on the symbolic level the tensions he dramatizes at the realistic one, for if Henry's identity is the fox as sly predator, the logic of the animal analogies suggests that March and Henry have no potential for sexual and emotional compatibility, but are trapped in a predator-prey relationship.

    This notion of the fox as demon or sly predator, however, distorts both the reality and the typical human perception of the animal itself. The common red fox, a member of the dog family, is a carnivore, but his diet is opportunistic, including insects, earthworms, fruits, eggs, and carrion, as well as birds and small mammals. Red foxes are small; in Britain, the average fox is not much larger than a domestic cat, and North American foxes are reported to be even smaller. Foxes themselves are sometimes preyed upon by wolves and other larger predators. Although they are canids, foxes have a number of catlike characteristics, such as not traveling in packs as other dogs do and typically stalking their prey and pouncing on it rather than running it down. Long thought to be monogamous (an assumption that Lawrence himself would have made), foxes establish dens in burrows, often made by other animals, during the breeding season, and while the young are being raised the male hunts for his mate and the offspring. Recent research suggests that foxes find a new mate each season but also that mating patterns might be quite ecologically sensitive. Widely distributed throughout the Northern Hemisphere, red foxes were introduced to Australia and the eastern United States solely for purposes of the hunt, but they have managed to thrive in those environments, extending well beyond the culture of those who would kill them for sport. Today, most people report that they like foxes, and it is hard to imagine that Lawrence felt otherwise. To humans, they appear smart and resourceful, nurturing yet independent, forceful but not vicious, beautiful yet sly and aggressive.

    It is the expression, perception, or realization of those characteristics in the story that marks each character's partial grasp of the full potentiality of the animal, which represents a complete union between March and Henry, one that entails tension as well as loving intimacy and the concurrent individual growth of each partner. If for Banford the fox is a demon who can snatch chickens from under her feet, for March he represents many things, including a sexual awakening that will connect her profoundly with the natural world: "She did not so much think of him: she was possessed by him. She saw his dark, shrewd, unabashed eye looking into her, knowing her. She felt him invisibly master her spirit. She knew the way he lowered his chin as he looked up, she knew his muzzle, the golden brown, and the greyish white. And again, she saw him glance over his shoulder at her, half inviting, half contemptuous and cunning. So she went, with her great startled eyes glowing, her gun under her arm, along the wood edge" (11). Although she has had the opportunity to shoot the fox, and although she carries the gun in pursuit of him, she cannot shoot him. When Henry arrives at Bailey Farm, it is March who associates him with the fox. "Whether it was the thrusting forward of the head, or the glisten of fine whitish hairs on the ruddy cheek-bones, or the bright, keen eyes, that can never be said: but the boy was to her the fox, and she could not see him otherwise" (14). Just as the aura and general characteristics of the fox call her to the world of nature and her awakening sexuality, the connection between Henry and the fox is, in Nellie March's consciousness, animalistic and sensuous yet still mysterious.

Even though many scholars have identified the fox with Henry or some aspect of his psyche, it is in fact March, not Henry, who is preoccupied with the animal, in her consciousness and in her dreams, and it is for her, as Brayfield notes, that he takes on new form and meaning as the novella develops. As March becomes passive in the face of Henry's proprietary sexual aggression, her response to the fox as both reality and symbol reveals her desire for individual growth within the relationship. Accordingly, any violence to the fox at any point in the story damages the developing relationship between March and Henry and all of the life-history potential therein contained. March's inability to shoot the fox either before or after Henry arrives signifies her generally growth-oriented direction, in spite of her hesitation and the fear of sexuality that Renner rightly stresses. Logically, shooting the fox before Henry's arrival could only constitute the destruction of her own emerging desires, because it is only with these that he has so far become associated early in the story. After Henry has come to the farm, March's first dream relates the fox, in part, to her sexual ambivalence, as he lures her outside, then bites and burns her with his brush. At the same time, however, that the dream fox represents the pain of sexual experience, he is unequivocally androgenous, representing the corn god and goddess: "He was very yellow and bright, like corn" (20). Fashioned from Lawrence's reading of Frazer, the dream fox reflects folk deities connected with rituals of fertility that alternately employ the corn mother, the corn maiden, and the corn fox (or other animal).[50] Lawrence's choice of the fox, with its combination of feline and canid, sly and aggressive, feminine and masculine characteristics, contains within a single symbol the chief

Jungian archetypes representative of both central male and female life-history phases associated with fecundity, fertility, and nurture. As Brayfield notes, the fox represents for March an expanding range of experience, and the experience she desires here happens to coincide with the evolved life-history goal of bearing and nurturing offspring in partnership with a mate. While female choice has eluded her in her isolated circumstances, Henry Grenfel, virile and resourceful, has appeared out of nowhere, and March will not turn away from him or destroy the potential embodied in that relationship. The feminized and beatific qualities of the corn fox, his glowing aura and the singing that nearly brings the dreaming March to tears, reinforce the androgynous, composite nature of the symbol, which represents the pain of sexual experience and fecundity simultaneously. Instructively, although "she awoke with the pain of it, and lay trembling as if she were really seared" (20), the memory soon dims.

The divine aura of the dream fox derives, most immediately, from the spiritual significance of the fertility rituals Frazer chronicles, but within the text it epitomizes the divinity of the natural world and the life force through procreative union, themes connected to the fiction of Lawrence's early and middle phases and to the vision of heterosexual union in *Study of Thomas Hardy*. Hence, it is with March's yearning toward such a union that the Christian imagery of the novella should be glossed. Whereas Good suggests that the Christmas wedding establishes Henry as a Christ figure, such an interpretation is questionable. Most saliently, March never perceives Henry as divine or redemptive; rather, Lawrence attributes divinity and erotic power to the animal, whose symbolic significance exceeds correspondence with Henry. Surely, to the extent that Lawrence invites an analogy between Henry and Christ, the comparison is ironical, and the key, again, is the author's focus on March's perception. After Henry has shot and skinned the animal, "[March] saw the fox's skin nailed flat on a board, as if crucified. It gave her an uneasy feeling" (42). Just as only March connects the fox with the natural world at large and, through her dream, with the male and female forces of procreation, it is only she who relates him to Christ and therefore only she who perceives the death of the divinity in the animal. That divinity is, in the first dream, conceptually coterminous with sexual fulfillment and its life function, genetic perpetuation through the pair bond. Since the animal betokens her awakening sexuality before Henry's arrival at Bailey Farm, the crucified fox plausibly represents the sacrifice of March's sexual fulfillment and psychic-emotional growth to Henry's predatory compulsiveness. That her stroking of the dead animal's tail just before he is skinned constitutes the story's most erotic scene signifies a potency still alive in March and, of course, nature as a whole but perhaps no longer alive in the relationship to which she has committed herself. This scene follows her second, morbid dream of laying Banford's body in the kindling box with the fox skin just after Henry has killed the animal. The second dream crucially identifies the death of the fox with the foreshadowed death of Banford and, as Brayfield suggests, expresses their basic wrongness.

Whereas in March's case the symbolism of the fox unfolds the young woman's ambivalent though seemingly determined effort to grow into shared reproductive adulthood, in Henry's case the symbolism generally confirms his actions at the realistic level of the story. Henry's perception of the fox, like Banford's, remains static and negative and thus defines the psychic gulf between him and his potential mate. In the conversation that precedes Henry's successful efforts to pressure March into accepting his marriage proposal, she admits that she has connected the fox singing around the cottage with Henry, and she tells him of her experience the previous summer, when she could not shoot the fox, who stared into her eyes and "made an impression on me" (32). March's responses provide several clues to the meaning of the fox for her to which Henry is not alert:

> "A laugh on his face!" repeated Henry, also laughing. "He frightened you, did he?"
>
> "No, he didn't frighten me. He made an impression on me, that's all."
>
> "And you thought I was the fox, did you?" he laughed, with the same queer, quick little laugh, like a puppy wrinkling its nose.
>
> "Yes, I did, for the moment," she said. "Perhaps he'd been in my mind without my knowing."
>
> "Perhaps you think I've come to steal your chickens or something," he said, with the same young laugh.
>
> But she only looked at him with a wide, dark, vacant eye. (32)

March's claims about the fox, her association of him with Henry, and her open gaze not only signal her receptivity to this particular man but intimate that he is already, in a sense, inside her ("in my mind without my knowing"), although the relationship requires psychic-physical consummation. But instructively, Henry, like Banford, sees the fox only as a predator and is incapable of grasping the opportunity for relationship and individuation, embodied in the fox, that March provides. If he could, he might not be so quick to disown the association of himself with the fox. The conversation connects his immaturity with his misapprehension; but puppyish and playful though he is, he is nonetheless still the "young hunter" who will "bring down March as his quarry" (24). The contrast between the perceptions of Henry and March, between the fox as externalized predator and as internalized image of natural union, could not be greater. Furthermore, Henry's determination to extract a promise of marriage that very evening through the manipulative tactics that centuries of folklore have associated with foxes prompts him to say, once again, "I'm sure you don't really think I'm like the fox" (33). Projecting his own concept of the animal onto March's revelations, Henry is evidently anxious to disclaim any likeness to the canid he defines only as predatory, sly, and manipulative, seeking to mask strategies he hardly needs to employ in his efforts to earn her assent.

Henry's subsequent extermination of the fox further articulates his compulsive destructiveness, his inability to develop, and his predatory perception of his relationship with March. Although he is not conscious of his motives, the narrative perspective emphasizes his destructive impulse. In fact, Henry's lust for blood exceeds the natural predatory instinct of the fox, who kills to feed his mate and the fox kits in the den (now left to fend for themselves, a point Lawrence likely expects his readers to note). Henry's only real motivation for shooting the fox is relief from the intense agitation caused by Banford telling March that he is unreliable and will make a fool of her, that he had never done any honest farm work for his grandfather, but "was off with the gun on every occasion, just as he is now" (37). Henry is profoundly agitated and hyper-attuned to the night world after eavesdropping at the women's bedroom door while Banford criticized him. He "[takes] the gun . . . [and does] not think to go away from the farm. No, he only took the gun. . . . He went stealthily away down a fence-side, looking for something to shoot. At the same time he remembered that he ought not to shoot and frighten the women" (38). Driven by a compulsive need to destroy when he is thwarted, he cannot modify his actions in light of his conscious awareness that the gunshots will alarm the sleeping women. This is the second time in the story that he has been unable to adjust his behavior in light of conscious insight, the first being when he recognized that he should take things slowly in his courtship of March.

When Henry kills the fox, he not only eliminates the potentiality of the relationship and his own opportunity for growth but solidifies the interpersonal dynamics in the story into the predator-prey mode. As Andrew Howe notes, the treatment of animals in Lawrence sometimes provides a key to the tenor of sexual relationships and to the treatment of the self; in this case, according to Granofsky, his action is clearly self-brutalizing.[51] Although Henry is only "looking for something to shoot" as he leaves the cottage, the barking dogs alert him to the fox's presence, and his sympathy for the fox, who "didn't have a chance," is briefly in tension with his impulse to kill, no matter how slight the challenge. Henry recognizes that the fox, far from being a terrible pest, represents the remnant of some-thing special: "It seemed to him it would be the last of the foxes in this loudly-barking, thick-voiced England, tight with innumerable little houses" (38–39). The parallels between the abundant barking dogs, houses, and substantial British populace on the one hand and the fox and Henry, "peering through the darkness with dilated eyes that seemed to be able to grow black and full of sight in the dark, like a cat's," on the other clearly identifies Henry with the fox and thus marks Henry's act as self-destructive. When he kills the part of himself that is like the fox, his compulsive aggression effectively marks him as a more vicious predator than the fox.

Because the fox of the story corresponds to the animal *as perceived,* there is a certain logic to expanding the conception of the animal beyond species bounds once the killing has occurred. When Henry receives March's letter asking to dis-solve the engagement, he instantly focuses on his battle with Banford, and the language Lawrence employs—first in externalized narration, then in Henry's perspective—implies vulpine transformation. Henry turns "yellow round the eyes with fury. . . . He wanted the woman, he had fixed like doom upon having her. . . . Sightless with rage and thwarted madness he got through the morning. . . . Deep in himself he felt like roaring and howling and gnashing his teeth and breaking things" (58). The increased sense of viciousness and threat carry over to the final scene of the story, although Henry is self-contained and controlled upon his ar-rival at Bailey Farm. As soon as March and Banford see him, they revert to the animal types with which they were identified in the beginning of the narrative. In effect, March turns back into a rabbit and Banford into a bird. March goes slack as he approaches, her eyes "wide and vacant, and her upper lip lifted from her teeth in that helpless, fascinated rabbit-look. The moment she saw his glowing red face it was all over with her. She was helpless as if she had been bound" (62).

There is, in the long run, nothing fablelike about *The Fox,* but it is character-istic of Lawrence's idiosyncratic sense of irony that these elements of the genre would literally come back to haunt us before the story's grotesque denouement. The modern novella is an amalgam of numerous modes and genres that have gone before, and while it cannot typically have the scope of a developed comedy or tragedy, it can contain many of their generic elements and evolved impulses. Those that Storey brings to bear on his descriptions of comedy and tragedy, the sense of mastery and the fine-tuning of the social emotions, certainly have a role here. It is true that *The Fox,* like all romantic comedies, ends with a marriage, but for the characters in the story the marriage has effectively ended before it has begun—ended with mating minus love, as the will to dominate robs a relationship of extraordinary erotic power and the potential for individual and relational growth. Not so for the reader: in the ethical questions raised by Henry's exertion of power, in the potent possibilities of the symbols, in the perplexing dissipation of sexual love, Lawrence provides each of us with opportunities to fine-tune the emotions of our most fundamental love relationships.

Chapter 1 · *Literature, Science, and Biocultural Interpretation*

1. M. Arnold, "Literature and Science," 72–73.
2. Scholes, "Presidential Address 2004," 728.
3. M. Arnold, *Culture and Anarchy.*
4. Steven Marcus explains that the present-day concept of the humanities only emerged after 1930. See "Humanities from Classics to Cultural Studies."
5. Scholes, Forum.
6. Menand, "Dangers Within and Without," 15. For Brian Boyd's reply, see "Getting It All Wrong."
7. Menand, *Metaphysical Club.*
8. Wilson, *Consilience;* Wilson, "Resuming the Enlightenment Quest"; Rorty, "Against Unity"; Gross, "Icarian Impulse"; Crain, "Artistic Animal"; Knapp, "Evolutionary Paradigm for Literary Study." Among the articles in the popular media are Shea, "Survivalist lit"; Max, "Literary Darwinists"; Gillespie, "When Darwin Meets Dickens"; Gottschall, "Measure for Measure"; Mooney, "A Science of Literature?"; B. Peterson, "Darwin to the Rescue"; and Cohen, "Next Big Thing in English."
9. B. Smith, "Figuring and Reconfiguring," 25.
10. Graff, *Professing Literature,* 55.
11. Scholes, *Rise and Fall of English,* 110.
12. Seamon, "Literary Darwinism as Science and Myth," 261.
13. William Wordsworth, Preface to *Lyrical Ballads* (1802), in Wordsworth, *Lyrical Ballads and Other Poems.*
14. Shelley, *Defence of Poetry,* 517.
15. R. Levin, "New Interdisciplinarity in Literary Criticism," 13.
16. James, *Pragmatism,* 108, 101.
17. For the argument that classical pragmatism is convergent with contemporary bioepistemology, and that bioepistemology offers a moderate solution to the seesaw of naïve realism versus nihilistic relativism in epistemology, see N. Easterlin, "Making Knowledge." Menand's intellectual history of American pragmatism, *The Metaphysical Club,* clarifies the extent to which William James especially was influenced by his knowledge of evolution in formulating his philosophy.

18. Jackson, "'Literary Interpretation' and Cognitive Literary Studies," 204. See also Jackson's other two important early essays expressing ambivalence about the interpretive potential of interdisciplinary paradigms, "Issues and Problems" and "Questioning Interdisciplinarity."

19. For Carroll's criticisms, see his review "Wilson's *Consilience* and Literary Study."

20. Carroll, "Evolutionary Paradigm for Literary Study," 105.

21. In his discussion of free will, Wilson suggests that while in a strict sense freedom might be a self-delusion, the human mind is too complex a structure for any intelligence to exist that could predict the behavior of individuals. See Wilson, *On Human Nature*, 76–77. My assumption is that any retroactive description of a complex human behavior confronts the same obstacle of overwhelming complexity.

22. Gottschall, "What Are Literary Scholars For?," 186, 187.

23. Gottschall, *Literature, Science, and the New Humanities*, 75. For my review of this work, see *Philosophy and Literature* 33.1 (2009): 230–33.

24. Slingerland, "Good and Bad Reductionism."

25. Carroll, "Rejoinder to the Responses," 327.

26. Carroll furthermore claims that Gottschall's scholarly oeuvre exemplifies "the range of activities in this program," but in fact Gottschall's work attests to the reorientation of the discipline that he himself champions. His fine book *The Rape of Troy*, the work Carroll describes as "a discursive historical and interpretive account of Homer's *Iliad* and *Odyssey*," is an anthropological rather than a literary critical enterprise. As Gottschall himself defines the book in the introduction, "It analyzes Homeric conflict from the perspective of modern anthropology and evolutionary biology; it is best described as an evolutionary anthropology of conflict in Homeric society.... [The] Homeric epics are not only precious as literary art; they are also our most important artifacts of life on island outcroppings and threads of coastal land in and surrounding the Aegean sea almost three thousand years ago" (3). Gottschall has also pioneered the use of quantitative studies to test human universals on the basis of literary evidence, and these studies are included in *Literature, Science, and the New Humanities*.

27. Carroll, "'Theory,' Anti-Theory, and Empirical Criticism," 34, 35.

28. Carroll, "Human Nature and Literary Meaning," 187–88.

29. Crews, "Apriorism for Empiricists," 159. For similar criticism that "neo-naturalists" (cognitive and evolutionary critics) misconstrue the nature of their objects of study as well as the aims of the humanities, see Frank Kelleter's trenchant essay "A Tale of Two Natures." See also Karl Eibl's reply, "On the Redskins of Scientism and the Aesthetes in the Circled Wagons."

30. Alan Richardson and Francis F. Steen similarly argue that literary works must be viewed as "cognitive artifacts." See "Reframing the Adjustment," quotation on 152.

31. Donald, *Origins of the Modern Mind*.

32. Williams, *Stoner*, 13.

33. Tooby and DeVore, "Reconstruction of Hominid Behavioral Evolution."

34. Huizinga, *Homo Ludens*.

35. Dutton, *Art Instinct*, 64–84.
36. Storey, "Art and Religion," 293.
37. N. Easterlin, "Play, Mutation, and Reality Acceptance."

Chapter 2 · *"It Is No Tale"*

1. van Peer, "Two Laws of Literary History," 124. Van Peer presents both of these conclusions as testable hypotheses and suggests as well that in terms of shaping the canon, "persons, groups, or institutions, matter relatively little over the long term" (128). Obviously, my argument suggests that I am hoping otherwise.
2. Shelley, *Defence of Poetry*, 513.
3. See, e.g., Barkow, Cosmides, and Tooby, *Adapted Mind;* and Wilson, *Consilience*, ch. 5.
4. Gottschall, "Quantitative Literary Study." See also idem, *Literature, Science, and the New Humanities*.
5. Frye, "Function of Criticism at the Present Time," 6.
6. Genette, "Frontiers of Narrative."
7. Herman, *Narrative Theory and the Cognitive Sciences*, introduction; Palmer, *Fictional Minds*, 42, 93.
8. Lloyd, *Simple Minds*, 210.
9. Bruner, *Acts of Meaning*.
10. Schank, *Tell Me a Story*.
11. Hume, *Enquiry concerning Human Understanding*, 17.
12. Carrithers, "Narrativity."
13. Harris, "Work of Imagination."
14. Storey, *Mimesis and the Human Animal*, 82.
15. See Sugiyama, "Predation, Narration, and Adaptation."
16. The functionalist account of mind inaugurated by nineteenth-century pragmatic philosophers, which holds that thought functions toward practical ends, was significantly influenced by Darwin's theory of evolution by natural selection, as Louis Menand explains in *The Metaphysical Club*. William James's influential *Principles of Psychology* argues for the functionalism of the mind's inherent conservatism. Late twentieth-century sociopsychological studies in consistency and attribution theory provide experimental support for the functionalist account of mind; see, e.g., Festinger, *Theory of Cognitive Dissonance*. Gerrig's findings, therefore, are consistent with the scientifically based theory of mind that has emerged in the past two hundred years and build on its recent experimental tradition.
17. Although arguing from a perspective distinctly different from Gerrig's, Ellen Spolsky similarly claims, in a rebuttal to the evolutionary psychologists Leda Cosmides and John Tooby, that narrative is too all-pervasive in cognition and function for an evolved algorithm to separate fictional from nonfictional representations. See "Why and How."
18. Mandler, *Stories, Scripts, and Scenes*, 14. The emergence of the embodied mind paradigm in cognitive neuroscience draws on numerous subfields of psychology that

take a more holistic and situated approach to cognitive processing and experimentation than earlier cognitive psychology. Some research results in these interrelated fields question earlier assertions about human reliance on scripts, schemas, and the like. I explore this new research and apply it in chapter 3 and especially chapter 4 of this book.

19. Cited in Hogan, *Mind and Its Stories,* 65.

20. See Palmer and Ryan, "Cognitive Maps."

21. The translated passage I have in mind reads as follows: "Perhaps, too, we should abandon a whole tradition that allows us to imagine that knowledge can exist only where the power relations are suspended and that knowledge can develop only outside its injunctions, its demands and its interests. Perhaps we should abandon the belief that power makes mad and that, by the same token, the renunciation of power is one of the conditions of knowledge. We should admit rather that power produces knowledge (and not simply by encouraging it because it serves power or by applying it because it is useful); that power and knowledge directly imply one another; that there is no power relation without the correlative constitution of a field of knowledge, nor any knowledge that does not presuppose and constitute at the same time power relations. These 'power-knowledge relations' are to be analysed, therefore, not on the basis of a subject of knowledge who is or is not free in relation to the power system, but, on the contrary, the subject who knows, the objects to be known and the modalities of knowledge must be regarded as so many effects of these fundamental implications of power-knowledge and their historical transformations. In short, it is not the activity of the subject of knowledge that produces a corpus of knowledge, useful or resistant to power, but power-knowledge, the processes and struggles that traverse it and of which it is made up, that determines the forms and possible domains of knowledge." From Foucault, *Discipline and Punish,* 27–28.

22. Zunshine, "Theory of Mind," 273.

23. Two early books focusing on the implications of psychology for aesthetics are Arnheim, *Toward a Psychology of Art;* and Peckham, *Man's Rage for Chaos.* Both of these works focus specifically on the visual arts, and the authors make opposite aesthetic claims: that art should not resist our prototypical modes of perceptual organization (Arnheim) and that art's function is to break up normative perceptual-cognitive modes (Peckham). More recently, Steven Pinker asserted that "the dominant theories of elite art and criticism in the twentieth century grew out of a militant denial of human nature" and that this denial was the source of declining interest in the arts. *Blank Slate,* 416. Pinker's dubious claim neglects, among other things, the impact of psychology (Freudian *and* Jamesian) and anthropology on modernist aesthetics, which indicates that the source of difficulty lies elsewhere.

24. For a discussion of the interrelationship between technological developments, economic modernization, and social change, see R. Easterlin, *Reluctant Economist,* ch. 4, or, for a somewhat more technical discussion, idem, *Growth Triumphant,* chs.1–6.

25. In contrast to the earlier major transition for the human species—that from nomadic to sedentary culture—the transition from rural, agricultural economies and

social structures to modern, industrialized structures is incredibly rapid. Shifts in climate with the retreat of the last ice age provided the opportunity for the beginnings of settled culture but also set limits on the viability of sedentism, so that it took about fifteen thousand years for settlement to become a firmly established way of life. For a comprehensive account based on the archaeological and paleoanthropological record, see Mithen, *After the Ice.*

26. The notion that literature provides a kind of practice ground for direct human action goes back at least to Hume's "Of Tragedy," but it has gained more force and currency with the emergence of possible-worlds theory and, more recently, the rise of cognitive-evolutionary approaches to literature. See Hume, "Of Tragedy"; and Pavel, *Fictional Worlds.* My essay in *After Poststructuralism* and Lisa Zunshine's use of contemporary theory of mind in *Why We Read Fiction* are just a couple of examples of the extension of this tradition via cognitive-evolutionary research.

27. William Blake, *Jerusalem*, ch. 1, plate 10, ll. 20–21, in *Blake's Poetry and Designs*, 316.

28. William Blake, *The Marriage of Heaven and Hell*, in *Blake's Poetry and Designs.*

29. Barbauld, *Anna Letitia Barbauld*, 143–47.

30. Wordsworth, *Lyrical Ballads and Other Poems*, 742–43. All references to poems from *Lyrical Ballads* are to this edition, and all quotations from this source incorporate changes Wordsworth made for the second edition (1800).

31. Wordsworth, *Prelude*, 5.259–60. All references are to the 1805 text.

32. This view of mind is therefore evident in much of Wordsworth's major poetry, but especially in that written during the period 1797–1807.

33. I make this argument about the spots of time in "Self-Qualification and Naturalistic Monism in *The Prelude*," ch. 2 of *Wordsworth and the Question of "Romantic Religion*," 78–115.

34. Shklovsky, "Art as Technique," 12.

35. The romanticist David Miall has drawn on Shklovsky's work to elucidate the defamiliarizing process in Shelley's "Mount Blanc." See "Shelley at Chamonix."

36. Abrams, "Structure and Style."

37. Jordan, *Why the "Lyrical Ballads"?*, 144. Jordan notes that in addition to the overlapping modes of ballad and tale, Wordsworth shunned the conventional, high-cultural literary forms enjoying popularity in 1798, the sonnet and the ode—an interesting contrast to his prodigious output of sonnets later in his career. Mary Jacobus explains that Wordsworth's approach to the ballad was partly a reaction to the supernaturalism and sensationalism of Gottfried Burger's ballads, which appeared in translation in the 1790s. See Jacobus, *Tradition and Experiment.* Tracing the emergent tradition of peasant poetry throughout the eighteenth century, Scott McEathron suggests that the originality of Wordsworth's poetry was in the pairing of elevated narrators with lowly subjects, enabling the poet to seek authenticity through a range of voices and sympathy. See McEathron, "Wordsworth, *Lyrical Ballads*."

38. Griffin, "Wordsworth and the Problem of Imaginative Story," 393.

39. Wordsworth was a notorious reviser, and the complicated history of revisions

to "Simon Lee" suggests careful attention to tone and thus to the persona or masks adopted in the poem. Over time, Wordsworth particularly rearranged and rewrote portions of stanzas 1–4, working out the tonal shifts to his satisfaction, resulting in a final poem whose opening stanzas differ substantially from those of the 1798 version. For instance, the Miltonic allusion in stanza 4, which Wordsworth added and then reinforced in 1827, greatly affects the reader's attitude toward the speaker of the poem. As late as 1845, Wordsworth further altered the final line of the first stanza, substituting the phrase "red as a ripe cherry" for "blooming as a cherry," thus accentuating the nursery-rhyme qualities with excessive alliteration and clipped vowels sounds. See Wordsworth, *Lyrical Ballads and Other Poems,* 64–71, for the history of these revisions. I have adopted the 1845 version for my reading of the poem.

40. Danby, *Simple Wordsworth,* 38.

41. Broadbent, *John Milton,* 186.

42. In a similar vein, Terry Gifford comments astutely on Wordsworth's criticism of pastoral convention in the dehumanizing characterization of rustics in the beginning of "Michael." See Gifford, *Pastoral,* 5–7.

43. Curran, "Mary Robinson's *Lyrical Tales* in Context."

44. For a brief overview of Robinson's life and literary relations, see Judith Pascoe's introduction to *Mary Robinson: Selected Poems,* 19–61. All quotations of Robinson's poetry are from this edition.

45. Pascoe, "Mary Robinson and the Literary Marketplace," 252, 253, 259.

46. For a discussion of Robinson's self-characterization as a romantic writer of genius, see L. Peterson, "Becoming an Author."

47. Arguing in 1995 that Robinson's work deserves to be examined in its own right rather than solely for its literary historical relations, Robin L. Miskolcze stresses the centrality of themes of alienation and exile in the poet's verse. See Miskolcze, "Snapshots of Contradiction." Both Curran and Pascoe rightly note Robinson's technical facility.

48. For an interesting essay on the contrast between the personae in the 1797–98 Tabitha Bramble poems and those published in *Lyrical Tales,* see D. Robinson, "Mary Robinson and the Trouble with Tabitha Bramble." Daniel Robinson suggests that the early Tabitha Bramble poems may not even have been written by Mary Robinson.

Chapter 3 · Minding Ecocriticism

1. Bennett, "Different Shades of Green," 208.

2. Marshall, "Literary Criticism as Ecological Thought," 2.

3. Quoted in Phillips, *Truth of Ecology,* 65.

4. Phillips's concern about the mismatch between ecocritical and scientific conceptualizations of nonhuman nature is echoed by Greg Garrard, who points to this discrepancy as a central challenge for developing interdisciplinary relations. See Garrard, *Ecocriticism,* 178.

5. Cheryll Glotfelty and Harold Fromm, introduction to Glotfelty and Fromm,

Ecocritical Reader, xviii; Lawrence Buell in Forum on Literatures of the Environment, by J. Arnold et al., 1091.

6. Slovic, "Nature Writing and Environmental Psychology." Slovic points out that nature writers such as Thoreau, Annie Dillard, and Barry Lopez are actually writing about human awareness rather than about nature itself, and he employs pragmatic and environmental psychology to support his argument.

7. Paul Gross and Norman Levitt make this helpfully clear distinction between commonsense weak constructivism (or constructionism) and strong constructivism (or constructionism). See *Higher Superstition,* ch. 3, "The Cultural Construction of Cultural Constructivism."

8. Hitt, "Ecocriticism and the Long Eighteenth Century," 134.

9. Buell, *Future of Environmental Criticism,* 31. See also idem, *Writing for an Endangered World.*

10. For the argument that comedy hews closer to our natural propensities than tragedy, see Meeker, *Comedy of Survival.*

11. Love, *Practical Ecocriticism.*

12. For an account of the history of pastoral, see Gifford.

13. J. Bate, *Romantic Ecology.* James McKusick's *Green Writing: Romanticism and Ecology* provides a comprehensive discussion of the origins of ecological writing in the British romantics and their influence on American environmental literature. Karl Kroeber argues in *Ecological Literary Criticism* that British romantic literature is proto-ecological, and he does so by emphasizing its holistic evolutionism. For a brief but incisive Darwinian critique of deep ecology's tendency to look to nature for moral guidance, as well as for a discussion of the value of teaching a poem like Wordsworth's "Nutting," which reveals the destructive result of idealizing nature, see Pite, "How Green Were the Romantics?"

14. J. Bate, "Culture and Environment," 554.

15. See, e.g., Manes, "Nature and Silence"; Hogarth, "Some Principles of Ecocriticism"; and Fromm, "From Transcendence to Obsolescence."

16. Bryson, "Ambivalent Discourse."

17. Darwin, *Origin of Species,* 108.

18. Mazel, "American Literary Environmentalism," 140.

19. In addition to J. Bate, "Culture and Environment," and Slovic, see, e.g., Evernden, *Natural Alien;* and Cantrell, "Locus of Compossibility." Influenced by phenomenology and environmental and ecological psychology, these scholars are sensitive to the situated nature of being and the relational dependence of organisms and physical places. For an evolutionary perspective emphasizing physical environments, see Carroll, "Ecology of Victorian Fiction."

One result of the emergence of feminist ecocriticism in particular has been a growing awareness that human relationships are central to the sense of valued place. See Armbruster, "Bringing Nature Writing Home"; Stein, "To Make the Visible World Your Conscience"; and Wallace, "All Things Natural Are Strange."

20. Kaplan, "Environmental Preference," 585.

21. McKillop, "Local Attachment and Cosmopolitanism."
22. Boym, *Future of Nostalgia*, xiii, xv.
23. Tuan, *Space and Place*, 29. See also Ogden, "From Spatial to Aesthetic Distance."
24. Bowlby, *Attachment*.
25. Stern, *First Relationship*, 36.
26. Trevarthen, "Interpersonal Abilities of Infants."
27. See, e.g., Orians and Heerwagen, "Evolved Responses to Landscapes." For a neurobiological overview of the life-regulating function of emotion, see Damasio, *Feeling of What Happens*, 33–81.
28. This account of human prehistory draws on numerous sources but is especially indebted to Kaplan's "Environmental Preference" and to Steven Mithen's "cognitive archaeology." See the following by Mithen: *Prehistory of the Mind; After the Ice;* and *Singing Neanderthals*.
29. H. Ross, *Behavior and Perception*, 109–14.
30. Stern, *Interpersonal World of the Infant*, 6. Stern's perspective is convergent with Antonio Damasio's more recent neurobiological account of the senses of the self and their function in enabling "continuity of reference across long periods of time." Damasio, 134–36. Damasio distinguishes between proto, core, and autobiographical selves, corresponding at the lowest level to a basic sense of organismic integrity and at the highest to an ongoing account based in individual memory (174–75).
31. A few brief examples from autobiographically and biographically based literature follow: Employing a psychoanalytic model, Richard J. Onorato hypothesized that Wordsworth's exceptional attachment to the environs of the Lake District was a symptom of infantile narcissism as a result of the death of his mother during his childhood. Although I would argue that the poet's capacity for adult love and friendship suggests that this attachment to nature was not regressive, his mother's death (and his removal to his uncongenial uncle Christopher's house) may well have contributed to his exceptional feeling for natural place. See Onorato, *Character of the Poet*. Likewise, the story of the contemporary American backwoodsman Eustace Conway suggests two reasons why this man has so single-mindedly pursued life in the woods: (1) a love of the natural world passed down from the families of both parents and (2) a brilliant, harsh, and disapproving father who trained him in the forms of suffering that only humans can produce. See Gilbert, *Last American Man*. Writing about how Anne LaBastille's divorce precipitated her wilderness regeneration, K. Wesley Berry maintains that outsider status is typical of regeneration through wilderness stories. Berry notes that the rustic cabin in LaBastille's narrative cures the author's sense of homelessness, and she pertinently asks whether wilderness escape is a bourgeois phenomenon. See "Regeneration in the Adirondacks."
32. For a fuller interpretation of this passage and its significance in *The Prelude*, see N. Easterlin, "Psychoanalysis and 'The Discipline of Love.'"
33. Libby argues, in fact, that ambivalence toward the natural world and disorientation are the creative conditions inspiring Terry Tempest Williams's *Refuge*, because

writing enables the simultaneous creation of self and natural world. See "Nature Writing as *Refuge*."

34. "Lines, Written a Few Miles above Tintern Abbey," ll. 96–98, in Wordsworth, *Lyrical Ballads and Other Poems*, 118–19.

35. The first four of these Lucy poems were initially published in the 1800 edition of *Lyrical Ballads*, and I have adopted the text in Butler and Green's edition of *Lyrical Ballads and Other Poems*, 163–64, 221–22. "Three years" was not grouped with the first three poems when it was initially published. Although the first four poems, and often all five, are today grouped together for pedagogical and scholarly purposes, see Wordsworth, *Lyrical Ballads and Other Poems*, 383–84, for a summary of the debates surrounding this grouping.

36. "Old Man travelling; Animal Tranquillity and Decay, a Sketch," published originally in the 1798 *Lyrical Ballads* (see Wordsworth, *Lyrical Ballads and Other Poems*, 110). Wordsworth originally wrote "Description of a Beggar," which evolved into the much more developed "Old Cumberland Beggar"; "Old Man travelling" was, according to the poet's recollection, the "overflow" from this process. In the final four lines, the old man tells the speaker that he is traveling to visit his dying son in the hospital. These lines undercutting the speaker's romantic image of the old man were deleted in 1815, possibly because they closely resemble lines from one of Robert Southey's *English Eclogues, The Sailor's Mother*. See *Lyrical Ballads and Other Poems*, 356; and "Resolution and Independence," in Wordsworth, *Poems, in Two Volumes*, 123–29.

37. In Wordsworth, *Poems*, 103–4.

38. Ibid., 266–68.

39. Sonnet 27 (untitled), ll. 7–8, and sonnet 5, "To the South Downs," ll. 6–8, in C. Smith, *Poems of Charlotte Smith*, 30, 15–16.

40. Samuel Taylor Coleridge, "Dejection: An Ode," ll. 47–49, in *Samuel Taylor Coleridge*, 180.

41. In an article published as I was finalizing the manuscript for this book, Kathleen Robin Hart and John H. Long Jr. describe how they explore these questions in an interdisciplinary environmental-studies course at Vassar College that draws on literary studies, biology, and cognitive science. The course includes cognitive work on metaphor and my theorization of place. See "Animal Metaphors and Metaphorizing Animals."

42. All text references to *Wide Sargasso Sea* are to the 1999 Norton Critical edition.

43. Mezei, "And it Kept its Secret." Also pointing attention to a narrative technique that moves between internal and external focalization (the child versus the adult narrating Antoinette), Carine Mardorossian emphasizes how this technique reveals colonialist assumptions. See "Shutting Up the Subaltern."

44. Mardorossian, "Double [De]Colonization," 81. Mary Louise Emory identifies dreams, memory, and madness as forms of resistance in "Politics of Form." Jan Curtis offers perhaps the most optimistic reading of Antoinette's demise, reading her death as a prophetic transformation. See "Secret of *Wide Sargasso Sea*."

45. Kaplan and Kaplan, *Cognition and Environment*.

46. In his comprehensive study of slave societies, Orlando Patterson identifies a common pattern, finding that, in E. O. Wilson's words, "true, formalized slavery passes repeatedly through approximately the same life cycle, at the end of which the peculiar circumstances stemming from its origin together with the stubborn qualities of human nature lead to its destruction." Unlike in species that are predisposed to accept low status, slavery among humans has "a disintegrating effect on slaves and masters alike." Discussed in Wilson, *On Human Nature*, 80–81.

47. Howells, *Jean Rhys*.

48. Anne B. Simpson offers a psychoanalytic interpretation of Rhys's novels that particularly emphasizes the impact of early mother-child interactions on the heroines. In her reading of *Voyage in the Dark* she connects fears of abandonment with perceived threats from the object world. See *Territories of Psyche*, 29.

49. The seminal work on mystical and related transport experiences is James, *Varieties of Religious Experience*.

50. Interdisciplinary research and courses in literature and biology or other scientific areas, for instance, offer a distinct but complementary approach to my emphasis on evolved psychology. For a description of methods and coursework with this focus, see Keir and Lewis, "Continuing Evolution of Literary Ecology."

Chapter 4 · *Remembering the Body*

1. Richardson, "Studies in Literature and Cognition," 1–2.

2. Gibson, *Senses Considered as Perceptual Systems*.

3. Quoted in Gibbs, *Embodiment and Cognitive Science*, 43.

4. Quoted in Johnson, *Meaning of the Body*, 94.

5. William Blake, "There is No Natural Religion," in *Blake's Poetry and Designs*, 14–15.

6. Coleridge, *Samuel Taylor Coleridge*, 179–83; Carver, *What We Talk about*, 31–36.

7. One sign of a shift away from this emphasis on language and toward an evolutionarily grounded theory of cognition is the recent focus on theory of mind or folk psychology, particularly in the work of Lisa Zunshine. See *Why We Read Fiction*.

8. Bizup and Kintgen, "Cognitive Paradigm in Literary Studies," 854.

9. Along these lines, both F. Elizabeth Hart and Richardson note that Turner's introduction of cognitive linguistics into literary studies in the guise of cognitive rhetoric offered an alternative to the dichotomized view of literal and figurative language that had gained currency via deconstructive theory. Whereas Paul de Man claimed metaphor as the lynchpin of textual indeterminacy, the theory of conceptual metaphor points to the fundamental coherence of figurative expression. See Richardson, "Apostrophe in Life and in Romantic Art." Hart's essay addresses, additionally, the implications of conceptual metaphor theory for the binary opposition between realist and relativist epistemologies. See "Cognitive Linguistics."

10. In "Beyond a Comparison of Two Distinct Things," Elena Tapia demonstrates how the incorporation of cognitive linguistics into literary analysis highlights the way selected cultural metaphors structure thoughts and attitudes. Responding to the emphasis on the everyday nature of metaphor in cognitive rhetoric, Line Brandt and Per Aage Brandt suggest that literary reading should be interrelated with cognitive research to explain meaning production rather than using poetry as evidence of theses in cognitive semantics. Brandt and Brandt demonstrate that literary metaphors reprocess basic metaphors and speculate that such reprocessing may be a general feature of literature. See "Cognitive Poetics and Imagery." In a response to Brandt and Brandt's criticism of blending, Seana Coulson and Todd Oakley attempt to explain how emergent inferences are generated through a revised network model that includes a concept of context (or ground) and builds a grounding box into the existing blending diagrams. Coulson and Oakley posit that processing novel metaphors requires analogical reasoning and the derivation of emergence, while conventional metaphors require only abstract retrieval, a theory that seems consistent with Brandt and Brandt's notion of reprocessing and Miall and Kuiken's work on defamiliarization. See below, n. 38. Importantly, however, Miall and Kuiken emphasize the role of feeling in the processing of novel literary language, a dimension of cognitive processing ignored by blending theorists. See Coulson and Oakley, "Blending and Coded Meaning."

In the application of conceptual blending and stylistics to poetical analysis, Margaret Freeman's work stands out for the quality of analysis produced by attention to linguistic structures, figurative expressions, and cognitive frames. Nothing in these readings, however, depends on the theory that metaphors are bodily based. See "Body in the Word" and "Poem as Complex Blend." Less successful efforts by other scholars combine blending with areas of evolutionary social science with which it is incompatible and use blending as a metaphor for phenomena better elucidated in a literary, sociohistorical, or naturalistic context. See Cook, "Staging Nothing"; and Weber, "Cognitive Poetics and Literary Criticism."

11. Fauconnier and Turner, *Way We Think.*

12. Ritchie, "Lost in 'Conceptual Space.'"

13. Fauconnier, *Mappings in Thought and Language,* 4.

14. Shen and Balaban, "Metaphorical (In)Coherence in Discourse," 152.

15. Orwell, "Politics and the English Language," 957. In response to the special status that the New Critics claimed for metaphor, Peckham countered that "the basic condition for the creation of a metaphor . . . is the presentation to the speaker's consciousness of a phenomenon for which there is no category and therefore are no attributes, or for which, in his judgment, the conventional category and attributes for that phenomenon are inadequate or . . . unusable." "Metaphor," 416. Peckham elaborates that this is "why the language of simple people tends to be highly metaphorical when they encounter novel phenomena" (417).

16. O'Connor, "Everything That Rises Must Converge," 486.

17. These criticisms apply as well to the modifications to Fauconnier and Turner's

theory by other blending theorists. In "Metaphor and the Space Structuring Model," Seana Coulson and Teenie Matlock propose and test such a model. See also Coulson and Oakley.

18. Carroll, "Deep Structure of Literary Representations," 104.

19. Donald recognizes that his use of the term *mimesis* is more specific than that of literary scholars (168, 169). As a literary term identifying the general imitation or representation of human life in works of imaginative literature, *mimesis* denotes the combined use of all evolved systems of representation, not a single aspect thereof.

20. Turner, *Literary Mind*, 4–5.

21. Within cognitive approaches to literature, several other scholars are developing perspectives that take a dynamic, holistic approach to cognition influenced by ecological psychology. For a critique of the traditional view that modernist narrative technique is simply inward and subjective, see Herman, "1880–1945." In *Cognition in the Globe*, Evelyn Tribble applies theories of distributed cognition and cognitive ecology to the dynamics of Shakespearean troupes and generally argues that the ecological model is useful for consideration of theater history. See also Tribble and Keene, *Cognitive Ecologies*.

22. For a gloss of Kaplan's experiment on environmental preference in the context of other related research, see chapter 3.

23. Both the theory and the reading to follow here are compatible with the flexible concept of reader simulation that Blakey Vermeule adopts, based partly on the work of Amy Coplan. See Vermeule, *Why Do We Care about Literary Characters?*, 42–43.

24. On the other hand, an author may choose at the outset as part of a narrative strategy to stall the epistemic process by confusing the basic principle of reader identification. See my discussion of narrative strategy in N. Easterlin, "Who Was It If It Wasn't Me?"

25. In an important essay published at the same time that Turner was developing the project of cognitive rhetoric, Benny Shanon argues against the fixedness assumption of traditional theories of metaphor and insists on the context-dependent nature of such figures, which operate as gestalts that trigger a range of associations. Like me, Shanon grounds such claims in Gibsonian ecological psychology. See "From Fixedness and Selection to Differentiation and Creation." Shanon's view of metaphor coheres with the perceiver-relative theory of cognitive categorization, or prototype theory, proposed by Eleanor Rosch. See George Lakoff's *Women, Fire, and Dangerous Things*, 136–38. G. Gabrielle Starr's recent essay on multisensory imagery, which draws on empirical research to suggest that people respond holistically rather than piecemeal to the sensory images of poetry, is also compatible with Shanon's insights. See "Multisensory Imagery."

26. Bouslog, "Structure and Theme in Coleridge's 'Dejection: An Ode,'" 43.

27. Richard Holmes reports that the poem was first published in 1947 and then later, in 1988, by Cornell University Press. *Samuel Taylor Coleridge*, 329n49. Bruce Lawder dates the discovery of the poem to a 1977 auction of Wordsworth's letters and papers that included a copy of the poem. "Secret(ing) Conversations," 74.

28. Miall and Kuiken, "What Is Literariness?," 136.

29. Fairbanks, "Form of Coleridge's 'Dejection Ode.'"

30. See H. Ross, 127.

31. In his analysis of Coleridge's critique of Wordsworth's poetic persona in "A Letter," Luther Tyler notes the "pattern of vacillation between open and covert aggression" toward Wordsworth. One sign (among many) that this pattern extends to "Dejection" is the shift in addressee from "Sara" in "A Letter" to "Edmund" in the first published version to "Lady" for the 1817 publication in *Sibylline Leaves*. "Losing 'A Letter,'" 436.

32. For an important early source on the parallels and interplay between the Immortality ode and "Dejection," see F. Smith, "Relation of Coleridge's *Ode on Dejection*."

33. For a reading text of the Immortality ode accompanied by the most detailed editorial reconstruction of Wordsworth's probable composition and amendations of the various portions of the poem, see Wordsworth, *Poems*, 271–77.

34. Miall and Kuiken summarize empirical work on these three central aspects of processing, 130.

35. In the conclusion to *Embodiment and Cognitive Science*, Gibbs cautiously asserts that consideration of representations has a place in a dynamical systems perspective in cognitive science: "An embodied approach to the study of cognition does not, in my view, demand that researchers either embrace or abandon representationalism in theories of mind. . . . I remain open to the possibility that some aspects of cognition may require internal mental representations, at least some of which should be deeply shaped by embodied experience. But I also reject the automatic reflex to posit representations as the driving causal force for human performance, as is done far too often in cognitive science" (282).

36. The end of this story is that Coleridge has sought escape from feeling through "abstruse research," generally understood as a reference to the pursuit of philosophy and, more elliptically, his laudanum addiction.

37. Coleridge's pattern of indentation in "Dejection," in contrast to the pattern in "A Letter," further accentuates the irregularity of the verse form and the twisting structure of the poem.

38. In their empirical research, Miall and Kuiken identify three elements of literariness—stylistic variation (foregrounding), defamiliarization, and modification of feeling—all of which are amply manifest in this passage. Although the third of these, the modification or transformation of a conventional feeling or concept, is the most individualized from reader to reader, I think it likely that readers undergo such a process in the comprehension of this passage.

39. "Lucy Gray," ll. 57–60, in Wordsworth, *Lyrical Ballads and Other Poems*, 172.

40. See, e.g., Meyer, "Now You See Him"; and Facknitiz, "'The Calm,' 'A Small, Good Thing,' and 'Cathedral.'"

41. Quoted in Trussler, "Narrowed Voice," 30.

42. Lainsbury, "Critical Context for the Carver Chronotype"; Leypoldt, "Raymond Carver's 'Epiphanic Moments'"; Powell, "Stories of Raymond Carver."

43. Bloom, *Descartes' Baby*, 171.

44. Fontana, "Insomnia in Raymond Carver's Fiction."

45. Leypoldt suggests, rather inexplicably, that "the text's metaphorical under-currents revolve around the fact that there may be an erotic tension between Nancy and Sam" and that her epiphany corresponds to subliminal sexual desires (538). Such a reading of the story's symbolic content is not supported by any indication of sexual tension or charge at the surface level of the story.

Chapter 5 · Endangered Daughters

1. In this conception, the idea of originator and organizing center, whether as self or author, is eliminated, but the idea of the subject as a discursive entity is retained. Subjects appear under certain conditions in the order of discourse; that is a reasonable topic of investigation, as is the place the subject occupies and the rules it obeys. See Foucault, "What Is an Author?," 221.

2. See Althusser, "On the Reproduction of the Conditions of Production." Although I hardly subscribe to Althusser's Marxist determinism, it does seem to describe what happens under certain conditions:

> The reproduction of labour power requires not only a reproduction of its skills, but also, at the same time, a reproduction of its submission to the rules of the established order, i.e. a reproduction of submission to the ruling ideology for the workers, and a reproduction of the ability to manipulate the ruling ideology correctly for the agents of exploitation and repression, so that they, too, will provide for the domination of the ruling class "in words".
>
> In other words, the school (but also other State institutions like the Church, or other apparatuses like the Army) teaches "know-how", but in forms which ensure *subjection to the ruling ideology* or the mastery of its "practice".
>
> (132–33)

Under the aegis of poststructuralism, its forms have ensured the subjection of most humanist academics to a strong constructivist stance.

3. Crews, "Grand Academy of Theory," 225.

4. For a helpful overview of the major subfields of evolutionary social science, see Laland and Brown, *Sense and Nonsense.*

5. Carroll, "Wilson's *Consilience* and Literary Study," 78.

6. See N. Easterlin, "Hans Christian Andersen's Fish Out of Water."

7. Cooke, *Human Nature in Utopia,* quotation from 26.

8. Other important recent additions to evolutionary approaches include Saunders, *Reading Edith Wharton through a Darwinian Lens;* Machann, *Masculinity in Four Victorian Epics;* Mellman and Mueller-Wood, "Biological Constraints on the Human Imagination"; and Austin, *Useful Fictions.* While the Saunders and Machann monographs employ content-based approaches, Mellman and Mueller-Wood explicitly aim to broaden the scope of evolutionary criticism to include concerns such as the narrative and metaphorical nature of cognitive processing, and thus their goals are aligned with this book as a whole. Similarly, Austin's monograph broadens inquiry into the nature and function of narrative cognition by focusing on the role of anxiety in facili-

tating useful (in contrast to necessarily true) narratives. For a recent attack on both evolutionary psychology and its application to literary studies, see Kramnick, "Against Literary Darwinism."

9. Carroll confronts the Derridean proposition that there is nothing outside the text *(il n'y a pas de hors-texte)* in several places in *Evolution and Literary Theory;* see, e.g., 62–67.

10. Of Carroll's many essays, two invoke the concept of intentionality, the first to discuss aesthetics and the second to discuss meaning. The *Hamlet* essay seems to suggest a direct correlation between intention and what Carroll refers to as the text's "meaning structure," a theoretically problematic concept I discussed in chapter 1. See "Adaptationist Criteria of Literary Value"; and "Intentional Meaning in *Hamlet.*"

11. For overviews of the literature on incest avoidance, see Brown, *Human Universals,* 118–29; and Wilson, *Consilience,* 173–80.

12. Abbott, "Unnarratable Knowledge."

13. Thormählen surmises that Brontë drew on Spurzheim's contemporaneous analyses of mental illness and applied them in her characterization of Catherine and Heathcliff and perhaps Mr. Earnshaw, especially in relating selfishness to insanity in the schizoid personality. Claiming that Catherine is "pathologically egotistical," Thormählen asserts that Catherine is both responsible for the dire events of the novel *and* mentally unstable. See Thormählen, "Lunatic and the Devil's Disciple." Also convinced that Brontë aims to show human manipulation of sympathy and reason, Graeme Tytler has provided several provocative analyses. In "Nelly, I *am* Heathcliff!" Tytler claims that all assertions or presumptions of sympathy or identity in the novel are problematic, whether they issue from the main characters, Lockwood, or Nelly, because they actually constitute acts of domination. In a separate article, Tytler analyzes the persistent claims that both Nelly and Lockwood make to reasonableness. As Tytler notes, the term *reason* becomes a flag for patriarchal thinking and hidebound conventionality that manages to contain superstition and egotistical lack of awareness. Tytler also argues that Heathcliff suffers from a commonly recognized form of insanity toward the end of the novel but that Nelly's blindness to his condition is at least partially attributable to her excessive emphasis on reason. See Tytler, "Parameters of Reason in *Wuthering Heights.*"

14. Thormählen insists that Brontë intentionally refuses to provide her readers with guidance, and the novel's narrative structure, the difficulty of establishing a consistent stance toward the characters, and the problematic characteristics of the two narrators lend support to this view. Marshall Gregory describes how his own understanding of this novel has evolved as he has read it at different phases of his development and of his sophistication as a literary and ethical reader. Although Gregory's reading is from a cultural and ethical perspective, his conclusion is remarkably similar to Carroll's: ignoring the younger generation, he finds that the novel "lacks an ethical vision that includes 'a theory of human flourishing'" and asks whether "'bogus' life after death" is a legitimate replacement for the middle-class hypocritical culture that Brontë has demolished in the novel. Gregory, "Ethical Engagements over Time," 298. This reading, of course, requires us to legitimize the narrative viewpoints of both

Nelly and Lockwood, themselves profoundly vested in the values the novel questions. For the best current narratological accounts of the ethical and epistemic problems embedded in processing first-person narration, see Phelan, *Living to Tell about It*.

15. The most widely accepted explanation for altruistic behaviors toward nonkin is the theory of reciprocal altruism, whereby a selfless deed in the present anticipates reciprocation at some point in the future. Other evolutionists, most notably David Sloan Wilson, have reintroduced the theoretically controversial concept of group selection to propose another mechanism for altruism. For a concise overview of reciprocal altruism, see Wright, *Moral Animal*, ch. 9, "Friends."

16. All references to *Wuthering Heights* are to the Norton Critical Edition, 4th ed., ed. Richard J. Dunn.

17. Among the romantics, William Blake and Percy Shelley both thematized the cyclical and self-perpetuating nature of tyranny and violence. Brontë may well have been influenced by Shelley's use of this theme in *Prometheus Unbound* or *The Cenci*, or both. In "Catherine Earnshaw's Journey," Patsy Stoneman points to another Shelley source for aspects of the novel in "Epipsychidion," which Brontë likely read as a teenager. Following Edward Chitham, Stoneman suggests that Catherine wants both Heathcliff and Edgar and that Brontë draws on Shelley's ideas of free love to construct this impossible female desire. In my view, however, Catherine's instability ironizes the text's Shelleyan idealism without nullifying the critique of patriarchy's "exclusive customs" (not to mention its double standards) astutely noted by Stoneman.

18. See Levy, "Psychology of Loneliness in *Wuthering Heights*." In this insightful essay, Levy explains how the attitudes toward love developed in childhood persist in adulthood in Heathcliff, Catherine, and Lockwood. Resistant to pity, Heathcliff is cruel not only to others but to himself, fusing pity with cruelty to avoid dependence and helplessness and avenging his "humiliating sense of neglect" through his obsession with the ghost, by "[making] death signify *his* rejection of life as unworthy of attention" (163).

19. I cannot make sense of Frye's bizarre contention that "Heathcliff . . . plunges through death into vampirism." *Anatomy*, 40.

20. Richardson, "Rethinking Romantic Incest," 561. For an earlier essay suggesting that in romantic poetry erotic passion seems at first to offer an intensification of sympathetic sibling identification, see idem, "Dangers of Sympathy."

21. Arguing that Wordsworth's best poetry arose from inner turmoil, Reiman suggests that Dorothy was the model for the child characters Emma and Lucy in his poetry, pointing out that the poet's sister rather than his wife is associated with Eden and romantic feeling. Reiman further surmises that the death of these characters within the poems was a means of controlling incestuous feelings. See Reiman, "Poetry of Familiarity."

22. Dunbar, *Grooming, Gossip, and the Evolution of Language*, 203.

23. Barash and Barash, *Madame Bovary's Ovaries*, 39.

24. Kasdan, *Body Heat*.

25. See Boyd, "Jane, Meet Charles"; and Stasio and Duncan, "Evolutionary Approach to Jane Austen."

26. Darwin himself was not free of the view that nurture was the sphere of woman's special accomplishment. In his words, "Whether requiring deep thought, reason, or imagination, or merely the use of the sense and hands, [man will attain] a higher eminence . . . than can woman." Quoted in Hrdy, *Mother Nature*, 19. As Hrdy points out, "Like Spencer, Darwin convinced himself that because females were especially equipped to nurture, males excelled at everything else. No wonder women turned away from biology" (19).

27. Geary, *Male, Female*.

28. The account of mating strategies presented here reflects the theoretical paradigm established in Robert Trivers's 1972 paper "Parental Investment and Sexual Selection," which draws on an overlooked paper by A. J. Bateman. See Trivers, "Parental Investment and Reproductive Success." However, the Bateman-Trivers parental-investment hypothesis is not undisputed and is currently the subject of productive debate. Commenting on the absence of female alliances among humans, Barbara Smuts is skeptical of the Bateman-Trivers parental-investment hypothesis and suggests instead that pair bonding evolved in humans as protection against rape. See Smuts, "Male Aggression against Women." The anthropologist Monique Borgerhoff-Mulder also finds evolutionary psychology overly dependent on the Bateman-Trivers model, noting that factors such as reliance on kin and genetic benefits of multiple mates have been neglected. In a sample study among the Tanzanian Pimbwe, Borgerhoff-Mulder found that women rather than men benefitted from multiple marriages. "Serial Monogamy as Polygyny or Polyandry?" It is significant, though, that the ecological conditions of this population are very poor (because of postcolonial regulation of resources).

29. Scheidel, "A Peculiar Institution?"

30. The following passage from *Study of Thomas Hardy* is just one of many that speaks to the point:

> I can think of no being in the world so transcendently male as Shelley. He is phenomenal. The rest of us have bodies which contain the male and the female. If we were so singled out as Shelley, we should not belong to life, as he did not belong to life. But it were impious to wish to be like the angels. So long as mankind exists it must exist in the body, and so long must each body pertain both to the male and the female. . . .
>
> A man who is well balanced between male and female, in his own nature, is as a rule, happy, easy to mate, easy to satisfy, and content to exist. It is only a disproportion, or a dissatisfaction, which makes the man struggle into articulation. And the articulation is of two sorts, the cry of desire or the cry of realization, the cry of satisfaction, the effort to prolong the sense of satisfaction, to prolong the moment of consummation. (71)

31. Edwards, "D. H. Lawrence and the Problem of Submission."

32. Brayfield, "Lawrence's 'Male and Female Principles,' " 50.

33. Quoted in Ruderman, "Prototypes for Lawrence's *The Fox*," 94.

34. All references to *The Fox* in this chapter are to the 1994 edition of Lawrence,

The Fox * *The Captain's Doll* * *The Ladybird*, which also contains the ending of the original short story.

35. Osborn, "Complexities of Gender and Genre in Lawrence's *The Fox*."

36. Granofsky, D. H. *Lawrence and Survival*, 48–49.

37. Leavis, D. H. *Lawrence*, 267–68.

38. Ruderman, D. H. *Lawrence and the Devouring Mother*, 251–69.

39. Renner, "Sexuality and the Unconscious."

40. For a discussion of the distinction between aggression and violence, see Tiger, *Men in Groups*, 166–76. As Tiger explains, "I define 'aggression' as a process of more or less conscious coercion against the will of any individual or group of animals or men by any individual or group of people." By contrast, violence is a different phenomenon, descriptive of "an event that is only one possible outcome of an aggressive interaction" (158).

41. Granofsky, *Survival*, 16–18.

42. H. Simpson, D. H. *Lawrence and Feminism*, 73.

43. Balbert, "Freud, Frazer, and Lawrence's Palimpsestic Novella."

44. In *D. H. Lawrence and the Paradoxes of Psychic Life*, Barbara Ann Schapiro claims that seeing March in the dress "inflames Henry's need to dominate and control" (35), but I agree instead with critics like Granofsky, who suggest that the opposite is the case. Henry's confirmed consciousness of March's female vulnerability makes him unwilling to use *direct* physical contact during the proposal.

45. Campbell, *Mind of Her Own*, 82.

46. Viewed from the neurochemical perspective, and considering Helen Fisher's hypothesis in *Why We Love* that "romantic love is a primary motivation system in the brain" (74) is probably correct, the typical behavioral results of romantic love chemistry (obsessive thinking, focused attention) are overridden by antisociality and aggression in Henry's case. Fischer posits that dopamine and related neurotransmitters (especially norepinephrine and perhaps low seratonin) are central to the production of romantic love.

47. Good, "Toward a Resolution of Gender Identity Confusion."

48. Quoted on The Fox Website, www.thefoxwebsite.org/ecology/ecologyfacts. html. Other information on foxes is drawn from Questia Library online, www.questia .com/library/encyclopedia/fox_in_zoology.jsp; and Henry, *Red Fox*.

49. As to the significance of March's surname, Renner notes that *march* is a term for marsh- or borderland, and Osborn points out that a March hare is a hare in heat. Since Nellie March is at a threshold of sexual experience, both associations are apt.

50. Frazer, "The Corn-Spirit in Animal Form," in *The New Golden Bough*, 520–22.

51. Howe, "Beastly Desire"; Granofsky, "Second Caveat."

Abbott, H. Porter. "Unnarratable Knowledge: The Difficulty of Understanding Evolution by Natural Selection." In Herman, *Narrative Theory,* 143–62.

Abrams, M. H. "Structure and Style in the Greater Romantic Lyric." In *Romanticism and Consciousness: Essays in Criticism,* ed. Harold Bloom, 201–29. New York: Norton, 1970.

Aldama, Frederick Luis. *Toward a Cognitive Theory of Narrative Acts.* Austin: University of Texas Press, 2010.

———. *Why the Humanities Matter: A Commonsense Approach.* Austin: University of Texas Press, 2008.

Althusser, Louis. "Ideology and the Ideological State Apparatuses (Notes towards an Investigation)." In *Lenin and Philosophy and Other Essays,* trans. Ben Brewster, 127–86. New York: Monthly Review Press, 1971.

Armbruster, Karla. "Bringing Nature Writing Home." In Tallmadge and Harrington, *Reading under the Sign of Nature,* 3–18.

Arnheim, Rudolph. *Toward a Psychology of Art.* Berkeley and Los Angeles: University of California Press, 1966.

Arnold, Jean, et al. Forum on Literatures of the Environment. *PMLA* 114.5 (1999): 1089–1104.

Arnold, Matthew. *Culture and Anarchy, with Friendship's Garland and Some Literary Essays.* Vol. 5 of *Complete Prose Works of Matthew Arnold,* ed. R. H. Super. Ann Arbor: University of Michigan Press, 1965.

———. "Literature and Science." In *Philistinism in England and America,* vol. 10 of *Complete Prose Works of Matthew Arnold,* ed. R. H. Super, 53–73. Ann Arbor: University of Michigan Press, 1965.

Austin, Michael. *Useful Fictions: Evolution, Anxiety, and the Origins of Literature.* Lincoln: University of Nebraska Press, 2011.

Balbert, Peter. "Freud, Frazer, and Lawrence's Palimpsestic Novella: Dreams and the Heaviness of Male Identity in *The Fox.*" *Studies in the Novel* 38.2 (2006): 211–33.

Barash, David P., and Nanelle R. Barash. *Madame Bovary's Ovaries: A Darwinian Look at Literature.* New York: Delacorte, 2005.

Barbauld, Anna Letitia. *Anna Letitia Barbauld: Selected Poetry and Prose.* Ed. William McCarthy and Elizabeth Kraft. Peterborough, ON: Broadview Literary Texts, 2002.

Barkow, Jerome, Leda Cosmides, and John Tooby. *The Adapted Mind: Evolutionary Psychology and the Generation of Culture.* New York: Oxford University Press, 1992.

Bate, Jonathan. "Culture and Environment: From Austen to Hardy." *New Literary History* 30.3 (1999): 561–76.

———. *Romantic Ecology: Wordsworth and the Environmental Tradition.* London: Routledge, 1991.

Bate, Walter Jackson. *Coleridge.* New York: Macmillan, 1968.

Bedaux, Jean Baptist, and Brett Cooke. *Sociobiology and the Arts.* Amsterdam: Rodopi, 1999.

Bennett, Michael. "Different Shades of Green." *College Literature* 31.3 (2004): 207–12.

Berry, K. Wesley. "Regeneration in the Adirondacks: Anne LaBastille's Woodswoman Trilogy." In "Literary Ecocriticism," ed. Ian Marshall, special issue, *Interdisciplinary Literary Studies: A Journal of Criticism and Theory* 3.1 (2001): 66–88.

Bizup, Joseph M., and Eugene R. Kintgen. "The Cognitive Paradigm in Literary Studies." *College English* 55.8 (1993): 841–57.

Blake, William. *Blake's Poetry and Designs.* Ed. Mary Lynn Johnson and John E. Grant. Norton Critical Editions. 1st ed. New York: Norton, 1979.

Bloom, Paul. *Descartes' Baby: How the Science of Child Development Explains What Makes Us Human.* New York: Basic Books, 2004.

Borgerhoff-Mulder, Monique. "Serial Monogamy as Polygyny or Polyandry? Marriage in the Tanzanian Pimbwe." *Human Nature* 20 (2009): 130–50.

Bouslog, Charles S. "Structure and Theme in Coleridge's 'Dejection: An Ode.'" *Modern Language Quarterly* 24 (1963): 42–52.

Bowlby, John. *Attachment.* New York: Basic Books, 1969.

Boyd, Brian. "Getting It All Wrong." *American Scholar* 75.4 (2006): 18–30.

———. "Jane, Meet Charles: Literature, Evolution, and Human Nature." *Philosophy and Literature* 22.1 (1998): 1–30.

———. "Literature and Evolution: A Bio-Cultural Approach." *Philosophy and Literature* 29.1 (2005): 1–23.

———. *On the Origin of Stories: Evolution, Cognition, and Fiction.* Cambridge, MA: Harvard University Press, 2009.

Boym, Svetlana. *The Future of Nostalgia.* New York: Basic Books, 2001.

Brandt, Line, and Per Aage Brandt. "Cognitive Poetics and Imagery." *European Journal of English Studies* 9.2 (2005): 117–30.

Brayfield, Peggy. "Lawrence's 'Male and Female Principles' and the Symbolism of *The Fox.*" *Mosaic: A Journal for the Interdisciplinary Study of Literature* 4.3 (1971): 41–51.

Brewer, William D. "Egalitarianism in Mary Robinson's Metropolis." *Wordsworth Circle* 41.3 (2010): 146–50.

Broadbent, J. B. *John Milton: Odes, Pastorals, Masques.* Cambridge: Cambridge University Press, 1975.

Brontë, Emily. *Wuthering Heights*. Ed. Richard J. Dunn. Norton Critical Editions. 4th ed. New York: Norton, 2003.

Brown, Donald E. *Human Universals*. Philadelphia: Temple University Press, 1991.

Bruner, Jerome. *Acts of Meaning*. Cambridge, MA: Harvard University Press, 1990.

Bryson, J. Scott. "The Ambivalent Discourse: Words, Language, and the Human-Nature Connection." In "Literary Ecocriticism," ed. Ian Marshall, special issue, *Interdisciplinary Literary Studies: A Journal of Criticism and Theory* 3.1 (2001): 41–52.

Buell, Lawrence. *The Future of Environmental Criticism: Environmental Crisis and Literary Imagination*. Oxford: Blackwell, 2005.

———. *Writing for an Endangered World: Literature, Culture, and Environment in the U.S. and Beyond*. Cambridge, MA: Belknap Press of Harvard University Press, 2001.

Campbell, Anne. *A Mind of Her Own: The Evolutionary Psychology of Women*. Oxford: Oxford University Press, 2002.

Cantrell, Carol H. "'The Locus of Compossibility': Virginia Woolf, Modernism, and Place." In *The ISLE Reader: Ecocriticism, 1993–2003*, ed. Michael P. Branch and Scott Slovic, 33–48. Athens: University of Georgia Press, 2003.

Carrithers, Michael. "Narrativity: Mindreading and Making Societies." In Whiten, *Natural Theories of Mind*, 305–17.

Carroll, Joseph. "Adaptationist Criteria of Literary Value: Assessing Kurtén's *Dance of the Tiger*, Auel's *The Clan of the Cave Bear*, and Golding's *The Inheritors*." In Carroll, *Literary Darwinism*, 163–85.

———. "The Cuckoo's History: Human Nature in *Wuthering Heights*." *Philosophy and Literature* 32.2 (2008): 241–57.

———. "The Deep Structure of Literary Representations." *Evolution and Human Behavior* 20.3 (1999): 159–73. Reprinted in Carroll, *Literary Darwinism*, 103–16.

———. "The Ecology of Victorian Fiction." In "Symposium: Evolution and Literature," ed. Nancy Easterlin, special issue, *Philosophy and Literature* 25.2 (2001): 295–313.

———. *Evolution and Literary Theory*. Columbia: University of Missouri Press, 1995.

———. "An Evolutionary Paradigm for Literary Study." *Style* 42.2–3 (2008): 103–35.

———. "Human Nature and Literary Meaning: A Theoretical Model Illustrated with a Critique of *Pride and Prejudice*." In Carroll, *Literary Darwinism*, 187–216.

———. "Intentional Meaning in *Hamlet*: An Evolutionary Perspective." *Style* 44.1–2 (2010): 230–60.

———. *Literary Darwinism: Evolution, Human Nature, and Literature*. New York: Routledge, 2004.

———. "Rejoinder to the Responses." *Style* 42.2–3 (2008): 308–411.

———. "'Theory,' Anti-Theory, and Empirical Criticism." In Carroll, *Literary Darwinism*, 29–40.

———. "Wilson's *Consilience* and Literary Study." *Philosophy and Literature* 23 (1999): 361–81. Reprinted in Carroll, *Literary Darwinism*, 69–84.

Carroll, Joseph, Jonathan Gottschall, John A. Johnson, and Daniel Kruger. "Hierarchy in the Library: Egalitarian Dynamics in Victorian Novels." *Evolutionary Psychology* 6.4 (2008): 715–38. Accessed June 28, 2011. www.epjournal.net/filestore/ep06715738.pdf.

Carver, Raymond. *What We Talk about When We Talk about Love*. 1974. Reprint, New York: Random House / Vintage Books, 1989.

Cohen, Patricia. "Next Big Thing in English: Knowing They Know That They Know." *New York Times*, March 31, 2010.

Coleridge, Samuel Taylor. *Samuel Taylor Coleridge: Selected Poems*. Ed. Richard Holmes. London: Penguin Books, 1996.

Cook, Amy. "Staging Nothing: *Hamlet* and Cognitive Science." *SubStance* 35.2 (2006): 83–99.

Cooke, Brett. *Human Nature in Utopia: Zamyatin's "We."* Evanston, IL: Northwestern University Press, 2002.

Coulson, Seana, and Teenie Matlock. "Metaphor and the Space Structuring Model." *Metaphor and Symbol* 16.3–4 (2001): 295–316.

Coulson, Seana, and Todd Oakley. "Blending and Coded Meaning: Literal and Figurative Meaning in Cognitive Semantics." *Journal of Pragmatics* 37 (2005): 1510–36.

Crain, Caleb. "The Artistic Animal: Is Creativity in Our Genes?" *LinguaFranca* 11.7 (2001): 28–37.

Crews, Frederick. "Apriorism for Empiricists." *Style* 42.2–3 (2008): 155–60.

———. "The Grand Academy of Theory." In Patai and Corral, *Theory's Empire*, 218–33.

Curran, Stuart. "Mary Robinson's *Lyrical Tales* in Context." In Wilson and Haefner, *Re-Visioning Romanticism*, 17–35.

Curtis, Jan. "The Secret of *Wide Sargasso Sea*." *Critique* 31.3 (1990): 185–97.

Damasio, Antonio. *The Feeling of What Happens: Body and Emotion in the Making of Consciousness*. New York: Harcourt, 1999.

Danby, John F. *The Simple Wordsworth: Studies in the Poems, 1797–1807*. London: Routledge and Kegan Paul, 1960.

Darwin, Charles. *The Origin of Species by Means of Natural Selection, or the Preservation of Favored Races in the Struggle for Life*. 1860. Reprint, ed. and intro. J. W. Burrow, Middlesex, UK: Penguin Books, 1968.

Dissanayake, Ellen. *Art and Intimacy: How the Arts Began*. Seattle: University of Washington Press, 2000.

———. *Homo Aestheticus: Where Art Comes From and Why*. New York: Free Press, 1992.

———. *What Is Art For?* Seattle: University of Washington Press, 1988.

Donald, Merlin. *The Origins of the Modern Mind: Three Stages in the Evolution of Culture and Cognition*. Cambridge, MA: Harvard University Press, 1991.

Dunbar, Robin. *Grooming, Gossip, and the Evolution of Language*. Cambridge, MA: Harvard University Press, 1996.

Dutton, Denis. *The Art Instinct: Beauty, Pleasure, and Human Evolution*. New York: Bloomsbury, 2009.

Easterlin, Nancy. "Cognitive Ecocriticism: Human Wayfinding, Sociality, and Literary Interpretation." In Zunshine, *Introduction to Cognitive Cultural Studies*, 257–74.

———. "Do Cognitive Predispositions Predict or Determine Literary Value Judgments? Narrativity, Plot, and Aesthetics." In *Biopoetics: Evolutionary Explorations in the Arts*, ed. Brett Cooke and Frederick Turner, 241–61. Lexington, KY: Paragon House, 1999.

———. "Hans Christian Andersen's Fish Out of Water." In "Symposium: Evolution and Literature," ed. Nancy Easterlin, special issue, *Philosophy and Literature* 25.2 (2001): 251–77.

———. "How to Write the Great Darwinian Novel: Cognitive Predispositions, Cultural Complexity, and Aesthetic Evaluation." In special issue, ed. Robin Dunbar, *Journal of Cultural and Evolutionary Psychology*, 3.1 (2005): 23–38.

———. "'Loving Ourselves Best of All': Ecocriticism and the Adapted Mind." *Mosaic: A Journal for the Interdisciplinary Study of Literature* 37.3 (2004): 1–18.

———. "Making Knowledge: Bioepistemology and the Foundations of Literary Theory." *Mosaic: A Journal for the Interdisciplinary Study of Literature* 32.1 (1999): 131–47. Reprinted in Patai and Corral, *Theory's Empire*, 621–35.

———. "Play, Mutation, and Reality Acceptance: Toward a Theory of Literary Experience." In N. Easterlin and Riebling, *After Poststructuralism*, 105–25.

———. "Psychoanalysis and 'The Discipline of Love.'" *Philosophy and Literature* 24.2 (2000): 261–79.

———. "Voyages in the Verbal Universe: The Role of Speculation in Darwinian Literary Criticism." In "Literary Biopoetics," ed. Brett Cooke, *Interdisciplinary Literary Studies: A Journal of Criticism and Theory* 2.2 (2001): 59–73.

———. "'Who Was It If It Wasn't Me?' The Problem of Orientation in Alice Munro's 'Trespasses': A Cognitive Ecological Analysis." In Mellman and Mueller-Wood, "Biological Constraints," 79–102.

———. *Wordsworth and the Question of "Romantic Religion."* Lewisburg, PA: Bucknell University Press, 1996.

Easterlin, Nancy, and Barbara Riebling, eds. *After Poststructuralism: Interdisciplinarity and Literary Theory.* Evanston, IL: Northwestern University Press, 1993.

Easterlin, Richard A. *Growth Triumphant: The Twenty-first Century in Historical Perspective.* Ann Arbor: University of Michigan Press, 1996.

———. *The Reluctant Economist: Perspectives on Economics, Economic History, and Demography.* Cambridge: Cambridge University Press, 2004.

Edwards, Duane. "D. H. Lawrence and the Problem of Submission." *Southern Humanities Review* 25.3 (1991): 205–15.

Eibl, Karl. "On the Redskins of Scientism and the Aesthetes in the Circled Wagons." *Journal of Literary Theory* 1.2 (2007): 421–41.

Emory, Mary Louise. "The Politics of Form: Jean Rhys's Social Vision in *Voyage in the Dark* and *Wide Sargasso Sea*." *Twentieth Century Literature* 28.4 (1982): 418–30.

Evernden, Neil. *The Natural Alien: Humankind and Environment.* Toronto: University of Toronto Press, 1985.

Facknitz, Mark A. R. "'The Calm,' 'A Small, Good Thing,' and 'Cathedral': Raymond

Carver and the Rediscovery of Human Worth." *Studies in Short Fiction* 23.3 (1986): 287–96.

Fairbanks, A. Harris. "The Form of Coleridge's 'Dejection Ode.'" *PMLA* 90.5 (1975): 874–84.

Fauconnier, Gilles. *Mappings in Thought and Language.* Cambridge: Cambridge University Press, 1997.

Fauconnier, Gilles, and Mark Turner. *The Way We Think: Conceptual Blending and the Mind's Hidden Complexities.* New York: Basic Books, 2002.

Festinger, Leon. *A Theory of Cognitive Dissonance.* Evanston, IL: Row, Peterson, 1957.

Fisher, Helen. *Why We Love: The Nature and Chemistry of Romantic Love.* New York: Henry Holt, 2004.

Flesch, William. *Comeuppance: Costly Signaling, Altruistic Punishment, and Other Biological Components of Fiction.* Cambridge, MA: Harvard University Press, 2007.

Fontana, Ernest. "Insomnia in Raymond Carver's Fiction." *Studies in Short Fiction* 26.4 (1989): 447–51.

Foucault, Michel. *Discipline and Punish: The Birth of the Prison.* Trans. Alan Sheridan. New York: Pantheon Books, 1977.

———. "What Is an Author?" In *Essential Works of Michel Foucault,* vol. 2, *Aesthetics, Method, and Epistemology,* ed. James D. Faubion, trans. Robert Hurley and others, 205–22. 1994. New York: New Press, 1998.

Frazer, Sir James. *The New Golden Bough.* Abr. and ed. Theodor H. Gastor. New York: Signet Classics, 1959.

Freeman, Margaret. "The Body in the Word: A Cognitive Approach to the Shape of a Poetic Text." In *Cognitive Stylistics: Language and Cognition in Text Analysis,* ed. Jonathan Culpepper and Elena Semino, 23–47. Amsterdam: Benjamins, 2002.

———. "The Poem as Complex Blend: Conceptual Mappings of Metaphor in Sylvia Plath's 'The Applicant.'" *Language and Literature* 14.1 (2005): 25–44.

Fromm, Harold. "From Transcendence to Obsolescence: A Route Map." In Glotfelty and Fromm, *Ecocriticism Reader,* 30–39.

Frye, Northrop. *Anatomy of Criticism: Four Essays.* 1957. Reprint, Princeton, NJ: Princeton University Press, 1971.

———. "The Function of Criticism at the Present Time." *University of Toronto Quarterly* 19 (1949): 1–16.

Garrard, Greg. *Ecocriticism.* London: Routledge, 2004.

Geary, David C. *Male, Female: The Evolution of Human Sex Differences.* Washington, DC: American Psychological Association, 1998.

Genette, Girard. "Frontiers of Narrative." In *Figures of Literary Discourse,* trans. Alan Sheridan, 127–44. New York: Columbia University Press, 1982.

Gerrig, Richard J. *Experiencing Narrative Worlds: On the Psychological Activities of Reading.* New Haven, CT: Yale University Press, 1993.

Gibbs, Raymond. *Embodiment and Cognitive Science.* Cambridge: Cambridge University Press, 2005.

Gibson, James J. *The Senses Considered as Perceptual Systems.* Boston: Houghton Mifflin, 1966.

Gifford, Terry. *Pastoral.* London: Routledge, 1999.

Gilbert, Elizabeth. *The Last American Man.* London: Penguin Books, 2002.

Gillespie, Nick. "When Darwin Meets Dickens." *TCS Daily,* December 29, 2005.

Glotfelty, Cheryll, and Harold Fromm, eds. *The Ecocriticism Reader: Landmarks in Literary Ecology.* Athens: University of Georgia Press, 1996.

Good, Jan. "Toward a Resolution of Gender Identity Confusion: The Relationship of Henry and March in *The Fox.*" *D. H. Lawrence Review* 18.2–3 (1986): 217–27.

Goodheart, Eugene. *Darwinian Misadventures in the Humanities.* New Brunswick, NJ: Transaction, 2007.

Gottschall, Jonathan. *Literature, Science, and the New Humanities.* New York: Palgrave Macmillan, 2008.

———. "Measure for Measure." *Boston Globe,* May 11, 2008.

———. "Quantitative Literary Study: A Modest Manifesto and Testing the Hypotheses of Feminist Fairy Tale Studies." In *The Literary Animal: Evolution and the Nature of Narrative,* 199–224. Evanston, IL: Northwestern University Press, 2005.

———. *The Rape of Troy: Evolution, Violence, and the World of Homer.* Cambridge: Cambridge University Press, 2008.

———. "What Are Literary Scholars For? What is Art For?" *Style* 42.2–3 (2008): 186–91.

Graff, Gerald. *Professing Literature: An Institutional History.* Chicago: University of Chicago Press, 1987.

Granofsky, Ronald. *D. H. Lawrence and Survival: Darwinism in the Fiction of the Transitional Period.* Montreal: McGill-Queen's University Press, 2003.

———. "A Second Caveat: D. H. Lawrence's *The Fox.*" *English Studies in Canada* 16.1 (1988): 49–63.

Gregory, Marshall. "Ethical Engagements over Time: Reading and Rereading *David Copperfield* and *Wuthering Heights.*" *Narrative* 12.3 (2004): 281–97.

Griffin, Andrew L. "Wordsworth and the Problem of Imaginative Story: The Case of 'Simon Lee.'" *PMLA* 92.3 (1977): 392–409.

Gross, Paul R. "The Icarian Impulse." *Wilson Quarterly: Surveying the World of Ideas* 22.1 (1998): 39–49.

Gross, Paul R., and Norman Levitt. *Higher Superstition: The Academic Left and Its Quarrels with Science.* Baltimore: Johns Hopkins University Press, 1994.

Harris, Paul L. "The Work of Imagination." In Whiten, *Natural Theories of Mind,* 283–304.

Hart, F. Elizabeth. "Cognitive Linguistics: The Experiential Dynamics of Metaphor." *Mosaic: A Journal for the Interdisciplinary Study of Literature* 28.1 (March 1995): 1–23.

Hart, Kathleen Robin, and John H. Long. "Animal Metaphors and Metaphorizing Animals: An Integrated Literary, Cognitive, and Evolutionary Analysis of Making and Partaking of Stories." *Evolution: Education and Outreach* 4.1 (2011): 52–63. Accessed February 3, 2011. doi: 10.1007/s12052-010-0301-6.

Henry, J. David. *Red Fox: The Catlike Canine.* 1986. Reprint, Washington, DC: Smithsonian Institute Press, 1996.

Herman, David. "1880–1945: Re-minding Modernism." In *The Emergence of Mind: Representations of Consciousness in Narrative Discourse in English*, ed. David Herman, 243–72. Lincoln: University of Nebraska Press, 2011.

———, ed. *Narrative Theory and the Cognitive Sciences*. Stanford, CA: CSLI, 2003.

———. "Stories as a Tool for Thinking." In Herman, *Narrative Theory*, 163–92.

Hitt, Christopher. "Ecocriticism and the Long Eighteenth Century." *College Literature* 31.3 (2004): 123–47.

Hogan, Patrick Colm. "Literary Universals." In Zunshine, *Introduction to Cognitive Cultural Studies*, 37–60.

———. *The Mind and Its Stories: Narrative Universals and Human Emotion*. Cambridge: Cambridge University Press, 2003.

———. "On Being Moved: Cognition and Emotion in Literature and Film." In Zunshine, *Introduction to Cognitive Cultural Studies*, 237–56.

Holland, Norman N. *The Brain of Robert Frost: A Cognitive Approach to Literature*. New York: Routledge, 1988.

Howarth, William. "Some Principles of Ecocriticism." In Glotfelty and Fromm, *Ecocriticism Reader*, 69–91.

Howe, Andrew. "Beastly Desire: Human/Animal Interactions in Lawrence's *Women in Love*." *Papers on Language and Literature* 38.4 (2002): 429–42.

Howells, Coral Ann. *Jean Rhys*. New York: St. Martin's, 1991.

Hrdy, Sarah Blaffer. *Mother Nature: A History of Mothers, Infants, and Natural Selection*. New York: Pantheon Books, 1999.

Huizinga, Johan. *Homo Ludens: The Play Element in Culture*. Boston: Beacon, 1950.

Hume, David. *An Enquiry concerning Human Understanding*. Ed. Tom L. Beauchamp. Oxford: Clarendon, 2000.

———. "Of Tragedy." In *Essays Moral, Political, and Literary*, 1:258–65. London: Longmans, Green, 1907.

Jackson, Tony E. "Issues and Problems in the Blending of Cognitive Science, Evolutionary Psychology, and Literary Study." *Poetics Today* 23.1 (2002): 161–79.

———. "'Literary Interpretation' and Cognitive Literary Studies." *Poetics Today* 24.2 (2003): 191–205.

———. "Questioning Interdisciplinarity: Cognitive Science, Evolutionary Psychology, and Literary Criticism." *Poetics Today* 21.2 (2000): 319–47.

Jacobus, Mary. *Tradition and Experiment in Wordsworth's "Lyrical Ballads."* Oxford: Clarendon, 1976.

James, William. *Pragmatism*. 1910. Cambridge, MA: Harvard University Press, 1975.

———. *Principles of Psychology*. New York: Henry Holt, 1899.

———. *The Varieties of Religious Experience*. 1902. Reprint, New York: New American Library, 1958.

Johnson, Mark. *The Body in the Mind: The Bodily Basis of Meaning, Imagination, and Reason*. Chicago: University of Chicago Press, 1987.

———. *The Meaning of the Body: Aesthetics of Human Understanding*. Chicago: University of Chicago Press, 2007.

Jordan, John E. *Why the "Lyrical Ballads"? The Background, Character, and Writing of*

Wordsworth's 1798 "Lyrical Ballads." Berkeley and Los Angeles: University of California Press, 1976.

Kaplan, Stephen. "Environmental Preference in a Knowledge-Seeking, Knowledge-Using Organism." In Barkow, Cosmides, and Tooby, *Adapted Mind,* 581–98.

Kaplan, Stephen, and Rachel Kaplan. *Cognition and Environment: Functioning in an Uncertain World.* New York: Praeger, 1982.

Kasdan, Lawrence. *Body Heat.* Los Angeles: Ladd Company, 1981.

Keir, Jerry, and Corey Lewis. "The Continuing Evolution of Literary Ecology." In "Literary Ecocriticism," ed. Ian Marshall, special issue, *Interdisciplinary Literary Studies: A Journal of Criticism and Theory* 3.1 (2001): 89–105.

Kelleter, Frank. "A Tale of Two Natures: Worried Reflections on the Study of Literature and Culture in an Age of Neuroscience and Neo-Darwinism." *Journal of Literary Theory* 1.1 (2007): 153–89.

Knapp, John V., ed. "An Evolutionary Paradigm for Literary Study." Special issue, *Style* 42.2–3 (2008).

Kramnick, Jonathan. "Against Literary Darwinism." *Critical Inquiry* 37.2 (2011): 315–47.

Kroeber, Karl. *Ecological Literary Criticism: Romantic Imagining and the Biology of Mind.* New York: Columbia University Press, 1994.

Lainsbury, G. P. "A Critical Context for the Carver Chronotype." *Canadian Review of American Studies* 27.1 (1997): 77–91.

Lakoff, George. *Women, Fire, and Dangerous Things: What Categories Reveal about the Mind.* Chicago: University of Chicago Press, 1987.

Lakoff, George, and Mark Johnson. *Metaphors We Live By.* Chicago: University of Chicago Press, 1980.

Lakoff, George, and Mark Turner. *More Than Cool Reason: A Field Guide to Poetic Metaphor.* Chicago: University of Chicago Press, 1989.

Laland, Kevin N., and Gillian R. Brown. *Sense and Nonsense: Evolutionary Perspectives on Human Behavior.* Oxford: Oxford University Press, 2002.

Lawder, Bruce. "Secret(ing) Conversations: Coleridge and Wordsworth." *New Literary History* 32.1 (2001): 67–89.

Lawrence, D. H. *The Fox * The Captain's Doll * The Ladybird.* 1923. Reprint, ed. Dieter Mehl, notes and intro. David Ellis, London: Penguin Books, 1994.

———. *"Psychoanalysis and the Unconscious" and "Fantasia of the Unconscious."* Ed. Bruce Steele. Cambridge: Cambridge University Press, 2004.

———. *Studies in Classic American Literature.* 1923. Reprint, Middlesex, UK: Penguin Books, 1977.

———. *Study of Thomas Hardy and Other Essays.* Ed. Bruce Steele. Cambridge: Cambridge University Press, 1985.

Leavis, F. R. *D. H. Lawrence: Novelist.* Harmondsworth, UK: Penguin Books, 1955.

Lehrer, Jonah. *Proust Was a Neuroscientist.* Boston: Houghton Mifflin, 2007.

Levin, Jonathan. "Beyond Nature? Recent Work in Ecocriticism." *Contemporary Literature* 43.1 (2002): 171–86.

Levin, Richard. "The New Interdisciplinarity in Literary Criticism." In N. Easterlin and Riebling, *After Poststructuralism,* 13–43.

Levy, Eric P. "The Psychology of Loneliness in *Wuthering Heights.*" *Studies in the Novel* 28.2 (2002): 158–77.

Leypoldt, Gunter. "Raymond Carver's 'Epiphanic Moments.'" *Style* 35.3 (2001): 531–47.

Libby, Brooke. "Nature Writing as *Refuge:* Autobiography in the Natural World." In Tallmadge and Harrington, *Reading under the Sign of Nature,* 251–64.

Lloyd, Dan Edward. *Simple Minds.* Cambridge: Massachusetts Institute of Technology Press, 1989.

Love, Glen A. *Practical Ecocriticism: Literature, Biology, and the Environment.* Charlottesville: University of Virginia Press, 2003.

Machann, Clinton. *Masculinity in Four Victorian Epics: A Darwinist Reading.* Burlington, VT: Ashgate, 2010.

Mandler, Jean Matter. *Stories, Scripts, and Scenes: Aspects of Schema Theory.* Hillsdale, NJ: Erlbaum, 1984.

Manes, Christopher. "Nature and Silence." In Glotfelty and Fromm, *Ecocriticism Reader,* 15–29.

Marcus, Steven. "Humanities from Classics to Cultural Studies: Notes toward the History of an Idea." *Daedalus* 135.2 (2006): 15–21.

Mardorossian, Carine Melkom. "Double [De]Colonization and the Feminist Criticism of *Wide Sargasso Sea.*" *College Literature* 26.2 (1999): 79–95.

———. "Shutting Up the Subaltern: Silences, Stereotypes, and Double-Entendres in Jean Rhys's *Wide Sargasso Sea.*" *Callaloo* 22.4 (1999): 1071–90.

Marshall, Ian. "New Connections in Ecocritisms." *Interdisciplinary Literary Studies* 7.1 (2005): 1–4.

Max, D. T. "The Literary Darwinists." *New York Times,* November 6, 2005.

Mazel, David. "American Literary Environmentalism as Domestic Orientalism." In Glotfelty and Fromm, *Ecocriticism Reader,* 137–46.

McEathron, Scott. "Wordsworth, *Lyrical Ballads,* and the Problem of Peasant Poetry." *Nineteenth-Century Literature* 54.1 (1999): 1–26.

McKillop, Alan D. "Local Attachment and Cosmopolitanism—The Eighteenth-Century Pattern." In *From Sensibility to Romanticism: Essays Presented to Frederick A. Pottle,* ed. Frederick W. Hillies and Harold Bloom, 191–218. New York: Oxford University Press, 1965.

McKusick, James. *Green Writing: Romanticism and Ecology.* New York: St. Martin's, 2000.

Meeker, Joseph. *The Comedy of Survival: Literary Ecology and the Play Ethic.* 3rd ed. Tucson: University of Arizona Press, 1997.

Mellman, Katja, and Anja Mueller-Wood, eds. "Biological Constraints on the Literary Imagination." Special issue, *Studies in the Literary Imagination* 42.2 (2009).

Menand, Louis. "Dangers Within and Without." *Profession 2005,* 2005, 10–17.

———. *The Metaphysical Club.* New York: Farrar, Straus and Giroux, 2001.

Meyer, Adam. "Now You See Him, Now You Don't, Now You Do Again: The Evolution of Raymond Carver's Minimalism." *Studies in Short Fiction* 30.4 (1989): 239–51.

Mezei, Kathy. "'And it Kept its Secret': Narration, Memory, and Madness in Jean Rhys' *Wide Sargasso Sea.*" *Critique* 28.4 (1987): 195–209.

Miall, David. "An Evolutionary Framework for Literary Reading." In *Psychology and Sociology of Literature: In Honour of Elrud Ibsch,* ed. Gerard Steen and Dick Schram, 407–19. Amsterdam: John Benjamins, 2001.

———. "Shelley at Chamonix: Reading the Sublime." Paper delivered at the annual meeting of the North American Society for the Study of Romanticism, Montreal, August 13–16, 2005.

Miall, David, and Don Kuiken. "What Is Literariness? Three Components of Literary Reading." In "Empirical Studies of Literature: Selected Papers from IGEL '98," ed. David Miall, special issue, *Discourse Processes* 28.2 (1999): 121–38.

Miskolcze, Robin L. "Snapshots of Contradiction in Mary Robinson's Poetical Works." *Papers on Language and Literature: A Journal for Scholars and Critics of Language and Literature* 31.2 (1995): 206–91.

Mithen, Steven. *After the Ice: A Global Human History, 20,000–5,000 B.C.* Cambridge, MA: Harvard University Press, 2003.

———. *The Prehistory of the Mind: The Cognitive Origins of Art and Science.* London: Thames and Hudson, 1996.

———. *The Singing Neanderthals: The Origins of Music, Language, Mind, and Body.* Cambridge, MA: Harvard University Press, 2006.

Mooney, Chris. "A Science of Literature? Great Idea, as Long as We Get Actual Scientists Involved." May 21, 2008. www.scienceprogress.org/2008/05/a-science-of-literature.

Nordlund, Marcus. "Consilient Literary Interpretation." *Philosophy and Literature* 26.2 (2002): 312–33.

———. *Shakespeare and the Nature of Love: Literature, Culture, Evolution.* Evanston, IL: Northwestern University Press, 2007.

O'Connor, Flannery. "Everything That Rises Must Converge." In *Collected Works,* ed. Sally Fitzgerald, 484–500. New York: Library of America, 1988.

Ogden, J. T. "From Spatial to Aesthetic Distance in the Eighteenth Century." *Journal of the History of Ideas* 35 (1974): 63–78.

Onorato, Richard J. *The Character of the Poet: Wordsworth in "The Prelude."* Princeton, NJ: Princeton University Press, 1971.

Orians, Gordon H., and Judith H. Heerwagen. "Evolved Responses to Landscapes." In Barkow, Cosmides, and Tooby, *Adapted Mind,* 555–79.

Orwell, George. "Politics and the English Language." In *Essays,* 954–67. 1968. Reprint, ed. and intro. John Carey, New York: Knopf, 2002.

Osborn, Marijane. "Complexities of Gender and Genre in Lawrence's *The Fox.*" *Essays in Literature* 19.1 (1992): 84–97.

Palmer, Alan. *Fictional Minds.* Lincoln: University of Nebraska Press, 2004.

Palmer, Alan, and Marie-Laure Ryan. "Cognitive Maps and the Construction of Narrative Space." In Herman, *Narrative Theory,* 214–42.

Pascoe, Judith. "Mary Robinson and the Literary Marketplace." In *Romantic Women Writers: Voices and Countervoices,* ed. Paula R. Feldman and Theresa M. Kelley, 252–68, 312–15. Hanover, NH: University Press of New England, 1995.

Patai, Daphne, and Will Corral, eds. *Theory's Empire: An Anthology of Dissent.* New York: Columbia University Press, 2005.

Pavel, Thomas. *Fictional Worlds.* Cambridge, MA: Harvard University Press, 1986.

Peckham, Morse. *Man's Rage for Chaos: Biology, Behavior, and the Arts.* Philadelphia: Chilton, 1965.

——. "Metaphor: A Little Speaking on a Weary Subject." In *The Triumph of Romanticism*, 401–20. Columbia: University of South Carolina Press, 1970.

Peterson, Britt. "Darwin to the Rescue." *Chronicle of Higher Education*, August 1, 2008.

Peterson, Linda H. "Becoming an Author: Mary Robinson's *Memoirs* and the Origins of the Woman Artist's Autobiography." In Wilson and Haefner, *Re-Visioning Romanticism*, 36–50.

Phelan, James. *Living to Tell about It: A Rhetoric and Ethics of Character Narration.* Ithaca, NY: Cornell University Press, 2005.

Phillips, Dana. *The Truth of Ecology: Nature, Culture, and Literature in America.* Oxford: Oxford University Press, 2003.

Pinker, Steven. *The Blank Slate.* New York: Viking, 2002.

——. *The Language Instinct: How the Mind Creates Language.* New York: Harper-Perrenial, 1995.

Pite, Ralph. "How Green Were the Romantics?" *Studies in Romanticism* 35.3 (1996): 357–73.

Powell, Jon. "The Stories of Raymond Carver: The Menace of Perpetual Uncertainty." *Studies in Short Fiction* 31.4 (1994): 647–56.

Reiman, Donald H. "Poetry of Familiarity: Wordsworth, Dorothy, and Mary Hutchinson." In *The Evidence of the Imagination: Studies of Interactions between Life and Art in English Literature*, ed. Donald H. Reiman, Michael C. Jage, and Betty Bennett, 142–77. New York: New York University Press, 1978.

Renner, Stanley. "Sexuality and the Unconscious: Psychosexual Drama and Conflict in *The Fox*." *D. H. Lawrence Review* 21.3 (1990): 245–73.

Rhys, Jean. *After Leaving Mr. Mackenzie.* 1931. Reprint, New York: Norton, 1997.

——. *The Collected Stories of Jean Rhys.* 1938. Reprint, New York: Norton, 1986.

——. *Good Morning, Midnight.* 1938. Reprint, New York: Norton, 1986.

——. *Quartet.* 1929. Reprint, New York: Norton, 1997.

——. *Voyage in the Dark.* New York: Norton, 1982.

——. *Wide Sargasso Sea.* Ed. Judith L. Raiskin. Norton Critical Editions. 1st. ed. New York: Norton, 1999.

Richardson, Alan. "Apostrophe in Life and in Romantic Art: Everyday Discourse, Overhearing, and Poetic Address." *Style* 36.3 (2002): 363–85.

——. "The Dangers of Sympathy: Sibling Incest in English Romantic Poetry." *Studies in English Literature* 25.4 (1985): 737–54.

——. "Rethinking Romantic Incest: Human Universals, Literary Representation, and the Biology of Mind." *New Literary History* 31.3 (2000): 553–72.

——. *Romanticism and the Science of Mind.* Cambridge: Cambridge University Press, 2001.

——. "Studies in Literature and Cognition: A Field Map." In *The Work of Fiction: Evolution, Cognition, and Complexity*, ed. Alan Richardson and Ellen Spolsky, 1–29. Aldershot, UK: Ashgate, 2004.

Richardson, Alan, and Francis F. Steen. "Reframing the Adjustment: A Response to Adler and Gross." *Poetics Today* 24.2 (2003): 151–59.

Richerson, Peter J., and Robert Boyd. *Not By Genes Alone: How Culture Transformed Human Evolution*. Chicago: University of Chicago Press, 2005.

Ritchie, L. David. "Lost in 'Conceptual Space': Metaphors of Conceptual Integration." *Metaphor and Symbol* 19.1 (2004): 31–50.

Robinson, Daniel. "Mary Robinson and the Trouble with Tabitha Bramble." *Wordsworth Circle* 41.3 (2010): 142–46.

Robinson, Mary. *Mary Robinson: Selected Poems*. Ed. Judith Pascoe. Peterborough, ON: Broadview Literary Texts, 2000.

Rorty, Richard. "Against Unity." *Wilson Quarterly: Surveying the World of Ideas* 22.1 (1998): 28–38.

Ross, Helen. *Behavior and Perception in Strange Environments*. New York: Basic Books, 1974.

Ross, Michael L. "Ladies and Foxes: D. H. Lawrence, David Garnett, and the Female of the Species." *D. H. Lawrence Review* 18.2–3 (1986): 229–38.

Ruderman, Judith. *D. H. Lawrence and the Devouring Mother: The Search for a Patriarchal Ideal of Leadership*. Durham, NC: Duke University Press, 1984.

——. "Prototypes for Lawrence's *The Fox*." *Journal of Modern Literature* 8.1 (1980): 77–98.

Ryan, Marie-Laure. "Cognitive Maps and the Construction of Narrative Space." In Herman, *Narrative Theory*, 214–42.

Saunders, Judith. *Reading Edith Wharton through a Darwinian Lens: Evolutionary Biological Issues in Her Fiction*. Jefferson, NC: McFarland, 2009.

Schank, Roger C. *Tell Me a Story: A New Look at Real and Artificial Memory*. New York: Charles Scribner's Sons, 1990.

Schapiro, Barbara Ann. *D. H. Lawrence and the Paradoxes of Psychic Life*. Albany: State University of New York Press, 1979.

Scheidel, Walter. "A Peculiar Institution? Greco-Roman Monogamy in Global Context." *History of the Family* 20 (2009): 1–12.

Scholes, Robert. Forum. *PMLA* 121.1 (2006): 297–98.

——. "Presidential Address 2004: The Humanities in a Posthumanist World." *PMLA* 120.3 (2004): 724–33.

——. *The Rise and Fall of English: Reconstructing English as a Discipline*. New Haven, CT: Yale University Press, 1998.

Seamon, Roger. "Literary Darwinism as Science and Myth." *Style* 42.2–3 (2008): 261–65.

Shanon, Benny. "From Fixedness and Selection to Differentiation and Creation." *Poetics Today* 13.4 (1992): 659–85.

Shea, Christopher. "Survivalist lit: Does Darwin have anything to say about Beowulf and Madam Bovary?" *Boston Globe*, November 6, 2005.

Shelley, Percy Bysshe. *A Defence of Poetry*. In *Shelley's Poetry and Prose*, ed. Donald H. Reiman and Neil Fraistat, 509–35. Norton Critical Editions. 2nd. ed. New York: Norton, 2002.

Shen, Yeshayahu, and Noga Balaban. "Metaphorical (In)Coherence in Discourse." *Discourse Processes* 28.2 (1999): 139–53.

Shklovsky, Viktor. "Art as Technique." In *Russian Formalist Criticism: Four Essays*, trans. and intro. Lee T. Lemon and Marion J. Reis, 3–24. Lincoln: University of Nebraska Press, 1965.

Simpson, Anne B. *Territories of Psyche: The Fiction of Jean Rhys*. New York: Palgrave Macmillan, 2005.

Simpson, Hilary. *D. H. Lawrence and Feminism*. DeKalb: Northern Illinois University Press, 1982.

Slingerland, Edward. "Good and Bad Reductionism: Acknowledging the Power of Culture." *Style* 42.2–3 (2008): 266–71.

Slovic, Scott. "Nature Writing and Environmental Psychology: The Interiority of Outdoor Experience." In Glotfelty and Fromm, *Ecocriticism Reader*, 351–70.

Smith, Barbara Herrnstein. "Figuring and Reconfiguring the Humanities and the Sciences." *Profession 2005*, 2005, 18–27.

Smith, Charlotte. *The Poems of Charlotte Smith*. Ed. Stuart Curran. Oxford: Oxford University Press, 1993.

Smith, Fred Manning. "The Relation of Coleridge's *Ode on Dejection* to Wordsworth's *Ode on Intimations of Immortality*." *PMLA* 50.1 (1935): 224–34.

Smuts, Barbara. "Male Aggression against Women: An Evolutionary Perspective." In *Sex, Power, and Conflict: Evolutionary and Feminist Perspectives*, ed. David M. Buss and Neil Malamuth, 231–68. Oxford: Oxford University Press, 1996.

Snow, C. P. *The Two Cultures*. Cambridge: Cambridge University Press, 1998.

Spolsky, Ellen. *Gaps in Nature: Literary Interpretation and the Modular Mind*. Albany: State University of New York Press, 1993.

———. "Why and How to Take the Fruit and Leave the Chaff." In "On the Origins of Fictions: Interdisciplinary Perspectives," ed. H. Porter Abbott, special issue, *SubStance* 30.1–2 (2001): 177–98.

Starr, G. Gabrielle. "Multisensory Imagery." In Zunshine, *Introduction to Cognitive Cultural Studies*, 275–91.

Stasio, Michael J., and Kathryn Duncan. "An Evolutionary Approach to Jane Austen: Prehistoric Preferences in *Pride and Prejudice*." *Studies in the Novel* 39.2 (2007): 133–46.

Stein, Rachel. "'To Make the Visible World Your Conscience': Adrienne Rich as Revolutionary Nature Writer." In Tallmadge and Harrington, *Reading under the Sign of Nature*, 198–207.

Stern, Daniel N. *The First Relationship: Infant and Mother*. Cambridge, MA: Harvard University Press, 1977.

———. *The Interpersonal World of the Infant: A View from Psychoanalysis and Developmental Psychology*. New York: Basic Books, 1985.

Stockwell, Peter. *Cognitive Poetics: An Introduction*. London: Routledge, 2002.

Stoneman, Patsy. "Catherine Earnshaw's Journey to her Home among the Dead: Fresh Thoughts on *Wuthering Heights* and 'Epipsychidion.'" *Review of English Studies* 47.188 (1996): 521–33.

Storey, Robert. "Art and Religion: Co-evolved Phenomena." *Style* 42.2–3 (2008): 290–95.

———. *Mimesis and the Human Animal: On the Biogenetic Foundations of Literary Representation.* Evanston, IL: Northwestern University Press, 1996.

Sugiyama, Michelle Scalise. "Predation, Narration, and Adaptation: 'Little Red Riding Hood' Revisited." *Interdisciplinary Literary Studies: A Journal of Criticism and Theory* 5.2 (2004): 110–19.

Tallmadge, John, and Henry Harrington, eds. *Reading under the Sign of Nature: New Essays in Ecocriticism.* Salt Lake City: University of Utah Press, 2000.

Tapia, Elena. "Beyond a Comparison of Two Distinct Things; or, What Students of Literature Gain from a Cognitive Linguistic Approach to Metaphor." *College Literature* 33.2 (2006): 135–53.

Thormählen, Marianne. "The Lunatic and the Devil's Disciple: The 'Lovers' in *Wuthering Heights.*" *Review of English Studies* 48.190 (1997): 183–97.

Tiger, Lionel. *Men in Groups.* 1969. 3rd ed. New Brunswick, NJ: Transaction, 2005.

Tooby, John, and Leda Cosmides. "Does Beauty Build Adapted Minds? Toward an Evolutionary Theory of Aesthetics, Fiction and the Arts." In "On the Origins of Fictions: Interdisciplinary Perspectives," ed. H. Porter Abbott, special issue, *SubStance* 30.1–2 (2001): 6–27.

Tooby, John, and Irven DeVore. "The Reconstruction of Hominid Behavioral Evolution through Strategic Modeling." In *The Evolution of Human Behavior: Primate Models,* ed. Warren G. Kinzey, 183–237. Albany: State University of New York Press, 1987.

Trevarthen, Colwyn. "Interpersonal Abilities of Infants as Generators for Transmission of Language and Culture." In *The Behavior of Human Infants,* ed. Alberto Oliverio and Michele Zappella, 145–76. New York: Plenum, 1983.

Tribble, Evelyn. *Cognition in the Globe: Memory and Attention in Shakespeare's Theatre.* New York: Palgrave Macmillan, 2011.

Tribble, Evelyn, and Nicholas Keene. *Cognitive Ecologies and the History of Remembering: Religion, Education, and Memory in Early Modern England.* New York: Palgrave Macmillan, 2011.

Trivers, Robert L. "Parental Investment and Reproductive Success." In *Natural Selection and Social Theory: Selected Papers of Robert Trivers,* 56–110. Oxford: Oxford University Press, 2002.

Trussler, Michael. "The Narrowed Voice: Minimalism and Raymond Carver." *Studies in Short Fiction* 31.1 (1994): 23–37.

Tuan, Yi-Fu. *Space and Place: The Perspective of Experience.* Minneapolis: University of Minnesota Press, 1977.

Turner, Mark. *The Literary Mind: The Origins of Thought and Language.* New York: Oxford University Press, 1996.

———. *Reading Minds: The Study of English in the Age of Cognitive Science.* Princeton, NJ: Princeton University Press, 1991.

Tyler, Luther. "Losing 'A Letter': The Contexts of Coleridge's 'Dejection.'" *English Literary History* 52.2 (1985): 419–45.

Tytler, Graeme. "'Nelly, I am Heathcliff!': The Problem of 'Identification' in *Wuthering Heights*." *Midwest Quarterly: A Journal of Contemporary Thought* 47.2 (2006): 167–81.

———. "The Parameters of Reason in *Wuthering Heights*." *Brontë Studies* 30.3 (2005): 231–42.

van Peer, Willie. "Two Laws of Literary History." *Mosaic: A Journal for the Interdisciplinary Study of Literature* 30.2 (1997): 113–32.

Vermeule, Blakey. *Why Do We Care about Literary Characters?* Baltimore: Johns Hopkins University Press, 2010.

Wallace, Kathleen R. "'All Things Natural Are Strange': Audre Lorde, Urban Nature, and Cultural Space." In *The Nature of Cities: Ecocriticism and Urban Environments*, ed. Michael Bennett and David W. Teague, 56–73. Tucson: University of Arizona Press, 1999.

Weber, Jean Jacques. "Cognitive Poetics and Literary Criticism: Types of Resolution in the Condition of England Novel." *European Journal of English Studies* 9.2 (2005): 131–41.

Whiten, Andrew, ed. *Natural Theories of Mind: Evolutionary Development and Simulation of Everyday Mindreading*. Oxford: Basil Blackwell, 1991.

Williams, John. *Stoner*. 1965. Reprint, intro. John McGahern, New York: New York Review Books Classics, 2003.

Wilson, Carol Shiner, and Joel Haefner, eds. *Re-Visioning Romanticism: British Women Writers, 1776–1837*. Philadelphia: University of Pennsylvania Press, 1994.

Wilson, E. O. *Consilience: The Unity of Knowledge*. New York: Knopf, 1998.

———. *On Human Nature*. Cambridge, MA: Harvard University Press, 1978.

———. "Resuming the Enlightenment Quest." *Wilson Quarterly: Surveying the World of Ideas* 22.1 (1998): 16–27.

Wordsworth, William. *Lyrical Ballads, and Other Poems, 1797–1800*. Ed. James Butler and Karen Green. Ithaca, NY: Cornell University Press, 1992.

———. *Poems, in Two Volumes, and Other Poems, 1800–1807*. Ed. Jared Curtis. Ithaca, NY: Cornell University Press, 1983.

———. *The Prelude: 1799, 1805, 1850*. Ed. Jonathan Wordsworth, M. H. Abrams, and Stephen Gill. Norton Critical Editions. 1st ed. New York: Norton, 1979.

Wright, Robert. *The Moral Animal: Evolutionary Psychology and Everyday Life*. New York: Random House / Vintage Books, 1994.

Zunshine, Lisa, ed. *Introduction to Cognitive Cultural Studies*. Baltimore: Johns Hopkins University Press, 2010.

———. "Theory of Mind and Experimental Representations of Fictional Consciousness." *Narrative* 11.3 (2003): 270–91.

———. *Why We Read Fiction: Theory of Mind and the Novel*. Columbus: Ohio State University Press, 2006.